CORPORATE SOCIAL RESPONSIBILITY

Win-win Propositions for Communities, Corporates and Agriculture

CORPORATE SOCIAL RESPONSIBILITY

Win-win Propositions for Communities, Corporates and Agriculture

Edited by

Suhas P. Wani and K.V. Raju

International Crops Research Institute for the Semi-Arid Tropics (ICRISAT), Patancheru, Telangana, India

CABI is a trading name of CAB International

CABI	CABI
Nosworthy Way	745 Atlantic Avenue
Wallingford	8th Floor
Oxfordshire OX10 8DE	Boston, MA 02111
UK	USA

Tel: +44 (0)1491 832111
Fax: +44 (0)1491 833508
E-mail: info@cabi.org
Website: www.cabi.org

Tel: +1 (617)682-9015
E-mail: cabi-nao@cabi.org

A catalogue record for this book is available from the British Library, London, UK.

Library of Congress Cataloging-in-Publication Data

Names: Wani, S. P. (Suhas Pralhad), 1952- editor. | Raju, K. V., editor.
Title: Corporate social responsibility : win-win propositions for communities, corporates and agriculture / edited by Suhas P. Wani and K.V. Raju.
Description: Boston, MA : CABI, [2018] | Includes bibliographical references and index.
Identifiers: LCCN 2018023224 (print) | LCCN 2018028768 (ebook) | ISBN 9781786394521 (ePDF) | ISBN 9781786394538 (ePub) | ISBN 9781786394514 (hbk : alk. paper)
Subjects: LCSH: Social responsibility of business--India--Case studies. | Natural resources--Management--Case studies. | Agriculture--India--Case studies.
Classification: LCC HD60.5.I4 (ebook) | LCC HD60.5.I4 C67 2018 (print) | DDC 658.4/08--dc23
LC record available at https://lccn.loc.gov/2018023224

ISBN-13: 978 1 78639 451 4

Commissioning editor: David Hemming
Editorial assistant: Emma McCann
Production editor: Shankari Wilford

Typeset by SPi, Pondicherry, India
Printed and bound in the UK by CPI Group (UK) Ltd, Croydon, CR0 4YY

Contents

Contributors

Nagaraju Budama, Senior Scientific officer, ICRISAT Development Centre, International Crop Research Institute for the Semi-Arid Tropics, Patancheru 502 324, Telangana, India. E-mail: b.nagaraju@cgiar.org

Girish Chander, Senior Scientist, ICRISAT Development Centre, International Crop Research Institute for the Semi-Arid Tropics, Patancheru 502 324, Telangana, India. E-mail: g.chander@cgiar.org

O.P. Chaturvedi, Director, CAFRI, ICAR-Central Agroforestry Research Institute (CAFRI), Jhansi, Uttar Pradesh, India. E-mail: chaturvediopc@gmail.com

S.K. Dasgupta, Consultant, ICRISAT Development Centre, International Crop Research Institute for the Semi-Arid Tropics, Patancheru 502 324, Telangana, India. E-mail: D.Swapankumar@cgiar.org

Aviraj Datta, Visiting Scientist, ICRISAT Development Centre, International Crop Research Institute for the Semi-Arid Tropics, Patancheru 502 324, Telangana, India. E-mail: a.datta@cgiar.org

Inder Dev, Principal Scientist, CAFRI, ICAR-Central Agroforestry Research Institute (CAFRI), Jhansi, Uttar Pradesh, India. E-mail: drinderdev@gmail.com

Kaushal K. Garg, Senior Scientist, ICRISAT Development Centre, International Crop Research Institute for the Semi-Arid Tropics, Patancheru 502 324, Telangana, India. E-mail: k.garg@cgiar.org

A.V.R. Kesava Rao, Honorary Fellow, ICRISAT Development Centre, International Crop Research Institute for the Semi-Arid Tropics, Patancheru 502 324, Telangana, India. E-mail: k.rao@cgiar.org

Rajesh Nune, Visiting Scientist, ICRISAT Development Centre, International Crop Research Institute for the Semi-Arid Tropics, Patancheru 502 324, Telangana, India. E-mail: r.nune@cgiar.org

G. Pardhasaradhi, Manager, ICRISAT Development Centre, International Crop Research Institute for the Semi-Arid Tropics, Patancheru 502 324, Telangana, India. E-mail: g.pardhasaradhi@cgiar.org

Prabhakar Pathak, Consultant, ICRISAT Development Centre, International Crop Research Institute for the Semi-Arid Tropics, Patancheru 502 324, Telangana, India. E-mail: p.pathak@cgiar.org

Mukund D. Patil, Senior Scientist, ICRISAT Development Centre, International Crop Research Institute for the Semi-Arid Tropics, Patancheru 502 324, Telangana, India. E-mail: m.patil@cgiar.org

Kiran J. Petare, Manager, ICRISAT Development Centre, International Crop Research Institute for the Semi-Arid Tropics, Patancheru 502 324, Telangana, India. E-mail: k.petare@cgiar.org

D.S. Prasad Rao, Senior Technical Officer, ICRISAT Development Centre, International Crop Research Institute for the Semi-Arid Tropics, Patancheru 502 324, Telangana, India. E-mail: p.doppalapudi@cgiar.org

K.V. Raju, Theme leader, Policy and Impact, Research Program-Asia, International Crop Research Institute for the Semi-Arid Tropics, Patancheru 502 324, Telangana, India. E-mail: kv.raju@cgiar.org

A.N. Rao, Consultant, International Crop Research Institute for the Semi-Arid Tropics, Patancheru 502 324, Telangana, India. E-mail: a.narayanarao@cgiar.org

Gajanan L. Sawargaonkar, Senior Scientist, ICRISAT Development Centre, International Crop Research Institute for the Semi-Arid Tropics, Patancheru 502 324, Telangana, India. E-mail: g.sawargaonkar@cgiar.org

Anand K. Singh, Research Project Staff, ICRISAT Development Centre, International Crop Research Institute for the Semi-Arid Tropics, Patancheru 502 324, Telangana, India; CAFRI, ICAR-Central Agroforestry Research Institute (CAFRI), Jhansi, Uttar Pradesh, India. E-mail: amananand22@gmail.com

Ramesh Singh, Principal Scientist, CAFRI, ICAR-Central Agroforestry Research Institute (CAFRI), Jhansi, Uttar Pradesh, India. E-mail: rameshsinghnrcaf@gmail.com

K. Srinivas, Lead Scientific Officer, ICRISAT Development Centre, International Crop Research Institute for the Semi-Arid Tropics, Patancheru 502 324, Telangana, India. E-mail: k.srinivas@cgiar.org

Ch. Srinivasa Rao, Lead Scientific Officer, ICRISAT Development Centre, International Crop Research Institute for the Semi-Arid Tropics, Patancheru 502 324, Telangana, India. E-mail: s.rao@cgiar.org

R. Sudi, Consultant, ICRISAT Development Centre, International Crop Research Institute for the Semi-Arid Tropics, Patancheru 502 324, Telangana, India. E-mail: s.r.rao@cgiar.org

Suhas P. Wani, Director, Research Program-Asia, International Crop Research Institute for the Semi-Arid Tropics, Patancheru 502 324, Telangana, India. E-mail: s.wani@cgiar.org

Foreword

Corporate Social Responsibility (CSR) partnerships are being applied today on an unprecedented scale for wider social good. But we do not hear much about their role in agriculture involving small-holder farmers. Therefore, I am particularly delighted to see a consolidation of the knowledge that the ICRISAT IDC team has gained while impacting the lives of millions of farmers through its corporate and multi-stakeholder partnerships.

This book, *Corporate Social Responsibility: Win-win Propositions for Communities, Corporates and Agriculture*, imbibes ICRISAT's motto 'from the science of discovery to the science of delivery'. It documents various initiatives and programmes developed over the years to enable adoption of technologies by small-holder farmers. It highlights real-life case studies, enabling actors, institutions, policies and partnerships that are needed for leveraging context-driven technologies to benefit farmers, particularly in dryland agriculture. The book details an innovative approach for building partnerships among various stakeholders to ensure delivery at the doorsteps of small-holder farmers through a consortium approach, bringing together public–private–people-centric partnerships (four Ps), convergence of different schemes and departments involved in knowledge/input distribution of collective action of smallholder farmers and capacity building on the ground.

This approach promises to be a win-win proposition for the corporates and public-sector undertakings in terms of leveraging their Corporate Social Responsibility programmes in the area of agriculture and synergizing with government to achieve food and nutritional security. The approach provides wider social benefits to women and youths in rural areas through skill building, creating employment and transforming subsistence agriculture into a business model using high-science tools for achieving food, nutrient and income security.

I am sure that a wide segment of audience and readers, comprising policy makers, donors/development investors, research managers, researchers, development workers and students, will benefit immensely from this book.

David Bergvinson
Director General
ICRISAT

Preface

This book is a unique initiative, covering the results of scaling-up work undertaken by a consortium led by ICRISAT Development Center (IDC), International Crops Research Institute for the Semi-Arid Tropics (ICRISAT). Over the years, it has become evident that there are large yield gaps between the farmers' fields and the achievable potential yields for various crops at different locations. Agrarian distress, largely for dryland agriculture farmers, was another trigger for undertaking the science of delivery for scaling-up science-led technologies to benefit farmers. Partnership with a number of state governments and the Government of India, along with funding support from a number of corporates and public-sector undertakings, enabled us to pilot scaling-up work. The approach has been widely adopted in the form of building partnerships between agriculture and allied sectors like horticulture and livestock, resulting in improvements to productivity and income for the farmers. The lessons from this initiative are immense and the scaling-up approach has evolved over time.

The results and the learnings at different agro-ecological locations under varying socioeconomic conditions, as well as the natural resource endowments and the approach of building partnerships for providing end-to-end solutions, has huge potential in parts of Asia and Africa. In India, government policy since 2014 has been to invest 2% of the profits of the large corporates and public-sector undertakings under CSR, which has enabled institutions like ICRISAT to develop the science of delivery, build the partnerships through consortia and collective action of the small farm holders through Farmer Producer Organizations (FPOs) and capacity building. This approach has resulted in intensifications of the existing systems, innovations, and inclusivity of the systems by adopting an integrated approach, resulting in economic gain and protection for the environment, and also addresses the issues of equity through efficient use of available resources. We are very pleased to share the learnings of these initiatives, which we are confident will benefit millions of farmers across Asia and Africa.

Suhas P. Wani and K.V. Raju
ICRISAT

Acknowledgements

This book is based solely on scaling-up work performed with a number of stakeholders, largely farmers at different locations, who have conducted participatory demonstrations and shared the data with us. We gratefully acknowledge the help of all these farmers and also the various consortium partners, namely NGOs (non-governmental organizations) and the state governments of Andhra Pradesh, Karnataka, Maharashtra, Telangana, Uttar Pradesh, for their support in conducting these science-of-delivery initiatives for scaling-up in different states.

We also acknowledge the financial support provided by the corporates and public-sector undertakings, namely SABMiller India, JSW Foundation, Asian Paints Limited, Coca Cola Foundation, Power Grid Corporation of India Limited, Rural Electrification Corporation Limited, India and Sir Rattan Tata Trust, Sir Dorabji Tata Trust, Mumbai and Department of Science and Technology of Government of India. We acknowledge the help of all the staff working at different locations in these projects for their support in collecting the data that forms the basis of this book.

We are thankful to all our scientists who wrote different chapters, and Ms Sheila Vijay Kumar for editing and Ms Suchita Vithlani for providing all the administrative support.

We are extremely thankful to ICRISAT for enabling us to design and execute the CSR projects across India and for continuously encouraging us. Finally, we earnestly thank the entire team at CABI, for meticulously working on the manuscript and beautifully bringing out this book.

1 Corporate Social Responsibility in India: Philosophy, Policy and Practice

K.V. Raju* and Suhas P. Wani

International Crop Research Institute for the Semi-Arid Tropics, Patancheru, India

1.1 Introduction

1.1.1 Philosophy

The world is changing, and by dimensions and at a pace never seen in the past. Consumers are evaluating products and services not only in terms of functionality and technology but also whether the producer is paying adequate attention to the environment and the community. Social media allows for quick person-to-person dissemination of data and 'experience', and for a positive or negative build-up, which far exceeds the power of mass-media-based inferences.

Despite these great improvements, the latent potential of a nation of more than a billion people continues to be stymied by developmental barriers. India's development goals are immense, and the challenges that lie ahead can only be overcome with the efforts of every stakeholder in the ecosystem. Every giver, no matter how large or small the contribution, plays a vital role in helping India move closer towards its development goals. It is only when every giver reaches his or her full potential that the billion people will achieve their goals.

India has witnessed high economic growth in the past two decades. India continues to be one of the fastest-growing economies in the world and has made progress on several development indicators. Despite progress, challenges persist. India continues to face several challenges in health, poverty, nutrition and sanitation, education, water, unemployment, environment and others. The passage of Companies' Act 2013, notification of corporate social responsibility (CSR) rules and further notifications (henceforth referred as the Act) can be seen as a move by the Government of India to strengthen the relation of the business with communities and also better transparency and governance around CSR (GoI, 2013). While the Act provides the overall guidance framework for the corporates to lead their CSR initiatives, it also provides ample autonomy and flexibility to design and implement programmes. Furthermore, India is one of the first few countries in the world which has mandated CSR spending as well as its reporting. Internationally, disclosures on CSR have been in place for quite a few years now. Sector-specific, mandatory CSR has also been in place. The mandatory CSR reporting has its unique advantages. Besides complying with regulatory requirements, it allows corporates to demonstrate their commitment towards organizational transparency. It can also be used as a communication tool to

---

* Corresponding author: kv.raju@cgiar.org

engage with different stakeholders including shareholders, regulators, communities, customers and the larger society. CSR reporting provides an opportunity for corporates to reflect on their internal processes as well as to compare their CSR performance with peers.

Corporate social responsibility should act as a bridge between 'haves and have-nots', given the wide disparity that exists in the society. In other words, it should not be seen as 'good to have' or as a 'requirement under law' instead, they have to think beyond their customers and shareholders, and focus on developing partnerships with other important stakeholders in the society. In addition to business which is the economic exchange with society, companies need to also focus upon CSR as their non-economic exchange.

Corporate social responsibility in India, as in many parts of the world, has for companies matured from a utopian concept to a must-do activity. Globalization of Indian business, localization of multinational companies in India, corporate reputation, risk management and business continuity/sustainability, and public policy on CSR are key drivers for the mainstreaming of CSR. Nevertheless, a substantial number of enterprises in India still need to move up the CSR curve. CSR is becoming an integral part of every business portfolio in India, and companies have made significant contributions to the development of the country through various initiatives in areas such as education, health care, water and sanitation, infrastructure, livelihoods, rural development and urban development (Warner, 2014; Sheth *et al.*, 2017).

Recently, CSR activities have been growing at a faster rate than expected. One of the reasons for this growth is the burgeoning corporate foundations. These foundations are usually nonprofit entities set up to conduct CSR activities. This structure enables them to partner with other organizations engaged in research and implementation activities. These entities also work with government departments to seek alignment with social, environment or economic development priorities. In recognizing the role of business in inclusive growth through sustainable development efforts, the government in recent years, (e.g. the Ministry of Corporate Affairs) has increased efforts to put in place a policy on CSR that will provide an enabling environment for business to conduct CSR activities.

A widely used definition of CSR in the business and social context has been given by the European Union (EU). It describes CSR as

> the concept that an enterprise is accountable for its impact on all relevant stakeholders. It is the continuing commitment by business to behave fairly and responsibly, and contribute to economic development while improving the quality of life of the work force and their families as well as of the local community and society at large (European Commission, 2011).

In other words, CSR refers to ensuring the success of the business by inclusion of socioeconomic and environmental considerations into a company's operations. It means satisfying the demands of shareholders and customers while also managing the expectation of other stakeholders such as employees, suppliers and the community at large. It also means contributing positively to society and managing the organization's environmental impact (European Commission, Directorate-General for Enterprise).

Over the years, the Indian philanthropy market has matured.[1] Funds contributed by individual philanthropists have been steadily rising, growing faster than funds from foreign sources and funds contributed through CSR. Philanthropists are also becoming more sophisticated in how they view giving and are proactively adopting new strategies for high-impact results.

Philanthropy has been on the upswing in India over the past five years. Although fundraising continues to be one of the primary concerns in the development sector, it has seen steady growth in the recent past, primarily due to private sources. Though the current trend is heartening, a greater push for more philanthropic funding and resources is needed, given that the required scale of development remains significantly large.

In terms of visible outcomes, India still has a long way to go on most fronts despite progressive government schemes such as Beti Bachao Beti Padhao, Jan Dhan Yojana and Swachh Bharat. The country ranked 130 on the Human Development Index in 2014 and 110 on the Sustainable Development Goals (SDGs) Index in 2016, lagging behind its peers on both readings (see Fig. 1.1). Conservative estimates indicate that India will face a financial shortfall of approximately ₹53.3 million crore (US$8.5 trillion) if it is to achieve the SDGs by 2030. It needs significant additional funds, along with systematic changes at the policy and service-delivery levels, to achieve these goals. Although the government remains the largest enabler of change, the role of private philanthropy is critical.

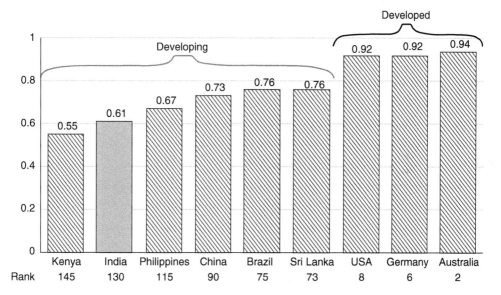

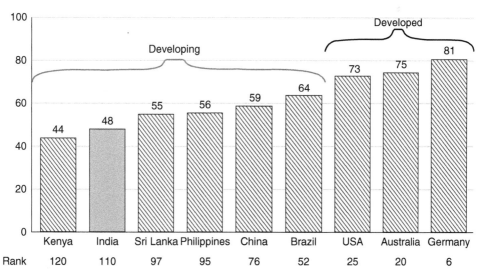

Fig. 1.1. India lags behind comparable peers on key social development indexes. From: CII, 2016; KPMG, 2017; Sheth *et al.*, 2017.

1.1.2 Growing funds

The *India Philanthropy Report* (Sheth *et al.*, 2017) observed that total funds for the development sector have grown approximately 9% over the past five years. In absolute terms, the funds have increased from approximately ₹150,000 crore to ₹220,000 crore with the combined efforts of both public and private sectors. While the public sector remains the largest contributor (₹150,000 crore in 2016), its share of total funding has been declining steadily. On the other hand, private-sector contributions primarily accounted for the ₹70,000 crore five-year growth. Private donations made up 32% of total contributions to the development sector in 2016, increasing from a mere 15% in 2011 (see Fig. 1.2).

To deal with increasing climate risks, environment degradation, lack of livelihood opportunities and widespread out-migration, the Ministry of Corporate Affairs, Government of India has recently notified the section 135 of the Companies Act, 2013 along with Companies (Corporate Social Responsibility Policy) Rules, 2014 (GoI, 2013). In response to the requirements of the Companies' Act 2013, companies have to set aside an amount of equal to 2% of the average net profits of the Company for annual CSR activities. However, the share of private corporate philanthropy in funds raised for the development sector has declined from 30% in 2011 to 15% in 2016. To create conducive environment to invest on CSR activities, the government has proposed amendments to the Companies' Act 2013 that seek to provide greater clarity on CSR provisions. Although philanthropy from foreign sources has continued to increase over the years, the rapid growth of philanthropy from individuals within the country promised for the sustained growth of Indian philanthropy. One of the estimates revealed that the new CSR mandate of 2% net profit has brought approximately ₹5,850 crore to local charities from 90 companies since 2014.

1.1.3 Individual philanthropist

In India, philanthropic funding from private individuals recorded a sixfold increase from approximately ₹6,000 crore in 2011 to ₹36,000 crore in 2016 (see Fig. 1.3). A large portion of

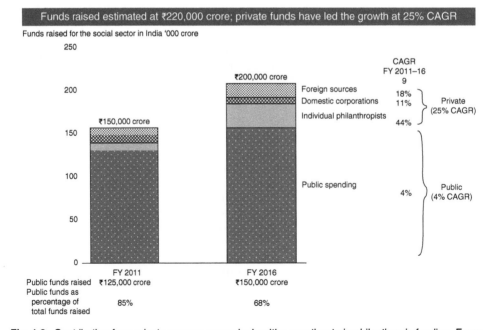

Fig. 1.2. Contribution from private sources caused a healthy growth rate in philanthropic funding. From: Sheth *et al.*, 2017.

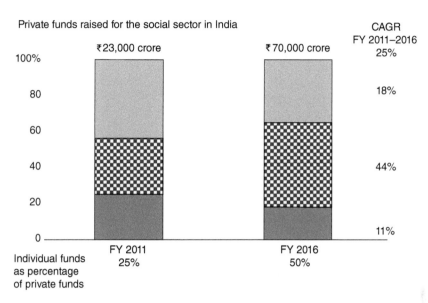

Private funds raised for the social sector in India

Fig. 1.3. The 44% growth in individual funds is the major reason for the 50% share increase in private funds. From: Sheth *et al.*, 2017.

this amount has come from a few established individuals who have pledged large sums of their net worth to philanthropy. This increase in private philanthropy is only expected to grow in the future, with government facilitating through policy and legal framework an environment conducive to investment on social and environmental issues. According to the *India Philanthropy Report* (Sheth *et al.*, 2017), the increased per capita gross domestic product has contributed to the increase in ultra-high net-worth individual (UHNWI) households, leading to more philanthropic activity. The number of UHNWI households has doubled since 2011, and their net worth has tripled during this period. The number of people who have volunteered their money and time between 2009 and 2015 has also increased 1.5 and 2 times respectively (see Fig. 1.4).

The growth of the Indian economy has contributed to the rise of individual philanthropists, which is an important phase in the growth of India's philanthropy sector. The growth-induced development is resulting in more Indians becoming wealthier, as reflected in the Forbes billionaires list, in which India ranks fourth among countries with the most billionaires. However, philanthropy is not a new concept in India, as the country has had a history and tradition of supporting and helping employee welfare activities and environmental sustainability through corporate houses. In today's environment, the philosophy of philanthropy is changing due to awareness of global issues and modernization has changed the attitude of new generations, and wealthy people are coming forward to address critical issues such as social and economic backwardness, environmental concerns and empowerment issues, thereby helping India to develop faster.

1.1.4 Contributing funds

Philanthropy is the way of helping to build stronger societies by protecting the environment, creating employment and providing basic amenities. In this process different philanthropists may opt for different methods, and this is the prerogative of each philanthropist, shaped in part by his or her unique giving philosophy, life experience, time availability, social interests and goals. Different philanthropists adopt different practices depending on time availability and interests, and some may invest their time and efforts into helping society in addition to monetary contributions. A philanthropic journey is

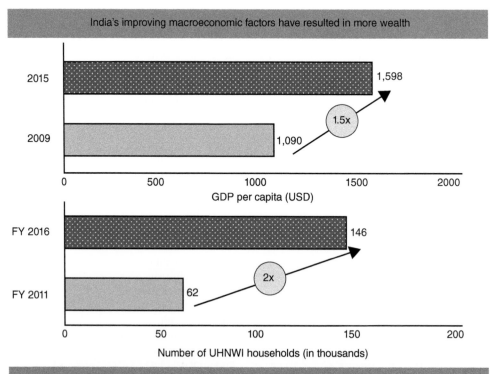

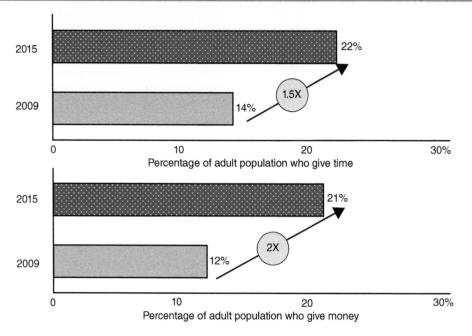

Fig. 1.4. Improving economic conditions and an increase in individual wealth have led to an increase in philanthropy. UHNWI = ultra-high net-worth individual; a UHNWI household is defined by Kotak Wealth Management as a household with a net worth >₹25 crore. From: Sheth *et al.*, 2017.

complex, and there are varied approaches that philanthropists can adopt. The *India Philanthropy Report* (Sheth *et al.*, 2017) outlined the framework and identified the ways that philanthropists may choose to engage with the sector. The report also highlighted how and where philanthropists give and manner in which their funds are used (Fig. 1.5) and lay out the various ways philanthropists can contribute beyond their financial contributions (Fig. 1.6). The confluence of the two can broadly illustrate the giving approach adopted by philanthropists (Sheth *et al.*, 2017).

1.2 Evolution of CSR Governance and Policies

Since CSR is gaining importance throughout the world,[2] governments are aware of the national competitive advantages won from a responsible business sector. Large corporations have progressively realized the benefit of implementing CSR initiatives, where their business operations are located. The Organisation for Economic Co-operation and Development (OECD) established a set of guidelines for multinational enterprises in 1976, and was thus a pioneer in developing the concept of CSR. The purpose of these guidelines was to improve the investment climate and encourage the positive contribution multinational enterprises can make to economic and social progress. In addition to the OECD's 30 member countries, 11 observer countries have endorsed the guidelines.[3]

It is observed that transparency in reporting enhances the focus on economic, social and environmental factors. It motivates companies to intensify their efforts in becoming socially responsible. Several efforts have been taken by various governments to encourage CSR reporting, such as incentivizing companies who voluntarily report their CSR activities or by taking measures such as mandating CSR reporting. In 2007, the Malaysian government passed a regulation to mandate all publicly listed companies to publish their CSR initiatives in their annual reports on a 'comply or explain' basis. Accordingly, all publicly listed companies in Malaysia have to either publish CSR information or explain why they should be exempted (Hauser Institute, 2015). In another example, in 2009

Denmark mandated CSR reporting, asking all state-owned companies and companies with total assets of more than €19 million, revenues of more than €38 million, and over 250 employees to report their social initiatives in their annual financial reports.

To enable transparency from businesses on the environment, social and governance front, France passed a law called Grenelle II, which mandates integrated sustainability and financial reporting for all companies listed on the French stock exchanges, including subsidiaries of foreign companies located in France and unlisted companies with sales revenue of more than €400 million and more than 2000 employees.

Although some CSR standards are mandatory, there are others, which comprise both mandatory and voluntary standards. For instance, in 2006 the British Companies Act mandated all companies listed in UK to include information about their CSR activities in their annual reports; however, a full-length CSR report was made voluntary (Maguire, 2011).

A corporate responsibility index challenges and supports large organizations to integrate responsible business practices. Emerging markets such as Brazil, China and South Africa have become forerunners in CSR reporting in the developing world in terms of their involvement in CSR-related activities in order to promote the listed companies' credibility, transparency and endurance. The Johannesburg stock exchange was the first emerging market stock exchange to create a socially responsible investing index in 2004. China has also encouraged CSR reporting in guidelines released through the Shanghai and Shenzhen Stock Exchange.

1.2.1 Evolution in India

India has a long tradition of paternalistic philanthropy. The process, though acclaimed recently, has been followed since ancient times, albeit informally. Philosophers such as Kautilya from India, and pre-Christian era philosophers in the West, preached and promoted ethical principles while doing business. The concept of helping the poor and disadvantaged was cited in several works of ancient literature. In the pre-industrial period, philanthropy, religion and

States of giving journey	← Early/Nascent →	← Transition →	← Mature stages →	
Vision	Gives in an unstructured manner across a broad range of sectors	Begins to reflect on and identify broad areas of interest to form a specific vision within the interest area	Develops and articulates a vision which could be based on geography, cause or theme	Solidifies vision, which becomes the source of all activity
	Giving is reactive and limited to individuals/nonprofits that might have sought him/her out	Giving begins to be more proactive, though some parts remain reactive	Investments tend to be more thought out proactive, and aligned to the vision	The giving approach becomes outcome-led and all giving is aligned to the vision
States of giving journey	← Early/Nascent →	← Transition →	← Mature stages →	
Percentage of potential giving	Low	Low to medium	Medium to high	High
	Is uncertain of the extent of funds they can commit to philanthropy and is more cautious about how much they contribute			Is certain of the extent of funds they commit and channels all funds over and above their needs, wants and desires (accounting for the future) towards philanthropy
States of giving journey	← Early/Nascent →	← Transition →	← Mature stages →	
Scope of giving	Giving is primarily limited to individuals	Gives to a few existing nonprofits or sets up own implementing foundation	Consolidates and engages deeper with a portfolio of programs/organizations	Giving is directed towards solving an issue at large
			This could involve exploring partnerships with peers, local government, etc., with the aim of supporting on organization's work	Identifies gaps at various levels (policy, research, capacity, delivery) and engages with multiple stakeholders (government, academics, intermediaries, nonprofits) to move the whole ecosystem
States of giving journey	← Early/Nascent →	← Transition →	← Mature stages →	
Type of funding	Only programmatic funding	Only programmatic funding	Largely provides programmatic funding and some institutional funding	Gives either programmatic or institutional funding
			(e.g. monitoring and evaluation, leadership development, systems, human resources), based mostly on one's own preference	Or a blend of both, based on the need
States of giving journey	← Early/Nascent →	← Transition →	← Mature stages →	
Time period of engagement	Short term	Short-medium term	Medium-long term	Long term
	Time horizon of 1 to 3 years	Time horizon of 3 to 5 years, with a focus on achievable outcomes and milestones	Time horizon of 3 to 5 years, with a focus on achievable outcomes and milestones	Time horizon of 5 years or more, with efforts made to catalyse the ecosystem to achieve outcomes

Fig. 1.5. The philanthropic pathways' framework: nature of giving. From: Sheth *et al.*, 2017.

States of giving journey	◄━━━ Early/Nascent ━━━►	◄━━ Transition ━━►	◄━━━━━━━ Mature stages ━━━━━━━►	
Time spent on philanthropic activities	<5%	5–10%	10–30%	>30%
	Often allocated in an ad hoc manner	Allocated in a conscious and regular manner	Allocated in a conscious and regular manner	Keeps increasing the amount of time allocated to philanthropy
States of giving journey	◄━━━ Early/Nascent ━━━►	◄━━ Transition ━━►	◄━━━━━━━ Mature stages ━━━━━━━►	
Monitoring, learning and evaluation (MLE)	**Is unable to spend time participating in MLE activities**	**Participates in MLE activities in an ad hoc manner**	**Regularly participates in MLE activities**	**Actively participates and encourages organizations to spend time on MLE activities**
	Does not track utilization of funds, is unable to find time to learn about the sector	Tracks utilization of funds and work done in sector when provided; participates in ad hoc learning opportunities by talking to peers and attending events	Proactively tracks utilization of funds and outputs; actively spends time learning about the sector by engaging with actors in the ecosystem	Proactively urges organizations to measure not just outputs, but outcomes; works with actors in the ecosystem to learn how best to make an impact in the sector
States of giving journey	◄━━━ Early/Nascent ━━━►	◄━━ Transition ━━►	◄━━━━━━━ Mature stages ━━━━━━━►	
Skills	**Volunteers with organizations based on their requirement**	**Consciously allocates mindspace and begins to align skills**	**Aligns skills and capabilities with how best to use allocated time**	**Constantly reviews and realigns the skills and capabilities**
	Does not attempt to align activities with one's capabilities and skills	Begins to reflect on how to best align his or her skills/capabilities with allocated time		That could be applied a cause/sector level
States of giving journey	◄━━━ Early/Nascent ━━━►	◄━━ Transition ━━►	◄━━━━━━━ Mature stages ━━━━━━━►	
Networks	**Discusses own philanthropy or the intent of philanthropy to inner circle of friends/family** In an unstructured environment (e.g. at dinners) and on an ad hoc basis	**Mobilizes network in a more structured, proactive manner** But limits this primarily to one's inner circle of friends and relatives	**Mobilizes One's larger peer group or professional network** (employees, own company resources, etc.) to support the development sector	**Proactively influences a much larger network** (e.g. friends of friends, industry) to participate in philanthropy
States of giving journey	◄━━━ Early/Nascent ━━━►	◄━━ Transition ━━►	◄━━━━━━━ Mature stages ━━━━━━━►	
Public outreach	Philanthropy is a **personal engagement** restricted to one's private networks	**Occasionally engages in the public domain** Speaks at smaller public events/forums, typically potential philanthropists when invited	**Proactively seeks opportunities to engage about philanthropy in the public domain** Speaks at larger public events/forums; proactively promotes philanthropic engagement in the public domain in interviews with media	**Proactively and regularly seeks to influence a much larger or higher level of audience** On sector-level trends and issues, thereby championing a specific cause;this could include doing television interviews, writing articles/editorials in newspapers or influencing the state/central government

Fig. 1.6. The philanthropic pathways' framework: engagement with the sector. From: Sheth *et al.*, 2017.

charity were the key drivers of CSR. The industrial families of the 19th century had a strong inclination towards charity and other social considerations. However, the donations, either monetary or otherwise, were sporadic activities of charity or philanthropy that were taken out of personal savings, which neither belonged to the shareholders nor constituted an integral part of business. During this period, the industrial families also established temples, schools, higher education institutions and other infrastructure of public use.

The term CSR itself came into common use in the early 1970s. The last decade of the 20th century witnessed a shift in focus from charity and traditional philanthropy toward more direct engagement of business in mainstream development and concern for disadvantaged groups in society. In India, there is a growing realization that business cannot succeed in isolation and social progress is necessary for sustainable growth. An ideal CSR practice has both ethical and philosophical dimensions, particularly in India where there exists a wide gap between sections of people in terms of income and standards as well as socioeconomic status (Bajpai, 2001).

Currently, there is an increased focus and a changing policy environment to enable sustainable practices and increased participation in the socially inclusive practices. Some of these enabling measures have been illustrated in the next section of this chapter.

Governance frameworks that focus on the social, environmental and ethical responsibilities of businesses help in ensuring long-term success, competitiveness and sustainability. This further helps to endorse the view that business is an integral part of the society and is essential for the development and sustenance of the society at large. There has been an influx of funding by the corporates in India to aid and uplift the Indian society for many decades. The 57th standing committee on finance highlighted the need for companies to contribute to the society as they depend on the society for obtaining the capital for their businesses. As a result, The Ministry of Corporate Affairs of the Government of India enforced the Act and the CSR Rules from 1 April 2014. The provision of Section 135 for CSR in the Act was introduced in order to enable companies to build social capital through a regulatory structure. By doing so, India became one of the first countries to have a regulatory requirement to spend on CSR and also one of the first to empower businesses to make an impact on the social front in a structured manner.

1.2.2 What qualifies as CSR?

With effect from 1 April, 2014, every private limited or public limited company, which either has a net worth of ₹500 crore or a turnover of ₹1000 crore or a net profit of ₹5 crore, is required to spend on CSR at least 2% of its average net profit for the immediately preceding three financial years' activities. The net worth, turnover and net profits are to be computed under Section 198 of Companies' Act 2013 as per the profit-and-loss statement prepared by the company in terms of Section 381 (1) (a) and Section 198 of the Companies' Act 2013.

The CSR activities should not be undertaken in the normal course of business and should be done according to Schedule VII of the 2013 Act. The Act mentions the following activities as part of CSR:

- Eradicating extreme hunger and poverty.
- Promotion of education.
- Promoting gender equality and empowering women.
- Reducing child mortality and improving maternal health.
- Combating HIV, AIDS, malaria and other diseases.
- Ensuring environmental sustainability.
- Employment enhancing vocational skills.
- Social business projects.
- Contribution to the Prime Minister's (PM's) national relief fund or any other fund set up by the central or state governments for socioeconomic development or relief, and funds for the welfare of Scheduled Caste, Scheduled Tribe, other backward classes, minorities and women.

To formulate and monitor the CSR policy of a company, Section 135 of the 2013 Act requires a CSR committee of the board to be constituted. The CSR Committee is to consist of at least three directors, including an independent director. However, CSR rules exempt unlisted public companies, and private companies that are not required to appoint an independent director, from having an independent director as a part of their CSR Committee, and stipulates that the committee for a private company and a foreign company need to have a minimum of only two members. The modalities require that the finance for spending on CSR activities shall be through a registered trust or society or by a holding/subsidiary or associate company, or through an outside entity having a track record of three years; if through an outside entity, then the company should specify the programme to be undertaken, modalities for utilization of funds and monitoring and reporting mechanism; it can give a donation to a corpus fund, if the entity is created exclusively to carry out CSR activities.

Incubators approved by the central government are considered as a CSR contribution. Examples of incubators are Villgro, a Department of Science and Technology-certified incubator with focus on social enterprises, and Centre for Innovation Incubation and Entrepreneurship (CIIE), the technology incubator at Indian Institute of Management, Ahmedabad. The 7th edition of Bain's *India Philanthropy Report* (Sheth *et al.*, 2017), focused on the growing importance of the individual philanthropist in the overall landscape of funding for the development sector. It goes beyond analysing how much philanthropists are giving and instead focuses on the evolving approaches that givers are adopting to maximize their philanthropic impact. Two examples (Infosys Foundation and Tata Group) are shown in Box 1.1 and Box 1.2.

1.3 Practice

It is a few years since the Companies' Act 2013 and notification of Section 135 was introduced in India. Since India was one of the first countries across the world to mandate CSR, there is a growing interest among various stakeholders to see how the scenario is progressing. What was earlier a voluntary pursuit for corporates has now become a regulatory requirement. The Act is quite comprehensive in nature and provides adequate framework and guidance for CSR project implementation. The Act focuses on implementing CSR in project mode and also requires a detailed disclosure as part of the annual report. The Act also brings in a higher level of governance requirements and hence accountability on CSR.

1.3.1 Estimated CSR expenditure

Estimates of the likely annual expenditure on activities defined in Schedule VII of the CSR Act and falling under the area of social development vary, ranging from ₹15,000 crore to ₹28,000 crore. It is anticipated that of 250 public-sector units (PSUs) in India, 70–80 may qualify for the CSR expenditure. Among nearly 20,000 private companies in India, 10,000–16,000 may qualify for CSR. Since 2010, PSUs have been required to spend a part of their profits, in a percentage slab based on the guidelines being issued by the

---

Box 1.1. Infosys Foundation.

Infosys' commitment to communities has led to the creation of the Infosys Foundation to support the underprivileged sections of society. A not-for-profit initiative aimed at fulfilling the social responsibility of Infosys Ltd, the Infosys Foundation creates opportunities and strives towards a more equitable society.

Established in 1996, the Foundation supports programmes in the areas of education, rural development, health care, arts and culture, and destitute care. Its mission is to work in remote regions of several states in India. The Foundation takes pride in working with all sections of society, selecting projects with infinite care and working in areas that were traditionally overlooked by society at large. Infosys has been an early adopter of a strong CSR agenda. Along with sustained economic performance and robust sustainability management, social stewardship is important to create a positive impact in the communities in which the project activities are undertaken. The key programmes are driven by the valuable CSR platforms built over the years.

To begin with, the Infosys Foundation implemented programmes in Karnataka, and subsequently extended its coverage to Andhra Pradesh, Arunachal Pradesh, Bihar, Delhi, Gujarat, Jammu and Kashmir, Kerala, Madhya Pradesh, Maharashtra, Odisha, Punjab, Rajasthan, Tamil Nadu, Uttarakhand and West Bengal.

Box 1.2. Tata philosophy for CSR.

The Tata Group's corporate social responsibility (CSR) activities are rooted in the knowledge that businesses have a duty to enable all living beings to get a fair share of the planet's resources. The Tata culture of giving back flows from the tradition of nation- and community-building developed more than a century ago by Jamsetji Tata, the Founder of the group. Tata companies are involved in a wide variety of community development and environment preservation projects. The group believes CSR is a critical mission that is at the heart of everything that it does, how it thinks and what it is. The Tata Group is committed to integrating environmental, social and ethical principles into the core business, thereby enhancing long-term stakeholder value and touching the lives of over a quarter of the world's population. The group's CSR programmes aim to be relevant to local, national and global contexts, keep disadvantaged communities as the focus, be based on globally agreed sustainable development principles and be implemented in partnership with governments, NGOs and other relevant stakeholders.

    The CSR approach adopted envisages that the group evolves and executes strategies to support communities in partnership with governments, civil society and relevant stakeholders. Key to this approach is that Tata employees generously give their time, experience and talent to serve communities; group companies encourage and facilitate them to do so. At the group level, the Tata Engage programme builds on this tradition. It is among the top 10 corporate volunteering programmes in the world. Tata companies work towards empowering people by helping them develop the skills they need to succeed in a global economy, which is now consolidated into a group CSR programme called Tata STRIVE. The group equips communities with information, technology and the capacity to achieve improved health, education and livelihood. It also works towards enabling other living things on the planet get their fair share of the resources. The core principles of CSR at Tata are diagrammatically represented below.

    (Based on: http://www.tata.com/sustainability/articlesinside/corporate-social-responsibility)

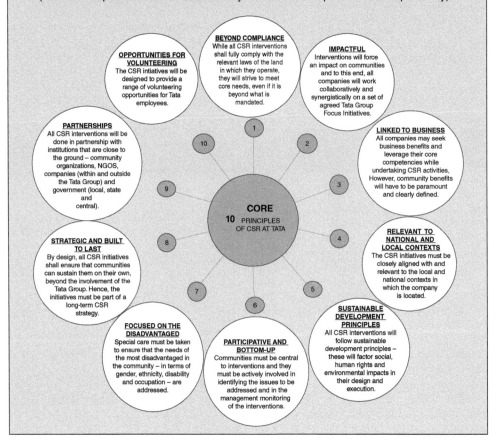

Department of Public Enterprises. The CSR expenditure ranged from 3% to 5% of the net profit of the previous year for PSUs, making a profit of less than ₹100 crore, and 2–3% (subject to minimum of ₹3 crore) in case of profit of ₹100–500 crore.

1.3.2   How are Indian companies doing on the CSR front?

The survey carried out in 2016, analyses and brings together findings from CSR reporting of the top 100 (N100) listed companies as per market capital as on 31 March 2016. All these companies are required to comply with the requirements of the Act. The CSR policy, CSR Committee, disclosure on CSR in the Annual Report, CSR expenditure and others were reviewed based on their availability in the public domain as on 30 September 2016. Key focus areas, compliance levels of companies and beyond compliance are summarized in Table 1.1.

1.3.3   Participation in Swachh Bharat campaign

As part of the Swachh Bharat campaign announced by the Prime Minister Shri Narendra Modi in October 2014, the government has set up a Swachh Bharat Kosh to collect contributions from individuals and organizations towards linking water supply to the constructed toilets, training and skill development to facilitate the maintenance of the toilets and to ensure its interlinkages with education on hygiene, and liquid waste management. Scientist R. Mashelkar chairs the 19-member expert committee to examine best technologies on sanitation and water, with affordability, sustainability, scalability and quality as the main criteria.

Corporate India has committed to construct 100,000 toilets, led by announcements from NTPC (24,000 units) and L&T (5000 toilets). Commitments have also been made by TCS, Toyota Kirloskar, Bharti Foundation, Ambuja Cements and other companies. As per statistics, over 114,000 government schools are without a girls' toilet, and 152,000 are without a boys' toilet. The average cost of construction of a toilet

block is about ₹130,000, while the maintenance cost stands at ₹ 20,000 per year.

1.3.4   Participation in other activities

Corporates in India are finding a range of CSR activities to participate in – they cover CSR being used for market development, to increase product penetration and tap first-time customers, to develop relationships and partnerships with local communities, to extend the supply chain to bring poor communities into the fold, and to enhance skills and capabilities of future customers. The benefits of CSR are given in Box 1.3.

1.3.5   CSR by type and nature of industry

The average prescribed 2% amount per company has gone up by 12% in case of PSU companies and 15% in case of non-PSU companies, according to KPMG (2017). The average expenditure against the prescribed 2% amount per company has gone up by 64% in case of PSU companies as compared to 15% in case of non-PSU companies. The average prescribed 2% amount per company has gone up by 7% in case of Indian origin companies and has reduced to above 20% in case of non-Indian origin companies. The average expenditure against the prescribed 2% amount per company has gone up by 18% in case of Indian origin companies and 30% in case of non-Indian origin companies. Interestingly, chemicals, construction, services, mining, automobile, media, cement and energy and power sector companies have spent more than the prescribed 2% CSR budget in the range of 101% to 119%. The telecom sector has increased spends from 18% to 31%, however, it still continues to lag behind other sectors.

1.3.6   How is the government supplementing CSR efforts?

According to data from the National Skill Development Agency (NSDA), 21 departments and ministries were supposed to train 10.5 million people in 2014–15, but it is estimated that only

Table 1.1. Focus and compliance of CSR. Source: summary based on KPMG (2017).

Focus	Details	Compliance	Beyond compliance
CSR Policy	The Act mandates companies to formulate CSR policies. The policy needs to list out projects/programmes it is planning to implement, execution mechanisms, monitoring and evaluation framework and others. The policy should be made available on the company's website	Three companies do not have their CSR policy available on their respective websites. Two companies have failed to make their CSR policy available in the public domain for the second year in a row. Eight per cent of these companies have failed to disclose details regarding the monitoring framework of their CSR policy	About 98% of companies have disclosed their vision/mission philosophy guiding their CSR programmes. Ninety per cent of companies have disclosed details regarding CSR governance
CSR Committee	The Act mandates that eligible companies must formulate a Corporate Social Responsibility (CSR) Committee. The CSR Committee needs to formulate and recommend the CSR policy to the board, list out and recommend CSR activities and their expenditure and periodically monitor the CSR policy	Ninety-eight companies have disclosed details regarding CSR committee in Directors' Annual Report, however, two Companies have failed to disclose CSR Committee details for the second year in a row. All companies have an independent director on the CSR Committee	Sixty-four per cent of companies have more than the prescribed number (three) of CSR Committee members; 47% of companies have more than the prescribed number (more than one) of independent CSR Committee members on board which is clearly a good indication from the governance front; 55% had women members in their CSR committee; 82% had held two or more CSR Committee meetings during the year
Disclosure on CSR in the Directors' Report	As per the Act, eligible companies must disclose CSR related details in their Directors' Report such as the composition of the CSR Committee, details about the policy developed and implemented by the company on CSR initiatives taken during the year as Annual Report on CSR containing particulars as specified by the Act, and in case of a failure to spend 2% towards CSR shall specify the reasons for same. Mandatory requirement as part of Act reflects the priority given to CSR at board level	During the current year, 98 companies have made disclosures on CSR in the Directors' Report. Four companies have failed to provide CSR details in the prescribed format. Forty-two companies have failed to disclose details regarding CSR Committee in the Directors' Report. Fifty-two% companies have failed to disclose details regarding CSR spend in the Directors' Report; 21% companies do not refer to the CSR policy in the Directors' Report	Forty-nine per cent of companies have presented their CSR vision/mission in the Directors' Report; 40% of the companies have disclosed details on the focus areas of CSR intervention in the Directors' Report. During the current year, 25% of the companies have reported details regarding the outreach/people impacted

---

Box 1.3. Benefits of CSR.

CSR is relevant because of not only a changing policy environment but also its ability to meet business objectives. Its key benefits are as follows:

- Strengthening relationships with stakeholders.
- Enabling continuous improvement and encouraging innovation.
- Attracting the best industry talent as a socially responsible company.
- Additional motivation to employees.
- Risk mitigation because of an effective corporate governance framework.
- Enhanced ability to manage stakeholder expectations.

---

a little more than 5 million people were actually trained. This includes nearly 1.5 million students passing out of ITIs every year. The government has moved the training and apprentice divisions of the labour ministry to the Skill Development and Entrepreneurship ministry formed in November 2014. The move brings over 11,000 ITIs and numerous other institutions, and the apprentice and training divisions, under the Skills ministry. The Skills ministry will implement the amended Apprentices Act, which allows students to get trained in shop floors and obtain financial assistance. The government has drawn up a target for skill-training 250 million people by 2022, including that for the National Skill Development Corporation (NSDC) under the Skills ministry, which will not only oversee the skill development activities of all ministries and departments but also actually implement the schemes. The findings of KPMG (2017) are fairly encouraging. According to KPMG research:

- Compliance to the requirements of the Act has improved.
- A positive trend in the availability of information can be seen as compared to previous year.
- Strengthening of governance mechanisms for CSR projects is visible.
- Overall CSR expenditure has increased and thematic areas of health, education and sanitation witnessed higher budget allocation from corporates.
- A few corporates have gone beyond the 2% mandate and spent more.
- Overall, this opportunity needs to be seized to demonstrate to the world that Indian businesses are contributing constructively to address India's development challenges and are doing it in an impactful way.

1.3.7 CII plays a pivotal role

Confederation of Indian Industry (CII) members need to go a step forwards to support establishing and executing social organizations and NGOs and all required tie-ups. CII also eminently influences the government to execute the legal frame in this regard. If companies see CSR as a legal requirement, and not as a strategic opportunity to enhance value to the society and to shareholders, then it will be an opportunity lost. The Companies' Act 2013 has opened a window to develop a new model by which businesses can make a real contribution towards finding lasting solutions to critical societal issues, and enhance their standing in the society. There should be a collaborative step towards propagating a CSR revolution in India. Even the subcommittee chairs[4] of CII, across the country, have clearly believed that CSR cannot be a law, it has to come from the heart. There is a lot of scope for social-sector development which would work only through public–private partnerships and joint community/corporate participation for social development (CII, 2014).

1.3.8 ICRISAT enabling CSR through win-win proposition

The International Crops Research Institute for the Semi-Arid Tropics (ICRISAT), Patancheru undertakes research for development in the area of agriculture in the semi-arid tropics for achieving food and nutrition security, reducing poverty and minimizing environment degradation in the dryland tropics. ICRISAT undertakes 'Science with a Human Face' by addressing the challenges of 'Science of Discovery' to 'Science of Delivery' by adopting a holistic approach in the water-scarce regions of semi-arid tropics, which is a hot spot of poverty, malnutrition and food insecurity. In this regard, ICRISAT is working with a number of corporates and private-sector companies to undertake CSR initiatives for improving water availability through rainwater harvesting, improving water quality through integrated watershed management, enhancing productivity through increased water and other inputs use efficiency, minimizing land degradation and increasing carbon (C) sequestration for mitigating the impacts of climate change while improving the social capital through cooperation and collective action. ICRISAT adopts science-led holistic development approach through sustainable management of natural resources for improving rural livelihoods. ICRISAT started working with corporates in 2002 long before the Companies' Act 2013 was passed for CSR by the Government of India. By integrating natural resources conservation, sustainability of livelihood as well as business, this approach helped in building good social capital and good relation with the surrounding communities as they were seeing the industries as supporting their livelihoods through sustainable development. Since 2013, after the Companies' Act on CSR, more companies are coming forward to help in rural development; more than 60% of the population reside in rural areas and their livelihoods are vulnerable to the impacts of climate change.

ICRISAT brings in the convergence of scientific approach with social engineering, government programmes, institutions, policies and enabling environment for achieving good impacts. In addition to the impacts on ground, ICRISAT helps in scientific data collection, systematic documentation and dissemination. This win-win approach for corporates and communities benefits not only the communities and corporates but also development researchers, policy makers and development agencies through learnings, feedback and evidences. There is a need to strengthen this approach by scaling-up such science-led development approach for CSR in other parts of the world.

1.4   Focus of this Book

The objective of this book is to present various efforts across India, made by different corporates

in collaboration with ICRISAT. It describes how in each location, cutting across the sectors, both the corporate and a research organization have meticulously designed and executed location-specific projects in the interest of enhancing livelihoods and improving natural resource use efficiency. The first chapter sets the stage to understand the CSR path of development, course corrections, policy support from the Government of India, refinements made over the years, key findings of the recent assessments made by leading agencies and critical role played by national-level corporate associations.

Chapter 2 presents why holistic solutions are needed to effectively address the issues of increasing land degradation, water scarcity and threat of climate change to bring in sustainable system intensification and diversification to high-yielding, climate-smart and high-value crops. Enhancing system productivity through crops and livestock and services in a holistic manner needs to be the focus rather than crops alone. The need to strengthen the 'Science of Delivery' of holistic solutions to farmers is emphasized. Capacity building of farmers involving traditional and modern tools like information and communication technology, collectivization as producer organization, on-farm mechanization and infrastructure for handling, storage and transport is the key to develop/promote significant control measures in production and effective linkages with the markets.

Chapter 3 deals with unabated soil degradation due to low soil organic C levels, multiple nutrient deficiencies including micro and secondary nutrients, rising salinity and soil loss due to erosion which jeopardize food security of swiftly rising global population projected to be 9.7 billion by 2050. Soils also play a major role in global C-cycling and huge C-sequestration potential offers opportunities for mitigating carbon dioxide and other greenhouse gas emissions. The lessons learnt from the CSR pilot and scaling-up initiatives indicated significant productivity benefits with soil health mapping-based management. The linkages of soil health and food quality are documented. Soil health mapping-based management increased C-sequestration with higher proportion of biomass-C and enhanced uptake and use efficiency of nitrogen fertilizers, and thereby reducing losses through runoff and gaseous emissions. Management at watershed level is proved as one of the most trusted approaches to manage natural resources and reduce runoff, soil loss and C and nutrients therein.

Chapter 4 describes the semi-arid tropical region as primarily agrarian with the dominance of rainfed traditional agricultural production systems. Jawhar, a tribal block in Maharashtra state is characterized by high rainfall, water scarcity, degraded soils and low crop productivity. ICRISAT in collaboration with JSW has initiated agricultural interventions with watershed approach, in both Jawhar in Maharashtra and Ballari in Karnataka. During the two-year period, the project has demonstrated various activities to build resilience against climate change to cope with varying climatic risks and to improve livelihoods. The interventions carried out are on conservation of available resources through various measures with active community participation. Agriculture is the main source of livelihood of the community. Soil health management, promotion of improved varieties introduction of new crops and promotion of agronomic practices are the major interventions carried out in the project villages. These have taken farmers towards the path of building resilience to cope with climatic risks.

Chapter 5 explains how water plays an important role in semi-arid tropical regions to address water scarcity, land degradation, and crop and livestock productivity which improve the rural livelihood system. The Charminar Breweries in Sangareddy district (formerly SABMiller; recently merged with AB InBev) has adopted an integrated approach to address the above issues in nearby villages of the plant under CSR initiative during 2009 to 2017 in a phased manner. The major interventions implemented in the project areas focused on rainwater harvesting, productivity enhancement through soil test-based fertilizer application, improved crop cultivars, enriching soil organic C and improved agronomic practices. Various *ex-situ* interventions have harvested nearly 150,000 m^3 water every year and facilitated groundwater recharge resulting in increasing the water table by 0.5–1 ft across the geographical extent of nearly 7000 ha. Further, productivity interventions have enhanced crop yield and cropping intensity by 30–50% compared to baseline situation. The livestock interventions enhanced milk yield by 1–2 l/day/animal. The watershed programme also

introduced various income-generating activities for women and the landless, such as distribution of spent malt as animal feed, kitchen garden, vermicomposting and nursery raising. The programme has benefited nearly 5000 households directly or indirectly and increased household income by ₹10,000 to 25,000 per annum.

Chapter 6 shows the initiative by Asian Paints Limited to improve rural livelihood through integrated watershed development programme in six villages in Patancheru mandal of Medak district, Telangana, covering an area of 7143 ha. The prime mitigation strategy for addressing water scarcity was initiated in the project by rainwater harvesting, efficient use of available water resources and recycling of grey water. Science-led interventions including soil test-based nutrient management, and improved crop cultivar and management practices were introduced for improving crop productivity. Rainwater harvesting structures of total water storage capacity 34,000 m^3 were utilized for groundwater recharge. Based on the observation, estimated groundwater recharge due to check-dams with total storage capacity of 12,700 m^3 during 2016 was 91,000 m^3. The improved agronomic practices demonstrated in farmers' fields have shown 30–50% increase in grain yield.

Chapter 7 emphasizes the development of the Bundelkhand region of Central India, which is the hot spot of water scarcity, land degradation and poor socioeconomic status. The Parasai-Sindh watershed, comprising three villages and covering nearly 1250 ha, was selected for developing a benchmark site in Jhansi district, Uttar Pradesh. ICRISAT and Central Agroforestry Research Institute with CSR funding from Coca-Cola India Foundation enabled science-led interventions. A series of check-dams on the main river stream were constructed which all together developed 125,000 m^3 of storage capacity; this enabled groundwater recharge by 2.5 m and in turn, supported increased cropping intensity by 30–50% in post-monsoon season. Fodder availability has drastically increased and therefore milch animal population has also increased by 30% within three years since the project started. Improved varieties of seeds of chickpea and wheat were introduced and this has improved the crop yield by 30–50%. It is estimated that watershed interventions in pilot villages enhanced average annual family income from ₹50,000 to ₹140,000 in a short span of 3–4 years.

Chapter 8 provides soil health mapping for enhancing water use efficiency in watersheds for sustainable improved livelihoods in Sir Dorabji Tata Trust-supported initiative across 16 districts of Madhya Pradesh and Rajasthan states of India. It showed widespread deficiencies of sulfur, boron, zinc and phosphorus. Soil test-based balanced nutrient management showed yield benefit of 10–40%, while the integrated nutrient approach showed still higher yield up to 20–50% along with 25–50% saving in chemical fertilizers. Promoting landform management enabled farmers to cultivate rainy season fallows and harvest 1270–1700 kg/ha soybean. Women mainstreaming was targeted through livelihood options like nutri-kitchen gardens, fodder promotion for livestock, seed banks, composting and dal-processing. The initiative built capacities of about 30,000 farmers through direct interventions and of around 4–5 times more farmers through information dissemination.

Chapter 9 describes a scaling-up approach in developing soil test-based fertilizer recommendations at block level, supported by the Sir Ratan Tata Trust in Jharkhand and Madhya Pradesh. The crop yield benefit with balanced nutrition was 27–44% in paddy, groundnut and maize with the benefit–cost (BC) ratio varying from 7.36 to 12.0. Balanced nutrition increased crop productivity by 11–57% in crops like soybean, paddy, green gram, black gram and groundnut with BC ratio of 1.97 to 9.35. Water harvesting through creation of farm ponds (~500) helped in supplemental irrigation during critical crop stages besides serving as reservoir for fish cultivation. The efforts towards off-season cultivation of vegetables, crop intensification, vermicompost units (~200) and seed bank was promoted in pilot villages and capacity development was carried out for ~15,000 farmers through direct demonstrations and around 2–3 times more through field days.

Chapter 10 explains innovative model of farmer-centric watershed management in Kurnool district, Andhra Pradesh and Vijayapura district, Karnataka for improving rural livelihoods and reducing degradation of natural resources. This model, supported by Power Grid Corporation of India Limited, uses holistic approach with science-led development in participatory mode with farmers. The watershed interventions have increased water availability by 25–30%, increased irrigated area by 15–25%, improved cropping intensity by 20–30%, increased crop yields by 15–35%, increased area under high-value crops by 10–15%, increased income, improved livelihoods and reduced runoff, soil loss and environment degradation. Innovative low-cost village-based wastewater treatment units were established at benchmark watersheds to increase the water availability for irrigation and improve the surface and groundwater quality.

Chapter 11 presents the success story the community and farm-based rainwater conservation (supported by RECL) have created a net storage capacity of about 18,000 m^3 with total conservation of about 50,000 m^3/year of surface runoff water in Anantapur watershed of Andhra Pradesh and 27,000 m^3 storage capacity with conservation of about 54,000 m^3/year of surface runoff water in Mahabubnagar watershed of Telangana. Soil health improvement with soil test-based addition of macro- and micronutrients and C-building, and varietal replacement are focused. The science-led management has resulted in increasing and sustaining crop and livestock productivity and diversification leading to increased incomes to farmers.

Chapter 12 demonstrates how improved sanitation and hygiene through proper wastewater management is critical to sustainable growth of rural communities. Traditional wastewater treatment technologies experience low penetration in these resource-poor semi-arid tropical villages with limited or no access to good-quality electricity and skilled supervision. The substandard performance of wastewater treatment efficiencies of traditional effluent treatment plants in the urban centres are testimony of their unviability in rural India. Constructed wetland (CW) is an age-old low-cost decentralized wastewater treatment technology. The absence of heavy metal and other xenobiotics in rural grey water highlights their reuse potential for growing jute, teak, etc. Lack of field-scale study with real wastewater thus far has made policy makers and professionals working in the sanitation sector sceptical about the long-term reliability of CWs with respect to wastewater treatment efficiencies. An attempt has been made to present the potential and challenges of CW implementation.

Chapter 13 summarizes, based on different case studies shown in earlier chapters, livelihood benefits and improved water use efficiency across various CSR sites. In Northern and Central Indian states (Madhya Pradesh, Rajasthan, Jharkhand and Odisha) the support of Sir Ratan Tata Trust and Sir Dorabji Tata Trust have benefited more than 50,000 farming families directly and indirectly in terms of enhancing crop productivity, water use efficiency and enhanced farmers' capacity about improved method of cultivation. A net storage capacity of nearly 400,000 m³ was developed through low-cost rainwater harvesting structures which is harvesting on an average 1 million m³ surface runoff annually or more and facilitated groundwater recharge. With enhanced green and blue water availability, increased cropping intensity was observed from 75–100% to 120–150% depending on rainfall variability. A large amount of green water which was unutilized before interventions (largely monocropping system) has been utilized through various water management interventions and resulted in higher cropping intensity and reduced water footprint by 35% and additional household income (by 30–100%). In addition to productivity and income gains, the natural resource management interventions also have helped in terms of strengthening various regulatory and supportive ecosystem services such as C sequestration, reducing soil erosion and stabilizing groundwater depletion, increasing water flow and green cover, and reducing land degradation. This clearly indicates a paradigm shift from low productive and susceptible system to productive, resilient and sustainable agroecosystem after watershed implementation. These case studies have also suggested that institutional issues are very important as they are catalysts for mobilizing collective participation of the community in managing natural resources and the key drivers of rural livelihood improvement.

Overall, this book provides an excellent insight into the early phase of CSR work undertaken by ICRISAT-led consortium for achieving the impacts and has gathered number of learnings by working in partnership. This can benefit development research as well as the corporates to have a win-win proposition for improving the livelihoods, protecting the environment and building the skills in rural areas by undertaking science of delivery which also serves as a feedback loop for the scientists to undertake the discovery phase of research – demand-driven research which will benefit the farmers.

Acknowledgement

We thank Dr K.H. Anantha for his help in reviewing the manuscript.

Notes

[1] The recent report on Indian philanthropy by Sheth *et al.* (2017) published by Bain & Company, based on 33 individual surveys and Dasra's in-depth interviews of 23 individuals, provides an overview of recent trends. Some of the relevant figures presented in this chapter were sourced from this report.
[2] For this section on across the world, some material is sourced from Ernst & Young and PHD Chamber (2013).
[3] The 11 observer countries are: Argentina, Brazil, Chile, Egypt, Estonia, Israel, Latvia, Lithuania, Peru, Romania and Slovenia.
[4] For example, Piruz Khambatta, Chair, Sub-committee on CSR & Affirmative Action, CII Western Region, India & Chairman & Managing Director, Rasna Pvt. Ltd, and Meher Pudumjee, Co-chair, Sub-committee on CSR & Affirmative Action, CII Western Region, India & Chairperson, Thermax Global.

References

Bajpai, G.N. (2001) *Corporate Social Responsibility in India and Europe: Cross Cultural Perspective.* Available at: http://www.ficci.com (accessed 7 November 2017).
CII (2014) *Public–Private Partnerships in CSR in India: Ten Demonstrative Case Studies.* Confederation of Indian Industry ITC Centre of Excellence for Sustainable Development, New Delhi.

CII (2016) *CSR Compendium*. Confederation of Indian Industry Western Region. Worli, Mumbai.

Ernst & Young and PHD Chamber (2013) *Corporate Social Responsibility in India: Potential to Contribute towards Inclusive Social Development*. Global CSR Summit 2013, An Agenda for Inclusive Growth. Ernst & Young and PHD Chamber, New Delhi.

Ernst & Young (2012) *How France's New Sustainability Reporting Law Impacts US Companies*. Ernst & Young report.

European Commission (2011) *Communication from the Commission to the European Parliament, the Council, the European Economic and Social Committee and the Committee of the Regions. A Renewed EU Strategy 2011–14 for Corporate Social Responsibility*. European Commission, 25 October 2011. Available at: http://eur-lex.europa.eu/LexUriServ/LexUriServ.do?uri=COM:2011:0681:FIN:en:PDF (accessed 6 April 2018).

Government of India (2013) *The Companies' Act 2013*. Ministry of Commerce, New Delhi.

Hauser Institute (2015) *Corporate Social Responsibility Disclosure Efforts by National Governments and Stock Exchanges*. Available at: http://iri.hks.harvard.edu/files/iri/files/corporate_social_responsibility_disclosure_3-27-15.pdf (accessed 6 April 2018).

KPMG (2017) *India's CSR Reporting Survey, 2016*. KPMG, New Delhi.

Maguire, Matthew (2011) *The Future of Corporate Social Responsibility Reporting*. Issues in Brief 34. Boston University, The Frederick S. Pardee Center for the Study of the Longer-Range Future. Available at: http://www.bu.edu/pardee/files/2011/01/PardeeIIB-019-Jan-2011.pdf (accessed 27 April 2018).

Rangan, K., Chase, L. and Karim, S. (2012) *Why Every Company Needs a CSR Strategy and How to Build it*. Working paper (12-088). Harvard Business School, Boston, MA.

Sheth, A., Sanghavi, D., Bhagwati, A., Srinivasan, S. and Dastoor, Pakzan (2017) *India Philanthropy Report*. Bain Insights, 4 March. Bain & Company, Boston, MA.

Warner, T. (2014) *Public–Private Partnership in CSR in India: Ten Demonstrative Case Studies*. Confederation of Indian Industry, New Delhi.

2 A Holistic Approach for Achieving Impact through CSR

Suhas P. Wani,* Girish Chander and Kaushal K. Garg

International Crops Research Institute for the Semi-Arid Tropics, Patancheru, India

Abstract

Food and nutritional security of projected population of 9.7 billion globally and 1.7 billion in India by 2050 is the major challenge of the 21st century. Alongside the challenge is to improve farmers' income and upgrade agriculture as a business to make it attractive to the youth and generate livelihood options through value chain, as 55% of the population in India is dependent on agriculture and allied sectors. Holistic solutions are needed to effectively address the issues of increasing land degradation, water scarcity and threat of climate change to bring in sustainable system intensification and diversification to high-yielding, climate-smart and high-value crops. There is a need to focus on enhancing system productivity through crops and livestock and services in a holistic manner rather than crops alone. In spite of availability of game-changing technologies, the farms are far from realizing the productivity potential mainly due to ineffective delivery of knowledge and scientific solutions. This necessitates the need to strengthen the 'Science of Delivery' of holistic solutions to farmers. Capacity building of farmers involving traditional and modern tools like information and communication technology, collectivization as producer organization, on-farm mechanization and infrastructure development for handling, storage and transport is the key to develop/promote significant control measures in production and effective linkages with the markets. Post-production is a sector that needs to be developed for income supplements at farm level as well as agro-zone-wise processing facilities to strengthen farming enterprise. Targeted generation of livelihood options in the process is important for inclusive development, including mainstreaming of women.

2.1 Why a Holistic Approach?

Securing food and nutritional security is a major challenge of the 21st century as the global human population is projected to increase from around 6.9 billion in 2010 to around 9.7 billion by 2050 (United Nations, 2016). In India, population is also rapidly growing and is expected to reach 1460 million by 2025 and 1700 million by 2050 in contrast to 1210 million in 2011 (FAOSTAT, 2017; Government of India, 2017).

Along with food security of the masses, another issue in the country is that nearly 55% of the population in India is dependent on agriculture and allied sectors for their livelihoods; agriculture, meanwhile, contributes only 15% to the nation's gross domestic product (Government of India, 2016). The issue is further compounded by degrading soil and water resources and impending climate change. Vulnerability of the rural poor to climate change is very high due to poverty, poor infrastructure and urban centric

---

* Corresponding author: s.wani@cgiar.org

development of service and manufacturing sectors. Large yield gaps especially in dryland agriculture (Wani *et al.*, 2003, 2011a), along with lack of holistic approach to target system-context productivity, value chains and market linkages add to the plight of smallholders in the country. There is evidence indicating that every 1% increase in agricultural yields translates to 0.6% to 1.2% decrease in the percentage of absolute poor (Thirtle *et al.*, 2002). So, a holistic approach for inclusive development in rural areas is needed that brings in agroecology-wise strategies along with framework of implementation, monitoring and evaluation for the desired impacts. Corporate social responsibility (CSR) resources are needed urgently for inclusive and sustainable development through improving rural livelihoods by investments in sustainable management of natural resources.

Significant growth has been achieved in agriculture since the green revolution, but it has also brought uncertainty in terms of sustainability, while there is an unfinished agenda of improving productivity and income of farmers. For example, groundwater and surface water resources in India are exploited to irrigate about 44 and 21 million ha of agricultural lands respectively that together cover nearly 46% of total cultivable land (Wani *et al.*, 2016a). The groundwater resources have been indiscriminately exploited with withdrawal of less than 25 km³ (km³ = 1 billion cubic metre) in the 1960s increasing to more than 250 km³ in 2008 (Shah *et al.*, 2009), and now threaten future sustainability. Per capita water availability in the country has decreased from 5177 m³ in 1951 to 1625 m³ in 2011, with an associated decrease in per capita water availability of 1345 m³ in 2025 and 1140 m³ by 2050 (Wani *et al.*, 2012b; FAOSTAT, 2017; Government of India, 2017). Even with irrigation expansion in India, still around 45% of the area by the year 2050 will continue to remain as rainfed (Amarasinghe *et al.*, 2007), where water scarcity is a major limiting factor and there are hot spot regions of poverty and malnutrition with potential opportunities in unexploited two- to fourfold yield gaps (Wani *et al.*, 2009). As regards the land resources, the cropping intensity has increased from about 1.17 in the late 1960s/early 1970s to 1.38 during 2011 and supported enhanced food production from 74 million tons during 1966–67 to 259 million tons during

2011–12 (Government of India, 2016). However, mismanagement has led to widespread land degradation such as nutrient mining and declining soil carbon levels, which is now a major hindrance in enhancing productivity levels. Due to prolonged nutrient mining, drylands are depleted not only in primary nutrients like nitrogen, phosphorus and potassium but also secondary and micronutrients like sulfur, zinc, iron and boron (Sahrawat *et al.*, 2007, 2010; Wani *et al.*, 2011b, 2015; Chander *et al.*, 2013a,b,c, 2014a). There are other important costs in terms of ecosystem services along with stagnation of yields. Farm productivity and resource use efficiency in both irrigated and rainfed systems are declining over the years, due to inappropriate water and land management practices, water scarcity, land degradation, land fragmentation, lack of access to credit and markets, etc. (Wani *et al.*, 2016a,b). Further, the projected climate-change scenario has increased the chances of water uncertainty and land degradation, leading to the vulnerability of food production in tropical countries like India. This necessitates the need for holistic solutions for resilience-building of production systems and livelihoods of smallholders.

2.2 Existing Death Valley of Impact – The Main Challenge

In spite of a large number of game-changing technologies, there are large yield gaps in farmers' fields mainly due to the lack of awareness and access to the technologies (Wani *et al.*, 2017). During development of a technology, it rarely moves ahead of proof-of-concept/pilot stage to reach hundred thousands or millions of farmers' fields for a significant effect and this gap acts like a death valley of impact for any technology (Fig. 2.1). Multiple exogenous factors, lack of synergy among actors and deficiencies in technology delivery mechanisms account for this gap. For a positive impact, the technologies need to be customized in the local context and so researchers can no longer remain external actors, but need to engage in action research to develop appropriate solutions together with resource users (Hagmann *et al.*, 2002). We need to go beyond the compartmental approach for a significant impact to emerge on the ground.

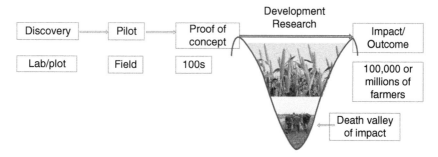

Fig. 2.1. Pictorial representation of the life cycle of a technology. From: Wani and Raju, 2016.

2.3 Framework of Holistic Solutions

2.3.1 Inclusive market-oriented development approach

Inclusive market-oriented development (IMOD) represents the development pathway of the International Crops Research Institute for the Semi-Arid Tropics (ICRISAT) to help the poor to harness markets while managing risks in order to most effectively reduce poverty, hunger, malnutrition and environmental degradation across the dryland tropics (ICRISAT, 2010). It encompasses harnessing markets for the poor and managing risks (Fig. 2.2). Innovations are required that help the poor gain economies of scale, work collectively for greater market coordination and clout, achieve innovative financing, increase technology and information flow and application, among other challenges. Innovations must also be dynamic rather than static. They must enable and incentivize the poor to move from left to right along the development curve rather than the old model of static innovations that may solve narrow technical problems yet still leave them poor because they are divorced from a development strategy. Further, risks are especially high for smallholders because they have few resources to fall back on. Risk management requires external help through development assistance and safety nets. As incomes increase through IMOD, smallholders increasingly reinvest in building their capacities to withstand and rebound from shocks by increasing various forms of capital (social, human, financial, institutional, environmental and others) and become more and more resilient.

2.3.2 Integrated watershed management – proven IMOD strategy for the drylands

Pilot studies have indicated that a participatory integrated watershed management approach is one of the tested, sustainable and ecofriendly options to upgrade rainfed agriculture to meet growing food demand along with additional multiple benefits in terms of improving livelihoods, addressing equity issues and biodiversity concerns (Wani *et al.*, 2012a,b, 2014). Water and soil conservation along with improved crop management opens up options for crop intensification and diversification, and strengthening the value chain for market-oriented development (Wani *et al.*, 2012a). Comprehensive assessment of watershed programmes in India undertaken by ICRISAT-led consortium has also revealed that 99% of watershed projects were economically remunerative and were silently revolutionizing rainfed agriculture with a benefit–cost ratio of 2, while reducing runoff by 45% and soil loss by 2–5 tons/ha/year, increasing agricultural productivity by 50% to 400%, and cropping intensity by 35% (Joshi *et al.*, 2008; Wani *et al.*, 2008). Additional benefits like generating rural employment of 151 days/ha/year were also noted. However, large scope existed for improving the performance of 68% of the watershed projects, which were performing below average. Programmes adopted uniform technologies, presuming that one size fits all. This resulted in good performance in only 700 to 1000 mm rainfall ecoregions, and the need for different strategies was indicated for low- and high-rainfall zones. There is also a need to consider climatic variability such as frequency of occurrence of

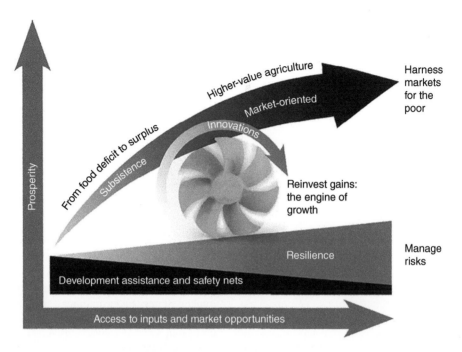

Fig. 2.2. Inclusive market oriented development pathway. From: ICRISAT, 2010.

extreme events while designing water-harvesting protocols. Experiences suggest that the implementation unit for watershed should be a micro-watershed (5000 to 10,000 ha), which can be further integrated for planning purposes into meso- and macro-watersheds and subsequently to subbasin and basin levels.

2.3.3   Strengthening the science of delivery of holistic solutions

Despite a large network of research and development institutions, there are serious deficiencies in the delivery of knowledge and scientific solutions to the farmers. Private companies and dealer networks mainly cover this gap to provide information on inputs such as crop seeds and varieties, pesticides, fertilizers, etc., but in most cases may not be well informed and may be guided mostly by business interests. Timely access to quality inputs like seeds and micronutrients is a limiting factor. Infrastructure for precise and thorough diagnosis of soil health is poorly developed. In the vast network of laboratories established, most are half-functional or dysfunctional and cost-ineffective and rarely the laboratories are equipped for thorough analysis of macro and micronutrients and other chemical, physical and biological parameters. Further, farmers rarely get information in time and mostly in a format that they fail to understand. Climate change scenario (Kesava Rao and Wani, 2016) requires reorientation of management practices as effective adaptation and mitigation strategies. Different geographies are likely to experience changes in length of growing period, rainfall pattern, water scarcity, soil erosion, loss of soil carbon and nutrients, emergence of new pests and diseases, etc. A weak delivery system threatens not only our food security but also livelihoods of smallholders especially in the drylands.

In view of current and emerging challenges, there is a strong need for strengthening the 'Science of Delivery' to ensure benefits of science to farmers in the country. It encompasses collective action among knowledge-generating and knowledge-disseminating institutions in public and private sectors, enhancing access to timely knowledge and inputs along with necessary policy orientation. *Bhoochetana*, in Karnataka state of India, is an exemplary initiative of showcasing the 'Science of Delivery' of innovative technologies. The concept of '4 Cs' was adopted in the project (Wani, 2016). The first C is 'Consortium' of research, education and field-based agencies to implement this programme effectively at ground level. The second C is 'Convergence' within the department schemes and other programmes. The third C is 'Capacity building' of the consortium partners, farm facilitators, lead farmers and other stakeholders. The fourth C is 'Collective action' at all levels during programme implementation in a mission mode. Apart from adopting '4 Cs' concept, efforts were also made to ensure that the '4 Es' – efficiency, economic gain, equity and environment protection – were also achieved at ground level.

There is a strong need of rejuvenating extension system with innovations to keep pace with current challenges and aspirations of people. Information and communication technology (ICT) has an important role in scaling-up the site-specific technologies. As an example in the *Bhoochetana* initiative in Karnataka, an App called *Krishi Gyan Sagar* was developed to provide up-to-date knowledge to the extension and para-extension workers in the local language as well as in English using tablets, smartphones and the web. This app had modules for plant protection and site-specific fertilizer recommendations, so proved quite effective in scaling-up the site-specific fertilizer recommendations. Farmer-to-farmer knowledge-sharing videos are another effective ICT tool. With a strong mobile phone network of nearly 500 million subscribers and the internet (>150 million internet users) spreading rapidly in rural India, these ICT-based tools can play a pivotal role in dissemination of real-time quality information and knowledge to farmers. Initiatives like Digital India and Soil Health Card schemes open up a serious opportunity for the use of ICT tools in agriculture. Investing in the 'Science of Delivery' of knowledge and timely access to inputs needed is the key to ensure food and nutritional security of the country.

2.4 Holistic Solutions for Impact

2.4.1 Rainwater conservation

Water is the major driver for food production. Efficient rainwater management especially in drylands is the key to alleviate severe water scarcity. *In-situ* water conservation (green water augmentation) is very important and contributes major share as globally green water used for food production is threefold more (5000 km³/year) than blue (irrigated) water (1800 km³/year). In integrated watershed management, the first and topmost priority is *in-situ* moisture conservation by adopting appropriate landforms (contour cultivation, bunding including gated bunds, broadbed and furrow, ridge and furrow, tied ridges, dead furrows, etc.), soil organic matter amendments, mulching, canopy management and other practices.

Runoff rainwater is harvested in various *ex-situ* water harvesting structures at community and farm levels depending on the runoff and soil strata. Due focus needs to be given to rainwater harvesting at farm level as a drought proofing strategy in the drylands. Pilot studies in drylands of Andhra Pradesh and other sites indicate that small low-cost farm ponds provide access to water for critical irrigation during drought and check yield losses up to 20–60% (see Chapter 11, this volume; ICRISAT, 2015; Dryland Systems, 2016), and also facilitate other farm operations like growing vegetable gardens, composting, etc. Realizing the benefits, the concept is catching up with policy makers and donors. The Government of Andhra Pradesh has piloted the construction of about 600,000 farm ponds during 2016–17. Similarly, by 2016–17 in the state of Karnataka, storing runoff rainwater from the farmer's field and using stored water for crops has been promoted under the *Krishi Bhagya* scheme with over 100,000 farmers. The *Jalyukt Shivar* scheme in Maharashtra aims to make 5000 villages free of water scarcity every year through digging of farm ponds and other water conservation works. Understanding the farm-level focus, the Government of India scheme, *Har Khet Ko Pani 'Pradhan Mantri Krishi Sinchayee Yojana (PMKSY)'*, has been formulated with the vision of extending the coverage of irrigation and improving water-use efficiency with end-to-end solutions on source creation, distribution and field application. Focused extensive efforts from all stakeholders including CSR partners are needed in this direction for drought-proofing of dryland farmers.

There is increasing evidence in the watershed sites that different interventions are effective in reducing rainwater runoff and the associated soil loss and improving groundwater recharge and other ecosystem services for human well-being (Joshi *et al.*, 2005; Wani *et al.*, 2011b, 2012a,b, 2014; Garg and Wani, 2013). In case of the *Kothapally* watershed pilot study in Telangana state, the soil loss in untreated area was 3.48 t/ha, while in treated watershed it was 1.62 t/ha only. Similarly, in the ICRISAT on-station watershed, long-term mean data shows soil loss of 6.64 t/ha in untreated area and only 1.60 t/ha in treated area.

In the present scenario, there is also an urgent need to develop a policy framework to govern the use of groundwater resources. Aquifer mapping and recharging needs to be undertaken on a priority basis. Also, groundwater quality deterioration with increased heavy metals, pesticides and salinity is a point of concern. Such problem areas need urgent attention.

2.4.2   Enhancing water-use efficiency

Pilot studies have shown that various watershed interventions enhanced productive transpiration and increased rainwater use efficiency for crop production by 13–160% (Wani *et al.*, 2012a). Enhancing the water-use efficiency and minimizing the unproductive evaporation loss of water through micro-irrigation (MI) systems (sprinklers and drip) is also a major opportunity in India (ICRISAT, 2016). Properly designed and managed MI systems can save up to 40–80% of water through increased water use efficiency up to 100% when compared to a mere 30–40% under the conventional surface irrigation system (Palanisami *et al.*, 2011). In India, total potential area coverage under MI is about 42 million ha through groundwater resources (Wani *et al.*, 2009; Palanisami *et al.*, 2011). Of this, about 30 million ha area is suitable for sprinkler irrigation for crops like cereals, pulses and oilseeds in addition to fodder crops, and 12 million ha for drip irrigation for cotton, sugarcane, fruits and vegetables, spices, condiments and some pulse crops like pigeonpea, etc. The percentage of actual area against the potential area estimated under drip irrigation in different states ranges from negligible in Nagaland to as much as 50% in undivided Andhra Pradesh (presently Andhra Pradesh and Telangana state), followed by Maharashtra

(43%) and Tamil Nadu with 24% (Palanisami *et al.*, 2011). In case of sprinkler irrigation, the percentage of actual area against the potential area estimated was as low as 0.01% (Bihar) and the highest was 52% (Andhra Pradesh). Compared to the potential of 42 million ha in the country, area under MI during 2011 was only 3.87 million ha (1.42 million ha under drip and 2.44 million ha under sprinkler) which is about 9% of the entire potential, which shows huge scope to harness the full potential.

2.4.3   Soil health

In view of widespread multiple nutrient deficiencies in Indian soils and exemplary impact seen under the *Bhoochetana* initiative in Karnataka and pilot sites across India, soil health mapping-based fertilizer management is a proven low-hanging entry point intervention for improving productivity and livelihoods, while strengthening the basic soil resource base. Under the *Bhoochetana*, the strategies to rejuvenate farm soil health through balancing the deficient micro- and secondary nutrients along with primary nutrients have shown 20% to 70% higher food production (Wani, 2012; Wani *et al.*, 2013; Chander *et al.*, 2016; ICRISAT, 2016). Even in comparatively drier years, application of balanced nutrients through including micro- and secondary nutrients significantly increased grain yield and aboveground dry matter which provides resilience against drought and food security (Uppal *et al.*, 2015). During 2009 to 2013, more than 5 million farmers benefited and net economic benefits through increased production were estimated as US$353 million (₹1963 crore). Taking the lead, the Government of Andhra Pradesh has also initiated the *Rythu Kosam* initiative with soil health rejuvenation as low-hanging technology to harness and build on it to improve primary-sector productivity and profitability along the value chain. Nutrient depletion also affects the quantity and quality of crop residue (Blümmel *et al.*, 2009a,b; Haileslassie *et al.*, 2011), which has an important role as feed components in the dominant mixed crop-livestock systems, and thereof affects the potential milk yield as high as 40% (Haileslassie *et al.*, 2013). There is also evidence of relation of soil quality and balanced fertilization with food quality, especially in terms of micronutrient contents (Sahrawat *et al.*, 2008, 2013; Chander *et al.*, 2013b) with a great scope to have widespread impact in reducing malnutrition in women and children, which is an important global issue. Integrated management of soil health not only increases food and nutritional security but also renders ecosystem benefits through increasing carbon sequestration, nutrient nitrogen and phosphorus use efficiency and decreasing fertilizer-based pollution (Wani *et al.*, 2003; Chander *et al.*, 2014b), and thereby ensures sustainability.

As smallholders dominate Indian agriculture and considering the practical difficulties, soil health mapping can be effective when adopted as a national strategy (Wani *et al.*, 2016b). Uniform sampling guidelines to collect samples in grids representing effectively the topography, soil texture, soil colour, farm size, cropping systems and management practices are important. In order to ensure quality, protocols and processes for accreditation of laboratories assume importance. The quality assurance standards as well as mechanisms to ensure quality analysis by the accredited labs by empowering leading institutions are important. Soil test-based fertilizer recommendations including deficient micro- and secondary nutrients should be developed at block (cluster of villages) level. Subsequently, village- and farmer-based recommendations should be made as awareness develops among the farmers, and the government is geared up to handle knowledge dissemination for villagers and individuals. Taking into account the benefits of integrated nutrient management, incentives are required to promote the use of organic manures as well as biofertilizers. There is an urgent need to look at policies and innovative institutional arrangements for ensuring quality supply of biofertilizers and organic manure to the farmers by recycling organic wastes generated both in urban and rural areas. As an example, crops like pigeonpea, cotton, maize, pearl millet and sorghum grown in around 37 million ha in India produce more than 100 million tons hardy straw biomass per year, which has little economic value or effective alternate use by farmers. This biomass is a potential opportunity to recycle plant nutrients worth more than ₹3000 crore per year through innovations in arranging shredders for chopping biomass on sharing basis and promoting accelerated vermicomposting technologies or aerobic composting which prove to be economically remunerative from the first year. Along with mapping for potential recyclable biomass, regions with current low chemical fertilizer use could also be prioritized and promoted as niche areas for organic farming without compromising with yield and harnessing premium price for the farmers. From sustainability point of view, land use planning based on land and agroecological capability is important and it can be promoted through incentivizing the farmers to adopt the recommended cropping system and applying penalties in terms of not providing the incentives and market support for crops that are not to be grown in a given agroecoregion.

2.4.4 Crops and cropping systems management

India has varying agroecologies from arid and semi-arid to subhumid and humid tropics with rainfall varying from 166 mm at Jaisalmer to 11,873 mm at Mawsynram, Meghalaya (Wani *et al.*, 2016a). In addition, soil types range from sandy soils in the desert to clayey to peat soils. The huge potential of these varying agroecologies can be harnessed through science-led planning and development, which would ensure sustainability as well as profitability to farmers, and ensuring food and nutritional security to the country. However, such land-use planning could be promoted through incentivizing farmers to adopt recommended cropping system and adopting coherent policies. Further evidence is emerging that climate change is making the rainfall variability more intense with increased frequency of extreme events such as drought and floods. Shifts in agroclimates observed (Kesava Rao and Wani, 2016) may necessitate redelineation of agro-eco-zones for effectives plans.

Most of the crop production systems in the country are characterized by low-yielding varieties and varietal replacement of cereals, pulses and oilseeds is an important opportunity to enhance food security and improve farmers' incomes (Chander *et al.*, 2016; Sawargaonkar *et al.*, 2016). Studies have shown a productivity advantage of 30–140% through using improved high-yielding cultivars and 1 rupee spent on improved variety seed resulted in an additional return of ₹3–50 in crops like finger millet, sorghum, pearl millet, groundnut, soybean, castor, pigeonpea and chickpea (Chander *et al.*, 2013c, 2016). Strengthening the seed systems along with decentralized on-farm seed production may be the key. Through addressing the issues of water and soil, policy support for market-led shift to high-value agriculture will empower smallholders economically, while enhancing food diversity (Chander *et al.*, 2013a).

Cropping system management to meet shortfall of protein needs of human diets in India through enhancing pulses production is also a priority area. Pulses are considered very important sources of proteins, vitamins and minerals, and are popularly known as 'poor man's meat' and 'rich man's vegetable'. They contribute significantly to the nutritional security of the country. In a short term of 3–5 years, the country needs to be made self-sufficient by intensification of area under pulses (~5 million ha rice fallows and increasing cropping intensity through intercropping). Efforts need to be made on intensification in pulses area through increasing productivity by scaling-up high-yielding cultivars, mechanization and efficient use of soil, water and nutrients, while simultaneously focusing on breeding lines to develop stress tolerant high-yielding cultivars to make pulses production systems climate resilient, profitable and sustainable to meet the growing demand in the country. Post-rainy fallow regions are potential opportunities for pulse revolution. Considerable amount of green water is available after the monsoon in these rice fallow systems, which could be easily utilized by introducing a short-duration legume crop with simple seed priming and micronutrient amendments (Kumar Rao *et al.*, 2008; Wani *et al.*, 2009; Singh *et al.*, 2010). Of the 14.29 million ha (30% of rice-growing area) rice fallows available in the Indo-Gangetic Plains, spread across Bangladesh, Nepal, Pakistan and India, about 11.4 million ha (82%) are in the Indian states of Bihar, Madhya Pradesh, Chhattisgarh, Jharkhand, West Bengal, Odisha and Assam (Subba Rao *et al.*, 2001). Taking advantage of the sufficiently available soil moisture, after harvesting rice crop, during the winter season in eastern India, growing early maturing chickpea with best-bet management practices provides opportunity for intensification (Harris *et al.*, 1999; Kumar Rao *et al.*, 2008). An economic analysis has shown that growing legumes in rice fallows is profitable for farmers with a benefit–cost ratio of more than 3 for many legumes. In addition, utilizing rice fallows for growing legumes could result in generating 584 million person-days employment for South Asia in addition to making India self-sufficient in pulses production.

Along with rice fallows, rainy season fallows are another opportunity for intensification and improving farm-based livelihoods. Vertisols and associated soils which occupy large areas are traditionally cultivated during the post-rainy season on stored soil moisture. Due to poor infiltration rates and waterlogging, farmers face difficulties in cultivating such lands during the rainy season. It is perceived that the practice of fallowing Vertisols and associated soils in Madhya Pradesh has decreased after the introduction of soybean. However, 2.02 million ha of cultivable land is still kept fallow in Central India, during *kharif* (rainy) season (Wani *et al.*, 2002; Dwivedi *et al.*, 2003). Vertisols with good moisture-holding capacity can be used to grow short-duration soybean by adopting reliable land management practices along with a good post-rainy season crop (Dwivedi *et al.*, 2003; Wani *et al.*, 2016c).

2.4.5 Inclusive system-context development

Inclusive system-context development signifies improving not only crop productivity but also the system productivity as such from agriculture, horticulture, animal husbandry and non-farm sector to improve overall income of farmers. This concept focuses on identifying and developing resilient, diversified and more productive combinations of crop, livestock, rangeland, aquatic and agroforestry systems that increase productivity, reduce hunger and malnutrition, and improve the quality of life of the rural people. Customized innovative technological solutions are needed for enhancing system productivity. The major focus of CSR pilot site activities in general is on not only productivity enhancement and value chain in agriculture but also targeting horticulture plantations in marginal lands and fodder promotion for livestock among other site-specific interventions.

Inclusive development focuses on not only landholders but also the landless, including the mainstreaming of women through developing livelihood options along the value chain. Livelihood approach is the main pillar for integrated watershed management to improve family income as well as food and nutritional security.

2.4.6 Modernizing agriculture: on-farm mechanization

How to attract youth to agriculture and promote agribusiness? This is the most important issue in agriculture. Mechanization in modern agriculture is essential to do away with the drudgery and to improve operational efficiency of farms. On-farm mechanization is a scalable technology to improve productivity and income through efficiency in on-farm operations like sowing, interculture, harvesting and threshing. Studies indicate that increase in power availability results in an increase in crop intensity and productivity, envisaging the importance of mechanization in improving farm-based livelihoods. The scope of mechanization is demonstrated in pilot sites through various low-cost machinery on a sharing basis like the tropicultor for sowing operations on a raised landform, shredders for chopping biomass, easy planters for vegetable transplanting, seed grading machines, groundnut dry/wet pod threshers, etc.

2.4.7 Value chain

Agriculture is a disorganized industry with little control over production. Science and technology along with modern business management are needed to bring in such control features in this enterprise. Development of handling, storage and transport infrastructure is need of the day for effective handling of markets by the farmers. Post-production is an area which is mostly neglected and is in infancy. Primary processing at farm/village level along with zone-wise centralized processing facilities may contribute significantly in strengthening the farm sector. A favourable policy and collective effort by government, private sector, and research and development institutions are needed for the desired change. The terms of trade which are generally biased towards farming sector need to be reexamined and brought in line with other sectors.

2.4.8 Collectivization: farmer producer organizations

The small size and little bargaining power of farmers in the country is the major cause for most of the problems. Hence, collectivization of producers, especially small and marginal farmers, into farmer producer organizations (FPOs) has emerged as one of the most effective pathways to address the many challenges of agriculture like improved access to investments, technology, inputs and markets. The FPOs may enable reaping the benefits of economies of scale, reduce the transaction costs, improve profit margins and effectively manage risks and uncertainties. However, strong stewardship for capacity building and strengthening the knowledge base of farmers along with help in formulating good business plans and management will be needed for the success. The Government of Andhra Pradesh along with ICRISAT as technical partner is promoting FPOs under *Rythu Kosam* as a possible mechanism to intervene at farmer level to aggregate the produce and increase the collective incomes of the farming community in agriculture, horticulture, fisheries and dairy sectors.

2.4.9 Capacity building and innovative extension system

One of the reasons for large yield gaps between current yield and the potential yield that researchers achieve in a pilot site is the knowledge gap between 'What to do' and 'How to do it'. In spite of a number of new/improved technologies and products available at research institutes and state agricultural universities, farmers continue to do their business in a traditional manner. The reasons are multifarious as the current knowledge delivery system, i.e. extension system, is inefficient and does not benefit the farmers. As per a recent national sample survey, over 59% of the farm households received no assistance from either government or private extension services (NSSO, 2013). Therefore, there is an urgent need to reform the knowledge delivery systems in the states and the country by using innovative partnerships, tools, approaches and methods.

The CSR pilot and scaling-up experiences demonstrated that the information delivery mechanism can be strengthened by utilizing the services of practising farmers in the villages through farmers' field schools and farmer facilitators who stay in the villages for most of their time, unlike external experts who visit villages once in a while. The mix of tools like soil health cards, leaflets, wall writings, awareness campaigns, media, learning sites, farmer-to-farmer videos, pico projectors and ICT tools like mobile and internet facility have proved very effective in disseminating improved management options in the watersheds. With increasing connectivity through Digital India initiative of the Government of India, there is wide scope for decision making, monitoring, impact analysis and knowledge dissemination for resource optimization in agriculture and allied sectors using ICT. As trained human resource is a major constraint in the agricultural extension system, various ICTs are available which can bridge the gap between farmer and knowledge generator. Rapidly evolving information technology industry and a favourable environment for ICT in agriculture are giving a great boost to agricultural extension in India. Coordination among government and private companies is needed by developing or bringing them on to a common platform. Moreover, scientific tools such as GIS (geographical information system), remote sensing and systems modelling can be integrated and used effectively to benefit farmers. Better agro-advisory services for crop production, markets and other issues may benefit farmers a lot. Agromet Advisory Services can be successfully rendered if the forecasts can be interpreted properly for taking on-farm decisions and educating farmers continuously. Currently, agrometeorology advisory content is limited to SMS (short message service)-based system. In future, innovative tablet-based or email-based agromet advisories along with detailed information as wall writings in local language need to be promoted. A consortium of partners comprising of India Metorological Department, national and state research organizations, state agricultural universities, international research organizations, government departments, non-governmental organizations (NGOs) and commercial companies (related to seed, fertilizer and plant protection) is needed for ensuring a better advisory service and identifying suitable adaptation strategies. An alternate cropping plan, critical inputs such as seeds, fertilizers, pesticides,

manures and postharvest strategies such as go-downs, cold storage and marketing information should be made available through information centres at the state and district levels with a 24/7 toll-free number to avail of the services.

The CSR pilot and scaling-up experiences proved that enhancing partnerships and institutional innovations through the consortium approach is the major impetus for harnessing the potential of community watershed management to reduce poverty and environmental degradation. The underlying element of the consortium approach is to engage a range of actors to harness their strengths and synergies with the local community as the primary implementing unit. Through the consortium approach, complex issues can be effectively addressed by the joint efforts of key partners like national agricultural research system, NGOs, government organizations, international institutions, agricultural universities, community-based organizations and other private-interest groups, with farm households as the key decision makers. Thus, the consortium approach brings together the expertise of different areas to expand the effectiveness of the various watershed initiatives and interventions. The public–private partnership (PPP) is an effective strategy to minimize transaction costs and to coordinate and enforce relations between the partners engaged in production of goods and services.

Working on 'seeing is believing', pilot sites of learning need to be developed in each district as exemplary sites for training as well as developmental purposes and CSR pilot sites are serving well. Such sites of learning need to be developed by the scientific institutions by adopting the consortium approach and building PPP. These sites of learning would also provide field laboratories for undertaking strategic research in the area of management strategies as well as impact assessment, monitoring and evaluation studies.

2.5   Summary and Key Findings

Ensuring food and nutritional security of the burgeoning population in India is a big challenge for the country. From the food point of view and mainstreaming of smallholders, the focus on drylands, which were bypassed during the green revolution, is now inevitable. There are large and economically exploitable yield gaps in the drylands, which can be easily bridged with current levels of technologies if holistic and integrated soil-crop-water-livestock-related solutions adapted to local conditions are made available to farmers. The 'Science of Delivery', involving timely end-to-end collective action along the value chain is the way forwards. There is an urgent need to transform rainfed agriculture, not only for increasing agricultural production and profits, but also to make it attractive for youth and women as a respectable profession by using scientific tools for mechanization, knowledge sharing, establishing market linkages and value addition. Such practices ensure a larger share of benefits through retaining processing in the villages with substantially increased investments, enabling policies and institutions. Projects such as *Bhoochetana* in Karnataka and *Rythu Kosam* in Andhra Pradesh are examples of scaling-up initiatives and harnessing benefits for the farmers. At the country level, such initiatives need to be scaled-up through innovative technology-driven institutional mechanisms with decentralized accountability for achieving large-scale impacts.

References

Amarasinghe, U.A., Shah, T., Turral, H. and Anand, B.K. (2007) *India's Water Future to 2025–2050: Business-as-Usual Scenario and Deviations*. IWMI Research Report 123. International Water Management Institute, Colombo, Sri Lanka.

Blümmel, M., Anandan, S. and Prasad, C.S. (2009a) Potential and limitations of by-product based feeding systems to mitigate greenhouse gases for improved livestock productivity. In: Gowda, N.K.S., Senani, S., Bhatta, R. and Pal, D.T. (eds) *Diversification of Animal Nutrition Research in the Changing Scenario*. Volume 1 (Lead papers). 13th Biennial Animal Nutrition Conference, 7–19 December 2009, Bangalore, India. ILRI, Hyderabad, India and Animal Nutrition Society of India, Bangalore, India, pp. 68–74.

Blümmel, M., Samad, M., Singh, O.P. and Amede, T. (2009b) Opportunities and limitations of food–feed crops for livestock feeding and implications for livestock–water productivity. *Rangeland Journal* 31, 207–213.

Chander, G., Wani, S.P., Maheshwer, D.L., Hemalatha, P., Sahrawat, K.L. *et al.* (2013a) Managing soil fertility constraints in market-led shift to high value agriculture for benefiting smallholders in the semi-arid tropics. *Journal of SAT Agricultural Research* 11, 1–11.

Chander, G., Wani, S.P., Sahrawat, K.L., Kamdi, P.J., Pal, C.K. *et al.* (2013b) Balanced and integrated nutrient management for enhanced and economic food production: case study from rainfed semi-arid tropics in India. *Archives of Agronomy and Soil Science* 59(12), 1643–1658.

Chander, G., Wani, S.P., Sahrawat, K.L., Pal, C.K. and Mathur, T.P. (2013c) Integrated plant genetic and balanced nutrient management enhances crop and water productivity of rainfed production systems in Rajasthan, India. *Communications in Soil Science and Plant Analysis* 44, 3456–3464.

Chander, G., Wani, S.P., Sahrawat, K.L., Dixit, S., Venkateswarlu, B. *et al.* (2014a) Soil test-based nutrient balancing improved crop productivity and rural livelihoods: case study from rainfed semi-arid tropics in Andhra Pradesh, India. *Archives of Agronomy and Soil Science* 60(8), 1051–1066.

Chander, G., Wani, S.P., Sahrawat, K.L. and Rajesh, C. (2014b) Enhanced nutrient and rainwater use efficiency in maize and soybean with secondary and micro nutrient amendments in the rainfed semi-arid tropics. *Archives of Agronomy and Soil Science* 61(3), 285–298.

Chander, G., Wani, S.P., Krishnappa, K., Sahrawat, K.L., Pardhasaradhi, G. and Jangawad, L.S. (2016) Soil mapping and variety based entry-point interventions for strengthening agriculture-based livelihoods – exemplar case of 'Bhoochetana' in India. *Current Science* 110(9), 1683–1691.

Dryland Systems (2016) Small ponds make for big progress among farmers in India. Available at: http://drylandsystems.cgiar.org/outcome-stories/small-ponds-make-big-progress-among-farmers-india (accessed 9 April 2018).

Dwivedi, R.S., Ramana, K.V., Wani, S.P. and Pathak, P. (2003) Use of satellite data for watershed management and impact assessment. In: Wani, S.P., Maglinao, A.R., Ramakrishna, A. and Rego, T.J. (eds) *Integrated Watershed Management for Land and Water Conservation and Sustainable Agricultural Production in Asia*. Proceedings of the ADB-ICRISAT-IWMI Project Review and Planning Meeting, 10–14 December 2001, Hanoi, Vietnam. International Crops Research Institute for the Semi-Arid Tropics, Patancheru, India, pp. 149–157.

FAOSTAT (2017) Data: Annual Population. Available at: http://faostat.fao.org/site/550/default.aspx#ancor (accessed 9 April 2018).

Garg, K.K. and Wani, S.P. (2013) Opportunities to build groundwater resilience in the semi-arid tropics. *Ground Water* 51(5), 679–691.

Government of India (2016) *Agricultural Statistics at a Glance 2016.* Directorate of Economics and Statistics, Department of Agriculture & Cooperation, Ministry of Agriculture, Government of India, New Delhi. Available at: http://eands.dacnet.nic.in/PDF/Glance-2016.pdf (accessed 9 April 2018).

Government of India (2017) *2011 Census Data.* Office of the Registrar General & Census Commissioner, Ministry of Home Affairs GoI, New Delhi. Available at: http://censusindia.gov.in (accessed 9 April 2018).

Hagmann, J., Chuma, E., Muriwira, K., Connolly, M. and Ficarelli, P. (2002) Success factors in integrated natural resource management R&D: lessons from practice. *Conservation Ecology* 5(2), 29.

Haileslassie, A., Blümmel, M., Clement, F., Descheemaeker, K., Amede, T. *et al.* (2011) Assessment of live-stock feed and water nexus across mixed crop livestock system's intensification gradient: an example from the Indo-Ganaga Basin. *Experimental Agriculture* 47, 113–132.

Haileslassie, A., Blümmel, M., Wani, S.P., Sahrawat, K.L., Pardhasaradhi, G. and Samireddypalle, A. (2013) Extractable soil nutrient effects on feed quality traits of crop residues in the semiarid rainfed mixed crop–livestock farming systems of Southern India. *Environment Development and Sustainability* 15, 723–741.

Harris, D., Joshi, A., Khan, P.A., Gothkar, P. and Sodhi, P.S. (1999) On-farm seed priming in semi-arid agri-culture: development and evaluation in maize, rice and chickpea in India using participatory methods. *Experimental Agriculture* 35, 15–29.

ICRISAT (2010) *ICRISAT Strategic Plan to 2020 – Inclusive Market Oriented Development for Smallholder Farmers in the Tropical Drylands.* International Crops Research Institute for the Semi-Arid Tropics, Patancheru, India. Available at: http://www.icrisat.org/who-we-are/sp/icrisat-sp-2020.pdf (accessed 9 April 2018).

ICRISAT (2015) Drylands get greener with low-cost agri interventions and shared resources in Andhra Pradesh, India. International Crops Research Institute for the Semi-Arid Tropics. Available at: http://www.icrisat.org/newsroom/latest-news/happenings/happenings1699.htm (accessed 9 April 2018).

ICRISAT (2016) *Annual Report 2015–16: Strengthening Bhoochetana: A Sustainable Agriculture Mission for Improved Livelihoods in Karnataka, Annual Report 2015–2016.* International Crops Research Insti-tute for the Semi-Arid Tropics. Available at: http://oar.icrisat.org/9919 (accessed 26 April 2018).

Joshi, P.K., Jha, A.K., Wani, S.P., Joshi, L. and Shiyani, R.L. (2005) *Meta-analysis to Assess Impact of Watershed Programme and People's Participation.* Research Report No. 8. International Crops Research Institute for the Semi-Arid Tropics, Patancheru, India/Asian Development Bank, Manila, Philippines.

Joshi, P.K., Jha, A.K., Wani, S.P., Sreedevi, T.K. and Shaheen, F.A. (2008) *Impact of Watershed Program and Conditions for Success: A Meta-Analysis Approach.* Global Theme on Agroecosystems, Report No. 46. International Crops Research Institute for the Semi-Arid Tropics, Patancheru, India/National Centre for Agricultural Economics and Policy Research, New Delhi.

Kesava Rao, A.V.R. and Wani, S.P. (2016) Impact of climate change on agriculture and food security. In: Juvvadi, Devi Prasad (ed.) *Capacity Building for Climate Smart Agriculture.* BS Publications, Hyderabad, India, pp. 27–52.

Kumar Rao, J.V.D.K., Harris, D., Kankal, M. and Gupta, B. (2008) Extending rabi cropping in rice fallows of eastern India. In: Riches, C.R., Harris, D., Johnson, D.E. and Hardy, B. (eds) *Improving Agricultural Productivity in Rice-based Systems of the High Barind Tract of Bangladesh.* International Rice Re-search Institute, Los Banos, Philippines, pp. 193–200.

National Sample Survey Organisation (NSSO) (2013) *Situation Assessment Survey of Agricultural House-holds in India (70th round: July 2012–June 2013).* Ministry of Statistics and Programme Implementation, New Delhi.

Palanisami, K., Mohan, K., Kakumanu, K.R. and Raman, S. (2011) Spread and economics of micro-irrigation in India: evidence from nine states. *Economic & Political Weekly* XLVI (26 & 27), 81–86.

Sahrawat, K.L., Wani, S.P., Rego, T.J., Pardhasaradhi, G. and Murthy, K.V.S. (2007) Widespread deficien-cies of sulphur, boron and zinc in dryland soils of the Indian semi-arid tropics. *Current Science* 93, 1428–1432.

Sahrawat, K.L., Rego, T.J., Wani, S.P. and Pardhasaradhi, G. (2008) Sulfur, boron, and zinc fertilization effects on grain and straw quality of maize and sorghum grown in semi-arid tropical region of India. *Journal of Plant Nutrition* 31(9), 1578–1584.

Sahrawat, K.L., Wani, S.P., Pardhasaradhi, G. and Murthy, K.V.S. (2010) Diagnosis of secondary and micro-nutrient deficiencies and their management in rainfed agroecosystems: case study from Indian semi-arid tropics. *Communications in Soil Science and Plant Analysis* 41(3), 346–360.

Sahrawat, K.L., Wani, S.P. and Pardhasaradhi, G. (2013) Balanced nutrient management: effects on plant zinc. *Journal of SAT Agricultural Research* 11, 1–3.

Sawargaonkar, G., Rao, S.R. and Wani, S.P. (2016) An integrated approach for productivity enhancement. In: Raju, K.V. and Wani, S.P. (eds) *Harnessing Dividends from Drylands: Innovative Scaling up with Soil Nutrients*. CAB International, Wallingford, Oxfordshire, pp. 201–235.

Shah, A., Wani, S.P. and Sreedevi, T.K. (2009) *Impact of Watershed Management on Women and Vulnerable Groups*. Proceedings of the Workshop on Comprehensive Assessment of Watershed Programs in India, 25 July 2007. International Crops Research Institute for the Semi-Arid Tropics, Patancheru, India.

Singh, P., Pathak, P., Wani, S.P. and Sahrawat, K.L. (2010) Integrated watershed management for increasing productivity and water use efficiency in semi-arid tropical India. In: Kang, Manjit S. (ed.) *Water and Agricultural Sustainability Strategies*. CRC Press, Boca Raton, FL, pp. 181–205.

Subba Rao, G.V., Kumar Rao, J.V.D.K. and Kumar, J. (2001) *Spatial Distribution and Quantification of Rice-fallows in South Asia – Potential for Legumes*. International Crops Research Institute for the Semi-Arid Tropics, Patancheru, India.

Thirtle, C., Beyers, L., Lin, L., McKenzie-Hill, V., Irz, X., Wiggins, S. and Piesse, J. (2002) *The Impacts of Changes in Agricultural Productivity on the Incidence of Poverty in Developing Countries*. DFID Report No. 7946. Department for International Development, London.

United Nations (2016) *World Population Prospects, the 2015 Revision*. UN Department of Economic and Social Affairs, Population Division, New York.

Uppal, R.K., Wani, S.P., Garg, K.K. and Alagarswamy, G. (2015) Balanced nutrition increases yield of pearl millet under drought. *Field Crops Research* 177, 86–97.

Wani, S.P. (2012) *Bhoochetana – Rejuvenating Land and Livelihoods in Karnataka*. International Crops Research Institute for the Semi-Arid Tropics, Patancheru, India.

Wani, S.P. (2016) Evolution of Bhoochetana. In: Raju, K.V. and Wani, S.P. (eds) *Harnessing Dividends from Drylands: Innovative Scaling up with Soil Nutrients*. CAB International, Wallingford, Oxfordshire, pp. 34–58.

Wani, S.P. and Raju, K.V. (2016) Lessons learnt and a way forward. In: Raju, K.V. and Wani, S.P. (eds) *Harnessing Dividends from Drylands: Innovative Scaling up with Soil Nutrients*. CAB International, Wallingford, Oxfordshire, pp. 290–305.

Wani, S.P., Pathak, P., Tam, H.M., Ramakrishna, A., Singh, P. and Sreedevi, T.K. (2002) Integrated watershed management for minimizing land degradation and sustaining productivity in Asia. In: Adeel, Z. (ed.) *Integrated Land Management in the Dry Areas*. Proceedings of a Joint UNU-CAS International Workshop, 8–13 September 2001, Beijing, China. United Nations University, Tokyo, Japan, pp. 207–230.

Wani, S.P., Pathak, P., Sreedevi, T., Singh, H. and Singh, P. (2003) Efficient management of rainwater for increased crop productivity and groundwater recharge in Asia. In: Kijne, J.W., Barker, R. and Molden, D. (eds) *Water Productivity in Agriculture: Limits and Opportunities for Improvement*. CAB International, Wallingford, Oxfordshire, pp. 199–215.

Wani, S.P., Sreedevi, T.K., Reddy, T.S.V., Venkateswarlu, B. and Prasad, C.S. (2008) Community watersheds for improved livelihoods through consortium approach in drought prone rainfed areas. *Journal of Hydrological Research and Development* 23, 55–77.

Wani, S.P., Sreedevi, T.K., Rockström, J. and Ramakrishna, Y.S. (2009) Rainfed agriculture – past trends and future prospects. In: Wani, S.P., Rockström, J. and Oweis, T. (eds) *Rainfed Agriculture: Unlocking the Potential*. Comprehensive Assessment of Water Management in Agriculture Series. CAB International, Wallingford, Oxfordshire, pp. 1–35.

Wani, S.P., Rockström, J., Venkateswarlu, B. and Singh, A.K. (2011a) New paradigm to unlock the potential of rainfed agriculture in the semi-arid tropics. In: Lal, R. and Stewart, B.A. (eds) *World Soil Resources and Food Security*. Advances in Soil Science. CRC Press, Boca Raton, FL, pp. 419–469.

Wani, S.P., Sahrawat, K.L., Sarvesh, K.V., Baburao Mudbi and Krishnappa, K. (2011b) *Soil Fertility Atlas for Karnataka, India*. International Crops Research Institute for the Semi-Arid Tropics, Patancheru, India.

Wani, S.P., Dixin, Y., Li, Z., Dar, W.D. and Chander, G. (2012a) Enhancing agricultural productivity and rural incomes through sustainable use of natural resources in the SAT. *Journal of the Science of Food and Agriculture* 92, 1054–1063.

Wani, S.P., Garg, K.K., Singh, A.K. and Rockström, J. (2012b) Sustainable management of scarce water resource in tropical rainfed agriculture. In: Lal, R. and Stewart, B.A. (eds) *Soil Water and Agronomic Productivity*. Advances in Soil Science. CRC Press, Boca Raton, FL, pp. 347–408.

Wani, S.P., Sarvesh, K.V., Sahrawat, K.L., Krishnappa, K., Dharmarajan, B.K., Raju, K.V., Kaushik Mukherjee and Dar, W.D. (2013) *Bhoochetana: Building Resilience and Livelihoods through Integrated Watershed Management*. Resilient Dryland Systems Report No. 62. International Crops Research Institute for the Semi-Arid Tropics, Patancheru, India.

Wani, S.P., Chander, G. and Sahrawat, K.L. (2014) Science-led interventions in integrated watersheds to improve smallholders' livelihoods. *NJAS – Wageningen Journal of Life Sciences* 70/71, 71–77.

Wani, S.P., Chander, G., Sahrawat, K.L. and Pardhasaradhi, G. (2015) Soil test-based balanced nutrient management for sustainable intensification and food security: case from Indian semi-arid tropics. *Communications in Soil Science and Plant Analysis* 46(S1), 20–33.

Wani, S.P., Anantha, K.H., Garg, K.K., Joshi, P.K., Sohani, G. *et al.* (2016a) *Pradhan Mantri Krishi Sinchai Yojana: Enhancing the Impact through Demand Driven Innovations*. Research Report IDC-7. International Crops Research Institute for the Semi-Arid Tropics, Patancheru, India.

Wani, S.P., Chander, G., Bhattacharyya, T. and Patil, M. (2016b) *Soil Health Mapping and Direct Benefit Transfer of Fertilizer Subsidy*. Research Report IDC-6. International Crops Research Institute for the Semi-Arid Tropics, Patancheru, India.

Wani, S.P., Chander, G., Sahrawat, K.L., Pal, D.K., Pathak, P. *et al.* (2016c) Sustainable use of natural resources for crop intensification and better livelihoods in the rainfed semi-arid tropics of Central India. *NJAS – Wageningen Journal of Life Sciences* 78, 13–19.

Wani, S.P., Chander, G. and Anantha, K.H. (2017) Enhancing resource use efficiency through soil management for improving livelihoods. In: Rakshit, A., Abhilash, P., Singh, H. and Ghosh, S. (eds) *Adaptive Soil Management: From Theory to Practices*. Springer, Singapore, pp. 413–451.

3

Building Soil Health, Improving Carbon Footprint and Minimizing Greenhouse Gas Emissions through CSR

GIRISH CHANDER,* SUHAS P. WANI, G. PARDHASARADHI, MUKUND D. PATIL AND A.N. RAO

International Crops Research Institute for the Semi-Arid Tropics, Patancheru, India

Abstract

Unabated soil degradation due to low soil organic carbon (C) levels, multiple nutrient deficiencies including micro- and secondary nutrients, rising salinity and soil loss due to erosion jeopardizes food security of swiftly rising global population projected to be 9.7 billion by 2050. Soils also play a major role in global C cycling and huge C sequestration potential offers opportunities for mitigating carbon dioxide and other greenhouse gas emissions. The lessons learnt from CSR pilot and scaling-up initiatives indicated significant productivity benefits with soil health mapping-based management. The linkages of soil health and food quality are documented. Soil mapping-based management increased C sequestration with higher proportion of biomass C and enhanced uptake and use efficiency of nitrogen fertilizers, and thereby reducing losses through runoff and gaseous emissions. Management at watershed level is proved as one of the most trusted approach to managing natural resources and reducing runoff, soil loss and C and nutrients therein.

3.1 Why Soil Health, Carbon and Greenhouse Gases are Important

Soils are fundamental to life on Earth and careful soil management is one essential element of sustainable agriculture and also a valuable lever for climate regulation and a pathway for safeguarding ecosystem services. Soils provide ecosystem services categorized into four broad classes: provisioning; regulating; supporting; and cultural services (Table 3.1). Provisioning services refer to the products obtained of direct benefit to people; regulating services to the benefits obtained from the regulation of ecosystem processes; supporting services are necessary for the production of all other ecosystem services (their impacts on people are often indirect or occur over a very long time); and cultural services refer to non-material benefits which people obtain from ecosystems (FAO and ITPS, 2015).

As defined in the World Soil Charter, sustainable soil management comprises activities that maintain or enhance the supporting, provisioning, regulating and cultural services provided by soils without significantly impairing either the soil functions that enable those

---

* Corresponding author: g.chander@cgiar.org

Table 3.1. Ecosystem services provided by the soil, and soil functions that support these services. From: FAO and ITPS (2015).

Ecosystem service	Soil function
Provisioning	
Food supply	Providing water, nutrients and physical support for growth of plants for human and animal consumption
Fibre and fuel supply	Providing water, nutrients and physical support for growth of plant for bioenergy and fibre
Refugia	Providing habitat for soil animals, birds, etc.
Genetic resources	Source of unique biological materials
Raw earth material supply	Provision of topsoil, aggregates, peat, etc.
Surface stability	Supporting human habitations and related infrastructure
Water supply	Retention and purification of water
Regulating	
Climate regulation	Regulation of CO_2, N_2O and CH_4 emissions
Water quality regulation	Filtering and buffering of substances in soil water
	Transformation of contaminants
Water supply regulation	Regulation of water infiltration into soil and water flow within the soil
	Drainage of excess water out of soil and into groundwater and surface water
Erosion regulation	Retention of soil on the land surface
Supporting	
Soil formation	Weathering of primary minerals and release of nutrients
	Transformation and accumulation of organic matter
	Creation of structures (aggregates, horizons) for gas and water flow and root growth
	Creation of charged surfaces for ion retention and exchange
Nutrient cycling	Transformation of organic materials by soil organisms
	Retention and release of nutrients on charged surfaces
Primary production	Medium for seed germination and root growth
	Supply of nutrients and water for plants
Cultural	
Aesthetic and spiritual	Preservation of natural and cultural landscape diversity
	Source of pigments and dyes
Heritage	Preservation of archaeological records

services or biodiversity. Major threats to soil functions include nutrient imbalances, soil organic carbon (C) loss, soil erosion, salinization, soil acidification, soil contamination, soil compaction, waterlogging, soil sealing and loss of soil biodiversity.

In recent times, increasing land degradation is one of the major challenges and debatable topic. 'Land degradation' refers to a temporary or permanent decline in the productive capacity of the land, or its potential for environmental management. The most important on-farm effects of land degradation are declining potential yields or need to use a higher level of inputs in order to maintain yields. The unabated land degradation jeopardizes food security of swiftly rising population. The world population of 7.2 billion in

mid-2013 is projected to increase to 8.2 billion by 2025, 9.7 billion by 2050, and to rise to 10.9 billion by 2100 (UN, 2016). Carbon storage is an important ecosystem function of soils that has gained increasing attention in recent years due to its direct relation with soil health and mitigation potential of greenhouse gases (GHGs). There are major opportunities for mitigation of carbon dioxide (CO_2) and other GHG emissions through changes in the use and management of agricultural lands by maintaining or increasing stocks of organic C in soils (and biomass), and reduced emissions by the agricultural sector itself (Paustian *et al.*, 1998; Whitmore *et al.*, 2014). Inefficient nitrogen (N) fertilizer-related pollution is an issue of concern worldwide. Nitrogen fertilizer inputs in excess of crop requirements are linked to the enhanced release of nitrous oxide (N_2O), a GHG 300 times more potent than CO_2, and agricultural soils are the dominant source, contributing over 80% of global anthropogenic N_2O emissions during the 1990s. Nitrous oxide emissions from agricultural soils are projected to increase from just over four million tons N_2O N per year in 2010 to over 5 million tons N_2O N per year by 2030.

The impact of land degradation is especially severe on livelihoods of the poor who heavily depend on natural resources. The annual cost of land degradation at the global level was about US$ 300 billion (Nkonya *et al.*, 2016). Sub-Saharan Africa accounts for the largest share (22%) of the total global cost of land degradation. The analysis of the cost of land degradation across the type of ecosystem services shows that 54% of the cost is due to the losses in regulating, supporting and cultural services which are considered as global public goods. And hence reversing land degradation trends while improving C footprints and reducing GHG emissions definitely makes economic sense with multiple social and environmental benefits.

3.2   How Soil Health and Ecosystem Service Issues are Aggravated

According to the National Bureau of Soil Survey and Land Use Planning (2005) assessment during 2004, ~146.8 million ha is degraded. Erosion is the most serious degradation problem in India covering around 93.7 million ha under water erosion and 9.5 million ha under wind erosion. Inappropriate land and water management practices in agriculture along with other human interventions like land clearing and careless management of forests, deforestation, overgrazing, surface mining, industrial development, etc. contribute to erosion problem. Further, in the post-Green Revolution era, nutrient mining along with imbalanced use of fertilizers has created multiple nutrient deficiencies which threaten sustainability. Soil fertility degradation coupled with indiscriminate use of N fertilizers is a major factor for low N use efficiency and losses in runoff and as GHG emission. Imbalanced use of fertilizers arises due to fertilizer subsidy, inadequate availability of the required fertilizers at the stipulated time in rural areas and lack of knowledge among farmers as to what nutrients are required by the crops and what is missing in their land. Due to cheaper chemical fertilizers, farmers have moved away from using organic manures, which has led to depletion of soil organic C also. The public infrastructure for soil analysis is also poorly developed and farmers rarely get quality information in time. A fragmented approach to soil analysis has restricted analysis to only macronutrients. Over-exploitation of groundwater has also emerged as one of the major factors contributing to secondary salinization. Out of 42 million ha irrigation through groundwater sources in the country, the surveys indicate that poor-quality waters being utilized in different states are 32–84% of the total groundwater development (Dagar, 2005). Such increase in irrigated area as envisaged would lead to secondary salinization consequentially leading to estimated 16.2 million ha salt affected area by 2050.

3.3   Soil Degradation Challenges in General and in CSR Sites

Increasing soil degradation, if not addressed properly, poses grave challenge to the realization of ambitious Sustainable Development Goals (SDGs), a set of seventeen aspirational 'Global Goals' with 169 targets between them (Wani *et al.*, 2015; UN, 2017). The SDGs came into effect in January 2016 and are largely interconnected. Soil degradation and related issues pose direct challenges in realization of certain goals like – no poverty; zero hunger; good health and well-being; clean water and sanitation; climate action; and life on land.

At global scale, out of 8.7 billion ha of agricultural land, pasture, forest and woodland, nearly 2 billion ha (22.5%) have been degraded since mid-century (Scherr and Yadav, 1996). Nearly half of this vegetated area is under forest, of which about 18% is degraded; 3.2 billion ha are under pasture, of which 21% is degraded; and nearly 1.5 billion ha are in cropland, of which 38% is degraded. Overall, water erosion is the principal cause of degradation and wind erosion is an important cause in drylands and areas with landforms conducive to high winds.

Chemical degradation such as nutrient loss and salinization, a result of cropping practices, accounts for a smaller overall proportion of degraded lands, but more than 40% of cropland degradation. Degradation of cropland appears to be most extensive in Africa, affecting 65% of cropland area, compared with 51% in Latin America and 38% in Asia (Scherr and Yadav, 1996).

The pilot studies supported by seven corporate social responsibility (CSR) projects across eight states in India, viz. Andhra Pradesh, Jharkhand, Karnataka, Madhya Pradesh, Maharashtra, Odisha, Rajasthan and Telangana (Fig. 3.1), showed still higher soil degradation compared to in general 40% of cropland degradation globally under chemical degradation (Table 3.2). Soil organic C is an indicator of general soil health and most fields (5–87% fields with low C levels across pilot sites) are detected with low soil organic C. Low soil organic C also indicate N deficiency. Available phosphorus (P) deficiency ranged between 10% and 89%, while potassium (K) is not an issue of concern in most fields adequate in it except pilot sites in Jharkhand. Along with macronutrients, there are widespread

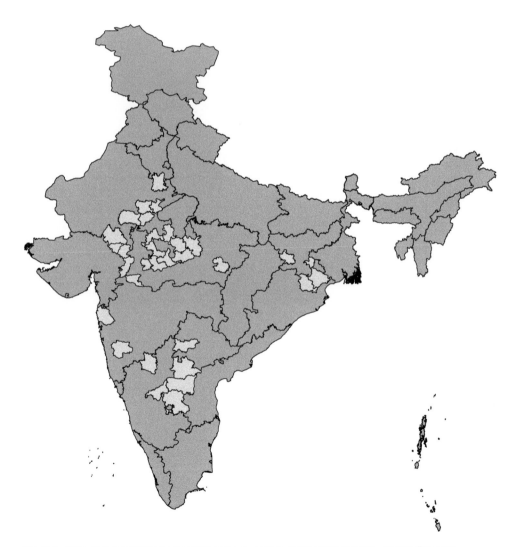

Fig. 3.1. Pilot sites supported under CSR projects across eight states in India: Andhra Pradesh, Jharkhand, Karnataka, Madhya Pradesh, Maharashtra, Odisha, Rajasthan and Telangana.

Table 3.2. Percentage of farm fields found deficient in available nutrients and having low levels of soil organic carbon (C) across CSR pilot sites in India.

CSR project	State	District	Mandal/Taluk/Block	% samples with low soil org C	pH	EC (dS/m)	P	K	S	Ca	Mg	Zn	B	Fe	Cu	Mn	No. of samples
Asian Paints	Telangana	Medak	Patancheru	59	8.06	0.44	10	0	35	1	0	62	19	1	0	0	189
Asian Paints	Maharashtra	Satara	Khandala	52	–	0.20	26	3	80	0	0	76	67	5	0	0	324
Jindal South West Steel Ltd	Karnataka	Bellary	Sandur	35	8.0	0.24	30	0	55	–	–	67	23	15	8	0	879
Jindal South West Steel Ltd	Maharashtra	Palghar	Jawhar	5	6.13	0.12	43	3	57	0	0	27	57	0	0	0	95
Rural Electrification Corporation Ltd	Telangana	Mahabubnagar	Wanaparthy	81	7.71	0.12	46	14	83	38	1	81	73	10	0	39	192
Rural Electrification Corporation Ltd	Andhra Pradesh	Anantapur	Penukonda	87	7.93	0.19	69	15	77	29	0	94	77	7	0	44	190
POWERGRID	Andhra Pradesh	Kurnool	Bethamcherla	50	7.48	0.19	15	8	76	80	0	75	35	4	0	12	169
POWERGRID	Karnataka	Bijapur	Basavan Bagewadi	49	8.16	0.27	89	0	71	0	0	94	16	8	0	0	187
SABMiller	Telangana	Medak	Pulkal, Sangareddy	71	7.76	0.29	28	6	55	6	0	66	45	0	0	2	246
Sir Dorabji Tata Trust	Rajasthan	Alwar, Banswara, Bhilwara, Bundi, Dungurpur, Jhalawar, Swai Madhopur, Tonk, Udaipur	Rajgarh, Kushalgarh, Jahajapur, Hindoli, Bichiwara, Jhalarapatal, Khandar, Deoli, Newai, Girwa	38	7.8	0.3	45	15	71	–	–	46	56	–	–	–	422
Sir Ratan Tata Trust	Jharkhand	Gumla, Kharsawan	Raidih, Saraikala	42	5.6	0.15	65	50	77	–	–	71	97	–	–	–	115
Sir Dorabji Tata Trust & Sir Ratan Tata Trust	Madhya Pradesh	Badwani, Dewas, Guna, Indore, Raisen, Rajgarh, Sagar, Sehore, Shajapur, Vidisha, Jhabua, Mandla	Badwani, Devas, Madusudangarh, Samer, Silwani, Rajgarh, JC Nagar, Sehore, Agar, Vidisha, Lateri, Meghnagar, Niwas	22	7.8	0.25	74	1	74	–	–	66	79	–	–	–	341
Sir Ratan Tata Trust	Odisha	Myurbhanj, Kyonjhar	Myurbhanj, Harichandanpur	18	5.5	0.12	73	10	96	–	–	7	99	–	–	–	177

deficiencies of secondary and micronutrients like 35–96% in sulfur (S), 16–99% in boron (B) and 7–94% in zinc (Zn), and 0–80% in calcium (Ca).

Most farmers are not aware of secondary and micronutrient deficiencies and their general practice is to add fertilizers containing only macronutrients NPK in suboptimal or indiscriminate amounts, which creates nutrient imbalances leading to increasing land degradation. Even with regard to macronutrients, the government fertilizer subsidy policy has promoted skewed fertilizer use in the country resulting in more application of N and P fertilizers in the NPK ratio of 8:2.7:1 (Government of India, 2014; Wani *et al.*, 2016). Inadequate availability of the required fertilizers at the stipulated time in rural areas and lack of knowledge is also promoting imbalanced fertilizer use. More importantly, while fertilizer consumption continues to rise substantially, the elasticity of output with respect to fertilizer use, especially N and P, has dropped sharply, i.e. declining fertilizer use efficiency. During the previous decade, while fertilizer consumption grew by 50%, the increase in food grain production was only 11% (Wani *et al.*, 2016). The increase in fertilizer use has increased the cost significantly. The fiscal burden of fertilizer subsidy was ₹60 crore in the years 1976–77, which shot up to over ₹70,000 crore in 2012–13. There are other important costs in the form of long-term soil degradation and stagnation of yields, low C-sequestration and degradation of water resources (in both quantity and quality). Besides, there is build-up of nutrients in pockets which is of concern today.

Along with agricultural fields, horticultural orchards and plantation crops also cover large tracts of land and are bypassed for any systematic soil health mapping and needs-based management. These are potential sites of increasing productivity and incomes, while improving C-footprints. For example, soil health mapping of fruit and plantation crops in Andhra Pradesh showed severely low levels of soil organic C and increasing nutrient deficiencies – 42–90% orchards/plantations in organic C, 3–70% in P, 1–40% in K, 10–89% in Ca, 21–96% in S, 18–80% in Zn, 8–85% in B, 0–45% in magnesium (Mg) and 0–63% in copper (Cu) (Table 3.3).

3.4 Building Soil Health and Ecosystem Services: A Low Hanging Technology

3.4.1 Soil health for food and nutritional security

One of the direct benefits that CSR scaling-up initiatives have demonstrated is improving food security. The strategies to rejuvenate farm soil health have shown significant productivity benefits that varied from 25% to 47% in cereals, 28% to 37% in pulses and 22% to 48% in oilseed crops (Chander *et al.*, 2016; Wani and Chander, 2016; Wani *et al.*, 2017). Even in comparatively drier years, soil health building through application of balanced fertilizers significantly increases grain yield and aboveground dry matter and adds to system resilience (Uppal *et al.*, 2015). Pilot

Table 3.3. Soil fertility status of soils in horticulture plantations across seven districts in Andhra Pradesh, India.

Crop	No. of samples	% samples with low soil C levels	% deficiency of available nutrients									
			P	K	Ca	Mg	S	Zn	B	Fe	Cu	Mn
East Godavari	720	76	63	36	81	9	88	64	71	0	37	2
Guntur	264	42	3	1	10	0	21	18	8	4	0	0
Krishna	2709	68	25	2	80	1	79	59	38	0	33	0
Srikakulam	641	90	41	40	89	45	95	59	85	1	63	1
Visakhapatnam	207	77	49	8	65	5	85	54	68	0	14	0
Vizianagaram	869	89	70	26	71	14	96	80	83	0	18	0
West Godavari	623	77	21	32	79	21	80	41	72	2	42	1
Grand total	6033	74	37	16	76	11	82	59	56	1	33	0

studies also show evidences of relation of soil health with food quality (Sahrawat *et al.*, 2008, 2013; Chander *et al.*, 2013a; Wani and Chander, 2016). Moreover, the outcome of soil degradation in predominant crop–livestock farming system in the drylands is far beyond reducing grain production; it also affects livestock feed quantity and quality (Blümmel *et al.*, 2009; Haileslassie *et al.*, 2011). In view of the increasingly important role of crop residue as feed components, the effects of soil health building through nutrient balancing on feed availability and feed quality are very important and show up in potential milk yield per ha by as high as 40% (Haileslassie *et al.*, 2013). The role of soil health building in enhancing food quantity and quality and helping individuals and communities to build sustainable food security is well demonstrated in Karnataka, India (Wani *et al.*, 2016).

Scaling-up soil health building in degraded drylands is important because out of 1.5 billion ha of cultivated land globally, about 1.1 billion ha (80% of world's physical agricultural area) is rainfed and generates about 60% of the world's staple food (Munir *et al.*, 2010). Evidences in the past few decades indicate that crop productivity growth in irrigated areas has slowed or stagnated and relying on irrigated agriculture for food security is not possible as data on water supply and demand are startling and as much as two-thirds of the world population could be water-stressed by 2025 (Seckler *et al.*, 1999; Richter *et al.*, 2003; Shah *et al.*, 2006). In Indian scenario, in spite of spectacular increase in food grain production from 74 million tons during 1966–67 to 259 million tons during 2011–12, the country still struggles for ensuring food security of its people who have grown from 361 million in 1951 to 1210 million in 2011 and are expected to reach the levels of 1460 million by 2025 and 1700 million by 2050 (Government of India, 2014; FAOSTAT, 2017). Therefore, consistent efforts are needed to increase the current food production levels to more than 300 million tons by 2025 and around 380 million tons by 2050 (Amarasinghe *et al.*, 2007). However, land resources are limited with almost no scope for expanding net sown area which has almost remained stagnant since the Green Revolution at about 141 million ha, but the cropping intensity has increased from about 1.17 in the late 1960s/early 1970s to 1.38 during 2011

(Government of India, 2014). Enhancing productivity is the way forward with limited opportunities in irrigated areas which are already near productivity plateau. The drylands with large yield gaps (Wani *et al.*, 2012b), thus, occupy centre stage and currently cover majority 54% (76 million ha) of cultivable land and in spite of irrigation expansion programmes are projected to still cover 45% (63 million ha) of area by 2050 (Amarasinghe *et al.*, 2007).

3.4.2 Improved nutrient and water use efficiency

Pilot studies (Chander *et al.*, 2014) show that soil health building through balanced fertilization including micro- and secondary nutrient amendments not only increase productivity, but also improve N and most importantly N use efficiency. The results show improvements in uptake and use efficiency of N and thereby reducing pollution through losses in runoff water and as GHG emissions. Moreover, improvements in agricultural productivity, resulting in yield increase and denser foliage will involve a vapour shift from nonproductive evaporation in favour of productive transpiration. Various CSR pilot studies also corroborate the benefits of soil health building in effectively utilizing available water to get higher crop yields (Chander *et al.*, 2013b, 2016).

3.4.3 Soil C sequestration and offsetting GHG emissions

Building soil health and managing C footprint is a great opportunity for CSR consortia to have a win-win proposition. Managing soil organic C is central because it influences numerous soil properties relevant to ecosystem functioning and crop growth. It is essential to improve soil resilience through beneficial impacts on the following processes (Lal, 2011):

- increase in soil aggregation and aggregate stability;
- improvement in total and macro-porosity;
- decrease in loss of soil water through increase in water infiltration rate and reduction in evaporation;

- improvement in plant available water capacity;
- reduction in susceptibility to crusting, compaction and erosion by water and wind, and decrease in non-point source pollution of rivers and lakes;
- increase in soil's cation and anion exchange capacity;
- increase in plant nutrient reserves, both capacity and intensity factors;
- increase in microbial biomass C, along with activity and species diversity of soil biota;
- increase in CH_4 oxidation capacity, and moderation of rates of nitrification and denitrification;
- reduction in leaching losses of soluble plant nutrients;
- increase in soil's buffering capacity, and moderation of elemental balance; and
- improvement in agronomic production, through increase in use efficiency of energy-based inputs (e.g. fertilizers, water and pesticides).

Even small changes in total C content can have disproportionately large impact on key soil physical properties (Powlson *et al.*, 2011). An increase of 1 ton of soil C pool of degraded cropland soils may increase crop yield by 200–400 kg/ha of maize, 20–70 kg/ha of wheat, 20–30 kg/ha of soybean, 5–10 kg/ha of cowpea, 10–50 kg/ha of rice, 50–60 kg/ha of millets and 20–30 kg/ha of beans (Lal, 2011). Thus, an increase in the soil organic C pool within the root zone by 1 ton C per ha per year can enhance food production in developing countries by 30–50 million tons per year including 24–40 million tons per year of cereal and legumes, and 6–10 million tons per year of roots and tubers (Lal *et al.*, 2007).

World soils play an important role in C cycling and represent the largest terrestrial pool of soil C of about 2500 pg/billion ton (1550 pg soil organic C and 950 pg soil inorganic C) compared to about 700 pg in the atmosphere and 600 pg in land biota (Lal and Kimble, 1997; Batjes, 1999; Lal, 2004a,b). Most of the cultivated soils are depleted of soil organic C and far from saturation as is determined by climate, pedological and terrain characteristics (Lal, 2004a,b). The soils of different agroecosystems have lost their original soil organic pool with a global loss of 78±12 billion tons C through historic land misuse and soil degradation (Lal, 2011). Agriculture is important because of not only the potential to reduce its own emissions but also its potentiality to reduce net emissions from other sectors and to enhance the quality of soil, water and other natural resources and resilience-building (Lal, 2011). The global potential of C sequestration in soils of agroecosystems is about 2.1 billion tons C per year and so if the soil organic C pool in world soils can be increased by 10% (+250 billion tons) over the 21st century, it implies a drawdown of about 110 ppm of atmospheric CO_2 (1 billion tons of soil C = 0.47 ppm of atmospheric CO_2).

Pilot studies prove that soil health building through balanced fertilization along with improved crop and water management can sequester 335 kg C per ha per year (Wani *et al.*, 2003). In degraded lands, biofuel plantations of *Jatropha* proved to have potential opportunities to rehabilitate degraded lands through adding to soil around 1450 kg C per ha through leaf fall, pruned twigs, de-oiled cake along with 230 kg C per ha replacement in fossil fuel and 5100 kg C per ha as live plantation (Wani *et al.*, 2012a).

3.5 Framework for Soil Health and Ecosystem Services

3.5.1 Soil health building as an entry point activity

Soil health mapping and building through need-based management addresses the widespread problem the farmers face and hence is one of the best entry point intervention for quick benefits and building rapport with the majority of farmers to initiate a collective action for technological upgradation of dryland agriculture (Wani *et al.*, 2009a; Chander *et al.*, 2016). The main attributes which make it the best entry point activity are: it is knowledge-based and does not involve direct cash payment; it has a high success probability (>80–90%); involves participatory research and development approach; it results in the measurable tangible economic benefits to the farming community with a relatively high benefit–cost ratio; is simple and easy for the participating farmers to undertake; involves participatory evaluation; has a reliable and cost-effective approach to assess the constraints; and most importantly it benefits the majority of farmers in the watershed.

3.5.2 Strengthening analytical framework

In a soil analysis process to start for building soil health, soil sampling is one of the most important and the weakest links. The smallest amount of sample collected must effectively represent the millions of kg soil in the field. Participatory stratified soil sampling method (Sahrawat et al., 2008) takes care of such errors. Under this method, the target region is divided into three topo-sequences. At each topo-sequence location, samples are taken proportionately from small, medium and large farm holdings to address the variations that may arise due to different management practices because of different economic status in each farm size class. Within each farm size class in a topo-sequence, the samples are chosen carefully to represent different soil colour, texture, cropping systems and agronomic management practices. At ultimate sampling unit in a farmer's field, 8–10 cores of surface (0–0.15 m) soil samples are collected and mixed together to make a composite sample.

Analysis is the next step followed and unless soil samples are thoroughly diagnosed for all essential elements and key parameters, holistic recommendations are unlikely to be developed. A fragmented approach of soil analysis is no longer workable. Precision is another important requirement as small errors in especially micronutrients may result in different interpretation and recommendations. Therefore, establishing state-of-the-art laboratories makes better sense technically as well as operationally as only one such laboratory can effectively cater to the requirements of a district. In current scenario, out of around 1600 laboratories (1500 static, 100 mobile) in the country, only about 150 are equipped to analyse B and about 450 for S and about 600 can analyse diethylene triamine pentaacetic acid (DTPA) extractable micronutrients (Zn, Cu, Fe, Mn). Therefore, streamlining soil-plant-water diagnostic services through upgrading current half-functional laboratories into state-of-the-art laboratories is better technically as well as

operationally and one such laboratory per district could be a better proposition to improve operational efficiency and precision, rather than many half or non-functional laboratories (Wani et al., 2016).

The GIS (geographical information system) interpolation of analysis results across CSR and other pilot sites show that individual nutrient deficiencies are scattered differently across regions, and multiple nutrient deficiencies are also observed. In this scenario, current general practice of fertilizer recommendations at state or agroecoregion level does not effectively meet soil requirement and hence more precise recommendations at block/cluster-of-villages/village/farmer level need to be developed and promoted.

The CSR pilot areas are sites of learning of using soil health building as an entry point activity, by using stratified soil sampling and promoting and evaluating block/village level soil test-based recommendations for soil health rejuvenation. The experience of International Crops Research Institute for the Semi-Arid Tropics (ICRISAT), Patancheru, Telangana in these pilots demonstrates the benefits of these and subsequently, as awareness develops amongst the farmers, and the government is geared up to handle knowledge dissemination especially for smallholders, farmer-based recommendations can be followed.

3.5.3 Regulating soil C pools

It is important to realize that low-input agricultural systems deplete soil organic C and accentuate the risk of greenhouse effects (Lal and Kimble, 1997). Long-term studies at ICRISAT (Wani et al., 2003) showed that improved system comprising landform management (broad-bed and furrow cultivation), soil test-based balanced fertilization and crop management increases not only crop productivity but also soil organic C content. In this historical study, an additional quantity of 7.3 tons C per ha (335 kg C per ha per year) was sequestered in soil under the improved system compared with the traditional system over the 24-year period (Table 3.4). The C inputs were found to increase with continuous cropping, particularly where fertilizers were applied and when legumes were included

Table 3.4. Biological and chemical properties of semi-arid tropical Vertisols after 24 years of cropping under improved and traditional system at ICRISAT, Patancheru, India. From: Wani *et al.* (2003).

| Properties | System | Soil depth (cm) | |
		0 to 60	60 to 120
Microbial biomass	Improved	2676	2137
C (kg/ha)	Traditional	1462	1088
Organic C (t/ha)	Improved	27.4	19.4
	Traditional	21.4	18.1
Microbial biomass	Improved	86.4	39.2
N (kg/ha)	Traditional	42.1	25.8
Total N (kg/ha)	Improved	2684	1928
	Traditional	2276	1884
Olsen-P (kg/ha)	Improved	6.1	1.6
	Traditional	1.5	1.0

in the system (Paustian *et al.*, 1997; Wani *et al.*, 2003). Leguminous plants are considered to have a competitive advantage under global climate change because of increased rates of symbiotic N fixation in response to increased atmospheric CO_2 (Serraj, 2003; Wani *et al.*, 2003). Soil microbial biomass responds more rapidly than soil organic matter as a whole to changes in management that alter the annual input of organic material into soil C (Powlson and Jenkinson, 1981). Although small in mass, microbial biomass is one of the most labile pools of organic matter and thus serves as an important reservoir of plant nutrients such as N and P (Jenkinson and Ladd, 1981; Marumato *et al.*, 1982). Biomass C, as a proportion of total soil C, serves as a surrogate for soil quality (Jenkinson and Ladd, 1981). In on-station study at ICRISAT (Wani *et al.*, 2003), improved management practices of Vertisols resulted in higher values (10.3 vs 6.4%) of biomass C as a proportion of soil organic C.

In a study on monitoring changes in soil C between 1980 and 2005 (Bhattacharyya *et al.*, 2007), in two important food production zones of India, viz. the Indo-Gangetic Plains (IGP) (Punjab, Haryana, Uttar Pradesh, Bihar and West Bengal) and the black and associated red soils (BSR) (Andhra Pradesh, Madhya Pradesh, Karnataka, Gujarat and Maharashtra), soil organic C stock of both the soils was found to increase due to the turnover of more biomass to the soils

(however, the increase was more in the IGP than the BSR). Thus, scaling-up improved management is needed as the soil organic C stocks of Indian soils demonstrate enough potential to sequester organic C (Pal *et al.*, 2015). It is observed that vast areas of land in arid, semi-arid and drier part of sub-humid India are impoverished in soil organic C, but are high in soil inorganic C up to 30 cm depth. These specified areas are the prioritized ones for organic C management in soil. These areas cover 155.8 million ha of which, arid areas cover 4.9, semi-arid 116.4 and dry sub-humid 34.5 million ha. Under different land use systems, soil organic C sequestration within the first 100 cm is observed to be higher in soils under forest, followed by horticultural and agricultural system (Pal *et al.*, 2015).

To maintain soil organic matter status, there is need to add organic materials including manures, and crop residues on a regular basis to compensate the loss of organic matter by various processes. On-farm studies at ICRISAT (Chander *et al.*, 2013a) have shown that the use of manures like vermicompost increased biomass production and apparently recycling and C sequestration, while cutting cost of chemical fertilizers and making it a profitable option for farmers to adopt. Recycling large quantities of C and nutrients contained in agricultural and domestic wastes (~700 million tons organic wastes are generated annually in India) (Bhiday, 1994) are needed to rejuvenate soil health for enhancing productivity (Nagavallemma *et al.*, 2006; Chander *et al.*, 2013a; Wani *et al.*, 2014) (Fig. 3.2). To start with, focus on agricultural regions, producing large quantities of residues which have little alternate uses, could be the best strategy. In this context, the hardy stems of crops like pigeonpea, cotton, maize, pearl millet, sorghum and others are best target biomass for recycling. These five crops are grown in around 37 million ha in India and produce more than 100 million t hardy straw biomass per year which has little economic value or effective alternate use by farmers. This biomass is a potential opportunity to recycle plant nutrients worth more than Rs 3000 crores per year. For effective composting, these hardy residues need to be chopped into small pieces. Pilot studies in Andhra Pradesh have shown that arranging shredder machines on a sharing basis could be a good business

Fig. 3.2. Shredder machine piloted in Kadapa, Andhra Pradesh used to chop hardy biomass for composting.

model for chopping biomass for composting which prove to be economically remunerative from the first year. Alongside, composting technologies need to be scaled-out to farmers. Vermicomposting is a proven technology, but in many case desired success is not achieved due to the need for continuously maintaining moisture and arranging feeding material to earthworms. So, technologies like use of microbial consortium culture for composting needs to be promoted for undertaking it as and when needed and adding convenience to the farmers. Along with mapping for potential recyclable biomass in agriculture and horticulture, regions with current low chemical fertilizer use could also be prioritized and promoted as niche areas for organic farming without compromising with yield and harnessing premium price for the farmers. Also converting biomass into *Biochar*, having highly stable form of C, may be a good option of building soil C for long term (Sohi *et al.*, 2009); however, the long-term effects need to be evaluated.

Conservation agriculture (CA) may be a suitable technique for control of soil and C through erosion, lesser exposure for decomposition along with increased inputs of C as mulch. Some other studies indicate that crop rotations also play an important role in improvement in soil C. However, the results in on-station experiment at ICRISAT showed no significant effect on maize, chickpea and pigeonpea yield with or without residue addition (Jat *et al.*, 2012). Retained residues reduced total seasonal runoff under both the tillage practices (Jat *et al.*, 2015). These results imply that under CA high rainwater filters into the soil to add to the green water. Similarly, peak rate of runoff, which indicates erosive capacity of runoff water is also decreased with residue addition. No significant benefit is observed of retaining residues in improving water use efficiency. The difficulty in sowing through surface retained residues and poor seed to soil contact under residue retained plots apparently led to lower plant stand and crop yield

(Jat *et al.*, 2015). The residue addition, though, tended to improve soil organic C levels.

In context of promoting biofuels for C replacement in fossil fuels, on-farm research results (Wani *et al.*, 2009b, 2012a; Wani and Chander, 2012) show plants like *Jatropha* (a hardy plant) to grow successfully and rejuvenate degraded lands without compromising on the food security in heavily populated countries like India which could help strengthen local livelihoods and income diversification. In wastelands planted with *Jatropha*, around 4000 kg/ha/year organic matter (through leaf fall, pruned twigs and de-oiled cake) added not only 1450 kg C per ha per year, but also 85.5 kg N, 7.67 kg P, 43.9 kg K, 5.20 kg S, 0.11 kg B and 0.12 kg Zn per ha per year plus other essential nutrients (Wani *et al.*, 2012a). Out of the total C accumulated by seeds, 185–230 kg C per ha per year is as biodiesel/oil C and an apparent replacement in the fossil fuel. The live plant (shoot and root) biomass in the fields serves as a sink for C at 5120 kg C per ha (Table 3.5). The soil samples from one on-farm plantation location (Velchal, Rangareddy district, Andhra Pradesh) recorded increased microbial biomass C by 22%, soil respiration by 2.46% and microbial biomass N by 24% as compared to the adjoining grasslands (Wani *et al.*, 2012a).

Management practices to reduce soil C loss by erosion is an important component as ecosystems in the semi-arid tropics are prone to land degradation, which may be aggravated by climate change. Soil erosion by water and loss of soil C and nutrients along with it is a major global environmental problem (Boardman and Favis-Mortlock, 2001). In climate change scenario, the frequency and intensity of extreme rainfall events are expected to increase in some regions, which could lead to increased erosion rates (Michael *et al.*, 2005). In general, a 1% change in precipitation is expected to result on average a 2.4% change in soil loss (Zhang *et al.*, 2005). In context of impending climate change scenario, development of the watershed/catchment is one of the most trusted and ecofriendly approaches to managing natural resources and reducing runoff, soil loss and C therein (Wani *et al.*, 2012b). Desilting water tanks and application of tank sediment to agricultural fields (which are integral part of villages especially in India) is also an economically feasible (benefit–cost ratio of 1.23) option to return organic C and nutrients (Padmaja *et al.*, 2003). The sediment samples in Medak district, Telangana contained 720 mg N, 320 mg P and 10.7 g C per kg of sediment. During 2001, under Government of Andhra Pradesh initiative, namely 'Neeru-Meeru', 246,831 tons of sediment desilted and added to the farms returned 183 tons N, 86 tons P and 2873 tons of organic C.

3.5.4 GHG emissions and management

Global warming induced climate change caused by CO_2 (and other GHGs) emissions through fossil fuel combustion (IPCC, 2007) is an issue of concern worldwide. The CO_2 concentration has increased markedly in the 21st century at a rate of 2 ppm (parts per million) per year during 2000 onwards. The CO_2 concentration was 280 ppm in the pre-industrial times, and has crossed 400 ppm (Fig. 3.3). Atmospheric CO_2 levels are increasing at a rate of 0.4% per year and are predicted to double by 2100 (Lal, 2005; IPCC, 2007). The Intergovernmental Panel on Climate Change has shown that the earth temperature has increased by 0.74°C between 1906 and 2005 due to the increase in anthropogenic emissions of GHGs (Aggarwal, 2008). Global temperatures are predicted to increase by 1.1 to 6.4°C between 1990 and 2100 depending on CO_2 emission scenarios, with CO_2 atmospheric concentration projected to increase in the range 550 to 850 ppm (Stockle *et al.*, 2011). These

Table 3.5. Balance sheet of carbon (C) under *Jatropha* plantation as C returned to soil, biodiesel C replacement per year and live plant C. From: Wani *et al.* (2012a).

C through *Jatropha* plantation	Plant part involved	Organic C (kg per ha)
C returned back to soil	Leaf fall	800[a]
	Pruned twigs	150[a]
	De-oiled cake	495[b]
C replacement in fossil fuel	*Jatropha* oil	230[b]
C in live plant	Shoots and roots	5120

[a]Leaf and pruned twigs added C every year.
[b]*Jatropha* oil C (fuel replacement) and de-oiled cake added C from fourth year onwards every year.

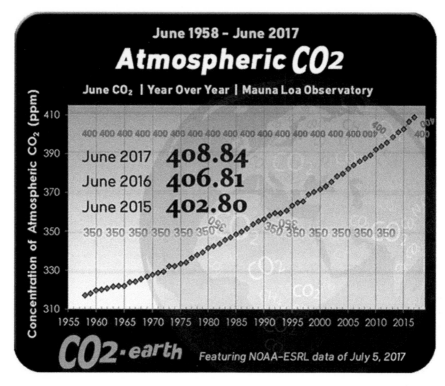

Fig. 3.3. Atmospheric CO_2 levels measured at Mauna Loa Observatory, Hawaii (NOAA-ESRL), 2017. From: Mauna Loa Observatory, 2017.

changes will have a profound impact on the natural resource base that agriculture depends upon. It is likely that climate variability and change will exacerbate food insecurity in areas currently vulnerable to hunger and undernutrition. Climate change is now being viewed as the single gravest threat to food security worldwide. There is a strong link between food insecurity, soil degradation and climate change, yet the twin crisis of climate change and food insecurity may be significantly addressed through restoration of soil organic C.

Current global GHG emissions (in terms of CO_2 equivalents (CO_2e)) are about 49 Gt CO_2e/year, 74% of which are CO_2, 16% of CH_4 and 10% of N_2O. Agriculture accounts for around 13.5% of the total global anthropogenic GHG emissions, contributing about 25%, 50% and 70 % of CO_2, CH_4 and N_2O respectively (Montzka *et al.*, 2011). As food crops production needs to be increased at a rate not less than 1.3% annually (Cassman *et al.*, 2003), GHG emissions are also expected to increase, if adequate measures to minimize the emissions are not taken. The GHG emissions from agriculture in the form of N_2O emit from fertilizer management practices. Agricultural activities add into the atmosphere about 4.2 to 7 Tg N annually in the form of N_2O (Del Grosso *et al.*, 2008). Nitrous oxide has high global warming potential of 298-fold. Increased soil temperatures coupled with high moisture conditions during cooler months will increase N_2O production in soil. Elevation in CO_2 concentrations is also projected to increase N_2O emissions from upland agricultural soils (Van Groeningen *et al.*, 2011). Regarding CO_2, soil respiration is an important source, but the majority of the farm operations and inputs, such as fertilizers, pesticides and energy, also have embodied CO_2 content. Rice cultivation is a major source of CH_4, currently accounting for 10–15% of all global GHG emissions from agriculture and 10–12% of the world's total anthropogenic CH_4 emissions (IPCC, 2014).

In agriculture, increasing soil C represents the greatest mitigation potential. About 50–66%

of the cumulative historic C loss from soil can be recovered through proper management (Lal, 2004a). Increasing soil organic C content in soil may lock the C out of the atmosphere for centuries by C sequestration. Managing agricultural land to increase soil C has a mitigation potential of 5340 million tons CO_2e/year. Much of this mitigation effort has an economic cost and this technical potential equates to an economic potential of 4300 million tons CO_2e/year at C price of US$100 per ton CO_2e (Murphy-Bokern and Kleemann, 2014). About 89% of this mitigation potential lies in soil C sequestration, and the remaining 11% arises from reducing emissions of methane (9%) and N_2O (2%). Identification and adoption of better management practices as discussed in the chapter can be used as a GHG offsetting tool. In rice cultivation, zero tillage reduces CH_4 and N_2O emissions, but increases CO_2 emissions (Pandey *et al.*, 2012; Ladha *et al.*, 2016). Tillage, moisture and aeration, and C supply affect CH_4 emissions (Wassmann *et al.*, 2000; Venterea *et al.*, 2005). The management practices such as alternate wetting and drying, alternative rice land preparation and crop establishment were reported to cause lower methane emissions from rice paddies (Adhya *et al.*, 2014; Linquist *et al.*, 2015; Ladha *et al.*, 2016). In areas where cropping system diversification is feasible, there is also scope for mitigation of GHG emissions in the rice-based ecosystem, while enhancing crop production (Ladha *et al.*, 2016). Improved agronomic practices, increased N use efficiency, use of diversified cropping systems, adoption of crop cultivars with high harvest index, and the use of soil bioresources such as P-solubilizers and arbuscular mycorrhizal fungi in crop production were reported to lower the average C footprint in semi-arid areas (Gan *et al.*, 2011). The over-exploitation of groundwater by agriculture for irrigation during recent years has lowered aquifer levels in many Asian countries, and pumping water from lower strata in the future would result in a greater use of energy, which is mostly generated by coal combustion, and would therefore result in increased emissions of GHG (Zhang *et al.*, 2013). Improved water use efficiency is likely to become a critical criterion for many grain-producing areas in South Asia, in part due to necessary adaptation to the anticipated adverse effects from climate change (Elliott *et al.*, 2014). Land use change and emission

reduction in agriculture will be key elements in achieving an 80% reduction in GHG emissions by 2050 (Rockström *et al.*, 2013).

The industry, with its high level of emissions, waste generation and fossil fuel consumption, is the major contributor to GHG emissions and climate change. However, industries in India are determined to become responsible corporations by undertaking CSR programmes. Data of the Ministry of Corporate Affairs on CSR expenditure of Indian companies in 2014–15 showed that 14% (₹1,213 crore) of total CSR expenses in India was made on activities focusing on conserving the environment. Carbon Disclosure Project survey conducted in UK by Doda *et al.* (2016) revealed little evidence that commonly adopted management practices by industry are reducing emissions. However, Murphy-Bokern and Kleemann (2014) felt that considering the commercial constraints and the obligations of firms to shareholders, CSR is contributing to climate protection. Corporates need to invest more in agricultural research and extension and should play a key role in enabling farmers to produce more food with minimal GHG emissions.

3.5.5 Scaling-out soil health management

Bhoochetana scaling-up initiative, with the support of Government of Karnataka and ICRISAT-led consortium as a technical partner, is an exemplary initiative of rejuvenating degraded farm lands and C-building which have shown significant productivity benefits. With this initiative in Karnataka state during 2009 to 2013, more than 5 million farmers benefited and net economic benefits through increased production were estimated at ~US$353 million (₹1963 crore) (Wani *et al.*, 2017).

Taking the lead from *Bhoochetana*, the government-supported Rythu Kosam initiative in Andhra Pradesh is unique in targeting system productivity through embracing allied sectors along with focus on core agricultural crops (i.e. Primary Sector). The Department of Agriculture, Government of Andhra Pradesh along with ICRISAT as a technical partner have used scaling-out soil health building to harness benefits due to these interventions having high levels of success in more than 2 million ha during 2015 and 2016, and pilot-tested innovative C-building technologies using microbial consortia cultures. Soil health building initiatives have monetary benefits through higher productivity in agricultural and horticultural crops to the tune of around ₹1100 crore.

Lessons learnt in such initiatives in Karnataka and Andhra Pradesh states in India indicated that improving food security and livelihoods of people need not wait for any new major scientific breakthrough, but a political will, collective action and innovations in technologies to reach farmers' doorsteps and soil health building and improving C footprints is the most effective entry point activity to harness benefits.

3.5.6 Innovative extension and information and communication technology in soil health management

Innovative extension ways for information dissemination have been explored during watershed projects and other productivity improvement programmes to improve the awareness and adoption rate among the farmers. In the context of soil health management, the key information dissemination tools were soil health cards, wall writings and android-based mobile App. Soil health cards are customized information cards of soil fertility status and crop-wise fertilizer recommendation. This is one of the entry point activities, which built good relationship with the community. The soil health card has information about the farmer, location information of the farm, status of major and micronutrients, and crop-wise fertilizer recommendation for the major crops based on fertility status. The soil health card programme is also widely adopted by Government of India for doubling the farmers' income.

Information related to soil fertility status has been also disseminated among the farmers through writing the information on the walls of common infrastructure in villages. This tool provides wider dissemination channel as all people from the village get access to this information. This tool has been also used in a watershed project for disseminating weather information and project details. Information written on the wall will be available for all the farmers from villages. However, this information is not customized like the crops or landholding. Soil health cards may provide customized fertilizer management solution, but that information is too static in nature. Thus, a dynamic information dissemination and monitoring tool is required to strengthen the local extension agent by providing a channel for information flow and to monitor the real time agriculture status on ground. In this context, the digital technologies with three important tools were piloted in *Bhoochetana* programme: *Krishi Gyan Sagar*, *Krishi Vani* and farmer-to-farmer video dissemination (Wani *et al.*, 2017).

A mobile App is another potential opportunity in soil health management and key features of this are the soil fertility maps and soil test-based fertilizer management (Fig. 3.4). Geospatial digital maps were prepared based on the results from state-wide soil samples. The same soil analysis data was adopted in mobile app in two forms: (i) district level soil fertility maps including status of organic C, P, K, S, B and Zn are embedded in the app; and (ii) site-specific fertilizer recommendation for the major crops. Thus, with the power of a geospatial database of soil fertility, this application provides dynamic customization that is not possible with soil health cards or information written on walls.

3.6 Summary and Key Findings

- Rejuvenating soil health is needed for food and nutritional security of the rising population, while contributing to improving C footprints through C sequestration and minimizing GHGs.
- A holistic soil health mapping and needs-based management that encompasses stratified sampling, quality analysis and timely availability of required inputs along with desired policy support are needed.
- Desired policies to promote quality organic manures by recycling organic wastes generated both in urban and rural areas along with biofertilizers are desired.
- For sustainability, land use planning based on land and agroecological capability is needed through policy.
- Pilot sites need to be established as exemplary sites for training as well as developmental purposes.

Fig. 3.4. District-wise soil fertility maps in *Krishi Gyan Sagar* App.

- There is an urgent need to reform the knowledge delivery systems by using innovative partnerships, tools, approaches and methods. Information and communication technology-based knowledge dissemination, etc. need to be developed.
- To address multifarious issues in soil health building and improving C footprints, a range of actors need to act together in a consortium model to harness their strengths and synergies with the local community as the primary implementing unit.

- Public–private partnerships are required as the governance strategy to minimize the transaction costs and coordinating and enforcing relations between the partners engaged in production of goods and services.

Acknowledgement

The authors duly acknowledge CSR partners for supporting soil health and C-building initiatives across the pilots.

References

Adhya, T.K., Linquist, B., Searchinger, T., Wassmann, R. and Yan, X. (2014) *Wetting and Drying: Reducing Greenhouse Gas Emissions and Saving Water from Rice Production*. Working paper, Installment 8 of Creating a Sustainable Food Future. World Resources Institute, Washington, DC.

Aggarwal, P.K. (2008) Global climate change and Indian agriculture: impacts, adaptation and mitigation. *Indian Journal of Agricultural Sciences* 78(11), 911–919.

Amarasinghe, U.A., Shah, T., Turral, H. and Anand, B.K. (2007) *India's Water Future to 2025–2050: Business As-usual Scenario and Deviations*. IWMI Research Report 123. International Water Management Institute, Colombo, Sri Lanka.

Batjes, N.H. (1999) *Management Options for Reducing CO_2 Concentrations in the Atmosphere by Increasing Carbon Sequestration in the Soil*. International Soil Reference and Information Centre, Wageningen, the Netherlands.

Bhattacharyya, T., Chandran, P., Ray, S.K., Pal, D.K., Venugopalan, M.V. *et al.* (2007) Changes in levels of carbon in soils over years of two important food production zones of India. *Current Science* 93(12), 1854–1863.

Bhiday, M.R. (1994) Earthworms in agriculture. *Indian Farming* 43(12), 31–34.

Blümmel, M., Samad, M., Singh, O.P. and Amede, T. (2009) Opportunities and limitations of food–feed crops for livestock feeding and implications for livestock–water productivity. *Rangeland Journal* 31, 207–213.

Boardman, J. and Favis-Mortlock, D.T. (2001) How will future climate change and land-use change affect rates of erosion on agricultural land? In: Ascough, J.C. and Flanagan, D.C. (eds) *Soil Erosion Research for the 21st Century. Proceedings of the International Symposium, 3–5 January 2001, Honolulu, Hawaii, USA.* ASAE, St Joseph, MI, pp. 498–501.

Cassman, K.G., Dobermann, A., Walters, D.T. and Yang, H. (2003) Meeting cereal demand while protecting natural resources and improving environmental quality. *Annual Review of Environment and Resources* 28, 315–358.

Chander, G., Wani, S.P., Sahrawat, K.L., Kamdi, P.J., Pal, C.K. *et al.* (2013a) Balanced and integrated nutrient management for enhanced and economic food production: case study from rainfed semi-arid tropics in India. *Archives of Agronomy and Soil Science* 59(12), 1643–1658.

Chander, G., Wani, S.P., Sahrawat, K.L., Pal, C.K. and Mathur, T.P. (2013b) Integrated plant genetic and balanced nutrient management enhances crop and water productivity of rainfed production systems in Rajasthan, India. *Communications in Soil Science and Plant Analysis* 44, 3456–3464.

Chander, G., Wani, S.P., Sahrawat, K.L. and Rajesh, C. (2014) Enhanced nutrient and rainwater use efficiency in maize and soybean with secondary and micro nutrient amendments in the rainfed semi-arid tropics. *Archives of Agronomy and Soil Science* 61(3), 285–298.

Chander, G., Wani, S.P., Krishnappa, K., Sahrawat, K.L., Pardhasaradhi, G. and Jangawad, L.S. (2016) Soil mapping and variety based entry-point interventions for strengthening agriculture-based livelihoods – exemplar case of 'Bhoochetana' in India. *Current Science* 110(9), 1683–1691.

Dagar, J.C. (2005) Salinity research in India: an overview. *Bulletin of the National Institute of Ecology* 15, 69–80.

Del Grosso, S.J., Wirt, T., Ogle, S.M. and Parton, W.J. (2008) Estimating agricultural nitrous oxide emissions. *Eos Transactions of the American Geophysical Union* 89, 529–530.

Doda, B., Gennaioli, C., Gouldson, A., Grover, D. and Sullivan, R. (2016) Are corporate carbon management practices reducing corporate carbon emissions? *Corporate Social Responsibility and Environmental Management* 23(5), 257–270.

Elliott, J., Deryng, D., Müller, C., Frieler, K., Konzmann, M. *et al.* (2014) Constraints and potentials of future irrigation water availability on agricultural production under climate change. *Proceedings of the National Academy of Science* 111, 3239–3244.

FAO and ITPS (2015) *Status of the World's Soil Resources (SWSR) – Main Report.* Food and Agriculture Organization of the United Nations and Intergovernmental Technical Panel on Soils, Rome.

FAOSTAT (2017) Annual population data. Available at: http://faostat.fao.org/site/550/default.aspx#ancor (accessed 9 April 2018).

Gan, Y., Liang, C., Hamel, C., Cutforth, H. and Wang, H. (2011) Strategies for reducing the carbon footprint of field crops for semiarid areas. A review. *Agronomy for Sustainable Development* 31, 643–656.

Government of India (2014) *Agricultural Statistics at a Glance 2014.* Directorate of Economics and Statistics, Ministry of Agriculture, New Delhi.

Haileslassie, A., Blümmel, M., Clement, F., Descheemaeker, K., Amede, T. *et al.* (2011) Assessment of livestock feed and water nexus across mixed crop livestock system's intensification gradient: an example from the Indo-Ganga Basin. *Experimental Agriculture* 47, 113–132.

Haileslassie, A., Blümmel, M., Wani, S.P., Sahrawat, K.L., Pardhasaradhi, G. and Anandan Samireddypalle (2013) Extractable soil nutrient effects on feed quality traits of crop residues in the semiarid rainfed mixed crop–livestock farming systems of Southern India. *Environment, Development and Sustainability* 15, 723–741.

IPCC (2007) *Climate Change 2007: Synthesis Report.* Intergovernmental Panel on Climate Change. Available at: https://www.ipcc.ch/pdf/assessment-report/ar4/syr/ar4_syr_full_report.pdf (accessed 9 April 2018).

IPCC (2014) *Climate Change 2014: Mitigation of Climate Change. Contribution of Working Group III to the Fifth Assessment Report of the Intergovernmental Panel on Climate Change.* Cambridge University Press, Cambridge.

Jat, R.A., Wani, S.P., Piara Singh, Pathak, P., Srinivas, K. *et al.* (2012) Effect of conservation agriculture on productivity and economics of different cropping systems under rainfed conditions in the semi-arid tropics. In: *Extended Summaries Vol. 3, 3rd International Agronomy Congress, Nov 26–30, 2012, New Delhi.* Indian Society of Agronomy, New Delhi, pp. 888–890.

Jat, R.A., Pathak, P., Wani, S.P., Piara Singh, Chander, G. and Sudi, R.S. (2015) Evaluating climate change mitigation and adaptation potential of conservation agriculture in semi-arid tropics of Southern India. *British Journal of Environment & Climate Change* 5(4), 324–338.

Jenkinson, D.S. and Ladd, J.N. (1981) Microbial biomass in soil: measurement and turnover. In: Paul, E.A. and Ladd, J.N. (eds) *Soil Biochemistry*, Vol. 5. Dekker, New York, pp. 415–471.

Ladha, J.K., Rao, A.N., Raman, A., Padre, A., Dobermann, A. *et al.* (2016) Agronomic improvements can make future cereal systems in South Asia far more productive and result in a lower environmental footprint. *Global Change Biology* 22, 1054–1074.

Lal, R. (2004a) Soil carbon sequestration impacts on global climate change and food security. *Science (Washington)* 304, 1623–1627.

Lal, R. (2004b) Carbon emission from farm operations. *Environment International* 30, 981–990.

Lal, R. (2005) Forest soils and carbon sequestration. *Forest Ecology and Management* 220, 242–258.

Lal, R. (2011) Sequestring carbon in soils of agro-ecosystems. *Food Policy* 36, S33–S39.

Lal, R. and Kimble, J.M. (1997) Conservation tillage for carbon sequestration. *Nutrient Cycling in Agroecosystems* 49, 243–253.

Lal, R., Follett, R.F., Stewart, B.A. and Kimble, J.M. (2007) Soil carbon sequestration to mitigate climate change and advance food security. *Soil Science* 172(12), 943–956.

Linquist, B.A., Anders, M.M., Adviento-Borbe, M.A.A., Chaney, R.L., Nalley, L.L. *et al.* (2015) Reducing greenhouse gas emissions, water-use, and grain arsenic levels in rice systems. *Global Change Biology* 21, 407–417.

Marumato, T., Anderson, J.P.E. and Domsch, K.H. (1982) Mineralisation of nutrients from soil microbial biomass. *Soil Biology and Biochemistry* 14, 469–475.

Mauna Loa Observatory (2017) Atmospheric CO_2. Available at: https://www.co2.earth (accessed 9 April 2018).

Michael, A., Schmidt, J., Enke, W., Deutschländer, T. and Malitz, G. (2005) Impact of expected increase in precipitation intensities on soil loss – results of comparative model simulations. *Catena* 61(2/3), 155–164.

Montzka, S.A., Dlugokencky, E.J. and Butler, J.H. (2011) Non-CO_2 greenhouse gases and climate change. *Nature* 476, 46–50.

Munir, A., Hanjra, M. and Qureshi, E.M. (2010) Global water crisis and future food security in an era of climate change. *Food Policy* 35, 365–377.

Murphy-Bokern, D. and Kleemann L. (2014) *The Role of Corporate Social Responsibility in Reducing Greenhouse Gas Emissions from Agriculture and Food*. Draft for public consultation. A study for the International Food Policy Research Institute. Available at: http://www.murphy-bokern.com/images/IFPRI_CR_Report_July_2015.pdf (accessed 9 April 2018).

Nagavallemma, K.P., Wani, S.P., Lacroix, S., Padmaja, V.V., Vineela, C. *et al.* (2006) Vermicomposting: recycling wastes into valuable organic fertilizer. *SAT eJournal* 2(1), 1–16.

National Bureau of Soil Survey and Land Use Planning (NBSS & LUP). (2005) *Annual Report 2005*. Nagpur, India: NBSS & LUP.

Nkonya, E.M., Mirzabaev, A. and von Braun, J. (2016) *Economics of Land Degradation and Improvement – A Global Assessment for Sustainable Development*. Springer International Publishing, Cham, Switzerland.

Padmaja, K.V., Wani, S.P., Lav Aggarval and Sahrawat, K.L. (2003) *Economic Assessment of Desilted Sediment in Terms of Plant Nutrients Equivalent: A Case Study in the Medak District of Andhra Pradesh*. Global Theme 3: Water, Soil and Agrodiversity Management for Ecosystem Resilience Report no. 4. International Crops Research Institute for the Semi-Arid Tropics, Patancheru, India.

Pal, D.K., Wani, S.P. and Sahrawat, K.L. (2015) Carbon sequestration in Indian soils: present status and the potential. *Proceedings of the National Academy of Science, India, Section B, Biological Sciences* 85(2), 337–358.

Pandey, D., Agrawal, M. and Bohra, J.S. (2012) Greenhouse gas emissions from rice crop with different tillage permutations in rice-wheat system. *Agriculture, Ecosystems & Environment* 159, 133–144.

Paustian, K., Colins, H.P. and Paul, E.A. (1997) Management controls on soil carbon. In: Paul, E.A., Paustian, K., Elliott, E.T. and Cole, C.V. (eds) *Soil Organic Matter in Temperate Agro-Ecosystems: Long-Term Experiments in North America*. CRC Press, Boca Raton, FL, pp. 15–49.

Paustian, K., Cole, C.V., Sauerbeck, D. and Sampson, N. (1998) CO_2 mitigation by agriculture: an overview. *Climatic Change* 40, 135–162.

Powlson, D.S. and Jenkinson, D.S. (1981) A comparison of the organic matter, biomass, adenosine triphosphate and mineralizable nitrogen contents of ploughed and direct drilled soils. *The Journal of Agricultural Science (Cambridge)* 97, 713–721.

Powlson, D.S., Gregory, P.J., Whalley, W.R., Quinton, J.N., Hopkins, D.W. *et al.* (2011) Soil management in relation to sustainable agriculture and ecosystem services. *Food Policy* 36(1), 72–87.

Richter, B.D., Mathews, R., Harrison, D.L. and Wigington, R. (2003) Ecologically sustainable water management: managing river flows for ecological integrity. *Ecological Applications* 13, 206–224.

Rockström, J., Sachs, J.D., Ohman, M.C. and Schmidt-Traub, G. (2013) *Sustainable Development and Planetary Boundaries*. Thematic group on agro-economics, population dynamics, and planetary boundaries. Background research paper prepared by the co-chairs of the Sustainable Development Solutions Network. High Level Panel on the Post-2015 Development Agenda, United Nations. Available at: http://www.post2015hlp.org/wp-content/uploads/2013/06/Rockstroem-Sachs-Oehman-Schmidt-Traub_Sustainable-Development-and-Planetary-Boundaries.pdf (accessed 9 April 2018).

Sahrawat, K.L., Rego, T.J., Wani, S.P. and Pardhasaradhi G. (2008) Stretching soil sampling to watershed: evaluation of soil-test parameters in a semi-arid tropical watershed. *Communications in Soil Science and Plant Analysis* 39, 2950–2960.

Sahrawat, K.L., Wani, S.P. and Pardhasaradhi, G. (2013) Balanced nutrient management: effects on plant zinc. *Journal of SAT Agricultural Research* 11, 1–3.

Scherr, S.J. and Yadav, S. (1996) *Land Degradation in the Developing World: Implications for Food, Agriculture, and the Environment to 2020*. Food, Agriculture, and the Environment Discussion Paper 14. International Food Policy Research Institute, Washington, DC.

Seckler, D., Barker, R. and Amarasinghe, U. (1999) Water scarcity in the twenty-first century. *International Journal of Water Resources Development* 15(1/2), 29–42.

Serraj, R. (2003) Atmospheric CO_2 increase benefits symbiotic N_2 fixation by legumes under drought. *Current Science* 85(9), 1341–1343.

Shah, T., Singh, O.P. and Mukherji, A. (2006) Some aspects of South Asia's groundwater irrigation economy: analyses from a survey in India, Pakistan, Nepal Terai and Bangladesh. *Hydrogeology Journal* 14(3), 286–309.

Sohi, S., Lopez-Capel, E., Krull, E. and Bol, R. (2009) *Biochar, Climate Change and Soil: A Review to Guide Future Research*. CSIRO Land and Water Science Report. Commonwealth Scientific and Industrial Research Organisation, Canberra, Australia.

Stockle, C.O., Marsal, J. and Villar, J.M. (2011) Impact of climate change on irrigated tree fruit production. *Acta Horticulturae* 889, 41–52.

UN (2016) *World Population Prospects, the 2015 Revision*. Department of Economic and Social Affairs, Population Division, New York.

UN (2017) *Sustainable Development Goals – 17 Goals to Transform Our World*. United Nations, New York. Available at: http://www.un.org/sustainabledevelopment/sustainable-development-goals (accessed 4 April 2017).

Uppal, R.K., Wani, S.P., Garg, K.K. and Alagarswamy, G. (2015) Balanced nutrition increases yield of pearl millet under drought. *Field Crops Research* 177, 86–97.

Van Groeningen, K.J., Osenberg, C.W. and Hungate, B.A. (2011) Increased soil emissions of potent greenhouse gases under increased atmospheric CO_2. *Nature* 475, 214–216.

Venterea, R.T., Burger, M. and Spoka, K.T. (2005) Nitrogen oxide and methane emissions under varying tillage and fertilizer management. *Journal of Environmental Quality* 34, 1467–1477.

Wani, S.P. and Chander, G. (2012) *Jatropha curcas* biodiesel – is it a panacea for energy crisis, ecosystem service and rural livelihoods? Challenges and opportunities. In: Bahadur, B., Sujatha, M. and Carels, N. (eds) *Jatropha – Challenges for a New Energy Crop*. Springer Science, New York, pp. 311–331.

Wani, S.P. and Chander, G. (2016) Role of micro and secondary nutrients in achieving food and nutritional security. *Advances in Plants & Agriculture Research* 4(2), 131.

Wani, S.P., Pathak, P., Jangawad, L.S., Eswaran, H. and Singh, P. (2003) Improved management of Vertisols in the semi-arid tropics for increased productivity and soil carbon sequestration. *Soil Use and Management* 19(3), 217–222.

Wani, S.P., Sahrawat, K.L., Sreedevi, T.K., Pardhasaradhi, G. and Dixit, S. (2009a) *Knowledge-based entry point for enhancing community participation in integrated watershed management*. In: *Best-bet Options for Integrated Watershed Management – Proceedings of the Comprehensive Assessment of Watershed Programs in India, 25–27 July 2007*. International Crops Research Institute for the Semi-Arid Tropics, Patancheru, India, pp. 53–68.

Wani, S.P., Sreedevi, T.K., Marimuthu, S., Kesava Rao, A.V.R. and Vineela, C. (2009b) Harnessing the potential of *Jatropha* and *Pongamia* plantations for improving livelihoods and rehabilitating degraded lands. In: *6th International Biofuels Conference, 4–5 March 2009, New Delhi*. Winrock International India, New Delhi.

Wani, S.P., Chander, G., Sahrawat, K.L., Srinivasa Rao Ch., Raghvendra, G., Susanna, P. and Pavani, M. (2012a) Carbon sequestration and land rehabilitation through *Jatropha curcus* (L.) plantation in degraded lands. *Agriculture, Ecosystems & Environment* 161, 112–120.

Wani, S.P. Dixin, Y., Li, Z., Dar, W.D. and Chander, G. (2012b) Enhancing agricultural productivity and rural incomes through sustainable use of natural resources in the SAT. *Journal of the Science of Food and Agriculture* 92, 1054–1063.

Wani, S.P., Chander, G. and Vineela, C. (2014) Vermicomposting: recycling wastes into valuable manure for sustained crop intensification in the semi-arid tropics. In: Chandra, R. and Raverkar, K.P. (eds) *Bioresources for Sustainable Plant Nutrient Management*. Satish Serial Publishing House, Delhi, pp. 123–151.

Wani, S.P., Chander, G., Sahrawat, K.L. and Pardhasaradhi, G. (2015) Soil test-based balanced nutrient management for sustainable intensification and food security: case from Indian semi-arid tropics. *Communications in Soil Science and Plant Analysis* 46(S1), 20–33.

Wani, S.P., Chander, G., Bhattacharyya, T. and Patil, M. (2016) *Soil Health Mapping and Direct Benefit Transfer of Fertilizer Subsidy*. Research Report IDC-6. International Crops Research Institute for the Semi-Arid Tropics, Patancheru, India. Available at: http://oar.icrisat.org/9747/1/2016-088%20Res%20Rep%20IDC%206%20soil%20health%20mapping.pdf (accessed 9 April 2018).

Wani, S.P., Chander, G. and Anantha, K.H. (2017) Enhancing resource use efficiency through soil management for improving livelihoods. In: Rakshit, A., Abhilash, P.C., Singh, H.B. and Ghosh, S. (eds) *Adaptive Soil Management: From Theory to Practices*. Springer, Singapore, pp. 413–451.

Wassmann, R., Neue, H.U., Lantin, R.S., Buendia, L.V. and Rennenberg, H. (2000) Characterization of methane emissions from rice fields in Asia. I. Comparison among field sites in five countries. *Nutrient Cycling in Agroecosystems* 58, 1–12.

Whitmore, A.P., Kirk, G.J.D. and Rawlins, B.G. (2014) Technologies for increasing carbon storage in soil to mitigate climate change. *Soil Use and Management* 31(S1), 62–71.

Zhang, G.H., Nearing, M.A. and Liu, B.Y. (2005) Potential effects of climate change on rainfall erosivity in the Yellow River basin of China. *Transactions of the American Society of Agricultural Engineers* 48, 511–517.

Zhang, F.S., Chen, X.P. and Vitousek, P. (2013) Chinese agriculture: an experiment for the world. *Nature* 497, 33–35.

4

CSR and Climate-resilient Agriculture – A JSW Case Study

KIRAN J. PETARE,* A.V.R. KESAVA RAO, MUKUND D. PATIL, SUHAS P. WANI, R. SUDI AND K. SRINIVAS

International Crops Research Institute for the Semi-Arid Tropics, Patancheru, India

Abstract

The semi-arid tropics being dominant region is primarily agrarian with rainfed traditional agricultural production systems. Jawhar is a tribal block in Maharashtra, India characterized by high rainfall, water scarcity, degraded soils and low crop productivity. ICRISAT in collaboration with JSW has initiated agricultural interventions with watershed approach. Over a two-year period, the project has demonstrated various activities to build the resilience against climate change to cope with varying climatic risks and to improve livelihoods. Conservation of available resources through various measures was carried out with active community participation. Agriculture is the main source of livelihood of the community. Soil health management, rainwater harvesting, soil conservation, promotion of improved cultivars, introduction of new crops (crop diversification), income-generating activities and promotion of agronomic practices were the major interventions carried out in the project villages. These have taken farmers towards the path of building resilience to cope with climatic risks.

4.1 High-rainfall Zone – Jawhar, Maharashtra

4.1.1 Challenges and opportunities

The semi-arid region is primarily agrarian with rainfed traditional agricultural production systems being dominant. In the semi-arid tropics (SAT) soil degradation along with water scarcity are the main causes for low crop yields; and inefficient utilization of existing water resources results in low water use efficiency. An integrated watershed management approach proved to be the suitable strategy for achieving holistic development in these regions through collective action (Wani *et al.*, 2003a). The very purpose of the watershed development programme is to reduce water-related risks in rainfed agriculture by improving the local soil–water balance by implementing both *in-situ* and *ex-situ* interventions. Since water and soil are important components of agricultural development, proper management of these resources is crucial to build the resilience of these systems to cope with varying climatic risks and to improve livelihoods. Rainfed soils are multinutrient deficient and need proper nutrient management strategies to bridge the existing gap between farmers' current yields and achievable potential yields (Sahrawat *et al.*, 2010).

---

* Corresponding author: k.petare@cgiar.org

Jawhar is situated in the Konkan region of India. The rainfall in the region is seasonal and generally comes as torrential downpour resulting in large runoff and causing severe soil erosion; its distribution is quite erratic. Even though annual average rainfall in the region is 2729 mm, most rural people face water scarcity and drinking water shortage in summer. The hilly terrain and subsurface basalt rock limit the subsurface water percolation, causing heavy surface runoff during a monsoon, leading to soil erosion and land degradation. About 92% of the population in Jawhar taluk, Maharashtra is indigenous (tribal). Landholding of farmers is low and most of the farmers are small and marginal. Malnutrition is a major issue in the taluk; 52.44% of children are underweight. Crop productivity levels are very low due to adoption of traditional practices. Agriculture is rainfed and is the main source of livelihood. Migration is predominant in the taluk after harvesting the *kharif* (rainy season) crops. The main issue for farmers is the scarcity of water in summer and due to undulated landscape, it is not possible to cultivate a second crop after rainy season. This situation in the region provides a unique opportunity to assess and address livelihood issues in the region by tapping the potential of rainfed agriculture through knowledge-based management of natural resources for increasing productivity.

4.1.2 Climatic situation

Palghar district was formed on 1 August 2014 (earlier it was part of Thane district, Maharashtra). Palghar district comprises eight taluks, viz. Dahanu, Jawhar, Palghar, Mokhada, Talasari, Vada, Vasai and Vikramgad. As per the agroecological classification, Palghar district falls under 'Central and South Sahyadris, hot moist subhumid to humid transitional Ecological Sub Region'. Palghar district has mostly deep, loamy to clayey red and lateritic soils with low to medium (200 mm) available water capacity. The length of the rainfed crop-growing period varies between 210 and 270 days. There is variation in the rainfed crop-growing period across the taluks due to the change in rainfall distribution and topography. Average annual rainfall for Jawhar taluk is about 2729 mm, and normal monthly rainfall ranges from 3 mm in May to 1042 mm in July; rainfall is nil during December to April.

The normal date of onset of the southwest monsoon over Jawhar taluk is around 10 June and the monsoon withdraws by the last week of September. Monthly rainfall distribution in Jawhar taluk indicates that July is the rainiest month of the year. Rainfall activity generally ceases by the end of October.

Weekly rainfall data of Jawhar taluk was collected by the Government of Maharashtra for 19 years (1998–2016) (http://maharain.gov.in) and the average weekly rainfall was computed. Two contrasting years were identified as a wet year (2011) and a dry year (1999) and the distribution of weekly rainfall during the major crop-growing period (10 June to 28 October) for these two years and for the 19-year average is shown in Fig. 4.1. Average total rainfall during the season is about 2699 mm; in the wet year (2011), the total seasonal rainfall was about 3932 mm which was 46% above the average while in the dry year (1999), the total seasonal rainfall was about 1565 mm, which was 42% below the average. In the wet year, three peaks with a rainfall of more than 500 mm per week were observed, and the total rainfall for these three peaks is about 1740 mm; even during the dry year, two peaks with rainfall of 230 mm and 300 mm per week were seen. This highlights the need for proper runoff water management to save crops from inundation and storage of excess water for use during the following non-rainy season.

4.1.3 Rainfed crop-growing period

The length of the rainfed crop-growing period is the period of the year in which crops could be grown successfully as both rainfall and moisture stored in the soil will meet the moisture demands of crops. Knowledge on crop-growing period and its variability helps in choosing the right crops and varieties for higher productivity as well as identifying the optimum sowing time. The beginning and end and length of the rainfed crop-growing period at Jawhar taluk were identified (Fig. 4.2). Crop-growing period can begin as early as 3 June, but could be delayed as late as

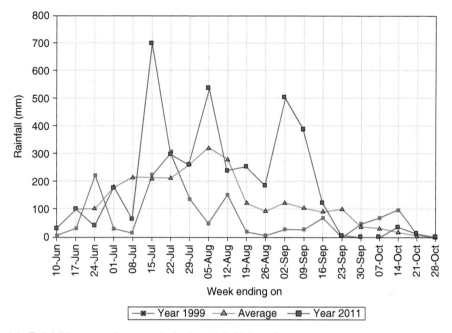

Fig. 4.1. Rainfall in contrasting years in Jawhar taluk, Maharashtra.

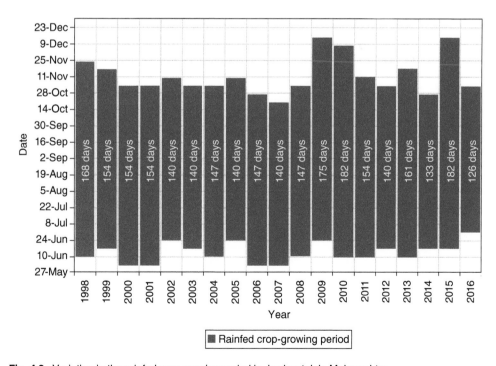

Fig. 4.2. Variation in the rainfed crop-growing period in Jawhar taluk, Maharashtra.

1 July; a difference of about 28 days. On average, the growing period begins by mid-June and ends by mid-November, so the length of the growing period is about 150–155 days.

Crop-growing period can end as early as 21 October and could extend up to 16 December; a difference of about 55 days. Thus, the beginning is more assured compared to the end of the growing period; there is a risk of end-of-season drought that can be managed by storing the excess water during the peak rainfall periods and with proper water management.

4.1.4   Projected climate change

Global atmospheric concentration of carbon dioxide has increased from a pre-industrial level of 280 ppm to 400 ppm in 2015. Various studies show that climate change in India is real and it is one of the major challenges faced by Indian agriculture. Climatic change in terms of water resource availability, changes in the length of crop-growing period and droughts is likely to aggravate the existing crop production risks. Both the strategic (longer-term) and tactical (seasonal) approaches are needed to manage climatic variability for sustainable crop production and rural incomes through efficient management of natural resources.

A study carried out by International Crops Research Institute for the Semi-Arid Tropics (ICRISAT), Patancheru, India revealed a net reduction in the dry subhumid area (10.7 million ha) in the country, of which about 5.1 million ha (47%) became drier and about 5.6 million ha (53%) became wetter, comparing the periods 1971–90 and 1991–2004 (Kesava Rao *et al.*, 2013). Results for Madhya Pradesh have shown the largest increase in semi-arid area (about 3.82 million ha) followed by Bihar (2.66 million ha) and Uttar Pradesh (1.57 million ha).

Relatively little changes occurred in Andhra Pradesh; semi-arid areas decreased by 0.24 million ha, which became both drier (0.13 million ha under arid type) and wetter (0.11 million ha under dry subhumid type). Results indicated that dryness and wetness are increasing in different parts of the country in place of moderate climates that existed earlier in these regions.

Projections of future climate are based on the output of atmosphere/ocean general circulation models and are used to simulate conditions in the future based on projected levels of greenhouse gases. There are several models available with different spatial resolutions. Majority of projections of future climate come from Global Circulation Models, which vary in the way they model the climate system, and so produce different projections about what will occur in the future. In the present study, Beijing Climate Center Climate System Model version 1.1 (BCC_CSM1.1) for the Coupled Model Intercomparison Project phase 5 (CMIP5) was considered. Monthly temperature and rainfall projections for the year 2030 for RCP 8.5 (Representative Concentration Pathways) were collected for the area representing Jawhar taluk, Palghar district and are shown in Figs 4.3 and 4.4.

Studies indicate that in addition to air temperature, rainfall amount and intensity are likely to change in future. These will impact the amount of water that can be stored as soil moisture and lost as runoff, thereby changing the water availability to crops at critical stages. Reduction in yields as a result of climate change is predicted to be more pronounced for rainfed crops as opposed to irrigated crops because of no coping mechanism for rainfall variability. Thus, rainfed agricultural crop production would become more challenging under future climatic conditions.

Projected changes in maximum and minimum temperatures and rainfall for Jawhar taluk show that there is great month-to-month variation. In the Jawhar taluk, the annual maximum temperature is expected to be higher by about 0.8°C and annual minimum temperature is likely to be highest by about 1.0°C. Maximum temperatures in July may increase by 1.2°C, while minimum temperatures during winter (November to February) are likely to increase by 1.2 to 1.5°C. A rise in temperature above a threshold level will cause a reduction in agricultural yields, but a change in the minimum temperature is even more crucial. Though the lands are mostly kept fallow in winter in this area, encouraging crop cultivation in winter is a way to enhance incomes of farmers. Higher minimum temperatures in winter are likely to hasten maturity and reduce crop yields in future and introduction of heat-tolerant varieties is likely to bring resilience.

Jawhar taluk is projected to have a positive change in annual rainfall of about 358 mm, mostly due to increase in rainfall during July and

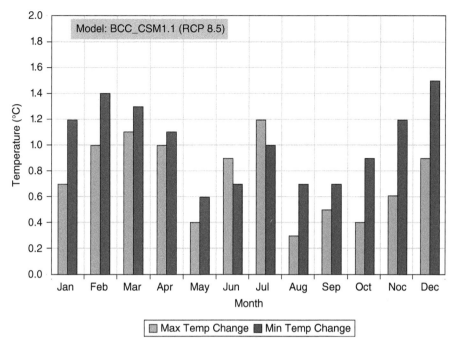

Fig. 4.3. Projected changes in temperature in Jawhar taluk, Maharashtra.

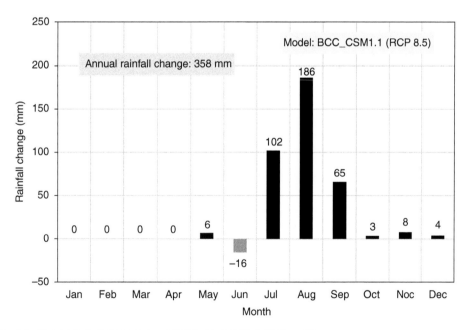

Fig. 4.4. Five projected changes in rainfall in Jawhar taluk, Maharashtra.

August. This is a positive indication for Jawhar taluk, as more water will be available for water harvesting and storing during these months. However, as June is likely to receive slightly lower rainfall and June is crucial for sowing and transplanting operations, more focus is needed for addressing the lower rainfall and variability in the sowing rains. Except for June, all other months are likely to have no change or higher rainfall compared to the present conditions (Kesava Rao *et al.*, 2013).

4.1.5   Corporate social responsibility opportunity

The JSW Foundation works consciously to support and empower communities by reducing social and economic inequalities by providing better opportunities through health, education, skill development and employment. It also works to tackle the issue of malnutrition, facilitate to make learning more effective and meaningful, empower the youth through employable skill programmes, ensure water security through long-term watershed development programmes and provide access to sanitation facilities in rural areas to make them open-defecation-free.

The JSW Foundation works with Government of Maharashtra to reduce malnutrition in Jawhar taluk, Palghar district. The interventions are mainly planned targeting the 0–6 age group children, pregnant women and lactating mothers. The focus of interventions are mainly on the dietary supplement provision to the targeted population. However, to eradicate malnutrion from Jawhar block, a long-term solution is required. Agriculture being the mainstay of the rural community in the region, agriculture-based interventions need to be planned. At a pilot scale, six villages, namely Ghivanda, Kogda, Jamsar, Dabheri, Sakharshet and Chambharshet were identified for malnutrition reduction through climate-resilient agriculture interventions (Fig. 4.5). The International Crops Research Institute for the Semi-Arid Tropics (ICRISAT), Patancheru, India initiated the preliminary work with participatory rural analysis to get an overall understanding of ground situation in consultation with the local community. Discussions were focused mainly on needs assessment and interventions.

4.1.6   Pre-project scenario – constraints

Jawhar is a tribal block in Maharashtra state characterized by high rainfall, water scarcity, degraded soils and low crop productivity. About 84% of the households are engaged in agriculture, which covers 64% of the geographical area (Table 4.1). Agriculture landholding is also fragmented, with 24% of the households with less than 1 ha and 37% of the households less than 3 ha.

The major crops in this region are paddy, finger millet, pigeonpea, black gram, groundnut, sesame and proso millet. The productivity levels of paddy and finger millet are low. Most of the area is under rainfed agriculture with sole cropping system. Few farmers also cultivate vegetables with irrigation. There are some plantation gardens with mango, sapota and coconut.

The economic condition of farmers in this region is poor. Agriculture is the main source of livelihood; however, agricultural produce is mainly used for household purposes. There are a few progressive farmers cultivating marketable vegetables and flowers.

Farmers' perception about fertilizer application is that their fields at the foothills get nutrients from runoff water as it flows through decomposed material in the forest area. Some farmers use organic manure in the form of farmyard manure, and chemical fertilizers such as urea and diammonium phosphate are also used. Except for rice, farmers do not use improved cultivars of crops. Farmers believe that the local traditional varieties are more suitable to their region than the improved cultivars. Improper use of chemical fertilizers and other inputs have increased the cost of cultivation, which results in poor economic returns.

Few farmers grow mango, cashew, sapota and guava; but their productivity is lower. Banana cultivation is picking up. Progressive farmers cultivating flowers and vegetables are getting more benefits through available resources. Even though farmers get profit, they cannot cultivate their farms in *rabi* (the post-rainy season) because of open grazing of cattle and crop damage. Due to low population density, farmers do not get enough labour during peak season, whereas during *rabi* season some people migrate to other places in search of employment.

Farmers are not aware of good agricultural practices. For example, farmers do not use fertilizer as per the soil and crop requirements. As a result, soils may be deficient in major and micronutrients. Soil fertility assessment needs to be carried out as a priority. Due to poor land management practices and high rainfall, agricultural

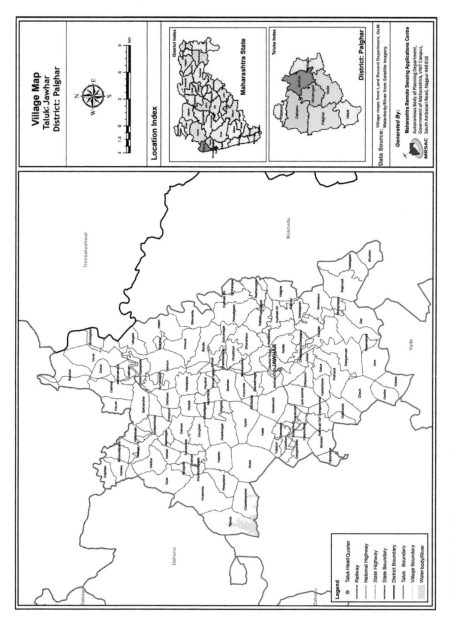

Fig. 4.5. Study sites in Jawhar taluk, Palghar district, Maharashtra. From: Maharashtra Remote Sensing Application Centre, Nagpur.

Table 4.1. Brief demographic information about the pilot villages.

Village	Households (no.)	Population (no.)		Land area (ha)
		Male	Female	
Ghivanda	323	805	844	808.52
Kogda	124	310	303	1405.07
Jamsar	305	730	731	941.12
Dabheri	321	938	882	875.15
Sakharshet	373	926	926	932.12
Chambharshet	288	829	845	807.95

land in these villages is degraded. Soil depths are shallow and low in organic carbon. Water-holding capacity is low to medium. Most of the farmers do not have an irrigation facility. Although the state government is providing 50% subsidy on irrigation pumps, farmers cannot afford to buy the pumps as farm holding size is very low.

4.1.7   Strategy and approach

Farm and land-based systems are complex with a multitude of problems. It requires a holistic approach that considers social, economic, political and institutional factors to achieve specific objectives. In this project, a holistic strategy has been adopted that considers all farm and land-based activities to take care of the multisectoral needs of farmers. The schemes and programmes initiated by central and state government have also been linked up to tap the resources for the welfare of the farming community. To gain community confidence on project interventions as a strategy, knowledge-based entry-point activity has been carried out in all the project villages; this has helped to promote confidence among the community members and generate awareness among the masses.

To achieve the overall goal of this initiative, emphasis was laid on increasing agricultural productivity and improving livelihoods on a sustainable basis by enhancing the impact of integrated watershed management programmes through capacity-building initiatives using site of learning in high rainfall agroecoregions. The project adopted consortium approach to bring together the expertise of different areas to expand effectiveness of various project interventions. In this project, the ICRISAT-led consortium has helped address complex issues effectively

addressed by the joint efforts of key partners, namely, Rural Commune as non-government organization (NGO), Krishi Vigyan Kendra (KVK), Dr Balasaheb Sawant Konkan Krishi Vidyapeeth Dapoli, government line department, community-based organizations and other private interest groups, with farm households as key decision makers.

Implementation of this integrated approach has been carried out through establishment of consortium of partners by adopting the concept of '4-C' principles. The first 'C' is consortium of research, education, field-based agencies and market players to implement this programme effectively on ground. The second 'C' is convergence with and within the agencies for providing programme support, execution and monitoring. The third 'C' is capacity building of the consortium partners, farmers, implementing agencies and other stakeholders. The fourth 'C' is collective action at all levels during programme implementation (Wani et al., 2003b, 2008).

In the overall programme partnership, the watershed committee is a major player for execution and monitoring of the programme activities. The watershed committee is empowered regularly towards programme activities. Considering the feminization of agriculture, the project placed efforts for representation of women members in watershed committee and also focused on capacity building of women farmers and female members of households. Also ICRISAT, along with the agriculture department and Krishi Vigyan Kendra of state agricultural university, has been working on crop improvement initiatives. The Rural Commune being the field implementation partner in the location is responsible for community capacity building and institutional support for implementation of activities in a sustainable manner.

4.1.8 Interventions

Interventions were initiated with the knowledge-based entry point activity (Dixit *et al.*, 2007). Constraint analysis has helped understand the issues related with the soil. Farmers were trained to collect the soil samples in their individual fields. A random stratified soil sampling methodology (Sahrawat *et al.*, 2008) was adopted to collect the soil samples. In the six project villages, 510 soil samples were collected with random stratified method, to get an overall understanding of soil health status in these project villages (Table 4.2). In the project villages, the farmers were trained on soil sample collection and details were shared on how to collect the sample. The soil sample analysis indicated that 8% of samples were deficient in organic carbon while 37% of soil samples were deficient in available phosphorus. For micronutrients, 93% of samples were observed deficient in available sulfur, 24% were deficient in available zinc and 78% deficient in available boron in the soils. Based on the soil sample analysis, in addition to NPK (nitrogen, phosphorus, potassium) 2.5 kg/ha borax, 25 kg/ha zinc sulphate and 100 kg/ha gypsum were recommended.

4.1.9 Soil and water conservation

As mentioned earlier, the region has high rainfall and due to inadequate soil and water conservation measures, soil erosion is a regular phenomenon. To arrest soil erosion, the project promoted soil conservation measures through continuous contour trenches, staggered contour trenches, gully plugs, etc. Over a period of two years, 41 ha area was treated with various soil and water conservation activities benefiting 102 households (Figs 4.6 and 4.7).

4.1.10 Rainwater harvesting

The villages face acute water shortage in summer. Hence, the project focused on desilting and repairing of existing water bodies in the project villages. The community was motivated for desilting of the water bodies in their respective villages and the project provided support for repair of the structures, if any (Table 4.3). This has led to water availability for drinking in summer in the project villages. The project also focused on desilting of existing check-dams in the project villages to create water storage facility (Fig. 4.8). Desilting has created additional storage capacity of 31,417 m^3. This would recharge 480,680 m^3 water considering 5 cm per day infiltration rate for 150 days (July to November). A success story in Kogda village is given in Box 4.1.

4.1.11 Crop management

Although agriculture is the main source of livelihood of the households in the project villages, the crop yields are below the district yields. Productivity of paddy, which is a staple crop in the villages, is 1.9 t/ha whereas the district average is 2.56 t/ha. Productivity of other crops is also low as compared to state and national averages. ICRISAT demonstrated crop management practices in the project villages with the major crops of the villages.

Paddy

Paddy is the major *kharif* crop in the villages and is the staple food of the community. To reduce the cost of cultivation and elevate the crop yield, demonstrations were carried out by promoting integrated crop management based on the science-led interventions as needed. In this context the project adopted line sowing as well as efficient water management along with soil test-based nutrient management practices for increasing the crop productivity (Fig. 4.9). Demonstration with 87 farmers was carried out with the variety Gujarat 4. Even though the rainfall was erratic and low with two long dry spells, yield was low but comparatively good over the traditional practice with an increase in yield of about 34% (Table 4.4). Farmers are now showing interest for the improved practices and are willing to scale-up the line sowing method.

Finger millet

Finger millet is the second-largest food crop of this region. Farmers usually grow the local variety using the broadcasting method. The average yield of the crop is very low, i.e. 350 kg/ha.

Table 4.2. Soil fertility status of farmers' fields in the project villages.[a]

Villages	No. of Samples	OC	Range of available contents (mg/kg soil)					
			Av P	Av K	Av S	Av Zn	Av B
Jamsar	50	0.49–2.15 (0)	3.8–25.0 (19)	52.46–565.05 (0)	0.80–7.91 (100)	0.28–4.06 (43)	0.22–0.89 (81)
Kogda	55	0.31–2.91 (0)	1.4–74.40 (47)	55.91–545.60 (0)	0.39–23.82 (95)	0.22–7.30 (66)	0.29–1.57 (75)
Sakharshet	97	0.27–3.50 (0)	1.4–89.80 (47)	47.55–561.80 (0)	0.47–43.57 (95)	0.44–7.72 (66)	0.24–1.14 (75)
Ghivanda	98	0.18–2.65 (14)	1.8–110.40 (51)	39.89–560.20 (2)	1.03–91.86 (92)	0.08–7.62 (7)	0.14–1.08 (67)
Dabheri	96	0.25–2.28 (9)	1.6–76.40 (29)	71.005–547.00 (1)	0.89–26.02 (84)	0.44–3.66 (11)	0.18–2.03 (73)
Chambharshet	98	0.26–3.50 (5)	0.8–120.40 (55)	47.27–539.76 (0)	0.41–267.53 (93)	0.24–10.13 (21)	0.07–3.31 (88)

[a]Note: Values in parentheses indicate % fields deficient in particular nutrient, i.e. baseline status of farmers' fields, and does not involve statistics or significance. Critical value adopted for delineating % deficiency are 0.5% for OC, 5 mg/kg for P, 50 mg/kg for K, 10 mg/kg for S, 0.58 mg/kg for B and 0.75 mg/kg for Zn. Based on the soil health assessment, for deficiency of micronutrients, 25 kg/ha zinc sulphate (20% Zn), 2.5 kg/ha borax (20% B) and 100 kg/ha gypsum (15% S) were recommended. The secondary nutrient recommendations were based on the crops.

Fig. 4.6. Soil and water conservation work in (a) Kogda and (b) Sakharshet villages.

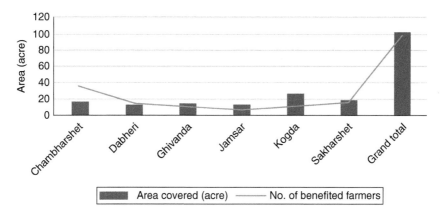

Fig. 4.7. Farmers benefiting from soil conservation work in the project villages.

Table 4.3. Repair and desiltation work in the project villages.

| Village | No. of structures | | | |
	Well repair	Well deepening	Desilting of check-dams	Desilting of lakes
Ghivanda	8	6	5	1
Jamsar	4	3	1	1
Kogda	4	5	6	0
Chambharshet	10	9	0	0
Sakharshet	4	4	5	0
Dabheri	5	3	0	0
Total	35	30	17	2

ICRISAT introduced long-duration high-yielding varieties MR 1 and GPU 28. Farmers were trained for nursery preparation and transplantation of crop. During *kharif* 2015, 44 finger millet demonstration trials covering 5.5 acres were carried out (Table 4.5). In 2015 scanty rainfall hampered crop growth; however, the demonstration plots showed 43% higher yield than the farmers' practice (Fig. 4.10).

Groundnut

A foliar-disease-tolerant new variety of groundnut ICGV 350 has been introduced to replace

Fig. 4.8. Desilted check-dam in Kogda village.

the traditional variety used by the farmers in the project villages. In addition to the varietal change, raised bed and broad-bed and furrow system have been introduced in groundnut crop. This has helped drain excess water from the field. With the recommended dose of fertilizers, the crop has shown encouraging results (Fig. 4.11). In the demonstration plots, 48% higher yield (1520 kg/ha) was obtained as compared to farmers' practice (1020 kg/ha).

Pigeonpea

Pigeonpea crop too has a prominent place in the diet of the local people. As a new initiative, demonstrations of pigeonpea and groundnut inter-cropping were carried out. Traditionally, farmers use the broadcasting method of sowing, so more seed is required. ICRISAT provided seed of improved varieties ICPL 88039, ICPL 87119 (Asha) and ICPH 2740. The hybrid ICPH 2740 performed very well in the project villages and produced 85% higher yield and ICPL 87119 and ICPL

88039 produced 51% higher yield as compared to the local variety (Fig. 4.12).

4.1.12   Crop diversification

Farmers' incomes were low with traditional crops. To enhance income at household level and for optimum utilization of available resources, ICRISAT promoted and demonstrated the post-monsoon crops as cash crops as well. The post-monsoon crops helped farmers to obtain more grain yield and cash crops helped gain additional income at household level. The project promoted cultivation of creeper vegetables in the project villages, initially focusing on bitter gourd covering 81 farmers in 15 ha (Fig. 4.13; also see Box 4.2). These interventions have helped farmers gain additional income at household level. Based on the experiences and output achieved in bitter gourd cultivation, the project supported the farmers for diversified vegetable cultivation in the project villages covering a 23.4 ha area (Table 4.6).

Box 4.1. Desilting old structures to enable fertile lands.

Mahadu Sakharam Bhoye is a farmer from Bhoyepada hamlet of Kogda panchayat in Jawhar taluk. He has a family consisting of nine members. With the introduction of the JSW project in his village, Rural Commune has started working in his village. A watershed committee has been elected in the village and a main watershed body of six villages was formed in which 12 members have been appointed and the farmer has been chosen as the secretary of the committee named 'Pragati Bahuudheshya Sevabhavi Sansthan'.

 Most of the agriculture in the village is rainfed and farmers are totally dependent on rainfall to raise their crops. In the village, there are three masonry check-dams which were built by the agriculture department in 2001. Despite this intervention, the village is facing water scarcity for agriculture purpose as the water was used as last source for irrigation in long dry spells during the rainy season. Due to rainfall of the past few years, silt had been deposited from 2001 and desiltation work had never been carried out. In 2015, with the help of Rural Commune, it was proposed to desilt two check-dams in the village. About ₹92,180 was spent to revive two check-dams with pitching in both sides. The community actively participated in the work and also donated ₹2,538 in the form of voluntary labour. The farmer later applied all the removed silt (i.e. approximately 250 tons) to his barren wasteland of about 0.2 ha, thus transforming it into highly fertile land. After the application, the farmer harvested vegetable crops like brinjal (513 kg), chilli (1620 kg) and pigeonpea (180 kg) and sold the vegetables for ₹12,825, ₹48,600 and ₹14,400 respectively.

 The farmer was surprised by the beneficial result of applying silt to his barren land and decided to apply silt to the rest of his agricultural land and motivated his colleagues to do the same to increase the productivity of their land. He says that this method can help retain lost fertility of soil; and old water-holding structures will be recycled, resulting in the increase of the groundwater table. During the *rabi* season, with the help of lift irrigation from the desilted check-dams, the farmer decided to harvest chickpea, onion, groundnut and maize in the silt applied area. Also, neighbouring farmers are lifting water from the desilted check-dam and growing vegetables like cabbage, okra, guar (cluster beans), tomato, onion, fenugreek and bottle gourd. In total, 3.04 ha of land was irrigated during the *rabi* season in 2015 after desilting of check-dams and vegetable crops were then cultivated.

Horticulture plantation

In the villages, most of the uplands remain barren. These are mostly cultivable wastelands where farmers cultivate finger millet and foxtail millet based on the availability of seed and time during the monsoon season. However, the land remains barren. After soil and water conservation works in the land, the project promoted cultivation of horticulture and forestry plantation. Horticulture plantation has been carried out in all the six project villages, covering 798 households (Table 4.7).

Rice fallow management

In the project villages, cultivating *rabi* crop is a bonus for small and marginal farmers. Due to lack of irrigation facilities at household level and non-availability of irrigation infrastructure the villagers were dependent only on the monsoon crops. Post-rainy season agriculture lands used to remain barren. The project helped the farmers to utilize the available soil moisture for the second crop and introduced chickpea (JG 11) in the project villages. About 135 farmers participated in the crop demonstration across six villages (Fig. 4.14). The crop was grown only on the available soil moisture after harvesting paddy. Chickpea yield was 46% higher in the demonstration plots as compared to farmers' practice.

Promotion of post-monsoon crops

The project has also focused on creating irrigation infrastructure in the project villages, mainly promotion of irrigation pumps, pipe lines, sprinklers, etc. Irrigation facilities were provided to the villagers on a group basis to generate ownership among the community and also revenue for future management and maintenance of the asset created. The project has provided six irrigation pumps and pipelines to women self-help groups (SHGs), who are caretakers of these assets and generate revenue by providing these pumps to individuals. After establishing irrigation

Fig. 4.9. Improved paddy crop management practice in Sakharshet village.

Table 4.4. Paddy yield and benefits with improved cultivation practices in project villages.[a]

Village	No. of trials	Crop yield (kg/ha)		Additional return with BN (₹)	Additional cost on BN (₹)	Benefit–cost ratio
		FP	BN			
Jamsar	9	1240	1680	6298	2100	3
Kogda	15	930	2220	18180	2100	8.66
Sakharshet	17	2950	3560	8626	2100	4.11
Ghivanda	14	2220	2820	8379	2100	3.99
Dabheri	9	2920	3650	10246	2100	4.88
Chambharshet	23	2200	2800	8411	2100	4.01

[a]FP = Farmers' practice; and BN = Balanced nutrition.

Table 4.5. Finger millet crop yield with balanced nutrient management.[a]

Village	No. of trials	Crop yield (kg/ha)		Additional return with BN (₹)	Additional cost on BN (₹)	Benefit-cost ratio
		FP	BN			
Kogda	18	320	690	6068	2100	2.89
Ghivanda	13	310	870	9193	2100	4.38
Dabheri	13	430	670	3935	2100	1.87

[a]FP = Farmers's practice; and BN = Balanced nutrition.

Fig. 4.10. High-yielding finger millet crop in Sakharshet village.

Fig. 4.11. Groundnut crop in Ghivanda village.

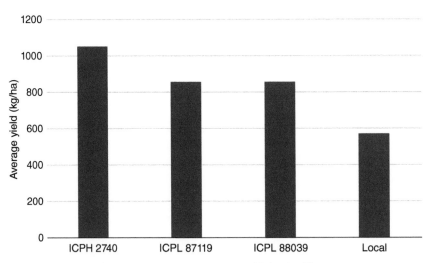

Fig. 4.12. Yield of improved pigeonpea varieties compared with local cultivar.

Fig. 4.13. Bitter gourd cultivation in Sakhershet village.

infrastructure, green gram (LGG 460) and wheat (HI 1531) were introduced in the project villages. Green gram has shown 24% higher yield with irrigation as compared to farmers' practice. In case of wheat, only three demonstrations could be worked out with assured irrigation possibility. Control plots with local variety available with the farmers were also established. The demonstration plots have recorded 29% higher yield as against the control plot (Fig. 4.15).

4.1.13 Graduation of tribal farmers to protected cultivation of vegetables

Vegetable cultivation has helped the farmers to gain confidence and understand the benefit of cash

crops. Building on the assurance, the project promoted cultivation of high-value cash crops. Following discussions with the community, a group-based net house was established in five villages based on the demand (Fig. 4.16). The project provided soft loan to these members for infrastructure establishment. The output of first year interventions is given in Table 4.8. In a span of 150 to 180 days, farmers earned ₹3000 to ₹10,000 from protected cultivation.

4.1.14 Microenterprises

Small-scale entrepreneurship through watershed development plays a significant role in poor people's lives and is one of the key factors to uplift people out of poverty (Anantha *et al.*, 2009). Some of the activities are the backbone on which the rural society survives in most arid and semi-arid regions. Watershed development is primarily aimed at sustainable management of natural resources contributing to overall agricultural development and livelihood promotion in rural areas. The project focuses on establishing microenterprises in the project villages. Village seed bank and nursery raising have been introduced in the project villages as income-generating activities.

Village seed bank

The introduction of hybrid technology made farmers depend on external sources for replenishing

---

Box 4.2. Technical guidance from JSW-ICRISAT programme helps farmer overcome debt trap.

Vijay Balwant Bhoye, a farmer from Kogda village has 3 acres of land. His family consists of six members and the entire family depends on agriculture for their livelihood. He usually harvests crops such as finger millet, paddy, pigeonpea, black gram and safflower, mainly grown under rainfed conditions. During the recent decade due to irregular rainfall and late arrival of the monsoon, sowing was delayed and resulted in reduced productivity for the farmer and his family, which eventually forced them to migrate to Thane or Palghar for earning their livelihood.

After migration, the farmer was in debt as the contractors did not pay him on time and his family was struggling for food. He was also burdened with the additional expenses of his children's education and his parents' health care. It was after the introduction of the JSW-ICRISAT programme, that the farmer's life gradually started to improve. Also, regular meetings by the Rural Commune (RC) staff helped motivate the farmer to improve productivity.

After a series of meetings with the RC staff, the farmer tried cultivating bitter gourd by the *mandav* (trellis system) method, which helped him make a regular income. During May 2015 in about 1 acre of land, the farmer dug pits and filled them with farmyard manure (FYM). He also procured a loan from neighbouring farmers for purchasing bamboo, strings, ropes and FYM for raising the *mandav* for bitter gourd. The expenditure incurred was ₹16,525.

The production of bitter gourd started from the first week of August. With proper guidance from the RC staff for collective marketing, the farmer took the produce to a common collection spot where they would weigh the produce. The vehicle used would take all the vegetable produce of his village and other neighbouring villages to Vashi wholesale vegetable market in Mumbai. The calculation of the profit was done on a weekly basis and he started to earn money from it. The farmer sold a total of 8500 kg of bitter gourd from 1 acre of land. Also, the RC staff had motivated him to keep a note on the details of expenditure and profit. He procured an income of ₹76,500 from selling bitter gourd, with net profit of ₹59,975.

The farmer's net profit helped him pay old debts. Due to the meetings with the RC, he was motivated and learnt new techniques and now he is growing more vegetables such as cabbage, tomato, cowpea and chilli in *rabi* season. In 2015 during 'Farmers' Day' farmers visited his farm. The event has made the farmer very proud. He is also working in watershed activities taken by the project and is thankful to ICRISAT for helping farmers.

Table 4.6. Vegetable cultivation in project villages.

Vegetable	No. of farmers	Area covered (ha)
Onion	29	2
Chilli	25	1
Brinjal	25	1.5
Tomato	49	2
Cowpea	2	0.2
Cluster bean	4	1
Cucumber	4	1
Okra	33	9
Broad bean	7	1.2
Bottle gourd	4	1.5
Sponge gourd	6	2.5
Pumpkin	2	0.5

seeds every season to gain higher productivity. The inability of small and marginal farmers to purchase hybrid seeds every season and availability of quality seeds in the rural market is a cause of concern. Therefore, the project made an attempt to establish village seed bank as an income-generating activity to meet self-sufficiency in production and distribution of quality seeds. This involved four women SHGs and one farmers' group. The current availability of seeds in the village level seed bank is given in Table 4.9.

Nursery raising

Nursery raising is a means of livelihood for a large number of people. It provides income-generating opportunities for the local communities. It also enables capacity building and upgrading skills of members of the communities. Nursery raising generates cash income for poverty alleviation. It provides an opportunity for women and aged people to contribute to income generation with flexible working hours. Overall, six nursery raising units in the project villages have been promoted covering six women SHGs. This has helped earn additional income of ₹20,000 to ₹50,000 per group.

Table 4.7. Horticulture plantation in project villages.

Village	No. of farmers	Mango	Cashew	Sapota	Guava	Lemon	Custard apple
Sakharshet	89	841	396	315	90	0	0
Chambharshet	110	110	230	110	110	0	0
Kogda	38	280	106	141	115	0	0
Jamsar	368	368	165	131	166	0	0
Ghivanda	1210	1210	369	252	302	70	34
Dabheri	325	325	112	55	55	0	0
Total	2140	3134	1378	1004	838	70	34

Fig. 4.14. Chickpea crop demonstration in Chambharshet village.

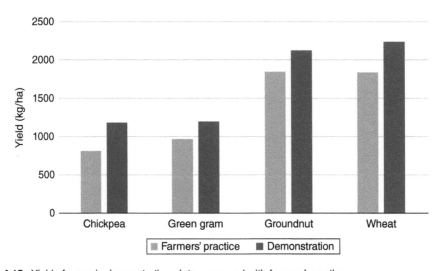

Fig. 4.15. Yield of crops in demonstration plots compared with farmers' practice.

Fig. 4.16. Protected cultivation of cucumber in Chambershet village.

Table 4.8. Farmer income from protected cultivation.

Village	No. of farmers	Net house area (m²)	Crop	Yield (kg)	Total income (₹)	Income per farmer (₹)
Kogda	4	784	Bitter gourd	1,078	42,385	10,596
Ghivanda	4	952	Cucumber	2,384	34,740	8,685
Jamsar	4	748	Cucumber	1,019	14,400	3,600
Sakharshet	2	352	Cucumber	350	6,200	3,100
Chambharshet	6	1,024	Cucumber	1,177	22,294	3,716

Table 4.9. Seed bank in project villages with seed (kg) of five crops.

Village	Pearl millet	Finger millet	Paddy	Groundnut	Pigeonpea
Ghivanda	0	4	8	70	3
Jamsar	0	3	5	100	2
Kogda	0	0	10	40	0
Sakharshet	0	10	7	93	0.5
Dabheri	1	0	0	55	3.5
Chambharshet	2	6	30	70	2
Total	3	23	60	428	11

4.1.15   Market linkages

The project has shown farmers the ways and means of improved production and to harvest additional benefits from the available resources within the villages. However, the project area being in the interior part of the district, accessibility to the market is an issue. The two nearest markets to the project locations are Nashik and Navi Mumbai. The project focuses on collectivization of the produce at the central place, the produce gets sorted and graded, farmer-wise quantity gets recorded and the produce is transported to the Navi Mumbai or Nashik Market. At both the markets, the identified dealer communicates the price and the produce is sold to the respective market. The transport cost incurred is divided among the farmers, based on the quantity each individual is sending to the market.

4.1.16   Overcoming malnutrition

As mentioned earlier, the project area has been facing a severe problem of malnutrition. The project exclusively targeted families having malnourished children as identified under the Government of Maharashtra's Integrated Child Development programme. Specific interventions, mainly vegetable cultivation as kitchen garden for consumption purpose were promoted. Under the cropping system, the project focused on introduction of its iron-rich pearl millet variety 'Dhanshakti' for consumption purpose along with the promotion of chickpea (see Box 4.3).

4.1.17   Marching towards mechanization

Farmers in the project villages mainly constitute small and marginal farmers having small landholdings. During the monsoon season availability of labour is an issue. The conventional tractor-based farm equipment are not suitable for field operations. The project invested in suitable small equipment like power tillers which help support easy farm operations.

4.1.18   Impact

The watershed project had positive impacts on the livelihoods of the community and on the natural resource base. Community-based organizations were strengthened and led to greater social capital for the rural population. Incomes and employment opportunities increased leading to reduction in outbound labour migration. Water availability significantly increased. Creation of water harvesting structures helped harvest 1,361,927 m³ of water. Improved agricultural practices showed increase in crop yields by 35% to 75% resulting in additional income of ₹15,000 to ₹25,000 per ha. Promotion of cash crops, mainly vegetable cultivation, helped gain additional ₹8,000 to ₹10,000. Capacity building measures and the empowerment of farmers, NGOs, extension workers and SHG members were enhanced.

4.2   Low-rainfall Zone – Ballari, Karnataka

4.2.1   Site specification

One of the requirements from JSW was to select villages in vicinity to their factory. The team comprising scientist from ICRISAT, officials from Department of Agriculture, Karnataka, and JSW have visited villages in Sandur taluk to identify the project locations. The four villages identified for the project were Dodda Anthapura, Chikka Anthapura, Kodalu and Joga. In these villages 1930 families are practising agriculture, while 293 families are landless. The villages are located about 25 km from the JSW factory in Toranagallu and 35 km from Ballari district headquarter.

There is a variation in resource endowments in these villages showing the opportunity to introduce different activities for the betterment of the community. The area is undulating and mainly depends on rainfall. The main sources of irrigation are bore well and open well. Each family generally has landholding of 2–5 acres, with a few families having up to 10 acres. Type of soil is red, loamy with few

---

Box 4.3. Preventing malnutrition through proper guidance.

Rajendra Mahale, a farmer from Sakharshet village, belongs to a joint family with 12 members. He is currently a watershed committee member in the village. He is working in the project implemented by ICRISAT and Rural Commune supported by JSW Foundation. The project team has been working extremely hard to eradicate malnutrition in the village and Rajendra regularly attends the monthly meetings in which the team takes decisions and brainstorm about the activities and issues happening in the project area. Rajendra's daughter, who is 3 years old, is severely underweight and it was only after attending the meetings that Rajendra became aware about the issue of malnutrition.

In September 2016, the project team had detailed the members about their approach towards eradicating malnutrition from the selected villages by motivating farmers to undertake nutrient enriched *rabi* crop and reduce migration of farmers to towns and cities during dry season. Rajendra decided to cultivate chickpea crop as it has good protein source. He cultivated the crop on 0.05 ha land as per the guidance of the project staff. He invested about ₹1094 for irrigation, labour and harvesting. He harvested about 62 kg of chickpea, which he utilized to feed his family. It was the first time Rajendra had cultivated chickpea crop and he is now thankful to JSW, ICRISAT and Rural Commune for helping his village to combat malnutrition and prevent migration.

---

patches of black soil. The decadal analysis of rainfall data (1996–2005) showed that the highest rainfall occurred in Sandur taluk (752 mm) and the lowest at Ballary (452 mm) with annual normal mean rainfall of 611 mm in the district. The southwest monsoon contributes 73% of the total rainfall in the district, while the northeast monsoon contributes 27% of total rainfall in the district. The mean maximum temperature in the district is 40.4°C and the mean minimum temperature is 14.3°C (January). Relative humidity ranges from 48% to 74% in the morning and 27% to 61% in the evening.

Agriculture contributes major portion of the income of the taluk. The main food crops are sorghum, paddy, maize and pulses, while the important commercial crops are sunflower, safflower and cotton. Though the productivity has shown a declining trend in the past few years, performance is better than the state average in terms of production and yield with reference to paddy, pulses, sorghum and cotton. Major horticultural crops grown in the district are chilli, coriander, pomegranate, mango and coconut. The current yield level is lower by 2–3 times the achievable potential yield of major dryland crops in the taluk. Even in irrigated belts of the taluk also the paddy yield is quite low. Overall, the yield of major dryland crops is far below the achievable yield.

4.2.2 Challenges and opportunities

Shift from agriculture to industry

The district is endowed with iron ore and famous for mining and related industrial activities which has provided employment opportunities for the young population. As a result of the available industrial employment opportunities, agriculture is left for elders and women, coupled with unavailability of labour force and falling returns due to low crop yields and price constraints.

Land use pattern

The average landholding is about 2.6 ha per household. In *kharif* season, 1.18 ha of land is irrigated, 1.14 ha is rainfed and rest is fallow land. During *rabi*, about 0.42 ha land is irrigated and rest is fallow. Similarly, in summer only 0.52 ha of land is irrigated and the rest is fallow. This land use pattern shows the lack of irrigation facility, which has implications on *rabi* and summer season cultivation.

Water resources

The unpredictable distribution of rainfall was affecting crop growth and total yield. Large numbers of bore wells and open wells are defunct, and need recharging structures. This provides an opportunity to improve groundwater resources by adopting proper land and water management interventions.

Market availability

Currently farmers sell their agricultural products in nearby district markets such as Ballary, Davanagere and Raichur. Good numbers of agricultural producers' marketing cooperatives are available to store their products. Apart from local markets, farmers sell their agricultural produce like horticultural produce to distant markets in Bengaluru and Hyderabad. The presence of JSW township is also a good opportunity to market their produce.

Land degradation

Due to persistent mining activities in and around the project villages and poor land management practices, agricultural lands in these villages are severely degraded. Lands are undulating with shallow soils and low in organic carbon. Water-holding capacity is poor. Thus, levelling and trench cum bunds (staggered trenches) across the slopes are required in order to conserve the soil and water.

4.2.3 Interventions

Soil test-based balanced nutrition trials

Farmer participatory approach was followed for collecting soil samples from selected villages. Stratified soil sampling methodology was adopted for sampling. The area was divided based on topography and cropping system. Farmers were trained for collecting soil samples from their fields. In total, 100 soil samples were collected in the selected villages. Analysis of soil for macro- and micronutrients was completed at ICRISAT laboratory.

The soil analysis results are presented in Table 4.10. Organic carbon is used as a proxy for nitrogen. The results revealed that most of the farmers' fields had sufficient amount of major nutrients. For example, none of the fields was deficient in potassium and very few fields were deficient in phosphorus and had low organic carbon content. Similarly, only 20% and 8% of fields were deficient in sulfur and boron respectively. The only deficient micronutrient was zinc. Based on these results, soil health cards were prepared and distributed to farmers in all four selected villages. The soil health cards include information on farmers' land, soil fertility status and nutrient recommendations for major crops grown in this region.

Soil test-based balanced fertilizer trials were conducted in famers' fields in selected villages to demonstrate the advantage of micronutrient application in addition to the application of nitrogen, phosphorus and potassium fertilizers. Farmers applied 200 kg gypsum, 12.5 kg zinc sulphate and 2.5 kg borax per hectare in improved practice and compared with farmers' practice. The treatments were imposed on plots, side by side and uniform crop management practices were ensured in all the treatments. Application of all the nutrients except nitrogen was made as basal: 50% of nitrogen dose to non-legumes was added as basal and the remaining in two equal splits at one-month intervals.

Farmer participatory evaluation of improved cultivars

Many farmers in selected villages use low-yielding old or local cultivars. Farmers' participatory varietal evaluation trials were conducted to demonstrate the yield advantage of improved crop cultivars as compared to existing low-yielding cultivars. The important crop cultivars included in these trials were with castor DCH 519, pearl millet

Table 4.10. Chemical analysis of soil from selected villages.

Village	Deficiency (%)					
	Organic carbon	Phosphorus	Potassium	Sulfur	Zinc	Boron
Chikanthapur	0	20	0	0	90	0
Doddanthapur	27	13	0	10	77	10
Joga	5	15	0	5	80	15
Kodalu	18	4	0	21	75	7

ICTP 8203, pigeonpea ICPL 87119, ICPH 2671 and ICPH 2740, groundnut ICGV 91114 and sorghum PVK 801, CHS 14, CSV 23 and CSV 15.

Rainwater harvesting

The ridge to valley approach was followed for achieving equity and access to water. The low-cost structures are proven for sustainability, equity as well as cost-effectiveness. The location, number of structures and designs were evaluated by ICRISAT and executed by locally appointed organization. The impact of rainwater harvesting on water resources was evaluated by monitoring groundwater levels. Fifty-two wells were selected across the topo-sequence for measuring groundwater level at a fortnightly interval. An automatic weather station has been established to collect weather data on rainfall, air and soil temperature, solar radiation and wind velocity and direction. Rainfall monitoring is necessary to help quantify the amount of moisture availability in different phenophases of crop growth, to estimate the crop water requirements, and also to assess runoff, soil loss and groundwater recharge. Most importantly, it helps the community to understand about crop water usage and for irrigation scheduling.

Capacity building programmes to improve livelihoods

Capacity building programme is very important activity in the watershed programme for sustainability of the interventions implemented and to carry forward the activities after the project period. Several capacity building programmes including technical training, field days, exposure visits were conducted for farmers and women's self-help groups (SHGs) to train and build their capacity for enhancing crop productivities and improving livelihoods. In addition to the formal training programme, awareness-building campaigns were organized on the occasions of events such as International Women's Day and World Environment Day. A total of 50 capacity-building programmes were conducted during the project period, benefiting all the farmers in the villages.

4.2.4   Impact

Increase in crop productivity with balanced nutrient management

In all the trials, yields were recorded at maturity by harvesting the crop at three spots in a treatment measuring 3 x 3 m and the average of three was used to compute yield in kg/ha. Results from farmers' field trials indicated that crop yield can be increased with improved agronomic practices. Figure 4.17 indicates grain yield increase from 8% to 29% for all the crops with the application of micronutrients. Maximum yield increase was observed in cotton (29%). The cost of micronutrient for 1 ha of land was ₹953 (₹2.2 per kg for gypsum, ₹33 per kg for zinc sulphate

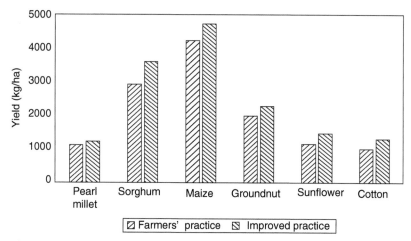

Fig. 4.17. Grain yield of major crops under farmers' practice (NPK only) and improved practice (NPK+Zn+S+B).

and ₹40 per kg for borax). The observed additional grain yield was 100, 660, 500, 280, 310 and 294 kg/ha for pearl millet, sorghum, maize, groundnut, sunflower and cotton respectively. This clearly indicated a return of ₹1.6, 10.4, 6.3, 10.9, 9.8 and 9.3 respectively on every rupee spent on micronutrients.

Soil analysis revealed a sufficient amount of phosphorus in the soils; however, farmers were using diammonium phosphate (DAP) fertilizer as source of nitrogen. Unknowingly, farmers were applying the phosphate fertilizer. In this context, phosphorus fertilizer trials were designed (with and without phosphorus application) for different crops to investigate the effect on crop performance. The results of these trials are presented in Fig. 4.18. Grain yield in the treatments was generally similar. Thus, it was scientifically established that crops cultivated in these soils do not require phosphorus fertilizer and DAP could be replaced by urea as source of nitrogen.

High-yielding improved cultivars

The grain yield of different crop cultivars is shown in Fig. 4.19. There was 28% grain yield advantage of castor hybrid DCH 519 over farmers' variety. Pearl millet variety ICTP 8203 gave

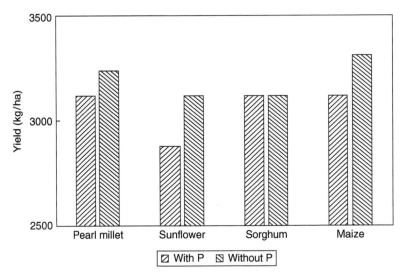

Fig. 4.18. Grain yield of different crops with and without phosphorus (P) application.

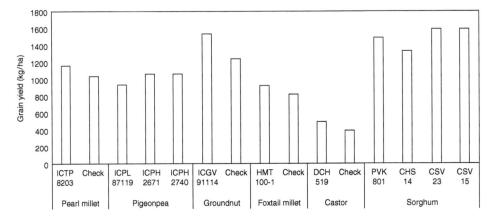

Fig. 4.19. Yield advantage of improved crop cultivars over existing cultivar in use.

17% grain yield increase over farmers' variety. Pigeonpea hybrids ICPH 2671 and ICPH 2740 and variety ICPL 87119 showed yield increase of 17, 38 and 17% respectively as compared to existing cultivars. In the case of sorghum, PVK 801 had increase in grain yield by 12% and CSV 23 by 16% compared to local varieties.

Increase in water availability

Various soil and water conservation structures were constructed in selected villages for minimizing land degradation and improving groundwater recharge. Rainwater harvesting structures such as farm ponds, check-dams (Fig. 4.20), bore well recharge pits and percolation tanks were established in consultation with the village community. Also, runoff was diverted to defunct open well and existing structures were rejuvenated. Similarly, gully plugs and field bunding were constructed for reducing soil erosion. Table 4.11 shows the total number of structures established during the three years of the project. Through these efforts a total of 33,000 m³ of rainwater is expected to be harvested during a normal monsoon season. The impact of these rainwater harvesting structures was clearly visible from observed groundwater levels near rainwater harvesting structure and levels away from the structure. Figure 4.21 clearly indicates the rise in groundwater level near the structure during monsoon as compared to level away from the structure. During the post-rainy season the levels for both the locations were similar indicating the depletion of level as a result of irrigation or groundwater recharge.

Livelihood activities

Several income-generating activities viz. *agarbathi* (incense sticks) making, kitchen gardening, Gliricidia nursery, vermicompost preparation have been introduced in the villages. The necessary training and financial support were provided to women self-help groups through the project. These activities have contributed to increase income of beneficiaries, for example, nursery preparation activity earned Rs 22,000 per year. Kitchen garden initiative has provided additional income of Rs 500–800 per month in addition to improved home nutrition through consumption of vegetables. Animal health developmental programmes and activities were also taken up in all the watershed villages for improvement of livestock in watershed villages every year. About 700–800 livestock were treated to prevent diseases and thus improved milk production (average 0.5–1.0 l/day/animal).

4.3   The Way Forward

The small farm holders in these regions have shown potential to bridge the large yield gaps by actively adopting to the change, and they continue to do so; however, these efforts need to be supported by capacity building efforts. As the terrain is undulating providing reduced space for traditional agriculture, tree-based farming needs to be considered on priority basis. The project has initiated market linkages, which need to be further strengthened with the value chain adaptation approach. Both the locations face

(a)

(b)

Fig. 4.20. Check-dam full with rainwater in (a) Kodalu and (b) Chikanthapur villages.

Table 4.11. Soil and water conservation and water harvesting structures constructed in selected villages.

Structure	2013–14	2014–15	2015–16	2016–17	Potential rainwater harvesting capacity (m³)	Beneficiaries (no.)
Gully plugs (no.)	90	0	0	6	480	46
Farm pond (no.)	9	3	5	7	6,000	24
Mini-percolation tank (no.)	2	1	0	0	300	4
Bore well recharge pit (no.)	15	1	0	3	60	19
Nala bund (no.)	1	0	0	1	12,000	20
Check wall (no.)	1	0	0	5	3,000	6
Check-dam (no.)	3	7	2	7	6,600	60
Wastewater treatment tank (no.)	1	0	0		1,500	5
Field bunding (m)	17,137	2,967	4,020	12,500	–	126
Silt removed from old check-dams (m³)	360	819	165	4,300	4,400	50
Open well recharging (no.)	0	4	0	2	300	6
Total	–	–	–		34,640	366

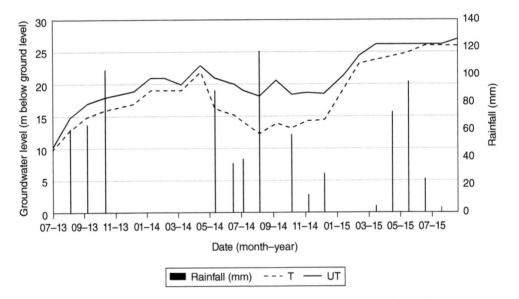

Fig. 4.21. Impact of rainwater harvesting (RWH) on groundwater level at Doddanthapur village. (T = near RWH structure; UT = away from REH structures.)

scarcity of water during the post-monsoon period irrespective of amount of rainfall received. Thus effective water management practices coupled with micro-irrigation practices need to be promoted.

The sustainability of the watershed programme after the project phase will be ensured by the four key factors, viz. effective participation of large numbers of community people (clearly indicating that they got tangible economic benefits

and the watershed interventions met their needs), presence of strong and effective community-based organizations, availability of watershed development fund (for repair and maintenance of the structures during the post-project phase) and strong linkage with the village panchayats. During the watershed programme, community-based organizations were given high priority to make them effective and strong. This will be further strengthened through capacity building

---

Box 4.4. Increasing yield through use of wastewater.

A decentralized wastewater treatment unit was constructed in Doddanthapur, which receives domestic wastewater from 250 households. This treated water was used by three farmers for irrigating cotton and pearl millet crops. Ms Thayamma, one of the farmers, harvested an additional 800 kg yield in cotton crop compared to non-irrigated crop. This has resulted in an additional income of Rs 34,000 with the use of treated wastewater. She also cultivated pearl millet in summer season using wastewater. Pearl millet crop gave higher yield (1000 kg) and earned income of about Rs 22,000. Before the project, Ms Thayamma used to cultivate one crop through wastewater without treatment and suffered skin problems. Now she is happy that the wastewater that accumulates around her house has been put to productive use while preventing health problems.

Box 4.5. JSW watershed initiative brings changes in SHG women's lives.

Mrs Vanajakshi is the group leader of *Manasa* women's self-help group in Joga village. Her husband works as an agricultural labourer. Under the active leadership of Manasa SHG has grown Gliricidia nursery. The saplings were provided to project and in the village, which gave an additional income of more than Rs 22,000 per year out of season.

Mrs Vanajakshi was also proactive and instrumental in taking up an income-generating activity of vegetable cultivation in a small piece of a land (100 sq m). These vegetables were primarily used for household consumption and excess quantity was sold in the village that also gave additional income of about Rs 500–800 per month.

The watershed project helped Vanajakshi to adopting income-generating activities, she became the proud owner of a small grocery store and net savings of about Rs 500 per month. Before the watershed project her financial condition was precarious. The additional income has helped to support her family expenditure.

---

and financial support, and by providing strong linkage with various institutions like market, banks, etc. These factors will go a long way in sustaining the impact of the watershed programme after the project phase.

Acknowledgements

The authors acknowledge the JSW Foundation for providing the funding support for implementing the watershed project; Mr Mukund Gorakshkar, Dr C.S. Kedar, Dr Vishwanath Palled, Mr Dharmesh Bhailal and Mr Rakesh Sharma from JSW for their support during the project implementation phase; Rural Commune as an implementation NGO at Jawhar and Pranati Rural Development Society at Ballari; the village-level watershed committee and all the farmers for active participation in watershed activities; and Mr Satish Gahukar and Ms Ganga for assisting in the watershed project.

References

Anantha, K.H., Wani, S.P. and Sreedevi, T.K. (2009) *Agriculture and Allied Micro-Enterprise for Livelihood Opportunities*. International Crops Research Institute for the Semi-Arid Tropics, Patancheru, India. Available at: http://oar.icrisat.org/3922/1/20._Agriculture_and_Allied_Micro-enterprise.pdf (accessed 5/10/2017).

Dixit, S., Wani, S.P., Rego, T.J. and Pardhasaradhi, G. (2007) Knowledge-based entry point and innovative up scaling strategy for watershed development projects. *Indian Journal of Dryland Agricultural Research and Development* 22(1), 22–31.

Kesava Rao, A.V.R., Wani, S.P., Singh, K.K., Irshad Ahmed, M., Srinivas, K. *et al.*(2013) Increased arid and semi-arid areas in India with associated shifts during 1971–2004. *Journal of Agrometeorology* 15(1), 11–18.

Sahrawat, K.L., Rego, T.J., Wani, S.P. and Pardhasaradhi, G. (2008) Stretching soil sampling to water-
    shed: evaluation of soil-test parameters in a semi-arid tropical watershed. *Communications in Soil
    Science and Plant Analysis* 39(19), 2950–2960.
Sahrawat, K.L., Wani, S.P., Pardhasaradhi, G. and Murthy, K.V.S. (2010) Diagnosis of secondary and
    micronutrient deficiencies and their management in rainfed agroecosystems: case study from Indian
    semi-arid tropics. *Communications in Soil Science and Plant Analysis* 41(3), 346–360.
Wani, S.P., Maglinao, A.R., Ramakrishna, A. and Rego, T.J. (eds) (2003a) Integrated Watershed Manage-
    ment for Land and Water Conservation and Sustainable Agricultural Production in Asia. *Proceedings
    of the ADB-ICRISAT-IWMI Annual Project Review and Planning Meeting*, Hanoi, Vietnam, 10–14
    December 2001. International Crops Research Institute for the Semi-Arid Tropics, Patancheru, India.
Wani, S.P., Singh, H.P., Sreedevi, T.K., Pathak, P., Rego T.J. *et al.* (2003b) Farmers participatory inte-
    grated watershed management: Adarsha watershed, Kothapally, India. An innovative and up-scaling
    approach. *Journal of SAT Agriculture Research* 2(1), 1–27.
Wani, S.P., Sreedevi, T.K., Reddy, T.S.V., Venkateshvarlu, B. and Prasad, C.S. (2008) Community water-
    sheds for improved livelihoods through consortium approach in drought prone rainfed areas. *Journal
    of Hydrological Research and Development* 23, 55–77.

5

Improving Livelihoods through Watershed Interventions: A Case Study of SABMiller India Project

RAJESH NUNE,* CH. SRINIVASA RAO, R. SUDI, SUHAS P. WANI, KAUSHAL K. GARG AND D.S. PRASAD RAO

International Crops Research Institute for the Semi-Arid Tropics, Patancheru, India

Abstract

Water plays an important role in the semi-arid tropical region to address water scarcity, land degradation, and crop and livestock productivity which improves the rural livelihood system. The Charminar Breweries (formerly SABMiller, and since merged with AB InBev) in Sangareddy district, Telangana, India has adopted an integrated approach to address the above issues in nearby villages of the plant under corporate social responsibility initiative between 2009 and 2017 in a phased manner. The major interventions implemented in the project focused on rainwater harvesting, productivity enhancement through soil test-based fertilizer application, improved crop cultivars, enriching soil organic carbon and improved agronomic practices. Further, livestock productivity was addressed by promoting spent malt (a by-product of the brewing industry, rich in carbohydrate, protein and other minerals) and improved breeding through artificial insemination. Various *ex-situ* interventions for water management enabled harvesting of nearly 150,000 m³ water every year and facilitated groundwater recharge, which resulted in increased water table of 0.5–1 ft across the geographical extent of nearly 7000 ha. Further, productivity interventions enhanced crop yield and cropping intensity by 30–50% compared to baseline situation. The livestock interventions enhanced milk yield by 1–2 l/day/animal. The watershed programme also introduced various income-generating activities for women and landless such as distribution of spent malt as animal feed, kitchen garden, vermicomposting and nursery raising. The programme has benefited nearly 5000 households directly or indirectly and increased household income by ₹10,000 to ₹25,000 per annum and contributed significantly towards improving rural livelihood along with strengthening various environmental services.

5.1 Introduction

Management of water resources has an important role in semi-arid regions, not only for increasing agricultural productivity and improving the livelihoods of the poor, but also for sustainable development of many water-based industries. The looming water scarcity as well as the projected increasing water demand by competing sectors like agriculture, environment and industry demonstrates that users are bound to put more pressure on the scarce and finite water resources. As there is a direct link between increasing agricultural productivity and economic

---

* Corresponding author: r.nune@cgiar.org

©CAB International 2018. *Corporate Social Responsibility: Win-win Propositions for Communities, Corporates and Agriculture* (eds S.P. Wani and K.V. Raju)

development for poverty reduction, it is evident that 1% increase in agricultural yields translates to 0.6–1.2% decrease in the number of absolute poor (Thirtle *et al.*, 2002; World Bank, 2005).

5.1.1   The initiative

The Charminar Breweries (formerly SABMiller, and since merged with AB InBev) is located on the bank of river Manjira, a perennial tributary of river Godavari, in the Sangareddy district of Telangana, India (Fig. 5.1). The Manjira river water is one of the major water resources. The farmers located near the river Manjira divert the river water to their fields for irrigation, especially during dry and *rabi* (post-rainy) seasons. It is critical to ensure that the surrounding communities do not view the factory as an exploiter of the water resources and for this necessary care needs to be taken to ensure sustainable development and management of the limited water resource in the surrounding areas. Under these circumstances, SABMiller and the International Crops Research Institute for the Semi-Arid Tropics (ICRISAT), Patancheru decided to adopt an integrated water resource management approach at catchment scale as a key to address water sustainability and management in the surrounding villages of Charminar Breweries for improving rural livelihoods as a win-win strategy.

5.1.2   Goal and objectives

The overall goal and objective of SABMiller initiative is to develop sustainable water resources in the surrounding areas of the factory while contributing to improving the livelihoods of the people dependent on agriculture. The specific objectives of the project are as follows.

(i) To improve water availability and agricultural productivity in selected villages through rainwater conservation, harvesting, its efficient use, and productivity enhancement measures for improving livelihoods.
(ii) To build capacity of the farmers in the selected villages to develop sustainable water management practices and enhance groundwater availability and use efficiency.

5.2   ICRISAT–SABMiller India Project

5.2.1   Background of the study area

The ICRISAT–SABMiller India Project has taken up integrated watershed management programme in a geographical area of around 7665 ha, spread across ten villages, located just 10–15 km away from Sangareddy town of Sangareddy district in Telangana state as shown in Fig. 5.1. The study area falls in one of the semi-arid tropical regions in the state, which is a hot spot for poverty, hunger, malnutrition, food insecurity, water scarcity and degraded land resources. This project was started in 2009 in four villages, namely Fasalvadi (Sangareddy mandal), Venkatakistapur, Shivampet and Chakriyal (Pulkal mandal). In 2013, the project expanded to three other villages, namely Sultanpur, Korpole and Vendikol (Pulkal mandal), and then in 2014, additional three villages, namely Chowtakur, Bommareddygudem and Upparigudem (Pulkal mandal) were added to the project. The project villages had a total population of 30,738 and 5754 households (Table 5.1). The average annual rainfall in the project area is around 895 mm. The villages are characterized by undulated topography with an average slope of 2.5%. Soil in these villages is dominated by Vertisol (black cotton soil) with medium to high water-holding capacity.

Of the total geographical area of the project villages, 90–92% of area is under agricultural use and the remaining area is under wasteland and non-agricultural use in the villages. Of the total agricultural area, 73% of area is rainfed and 23% of area is under irrigation condition (Table 5.2). The farmers grow cotton and maize predominantly in rainfed areas, and paddy and sugarcane in irrigated areas of these villages.

5.2.2   Identification of constraints

During rapid rural appraisal assessment done by the team of ICRISAT scientists in the selected villages, the following constraints were identified.

●   The soils were low in fertility because of imbalanced use of inputs of plant nutrients

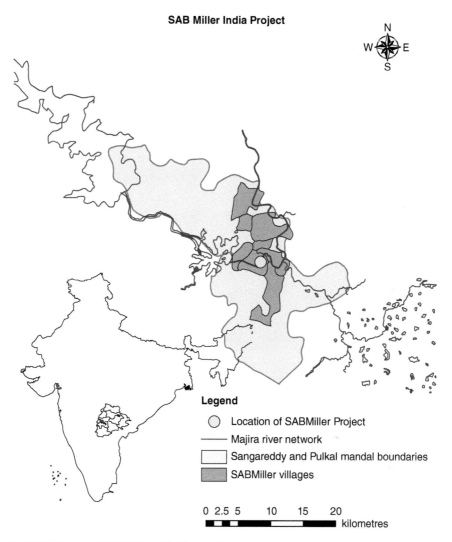

SAB Miller India Project

Legend

○ Location of SABMiller Project

—— Majira river network

▭ Sangareddy and Pulkal mandal boundaries

▮ SABMiller villages

0 2.5 5   10   15   20   kilometres

Fig. 5.1. Location map of SABMiller India Project villages.

through external sources and very low addition of organic matter.

- Inappropriate land and water management systems and insufficient water harvesting structures have led to a decrease in groundwater levels with time.
- There was hardly any evidence of efforts being made for water conservation, harvesting, storage and recharge of groundwater.
- The storage capacities of traditional water harvesting structures used by the community for domestic and cattle uses were reduced by siltation and poor maintenance.

- Besides water scarcity, fields were deficient in secondary and micronutrients like sulfur, zinc and boron in addition to organic carbon, nitrogen and phosphorus.

5.3 The Process

5.3.1 Strategy

- Use integrated genetic and natural resource management approach to bring about

Table 5.1. Demographic details of the project villages.

Village	Households (no.)	Population (no.)	Livestock (no.)	Milch animals (no.)	Year of project start
Fasalvadi	1,050	5,360	850	190	2009
Shivampet	841	4,220	1,050	210	2009
Venkatakistapur	275	1,160	410	70	2009
Chakriyal	360	2,200	1,010	255	2009
Korpole	816	4,159	680	68	2013
Sultanpur	384	2,980	320	32	2013
Vendikol	372	1,420	146	15	2013
Chowtakur	1,020	6,890	380	38	2014
Upparigudem	326	1,259	140	14	2014
Bommareddygudem	310	1,090	162	16	2014
Total	5,754	30,738	5,148	908	–

Table 5.2. Land use in the project villages.

Village	Rainfed area (ha)	Irrigated area (ha)	Wasteland (ha)	Nonagricultural land (ha)	Total watershed area (ha)
Fasalvadi	716	247	292	57	1312
Shivampet	853	170	14	8	1045
Venkatakistapur	237	59	2	0	298
Chakriyal	74	559	25	0	658
Korpole	1100	368	0	52	1520
Sultanpur	844	95	0	21	960
Vendikol	272.6	72	0	15	360
Chowtakur	793	164	0	35	992
Upparigudem	174	76	4	18	272
Bommareddygudem	143	78	8	15	244
Total	5207	1888	345	221	7661

sustainable management of water and enhance livelihoods within the watershed.

- Consortium approach to implement holistic and integrated development of watershed.
- Knowledge-based entry point for building rapport with the communities.
- Nothing is made available free for experimentation or evaluation except knowledge. Farmers need to pay for material support and the project would provide a small incentive. Farmers contribute 60% of the cost for the inputs to test improved technologies.
- Demand-driven interventions rather than supply-driven provision of technologies and products.
- Ensure involvement of small and marginal farmers as well as women for enhancing their incomes.

- Enhance rainwater conservation, improve water use efficiency and manage the water demand while improving the livelihoods.
- Farmers' participatory research for development and inclusive market-oriented development approach.
- Microenterprises as income-generating activities for enhancing incomes of the community members.

5.3.2   Partner consortia

- District Water Management Agency, Sangareddy, Government of Telangana
- Watershed committee and village organizations

- BAIF Development Research Foundation – BIRD (BAIF Institute for Rural Development)
- SABMiller India
- Rural Education & Agriculture Development (READ), a non-governmental organization (NGO)
- ICRISAT

5.3.3 Community mobilization and formation of watershed committee

Watershed committee of SABMiller India villages was formed to implement the watershed work along with READ, the selected NGO. Farmers are the primary stakeholders and beneficiaries. Hence, involvement of community was important for successful execution of project activity/interventions and to ensure long-term sustainability of the project. Women and Scheduled Caste/Scheduled Tribe candidates and members from the panchayat were also involved in the formation of watershed committee, as per common guidelines (GoI, 2011).

The committee was constituted in an open meeting and the objectives were briefed clearly. The committee members and villagers along with NGO staff were involved in each and every stage of project planning and execution of proposed interventions.

5.3.4 Entry-point activity: soil test

Soil testing as a knowledge-based entry point built strong trust between farmers, NGO and agency, and helped in effective planning and implementation of watershed activities. Farmers were trained to collect soil samples from their villages for analysing soil nutrient status using stratified random soil sampling method and samples were analysed in state-of-the-art laboratory at ICRISAT (Sahrawat *et al.*, 2008). Soil test results showed that large numbers of farmers' fields (50–80%) were deficient in organic carbon and also in secondary and micronutrients such as zinc, sulfur and boron (Table 5.3). The total number of soil samples collected from the first 4

Table 5.3. Nutrient analysis of soil samples collected from farmers' fields in project villages.

Village	Indicator	pH	EC (dS/m)	Organic C (%)	Olsen P (mg/kg)	Exch. K[a] (mg/kg)	Extractable nutrient elements (mg/kg)		
							S	B	Zn
Fasalvadi	Mean	7.4	0.6	0.43	18	187	39.1	0.36	0.8
	% fields deficient			75	35	0	50	80	55
Venkatakistapur	Mean	7.8	0.5	0.49	13.2	163	48.5	0.47	0.62
	% fields deficient			67	20	0	27	73	80
Shivampet	Mean	7.8	0.2	0.38	10.5	199	10.2	0.49	0.53
	% fields deficient			83	26	0	74	70	83
Chakriyal	Mean	7.9	0.6	0.52	21.2	130	62.1	0.89	0.69
	% fields deficient			47	5	5	26	26	63
Sultanpur	Mean	7.8	0.18	0.45	10.5	151	9.5	1.99	0.69
	% fields deficient			70	25	5	55	30	70
Korpole	Mean	7.9	0.36	0.44	14.9	216	27.5	1.13	1.31
	% fields deficient			70	35	5	48	30	35
Vendikol	Mean	7.9	0.14	0.33	7.8	263	15.1	1.06	0.8
	% fields deficient			100	40	0	90	35	80
Bommareddygudem	Mean	7.5	0.18	0.53	7.7	118	17	0.57	1.15
	% fields deficient			50	50	20	45	45	50
Upparigudem	Mean	7.9	0.16	0.42	7.7	79	11.5	0.55	0.7
	% fields deficient			65	45	25	70	60	85
Chowtakur	Mean	7.6	0.17	0.42	14.6	198	21.9	0.88	0.59
	% fields deficient			70	8	5	55	35	70

[a]Exch. K = exchangeable potassium

villages selected in 2009, 3 villages selected in 2013 and 3 villages selected in 2014 were 77, 80 and 89 respectively.

5.3.5 Awareness and capacity building

Several awareness programmes and regular interactions were conducted with the farming community on various project interventions and agricultural practices. The community was exposed to ICRISAT campus, Patancheru and Adarsha watershed, Kothapally to develop awareness of improved method of cultivation, best agricultural practices, soil and water conservation interventions, crop demonstration trials, etc. Nearly 3340 farmers participated in various training programmes, field exposure visits and field days during 2009–16 (Table 5.4).

5.4 Interventions

5.4.1 Productivity enhancement through application of soil test-based fertilizers

Based on soil test results, crop specific nutrient recommendations were provided to all the farmers in the villages. More importantly, use of micronutrients for different cereal (paddy, maize, etc.) and cash crops (sugarcane and cotton) were promoted. A number of farmers' participatory demonstration trials were undertaken in *kharif* (rainy) and *rabi* seasons since the project inception. Figure 5.2 shows the amount of micronutrients supplied under the farmers' demonstration trials during the seven-year period. Nearly 31,400 kg of gypsum, 9740 kg of zinc sulphate and 708 kg of agribor were made available in pilot villages during the project period. The total area covered so far in all the villages

with micronutrient usage is nearly 5430 acres (Table 5.5). The usage of micronutrients such as zinc sulphate and agribor in each of the villages was more or less same (1391 kg of zinc sulphate and 101 kg of agribor). The usage of micronutrients for paddy, sugarcane and cotton was more than other crops in the villages (Table 5.5).

5.4.2 Enhancing water resources availability

With the technical support of ICRISAT staff, potential locations for soil and water conservation structures were identified by the watershed committee, NGO and villagers. Several water harvesting structures such as check-dams, gully control structures, farm ponds, percolation tanks, mini-percolation tanks, sunken ponds, well recharge pits, water absorption trenches, etc. were constructed (Fig. 5.3). About 94,000 m³ water storage capacity was developed in the pilot villages during 2010–16 with different soil and water harvesting structures. The major water-harvesting structures created (84,800 m³) in these villages vary in storage capacities based on the size of the structure and purpose. The average storage capacities of these structures are 50 m³ for loose boulders; 150 m³ for sunken ponds; 100 m³ for rock-fill dams; 150 m³ for gabion structures; 350 m³ for mini-percolation tanks; 3500–5500 m³ for percolation tanks; 850 m³ for open well recharge structures; and 3000–12,000 m³ for check-dams. A total number of 347 structures have been created by the ICRISAT–SABMiller India Project in the pilot villages since 2010 (Table 5.6).

The total coverage area of all ten villages in this project is hydrologically divided into two small watersheds as shown in Fig. 5.4. The first watershed (Watershed 2009) covers around

Table 5.4. Awareness and capacity-building programmes conducted during the project period.

Particulars	2009	2010	2011	2012	2013	2014	2015	2016	Total
No. of training programmes	3	2	3	3	4	3	4	6	28
Exposure visits (ICRISAT and Kothapally)	–	2	–	–	2	3	2	1	10
Field days	–	1	–	–	1	–	–	–	2
No. of participants/trainees	200	350	450	460	430	660	390	396	3336

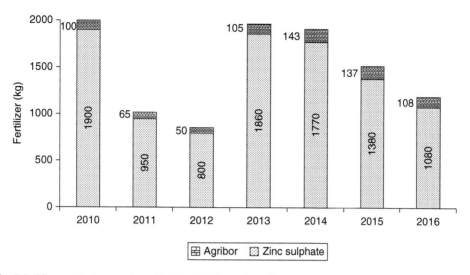

Agribor   Zinc sulphate

Fig. 5.2. Micronutrient usage from 2010 to 2016 in project villages.

Table 5.5. Crop area (acres) with application of micronutrients in SABMiller India pilot villages since project inception.

Village	Cotton	Maize	Pigeonpea	Sorghum	Paddy	Sugarcane	Others	Total
Fasalvadi	180	59	25	58	344	378	50	1094
Shivampet	138	26	18	19	303	297	28	829
Venkatakistapur	124	45	15	11	86	62	10	353
Chakriyal	20	6	8	2	223	296	25	580
Vendikol	98	13	27	11	172	127	16	464
Sultanpur	87	22	38	12	104	63	32	358
Korpole	154	28	32	8	195	150	15	582
Upparigudem	14	9	22	12	100	48	4	209
Bommareddygudem	6	4	14	0	55	14	0	93
Chowtakur	88	12	31	0	373	314	50	868
Total	909	224	230	133	1955	1749	230	5430

3420 ha with four villages (Fasalvadi, Shivampet, Venkatakistapur and Chakriyal) and the second watershed (Watershed 2013–14) covers 6560 ha with six villages (Vendikol, Sultanpur, Korpole, Upparigudem, Bommareddygudem and Chowtakur) in Pulkal mandal. The stream-flow of Watershed 2009 flows towards south and joins Manjira river at downstream of Manjira reservoir, whereas the stream-flow of Watershed 2013–14 flows towards north and joins Manjira river at downstream of Watershed 2009 as shown in Fig. 5.5. The total hydrological coverage area of the two watersheds is 9980 ha. The total capacity of major water-harvesting structures created in all ten villages is 84,800 m³, in which 47,700 m³ has been created in Watershed 2009

and 37,100 m³ has been created in Watershed 2013–14 as given in Tables 5.7 and 5.8.

5.4.3   Agroforestry and tree plantation

Agroforestry was promoted by planting trees on farm bunds, common lands and wasteland and was strengthened with community participation and also with the help of various government schemes in the project villages. Nearly 53,000 trees of different species were planted during the project period (Table 5.9). Moreover, 14,000 plants were cultivated under horticulture promotion in pilot villages.

Fig. 5.3. Water-harvesting structures constructed in project villages: (a) check-dam in Shivampet; (b) rock-fill dam in Fasalvadi; (c) percolation tank in Chowtakur; (d) sunken pond in Sultanpur.

Table 5.6. Water harvesting structures (no.) constructed in the pilot villages during 2010–16.

Village	2010	2011	2012	2013	2014	2015	2016	Total
Fasalvadi	18	26	6	9				59
Shivampet	34	56	4	14	2			110
Venkatakistapur		7			22			29
Vendikol				1	9	19		29
Korpole					29	4	4	37
Sultanpur					30	6		36
Upparigudem						2	10	12
Chowtakur						35		35
Total	52	89	10	24	92	66	14	347

5.5 Investments and Incremental Benefits

5.5.1 Productivity enhancement through soil test-based fertilizer application

Crop yields in the project villages increased with application of balanced and micronutrient fertilizers (Table 5.10). On average (2010–16), the response (increase in yield) to the application of balanced and micronutrient fertilizers of rainfed crops especially pulses such as chickpea and pigeonpea (27% to 28%) was more than irrigated crops such as sugarcane, paddy, maize and cotton (11% to 19%). The average cost of micronutrients applied in the improved practice was ₹2350 per ha. The farmer gained net income

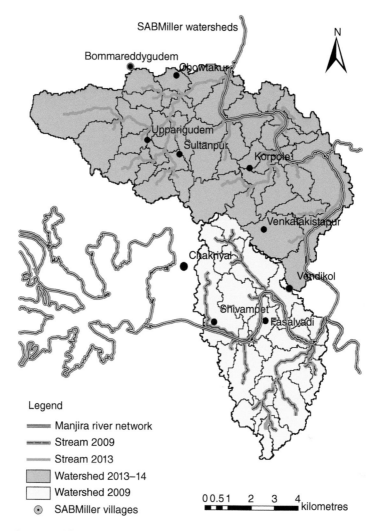

Fig. 5.4. Location map of SABMiller India Project watersheds started in 2009 and 2013–14.

of ₹13,500 and ₹11,800 per ha for chickpea and pigeonpea respectively in addition to the gain followed by farmers' practice (Table 5.11). Application of small quantity of micronutrients has significantly benefited in increasing crop yields and consequently farmers' income (Srinivasa Rao *et al.*, 2014).

5.5.2   Enhancing water resource availability

The daily rainfall data that occurred in Sangareddy mandal was collected and analysed. The average annual rainfall in both the watersheds was 895 mm. The rainfall from 2010 to 2016 was separated and normal, wet and dry years were indicated based on the annual rainfall. If annual rainfall is less than 671 mm (<0.75 times average annual rainfall) that year is considered as dry, if annual rainfall is more than 1118 mm (>1.25 times average annual rainfall) that year is considered as wet and if annual rainfall is 671–1118 mm that year is considered as normal. As per annual rainfall and observations made by field staff in the villages, the average number of water fillings in the water-harvesting structures was noted down for few years during the project implementation and the same was assumed for all the years. The effective recharge made in the villages was considered as 80% of

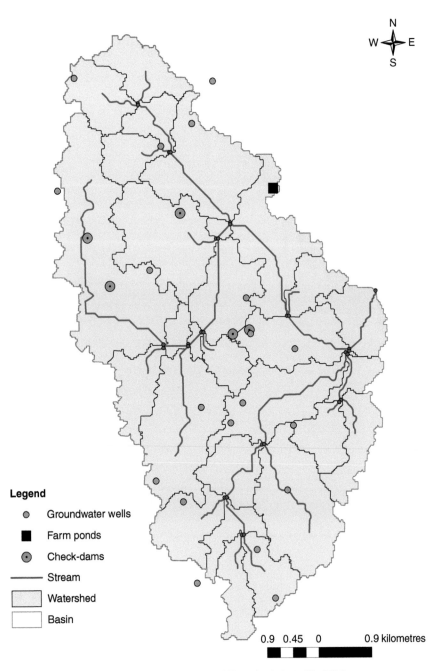

Legend

- ◉ Groundwater wells
- ■ Farm ponds
- ⊙ Check-dams
- —— Stream
- ▢ Watershed
- ▢ Basin

0.9 0.45   0   0.9 kilometres

Fig. 5.5. Hydrological map of SABMiller India Project Watershed started in 2009.

total recharge made and remaining 20% was as-sumed to be evapotranspiration losses from the structures.

In Watershed 2009 (Fig. 5.5), treatment of the agricultural lands with different interven-tions, especially with water-harvesting structures

was started in 2010 with a storage capacity of 3400 m³ and reached 47,700 m³ by 2014. The increase in water table due to annual recharge by all the structures in Watershed 2009 was 17 mm in 2010 and then rose to 173 mm (0.17 m) by 2014. The average watershed area that could

Table 5.7. Water-harvesting capacity created from 2010 to 2016 in Watershed 2009.

Particulars	Geographical area (ha)	Agricultural land (ha)	Storage capacity created (m³)						
			2010	2011	2012	2013	2014	2015	2016
Village									
Fasalvadi	1,312	963	1,450	13,400	5,750	8,200			
Shivampet	1,045	1,023	1,950	6,400	3,650	4,550	300		
Venkatakistapur	298	296		350			1,700		
Chakriyal	658	633							
Total area	3,313	2,915							
Annual storage capacity Created			3,400	20,150	9,400	12,750	2,000	0	0
Cumulative storage capacity created (m³)			3,400	23,550	32,950	45,700	47,700	47,700	47,700

Table 5.8. Water harvesting capacity created from 2013 to 2016 in Watershed 2013–14.

Particulars	Geographical area (ha)	Agricultural land (ha)	Storage capacity created (m³)			
			2013	2014	2015	2016
Village						
Vendikole	360	345	150	450	4,300	
Korpole	1,520	1,468		1,800	9,350	1,300
Sultanpur	960	939		6,550	1,900	
Upparigudem	272	250			100	3,550
Chowtakur	992	957			7,650	
Bommareddygudem	244	221				
Total area	4,348	4,180				
Annual storage			150	8,800	23,300	4,850

Table 5.9. Number of plants planted in the project villages during 2010–16.

Type of plants	2010	2011	2012	2013	2014	2015	2016	Total
Tree plantation	12,200	7,100	1,500	13,160	16,500	–	2,500	52,960
Fruit/horticulture trees	3,200	2,960	1,200	2,900	1,200	1,200	1,400	14,060

be sown in *rabi* due to recharged amount of water with chickpea crop was 5% in 2010, and then increased to 54% of watershed area by 2016 due to water-harvesting structures in Watershed 2009 (Table 5.12).

In Watershed 2013–14 (Fig. 5.6), treatment of the agricultural lands with different interventions, especially with water harvesting structures was started in 2013 with a storage capacity of 150 m³ and reached 37,100 m³ by 2016. The increase in water table due to annual recharge by all the structures in Watershed 2013–14 was 7 mm in 2010 and then rose to

102 mm (0.1 m) by 2016. The average watershed area that could be sown in *rabi* due to recharged amount of water with chickpea crop was 2% in 2013, and then increased to 32% of watershed area by 2016 due to water harvesting structures in Watershed 2013–14 (Table 5.13).

5.5.3 Agroforestry and tree plantation

Considering 50% survival rate and estimates based on biomass generation, nearly 132 tons

Table 5.10. Crop yields (t/ha) with farmers' practice (FP) and improved practice (IP) in project villages during 2010–16.

Crop treatment	2010–11	2011–12	2012–13	2013–14	2014–15	2015–16	2016–17	Maximum	Minimum	Mean	Increase in yield
Chickpea-FP	0.93		1.5				1.8	1.80	0.93	1.41	0.40
Chickpea-IP	1.23		1.9				2.3	2.30	1.23	1.81	
Cotton-FP	1.6	1.4	2.4	2.2	2.4	2.1	2.2	2.40	1.40	2.04	0.39
Cotton-IP	1.8	1.6	2.9	2.6	2.8	2.6	2.7	2.90	1.60	2.43	
Maize-FP						4.2	4	4.20	4.00	4.10	0.75
Maize-IP						4.9	4.8	4.90	4.80	4.85	
Paddy-FP	4.8	5.4	6.1	5.3	4.3	2.7	4.2	6.10	2.70	4.69	0.82
Paddy-IP	5.5	6.1	7.4	6	5.2	3.4	5	7.40	3.40	5.51	
Pigeonpea-FP						0.6	1.6	1.60	0.60	1.10	0.30
Pigeonpea-IP						0.8	2	2.00	0.80	1.40	
Sugarcane-FP	146	108	101	86	92	65.6	64.3	146.0	64.30	94.70	10.06
Sugarcane-IP	158	116	114	97	100	75.2	73.1	158.0	73.10	104.76	

Table 5.11. Farmers' income (in ₹000s per ha) with farmers' practice (FP) and improved practice (IP) in project villages during 2010–16.

Crop treatment	2010–11	2011–12	2012–13	2013–14	2014–15	2015–16	2016–17	Maximum	Minimum	Mean	Increase in net income[a]
Chickpea-FP	21.4		52.4				87.3	87.3	21.4	53.7	
Chickpea-IP	28.4		65.4				114.9	114.9	28.4	69.6	15.9 (30)
Cotton-FP	62.0	43.2	88.2	101.5	95.4	87.9	108.2	108.2	43.2	83.8	
Cotton-IP	72.0	49.6	106.7	121.7	111.7	107.1	133.8	133.8	49.6	100.4	16.6 (20)
Maize-FP						58.6	56.2	58.6	56.2	57.4	
Maize-IP						68.1	67.3	68.1	67.3	67.7	10.3 (18)
Paddy-FP	43.2	48.5	95.1	68.5	47.7	40.9	65.6	95.1	40.9	58.5	
Paddy-IP	49.3	55.1	115.4	78.4	56.9	50.5	77.1	115.4	49.3	69.0	10.5 (18)
Pigeonpea-FP						48.2	77.5	77.5	48.2	62.9	
Pigeonpea-IP						60.3	93.7	93.7	60.3	77.0	14.2 (23)
Sugarcane-FP	306.6	226.8	261.9	222.4	239.5	170.5	190.2	306.6	170.5	231.1	
Sugarcane-IP	332.2	243.6	295.9	252.2	260.6	195.5	216.3	332.2	195.5	256.6	25.5 (11)

[a]Figures in parentheses are percentage values.

Table 5.12. Benefits of water harvesting structures in Watershed 2009.

Particulars	2010	2011	2012	2013	2014	2015	2016
Geographical area (ha)	2,357	3,313	3,313	3,313	3,313	3,313	3,313
Agricultural land (ha)	1,986	2,915	2,915	2,915	2,915	2,915	2,915
Storage capacity created (m³)	3,400	20,150	9,400	12,750	2,000	0	0
Cumulative storage capacity created (m³)	3,400	23,550	32,950	45,700	47,700	47,700	47,700
Rainfall (mm)	1,093	605	768	1,251	904	605	1,037.7
Rainy year	Normal	Dry	Normal	Wet	Normal	Dry	Normal
No. of water fillings at structures	3	2	2	4	3	2	3
Total quantity of recharge (m³)	10,200	47,100	65,900	182,800	143,100	95,400	143,100
Total quantity of recharge (mm)	0.43	1.42	1.99	5.52	4.32	2.88	4.32
Effective recharge (mm) (reducing Et[a] 20%)	0.35	1.14	1.59	4.41	3.46	2.30	3.46
Increase in water table (specific yield 0.02) (mm)	17.31	56.87	79.57	220.71	172.77	115.18	172.77
Increase in water table (m)	0.02	0.06	0.08	0.22	0.17	0.12	0.17
Effective groundwater available for *rabi* (70%) (mm)	12.12	39.81	55.70	154.49	120.94	80.63	120.94
Post-monsoonal soil moisture (mm)	25	25	25	25	25	25	25
Chickpea water requirement (mm)	250	250	250	250	250	250	250
Extra water requirement for chickpea in *rabi* (mm)	225	225	225	225	225	225	225
Extra area could be sown with chickpea (%)	5.39	17.69	24.75	68.66	53.75	35.83	53.75

[a]Et = evapotranspiration

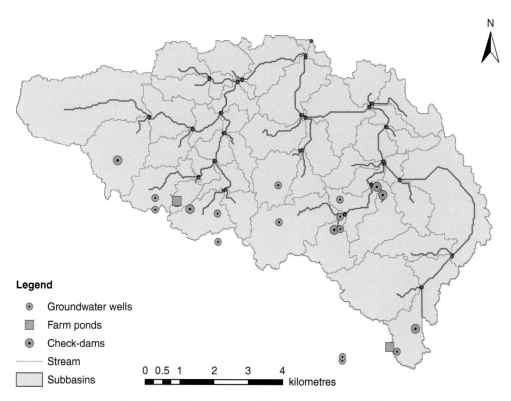

Legend

⊙ Groundwater wells

◼ Farm ponds

⊙ Check-dams

—— Stream

▢ Subbasins

0 0.5 1   2   3   4   kilometres

Fig. 5.6. Hydrological map of SABMiller India Project Watershed started in 2013–14.

Table 5.13. Benefits of water harvesting structures in Watershed 2013–14.

Particulars	2013	2014	2015	2016
Geographical area (ha)	360	2,840	4,348	4,348
Agricultural land (ha)	345	2,752	4,180	4,180
Storage capacity created (m³)	150	8,800	23,300	4,850
Cumulative storage capacity created (m³)	150	8,950	32,250	37,100
Rainfall (mm)	1,251	904	605	1,038
Rainy year	Wet	Normal	Dry	Normal
No. of water fillings at structures	4	3	2	3
Total quantity of recharge (m³)	600	26,850	64,500	111,300
Total quantity of recharge (mm)	0.17	0.95	1.48	2.56
Effective recharge (mm) (reducing Et[a] 20%)	0.13	0.76	1.19	2.05
Increase in water table (specific yield 0.02) (mm)	6.67	37.82	59.34	102.39
Increase in water table (m)	0.01	0.04	0.06	0.10
Effective groundwater available for *rabi* (70%) (mm)	4.67	26.47	41.54	71.67
Post-monsoonal soil moisture (mm)	25	25	25	25
Chickpea water requirement (mm)	250	250	250	250
Extra water requirement for chickpea in *rabi* (mm)	225	225	225	225
Extra area could be sown with chickpea (%)	2.07	11.77	18.46	31.86

[a]Et = evapotranspiration

of carbon was sequestered during the project period (Table 5.14). As most of the plants are about 6 years old, biomass accumulation will accelerate in subsequent years with increasing tree age. Due to various agricultural water management interventions, soil loss has been reduced from 10 t/ha to 3 t/ha, thus significantly contributing to reduction in land degradation and increase in crop productivity.

5.5.4 Livestock-based activities

As livestock is the integral part of the rural community, special emphasis was laid on livestock-based activities and increase in milk yield. Breed improvement of cattle was undertaken on a large scale in pilot villages (Fig. 5.7). Nearly 2421 animals were inseminated artificially and of those 1151 confirmed pregnancy. This has increased milk yield by 2–3 l/day/animal more than the local breed. Also, spent malt (a byproduct of the brewing industry, rich in carbohydrate, protein and other minerals) was promoted for use as animal feed. Four women's self-help groups (SHGs) were engaged in procuring, transporting

Table 5.14. Impact of agricultural water management interventions on various ecosystem services.

Parameter	Amount
Rainfall (mm)	895
Reduced soil erosion (t/ha)	From 10 to 3
No. of trees planted	52,960
No. of trees established (50% survival rate)	26,480
Average biomass accumulated (considering 10 kg wood/tree) (tons)	265
Carbon sequestered (tons)	132

Fig. 5.7. Cattle improvement in Fasalvadi village: (a) first generation crossbreed; (b) spent malt used as feed for animals; (c) sale of spent malt to farmers; (d) milk collection in the village.

and distributing the spent malt as a business model in the villages and households and women's SHGs are benefiting from this intervention (Table 5.15).

5.5.5 Income-generating activities by women

Various income-generating activities such as vermicomposting (11 units), nursery raising and other microenterprises helped farmers to earn additional income. Kitchen gardens have been promoted to address nutritional issues, especially for women and children.

Nursery raising

The project provided opportunities to women's SHGs to strengthen their livelihoods. Women's SHG Manjeera in Venkatakistapur village has undertaken nursery raising and grown about 12,000 saplings of teak, *Pongamia*, rain trees, *Gliricidia*, tamarind and *Pithecellobium dulce* to plant them in the project villages. Besides attending to their regular jobs, the SHG members supplied 10,056 saplings at ₹6 per sapling and earned ₹60,336 as additional income.

Table 5.15. Increase in milk yield and income in Fasalvadi village with spent malt as animal feed during 2011 to 2016.[a]

Particulars	Quantity/ Amount
No. of beneficiary households using spent malt	58
No. of cattle (feeding)	395
Average use of spent malt in the village (kg/day)	1,440
Milk production in the village (l/day)	1,570
Increase in milk production by feeding spent malt (l/animal/day)	1
Increase in gross income due to spent malt (₹/day)	17,800
Increase in net income due to spent malt (₹/day)	12,800
Increase in average net income due to spent malt (₹/family/month)	6,640
Increase in average net income due to artificial insemination (₹/family/ month)	3,375
Total increase in income due to spent malt and artificial insemination (₹/family/month)	10,015
Spent malt sold by the SHG (tons)	2,610
Net profit to SHG (₹)	140,069

[a]Intervention by women's self-help group (SHG) Priyadarshini.

Fig. 5.8. Awareness programme for school children on balanced nutrition in Korpole government school.

Nutri-kitchen gardens

In India, the problem of malnutrition in women and children is a serious issue, as 42% of children and about 34% of women in the country are malnourished. At the same time, many women and children are becoming disconnected from nature and there is an urgent need to increase awareness about balanced nutrition as well as environmental protection. To address the issue of malnutrition in children and women, there is a need to promote sustainable kitchen gardens for effective utilization of available natural resources like water and land by using organic farming methods, as well as to improve diet by the inclusion of fresh and safe nutritious vegetables produced in kitchen gardens. By taking up this activity, school children will gain hands-on experience in some areas of the school curriculum (e.g. science, agriculture, environmental science and home economics) (Fig. 5.8).

Interested women's SHG members and school children were identified to undertake this activity and registered for seed kits to initiate this activity in their backyards. Each member was provided with seed kits of nine vegetables (tomato, brinjal, okra, cluster bean, bottle gourd, bitter gourd, ridge gourd, spinach and amaranth) of their choice to grow in their kitchen gardens (Fig. 5.9). About 168 kitchen gardens were promoted during the rainy season of 2015, and 6300 kg vegetables were produced. During the rainy season of 2016, 178 kitchen gardens were promoted and 7480 kg vegetables were produced and used for consumption in the project villages (Table 5.16). This activity has helped in reducing the expenditure on vegetables.

Fig. 5.9. Kitchen garden grown by women in (a) Chowtakur and (b) Sultanpur villages.

Table 5.16. Progress of kitchen gardens in the project villages.

Village	2015		2016	
	No. of units promoted	Vegetable production (kg)	No. of units promoted	Vegetable production (kg)
Fasalvadi	10	490	20	830
Shivampet	80	2400	15	590
Chakriyal	–	–	15	620
Venkatakistapur	10	410	15	670
Korpole	13	590	20	730
Sultanpur	10	430	18	710
Chowtakur	18	720	25	1140
Vendikol	–	–	20	890
Bommareddygudem	13	590	15	640
Upparigudem	14	670	15	660
Total	168	6300	178	7480

Acknowledgements

The authors would like to thank SABMiller India, now AB InBev, for the finance and spent malt supply to the farmers; thanks to Government of Telangana officers for their constant support to the farmers and the project; and thanks to all the farmers in the SABMiller Project villages for the participation and contribution in the success of the project.

References

Government of India (2011) *Common Guidelines for Watershed Development Projects – 2008 (Revised Edition – 2011)* New Delhi: National Rainfed Area Authority, Planning Commission. Available at: http://dolr.nic.in/dolr/downloads/pdfs/Common%20Guidelines%20for%20WDP%202008%20Re-vised%20Edition%202011.pdf (accessed 12 April 2018).

Sahrawat, K.L., Rego, T.J., Wani, S.P. and Pardhasaradhi, G. (2008) Stretching soil sampling to watershed: evaluation of soil-test parameters in a semi-arid tropical watershed. *Communications in Soil Science and Plant Analysis* 39(19–20), 2950–2960.

Srinivasa Rao, C., Wani, S.P., Chander, G. and Sahrawat, K.L. (2014) Balanced nutrient management for crop intensification and livelihood improvement: a case study from watershed in Andhra Pradesh, India. *Communications in Soil Science and Plant Analysis* 45(19), 2515–2528. DOI: 10.1080/00103624.2014.912298.

Thirtle, C., Beyers, L., McKenzie-Hill, V., Irz, X., Wiggins, S. and Piesse, J. (2002) *The Impacts of Changes in Agricultural Productivity on the Incidence of Poverty in Developing Countries.* DFID Report No. 7946. Department for International Development, London.

World Bank (2005) *Agricultural Growth for the Poor: An Agenda for Development.* International Bank for Reconstruction and Development/The World Bank, Washington, DC.

6 Improved Livelihoods – A Case Study from Asian Paints Limited

MUKUND D. PATIL,* SUHAS P. WANI, KAUSHAL K. GARG AND RAJESH NUNE

International Crops Research Institute for the Semi-Arid Tropics, Patancheru, India

Abstract

Asian Paints Limited and International Crops Research Institute for the Semi-Arid Tropics (ICRISAT) collaborated to improve rural livelihoods through integrated watershed development programme. Six villages in Patancheru mandal of Medak district, Telangana, India covering an area of 7143 ha were selected in consultation with the local community for Asian Paints Limited–ICRISAT watershed. The prime mitigation strategy for addressing water scarcity was initiated in the project by rainwater harvesting, efficient use of available water resources and recycling of grey water. Science-led interventions including soil test-based nutrient management, and improved crop cultivars and management practices were introduced for improving crop productivity. Rainwater harvesting structures of a total water storage capacity of 34,000 m³ were utilized for groundwater recharge. Based on the observation, estimated groundwater recharge due to check-dams with total storage capacity of 12,700 m³ during 2016 was 91,000 m³. The improved agronomic practices demonstrated in farmers' fields have shown 30–50% increase in grain yield.

6.1 Background

6.1.1 Why? Problem statement

Water, food and energy securities are emerging as increasingly important issues for the world. Especially, rainfed agriculture in arid and semi-arid regions is experiencing moderate to severe water shortage and land degradation, due to the simultaneous effects of increasing food demand, industrialization and urbanization. The complexity of the problem is further increased by factors such as population rise, rapid and unplanned urbanization, change in cropping pattern towards water intensive cash crops, change of food preference towards water-intensive food products such as dairy and meat, and climate change.

For India, agriculture is the single largest sector, which provides employment to over 65% population, but at low net returns per hectare of cultivated land. The declining or low agricultural productivity is also affecting environmental sustainability as there is mismanagement of soil and water resources along with the negligence of local strategies. These trends however, showed increase in total agricultural production but decline in water productivity and other ecosystem services due to inefficient water use.

---

* Corresponding author: m.patil@cgiar.org

If such trends continue, the system may lose its resilience ability and will be vulnerable to further degradation. Thus, it is necessary to strengthen the ecosystem services through natural resource management with people's participation in dryland areas.

6.1.2 Integrated water resource management approach

Watershed is a natural entity and comprises different types of land use from where rainwater is drained through a common outlet (lake, river) and therefore, can vary from several ha to 1 million ha. However, it is also a sociopolitical-ecological entity, which plays a crucial role in determining food, social and economic security and provides life support services to rural people (Wani *et al.*, 2008). These watersheds provide various ecosystem services in uplands and the generated inflow supports downstream ecosystem. The holistic management of natural resources have shown greater resilience of crop income during the drought-like scenarios too. For example, while the share of crops in household income declined from 44% to 12% in the non-watershed project villages, crop income remained largely unchanged from 36% to 37% in the watershed village (Wani *et al.*, 2009).

Integrated watershed management approach proved to be the suitable strategy for achieving holistic development in these regions through collective action (Wani *et al.*, 2003). The very purpose of the watershed development programmes is to reduce water related risks in rainfed agriculture by improving the local soil–water balance by implementing both *in-situ* and *ex-situ* interventions. Since water and soil are important components of agricultural development, proper management of these resources is crucial to build the resilience of these systems to cope with varying climatic risks and to improve livelihoods. The International Crops Research Institute for the Semi-Arid Tropics (ICRISAT), Patancheru, Telangana, India has established model watersheds as learning sites for integrated watershed management programme in various agroclimatic regions of India. On similar grounds, Asian Paints Limited, Patancheru requested ICRISAT to develop an action site at their Patancheru works in Sanga Reddy district.

6.1.3 Objectives

The overall goal of this initiative is to increase agricultural productivity and improve the livelihoods of rural poor in fragile dryland areas on a sustainable basis by enhancing the impact of integrated watershed management programmes through capacity building initiatives using site of learning in low-rainfall agroecoregions. The specific goal of this initiative is to enhance the water resources availability (surface and groundwater), water productivity, income and livelihood in the selected villages of Patancheru mandal, Sangareddy district in Telangana. The objectives of the initiative are:

- To establish a 'Model Site of Learning' in Sangareddy district for demonstrating the potential of rainfed areas by adopting integrated water resource management approach.
- To enhance the water resource availability and its use efficiency through low-cost water-harvesting structures and to enhance capacity of existing water harvesting structures.
- To enhance agricultural productivity through land, water and nutrient management interventions.
- To build capacity of the farmers in the region for improving rural livelihoods through knowledge sharing and dissemination.

6.1.4 Site selection

Asian Paints Limited requested ICRISAT to select a project site in the vicinity of their factory in Patancheru mandal. The Patancheru mandal lies between 78.14° to 78.351° and 17.467° to 17.624° in Sangareddy district of Telangana state. Figure 6.1 shows Patancheru mandal and identified village locations (southwest) for the proposed watershed interventions. Field visits were conducted in four (north, east, west and southwest) directions to select villages for watershed (Fig. 6.1). ICRISAT team interacted with farmers during field visits to understand the farming system. Land resources in eastern villages were degraded due to high industrialization and real estate business. Agricultural land area in western villages decreased drastically due to groundwater pollution. In northern villages, only the area under tank irrigation is dominating as each village has two big water tanks. The rainfed area in southwestern villages is becoming fallow due to

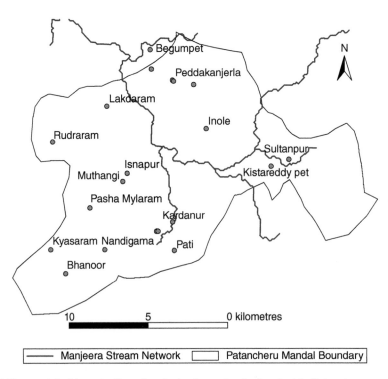

Fig. 6.1. Villages visited for selection of a site for the watershed project in Patancheru mandal, Sanga Reddy district, Telangana.

scarcity of surface and groundwater resources. The southwest region of Patancheru mandal (Bhanoor, Kyasaram, Nandigama, Kardanur, Pati and Ghanapur villages) had potential for implementing watershed interventions to enhance water resources availability, agricultural productivity and income.

6.1.5 Site specification

The project villages are located in and around Asian Paints Limited, Patancheru. Six villages were selected for implementation of watershed activities. The selected villages, covering a 7143 ha geographic area, are located 9 km west of ICRISAT campus. The rainfed area in these villages is 84% of total cultivable area while irrigated area is 9% and fallow land is 6% (Table 6.1). The main sources of irrigation are bore well and open well. Out of 4659 households, 56% households are small and marginal farmers, 8% are landless, and 34% are medium and large farmers (Table 6.2). Major crops in selected villages are

maize, paddy, pigeonpea, cotton, sorghum and vegetables. Livestock is also a major component for livelihoods in these villages. Buffalo, sheep and goats constitute the major population of livestock (Table 6.3).

6.2   Baseline Situation

A primary household baseline survey was conducted from representative sample farmers (534 households) in the watershed villages. Information on socioeconomic status, area allocation under different crops, average productivity levels and prices, water utilization pattern at household and farm level, accessibility to credit, etc. was collected and summarized. The household data collected will be used as 'benchmark values' for monitoring the project progress over a period of time. The project impact assessment studies if any could be undertaken in future using baseline information. Overall, the comprehensive baseline report also helps in identifying major constraints and devising suitable strategies in

Table 6.1. Land use pattern in selected watershed villages in Patancheru mandal, Telangana, India. From: Mandal Panchayat of Patancheru mandal, 2015.

Village	Irrigated (ha)	Rainfed (ha)	Fallow land (ha)	Common property resource (ha)	Industrial use (ha)	Total (ha)
Pati	82	442	38	32	202	796
Bhanoor	93	842	44	130	414	1523
Kyasaram	86	640	32	64	142	964
Kardhanur	54	422	42	24	140	682
Ghanapur	96	740	52	96	268	1252
Nandigama	90	1264	102	110	360	1926
Total	501	4350	310	456	1526	7143

Table 6.2. Landholdings in selected watershed villages in Patancheru mandal, Telangana, India. From: Gram Panchayats of respective villages, 2015.

Village	No. of households					
	Large	Medium	Small	Marginal	Landless	Total
Pati	8	72	280	302	62	724
Bhanoor	22	602	220	355	149	1348
Kyasaram	14	222	204	248	64	752
Kardanur	4	42	122	120	28	316
Ghanapur	12	124	212	248	46	642
Nandigama	18	412	252	148	47	877
Total	78	1474	1290	1421	396	4659

Table 6.3. Livestock population (numbers) in selected villages of watershed in Patancheru mandal, Telangana, India. From: Mandal Panchayat of Patancheru mandal, 2015.

Village	Cow	Buffalo	Bullock	Others (goat, sheep, etc.)	Total
Pati	2	129	12	312	455
Bhanoor	18	180	24	280	502
Kyasaram	8	160	12	160	340
Kardanur	4	45	10	80	139
Ghanapur	8	142	12	265	427
Nandigama	12	168	24	242	446
Total	52	824	94	1339	2309

the pilot site and district as a whole. The key findings from baseline survey are discussed.

6.2.1 Crop production

Cropping pattern

Maize is the major crop under cultivation across all sample villages followed by paddy and cotton. *Rabi* (post-rainy season) area constitutes nearly 4% of the rainy season area and chickpea is the predominant crop cultivated during the season. The cultivable area under summer is very low and leafy vegetables are grown during the season. This shows the dependency of farmers on rainfall for their livelihood and if irrigation is assured the remaining 96% of the land can be brought under cultivation.

Crop yield

The crop productivity data was collected from farmers on one year recall basis. The average productivity of crops is almost same across the villages with marginal variations. With average yield less than 1000 kg/ha, cotton is the most affected crop due to pest infestation across the villages.

Fertilizer usage

High utilization of urea was observed for cotton and maize. In addition to urea and diammonium phosphate, complex fertilizers were administered to cotton for higher returns. This exposes the risk of soil degradation and economic returns in cotton cultivation. Very few farmers reported use of micronutrients across the crops, which necessitates the need for educating the farmers on importance of micronutrient application for better growth and yield of crops.

Incidence of insects and diseases

Nearly 25% of the crops are getting infested with pests incurring an economic loss to farmers. Large-scale cultivation of high-yielding varieties and excessive use of nitrogenous fertilizers may further aggravate the incidence of pests. Farmers need to be educated on integrated pest management along with optimum utilization of fertilizers.

Economics of different crop enterprises

Among all crops, pigeonpea realized highest market price due to shortage of supply in the market. Majority of farmers complained of falling prices as cotton, paddy, maize and sorghum realized lesser price than the minimum support price announced by Government of India. Maize exhibited better benefit–cost ratio followed by pigeonpea, paddy and chickpea crops. Farmers were able to cover the variable costs of sorghum and recovered costs marginally. Cotton performed very badly among all crops in the study villages. Farmers were just able to recover their investments because of low productivity and higher costs of cultivation per acre.

6.2.2 Household income

The average household income of the pooled sample household was ₹162,000 per annum.

Around 40% of the total household income was contributed by agriculture, followed by salaried work (27%) and daily wage income (19%). Government development programmes, rentals from land and machinery, business and others together accounted for 14% share in the total household income. The average income per household was the highest in Nandigama followed by Kyasaram, Bhanoor, Pati, Ghanapur and Kardanur. The share of agriculture and allied sources income in the total household income was much higher in Kardanur (47%) followed by Bhanoor (43%), Kyasaram (41.1%), Nandigama and Pati (37%) and Ghanapur (36%). Large area under profitable crops like maize, pigeonpea and vegetables have contributed to higher income in Bhanoor and Kyasaram as compared to other pilot site villages.

6.2.3 Sources of water and utilization pattern

The villages are getting water both from open and bore wells. Open wells have an average depth of 25 m with water table of 20 m whereas bore wells are tapping water from nearly 85 m depth with water table of 50 m. Watershed belongs to hard rock aquifer and therefore has poor specific yield. Perched water table generally forms during the monsoon period in top 10–30 m depth and helps to recharge open wells. But most of the open wells do not retain water during post-monsoon period because of the depletion of groundwater level. Bore wells tap water from underlying layers of hard rock aquifer. Average area irrigated from each of the open or bore wells is about 1–1.5 ha providing 4–5 irrigations in a season. The average initial investment for bore wells is ₹19,000 with total investment of ₹77,000 to date. The declining water table may not only raise the marginal operational cost but also give rise to a situation of diminished water availability, resulting in loss of farm output and decline in net returns.

6.2.4 Perceptions about production problems and future interventions

A large percentage of sample farmers in the villages felt that water scarcity particularly during crop production period is the major problem followed by lack of scientific information. Farmers opined that they can improve their net returns if credit is available at lower interest rates. With significant movement of rural labour from farm to nonfarm activities, labour scarcity has emerged as one of the burning constraints to agricultural production. This is again impacting their net returns as the farmers have to pay high wage returns during peak crop season.

Harvesting surplus runoff in dugout ponds and recycling the same for providing supplemental irrigation to rainy season crops or pre-sowing irrigation to *rabi* crops have proved to be the most successful technologies for adoption. Majority of farmers expressed need for farm ponds but are not willing to share their land for the same as nearly 60% of the farmers are small and medium farmers. Area grown under pigeonpea and vegetables almost occupies 26% of the cropped area under major crops. Farmers opined the need for availability of high-yielding varieties. Majority of farmers opined that nursery raising can be a sustainable livelihood option for youth. Farmers' perception about any developmental activity has to be prioritized and policy makers should design policies in order to reduce vulnerability of farmers to financial risk.

6.3 Process

6.3.1 Partnerships

The consortium approach is adopted to enhance the impact of integrated watershed management. The important partners in ICRISAT-led consortium were district administration, Watershed Department of Government of Telangana, Rural Education & Agriculture Development (READ), a non-governmental organization (NGO) and community-based organizations. This project has adopted four principles: convergence; capacity building; collective action; and consortium for technical backstopping. Participatory research and development (PR&D) was the key strategy to build the capacity of different stakeholders, namely community, NGO staff and line department staff. The PR&D approach was also adopted for the integrated nutrient management (INM) and integrated pest management (IPM) trials

considering the local resources to be used as sources of plant nutrients and for biopesticide production. All the PR&D trials involved large number of farmers including small and marginal farmers. All the trials were conducted based on contributions in cash or kind by the participating farmers and efforts were made to involve as many farmers as possible during the project phase. In order to bring in transparency in the watershed development operations, participatory monitoring and evaluation approach was adopted along with the consortium partners. The community members were also involved in participatory groundwater monitoring as well as recording the yields from the PR&D trials of INM, IPM and cultivar selection. Participatory monitoring and evaluation will be a continuous process to do mid-course corrections in the interventions as well as for the approach.

6.3.2 Community mobilization

Watershed committee

Gram sabhas (village meeting with farmers) were conducted to inform the community about watershed initiatives to improve livelihoods. ICRISAT team and resource person from NGO along with panchayat member participated in *Gram sabhas* to facilitate the formation of user groups (UGs). The approach of voluntary membership in the UGs was adopted to ensure sustainability. The UGs and existing self-help groups (SHGs) have representation on the decision-making body of the watershed, i.e. Watershed Committee. Each watershed village has one village-level committee (4–5 members) and from each village-level committee 2–3 members were appointed on executive committee for entire watershed.

The committee was constituted in an open meeting and the objectives were briefed clearly. The committee members and villagers were involved at each and every stage of project planning and execution of proposed interventions. For example, selection and construction of water harvesting sites and types of structure, procurement of the materials, record keeping, and verification of bills and payment delivery, etc. were handled by the Watershed Committee under the guidance of the consortium team. Transparency at every step established good rapport and resulted in large and active participation of the village community in watershed management and development.

Inclusion of women

For the success of watershed development programme and livelihood improvement, inclusion of women from the villages has prime importance. Importance of water conservation, once understood by women, may bring water literacy in the entire family. Judicious use of water for domestic needs is equally important as that in agriculture. In this project, the strength of women SHGs was harnessed through facilitation of the groups for different income-generating activities. Women were also actively involved in key watershed development activities, including construction of rainwater harvesting structures.

6.3.3 Entry point activities

Community participation for success of any research for development programme is very critical which to a large extent is affected by the initial actions/interventions in the programme. Thereby, introducing any programme to the community has always been a challenging and an important activity which is done through what are called 'entry point activities' (EPA). Studies indicate that knowledge-based rather than investment-focused EPAs to solve farmers' issues are more effective for rapport building and initiating collective action with the farmers for progressive development (Dixit *et al.*, 2007). The main purpose of KBEPA is to build the sustainability and give a clear signal to the community that they should not be expecting dole-outs from the project for development of private farms. The important constraint which can provide tangible economic benefit to the community will be identified and implemented to build the trust and rapport with the community.

Soil health degradation is an important issue and studies show that most of the farmers are affected by it. As good soil health is a prerequisite to strengthen agri-based enterprises and this intervention fits well in the criteria of a good EPA. In this activity, farmers participated in collection of surface soil sample. Collected soil samples were analysed at ICRISAT Laboratory. Soil fertility status was shared with farmers through village level meeting during awareness-building programmes and by writing the information on walls of common buildings. Further, soil fertility information was used to provide village-wise and crop-wise fertilizer recommendation. Moreover, with these recommendation demonstrations were conducted in farmers' field. In addition to soil fertility management, rainwater harvesting was also considered as EPA as water scarcity and depleted groundwater level were the key issues identified by the community.

6.3.4 Dissemination

Farmers in the villages are aware about the problems in agriculture, but they do not have complete information about crop production constraints and measures to alleviate these problems. For example, farmers understand that the yield of groundwater wells (bore/tube wells) was decreasing; however, they try to resolve this problem by digging another well or extending the depth of existing bore well. Another classic example is about fertilizer usage; farmers know the importance of fertilizer for crop growth but they do not understand that fertilizers are nutrient supplements in addition to available nutrients in the soil. Thus, fertilizer application should be done based on soil fertility status. In this watershed project, both traditional and innovative extension ways for information dissemination have been explored to improve the awareness and adoption rate among the farmers.

Community programmes

Publicity of watershed implementation programme among the targeted villages was the first priority in the project for getting full cooperation from the community. Thus, the project was formally launched on 21 October 2014 at Bhanoor village, Telangana in the presence of Joint Collector, Medak district, Commissioner, Rural Development, Telangana, President of Home Improvement, Supply Chain and IT, Asian Paints Limited, *sarpanch* of all watershed villages, Director, ICRISAT Development Center, other officials and community members, and senior officials of Asian

Paints Limited (Fig. 6.2). During the launch programme, the work of check-dam construction was also inaugurated in the presence of dignitaries. Such small-scale functions were organized while initiating or inaugurating watershed activities; for example, seed distribution, soil health card distribution, the laying of foundation stones of rainwater harvesting structures, etc. These programmes have provided a good platform for awareness building and strengthening partnerships.

Soil health cards

In the context of soil health management, the key information dissemination tool was soil health cards. Soil health cards are customized information cards of soil fertility status and crop-wise fertilizer recommendation. This is one of the entry point activities, which built good relationship with the community. The soil health card (Fig. 6.3) has information about the farmer, location information of the farm,

Fig. 6.2. Launch programme of Asian Paints Limited–ICRISAT watershed project in Bhanoor village.

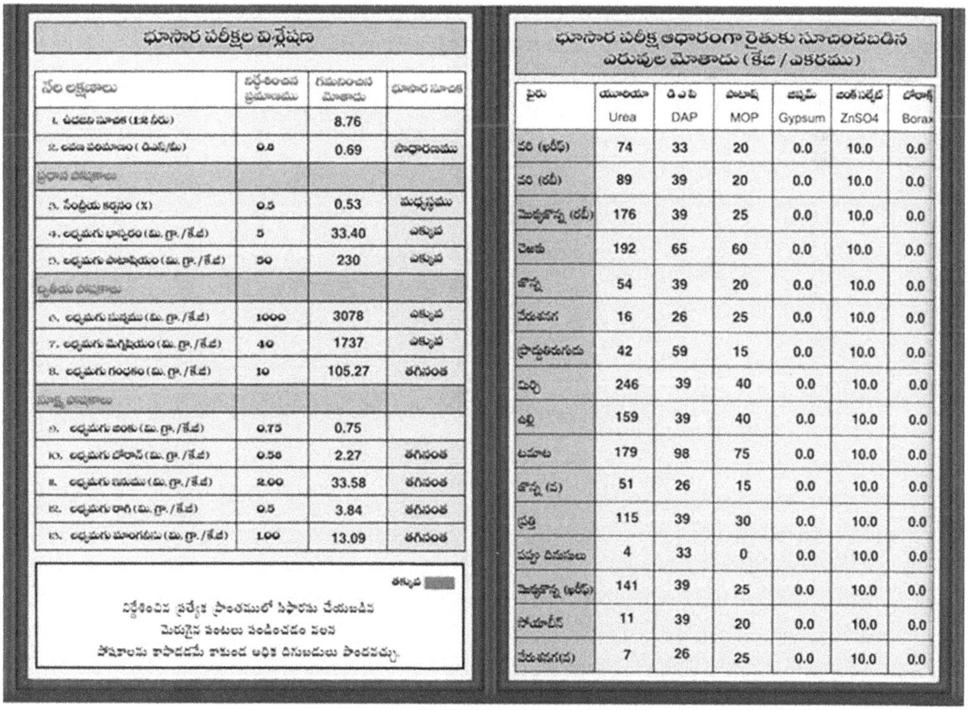

పంట	Urea	DAP	MOP	Gypsum	ZnSO4	Borax
పత్తి (ఖరీఫ్)	74	33	20	0.0	10.0	0.0
పత్తి (రబీ)	89	39	20	0.0	10.0	0.0
మొక్కజొన్న (రబీ)	176	39	25	0.0	10.0	0.0
వరి	192	65	60	0.0	10.0	0.0
జొన్న	54	39	20	0.0	10.0	0.0
వేరుశనగ	16	26	25	0.0	10.0	0.0
ప్రొద్దుతిరుగుడు	42	59	15	0.0	10.0	0.0
మిర్చి	246	39	40	0.0	10.0	0.0
ఉల్లి	159	39	40	0.0	10.0	0.0
టమాట	179	98	75	0.0	10.0	0.0
జొన్న (చ)	51	26	15	0.0	10.0	0.0
చెరకు	115	39	30	0.0	10.0	0.0
పప్పు దినుసులు	4	33	0	0.0	10.0	0.0
మొక్కజొన్న (ఖరీఫ్)	141	39	25	0.0	10.0	0.0
కూరగాయలు	11	39	20	0.0	10.0	0.0
వేరుశనగ(చ)	7	26	25	0.0	10.0	0.0

Fig. 6.3. Customized soil health card prepared for farmers in watershed villages.

status of major and micronutrients, and crop-wise fertilizer recommendation for the major crops based on fertility status. The soil health card programme is also widely adopted by the Government of India for doubling the farmers' income.

Wall writing

Information related to soil fertility status has been also disseminated among the farmers through writing the information in Telugu (the local language) on the public walls in villages. This tool provides a wider dissemination channel, as all people from the village get access to this information. Although this information is not customized as per the crops or landholding, this tool has been also used in the watershed project for disseminating weather information and project details. Information written on the wall will be available for all farmers in the villages.

6.3.5   Capacity development

Every year, exposure to the visit-cum-training programme was organized for farmers from watershed villages (Fig. 6.4). The topics covered during this programme were integrated watershed management concept with improved land and water management, INM, improved crop management and practices IMP. Farmers visited the established model watershed where science-based farmer participatory consortium model for efficient

management of natural resources for improving livelihoods of poor rural households was implemented by ICRISAT and its partners. Farmers have observed various interventions, including soil and water conservation measures, rainwater-harvesting structures, well recharging, improved crop varieties and cropping systems, crop diversification with high-value crops, productivity enhancement, livestock-based improvement and livelihood initiatives, and interacted with the local community. Farmers were impressed with the salient impacts that resulted due to the implementation of this model and appreciated the success due to collective action of the farmers in Kothapally village, Rangareddy district, Telangana and said that the visit provided an excellent learning opportunity.

6.4   Interventions

6.4.1   Rainwater harvesting

The excess rainwater taken out from the individual farms in a guided manner was stored at suitable sites. The potential sites for rainwater harvesting were identified by the village-level committee. The ridge to valley approach was followed for achieving equity and access to water. The site proposed for major water harvesting structures were technically evaluated by ICRISAT team of experts. Based on the technical evaluation, low-cost rainwater-harvesting structures such as farm ponds, loose boulder dams, check-dams, rock-filled dams, earthen check-dams, bore wells and open

Fig. 6.4. Field visits of farmers from watershed villages to Kothapally (a) and ICRISAT campus (b).

well recharging structures, etc. were established in the watershed (Table 6.4; Fig. 6.5). The low-cost structures are proven for sustainability, equity as well as cost-effectiveness. The impact of rainwater harvesting on water resources was evaluated by monitoring groundwater levels in existing bore well and monitoring the runoff at selected check-dams.

6.4.2   Safe reuse of domestic wastewater for agriculture

Safe use of wastewater could be a potential source of water. There are, however, numerous limitations for wastewater treatment and reuse in agriculture, such as a mismatch between demand and water supply, salinity, treatment capacity, over-application of nutrients, etc. We believe that the decentralized wastewater treatment (DWAT) system will address some of these problems and water scarcity issues at local scale. The rationale behind developing the DWAT system is water scarcity; the direct use of wastewater in agriculture is not good for farmers and consumers, disposal of untreated wastewater pollutes environment, and all localities do not have sewage treatment plants.

A wastewater treatment system has been established in Bhanoor village (Fig. 6.6). Domestic wastewater empties into a common drain that carries it to the end of the village. Few farmers were pumping this wastewater into their open wells and agricultural field, which is not advisable considering the harmful effect on farmers and consumers. Coupling wastewater treatment with the integrated watershed management

Table 6.4. Soil and water conservation structures in watershed villages in Patancheru mandal up to 2016.

Structure	Number of structures						Storage capacity (m³)
	Bhanoor	Pati	Kardanur	Kyasaram	Nandigama	Ghanapur	
Check-dam	3	1	1	3	2	1	12,700
Earthen check-dam	0	0	0	0	0	1	1,200
Desiltation of check-dam	2	0	0	0	0	2	–
Rock-filled dam	1	0	0	0	2	0	430
Loose boulder dam	14	0	7	12	40	0	5,100
Open well recharge pit	9	0	0	7	0	0	12,700
Bore well recharge pit	10	5	2	0	5	0	1,000
Farm pond	4	0	0	1	0	0	1,000
Wastewater treatment	1	0	0	0	0	0	–

Fig. 6.5. Check-dam filled with water during the rainy season in September 2016 in Bhanoor village.

programme is helpful in not only enhancing crop production and the income of smallholders but also improving the water quality of groundwater wells and downstream water bodies while partly addressing the issues of human health. Experts have visited the location and collected wastewater samples. The DWAT system is designed and constructed based on wastewater characteristics (see Box 6.1). Two types of vegetation, *Typha latifolia* and *Canna indica*, are transplanted in the constructed wetland. Now, wastewater flows through the wetland. After stabilization of the wetland, treated wastewater is available for irrigation. In addition, wastewater is safely disposed of without harming the environment.

6.4.3 Improving crop productivity

Soil test-based fertilizer application

A participatory demonstration of good agricultural practices was initiated with soil sampling as an entry point activity in watershed villages. Farmer participatory approach was followed for collecting soil samples from selected villages. Stratified soil sampling methodology was adopted for sampling (Sahrawat *et al.*, 2008). The area was divided based on topography and cropping system. Farmers were trained for collecting soil samples from their fields. A total of 189 soil samples were collected and analysed for the selected villages. Analysis of the soil for macro- and

Fig. 6.6. Construction of wastewater treatment plant in Bhanoor village: (a) in progress; (b) completed structure.

Box 6.1. Design parameters for decentralized wastewater treatment system.

Number of households connected to common drainage = 700
Domestic water consumption per household = 200 l per day
Wastewater generation per household (80% of consumption) = 160 l per day
Total wastewater generation = 160 x 700 = 112,000 l per day = 112 m³ per day
Initial design hydraulic retention time (HRT) = 5 days
Required volume of wetland considering 5 days HRT and 0.5 porosity = $\frac{112 \times 5}{0.5}$ = 1120 m³
Available space for wetland: The wetland may be constructed into existing drain. Width of drain is 3–4 m.
Bed of drain is 1–2 m below normal ground level.
Dimensions of constructed wetland: Width = 4 m; depth = 1 m; length = 280 m.
Construction:

- As the required length of wetland is more, three phases are proposed to construct wetland. Based on the performance of first phase wetland, the design may be modified for remaining phases.
- One sedimentation tank (3 x 3 x 3 m) needs to be constructed for trapping solid waste flowing into drain.
- Walls on both sides of wetland along the length should be retained.
- Bottom face should be sealed by compaction or clay or cement concrete.
- Filter media: 80 m³ each of 40 mm gravel, 20 mm gravel, 10 mm gravel and coarse sand.
- Wetland plant species: *Canna indica* and *Typha latifolia*.

micronutrients was completed at the ICRISAT laboratory. The soil analysis results indicated that soils of watershed villages are not deficient in phosphate and potash, but low organic carbon indicates low level of nitrogen (N) in soil. In addition to major nutrients, soils are deficient in micronutrients. Out of the 189 soil samples collected from watershed villages, 62%, 35% and 19% soil samples were deficient in zinc, sulfur and boron respectively (Table 6.5). The geospatial maps for different soil parameters were prepared for watershed villages (Fig. 6.7).

The results of the soil analysis were distributed among farmers during a group meeting and crop-wise fertilizer recommendations were provided for each village. Soil test-based balanced fertilizer trials were conducted in famers' fields in selected villages to demonstrate the advantage of micronutrient application in addition to the application of N, phosphorus, and potassium fertilizers. Farmers applied 200 kg gypsum, 12.5 kg zinc sulphate and 2.5 kg borax per ha in improved practice compared with farmers' standard practice. The treatments were imposed on plots, side by side and uniform crop management practices were ensured in all the treatments. Application of all the nutrients except N was made as basal: 50% of N dose to non-legumes was added as basal and the remaining in two equal splits at one-month intervals.

On-farm demonstrations

The on-farm demonstrations of improved practices were carried out for maize and pigeonpea intercropping. During post-rainy season, chickpea trials were conducted along with another set of farmers. These demonstrations included improved cultivars, soil test-based nutrient application and IPM practices. In addition to micronutrient application, farmers were trained on IPM, for example, monitoring insect and pest incidence using pheromone traps (Fig. 6.8). Regular monitoring of insect and pest occurrence allows farmers to plan for plant protection measures before any major damage to crop, and thus save crop loss. To ensure nutritional diet to families, concept of kitchen garden was also implemented in the villages. Under this activity, a small quantity of seeds of different vegetables were distributed to women farmers. Depending upon the availability of space, farmers have grown the vegetables near their house or on farm bunds.

Kitchen garden

To address the issue of malnutrition in children and women to some extent there is a need to promote sustainable kitchen gardens for effective utilization of available natural resources like water and land by using organic farming methods as well as to improve diet by inclusion of fresh and safe nutritious vegetables produced in kitchen gardens. By taking up this activity, school children will gain hands-on experience in some areas of the school curriculum (e.g. science, agriculture, environmental science and home economics) as well as developing an understanding of nature. Kitchen garden kits consisting of different vegetable seeds like tomato, brinjal, okra, amaranth, spinach, bottle gourd and bitter gourd were distributed to women SHGs, and primary and high school children in the watershed villages. A total of 150 vegetable kits were distributed to school children and SHGs. Women grew the vegetables in their backyards and harvested the vegetables, which were used for their own family consumption.

Table 6.5. Percentages of soil samples deficient in macro- and micronutrients in watershed villages.

Village	Organic carbon	Available phosphorus	Available potassium	Available sulfur	Available zinc	Available boron
Bhanoor	33	9	0	36	51	20
Ghanapur	52	13	0	26	58	13
Kardanur	59	5	0	41	50	18
Kyasaram	79	9	0	30	76	30
Nandigama	67	17	0	44	94	17
Pati	73	8	0	40	60	13
Average	59	10	0	35	62	19

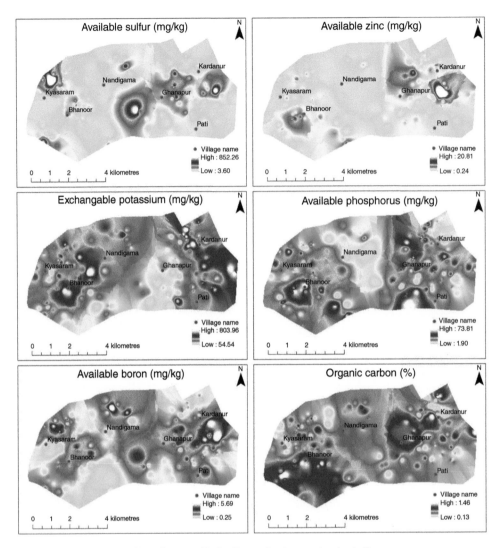

Fig. 6.7. Soil fertility maps based on stratified soil samples from watershed villages.

Promoting organic manure

Soils are degraded due to low levels of organic carbon, which is critical for the physical, chemical and biological processes indicative of soil fertility and soil health. Vermicomposting units were established for recycling farm waste. In addition, *Gliricidia* saplings were transplanted on community land and will be a rich source of green manure in future. These saplings were grown by SHGs from watershed villages that also provided additional income to SHG members. In total, 5500 saplings were grown in the nursery by SHGs in five villages.

Income-generating activity: spent malt-based business model

Spent malt is one of the byproducts generated from the brewery. It consists of malt residues and grain which contains carbohydrates, proteins and lignin, and water-soluble vitamins and is used as animal feed. It is palatable and is readily consumed by animals. In Bhanoor village, the spent malt unit was started by Mrugasheela SHG with 37 beneficiaries. The SHG group sold 354 tons of spent malt during 25 months till February 2017 and earned a net benefit of ₹75,611 after deducting all the expenditure costs, such as transportation, maintenance, equipment and labour charges (Table 6.6). Similarly, in Kyasaram village, the spent malt unit was started by Sri Bhavani SHG with 36 beneficiaries. The group sold 438 tons and earned a net benefit of ₹85,360. This business model of spent malt establishment in the villages helped in improving and strengthening the SHG group's capital and also the financial status of the group members due to the profits gained with spent malt. Moreover, farmers have also observed at least 1 l increase in milk production per animal due to feeding of spent malt.

Similar activities have been initiated in Nandigama village targeting 20 beneficiary farmers with 250 kg/day of spent malt feeding 90 milch animals.

6.5 Sustainability

6.5.1 Increased yield

On-farm demonstrations of improved practices were carried out for maize, pigeonpea and chickpea

Fig. 6.8. Brinjal field in Bhanoor village; (inset) a farmer using a pheromone trap to monitor insect and pest incidence.

Table 6.6. Increased milk yield and income in Bhanoor and Kyasaram villages due to use of spent malt as animal feed (the 25 months up to February 2017).

Particulars	Bhanoor	Kyasaram
Self-help group	Mrugasheela	Sri Bhavani
Number of farmers	37	46
Number of cattle (feeding)	177	292
Average use of spent malt in the village (kg/day)	860	1,380
Milk production in the village (l/day)	960	1,180
Increase in milk production by feeding spent malt (l/animal/day)	1	1
Increase in gross income due to spent malt (₹/day/village)	8,550	15,280
Increase in net income due to spent malt (₹/day/village)	4,670	9,070
Increase in family average net income due to proposed intervention (₹/family/ month)	3,780	5,910
Spent malt sold by the SHG (cumulative) (tons)	354	438
Net profit to SHG (cumulative) (₹)	75,611	85,360

crops. A total of 50 demonstrations were conducted for maize, pigeonpea and chickpea crops with improved cultivars and micronutrients. The observed data of crop-cutting experiments indicated up to 31%, 50% and 37 % increase in grain yield of maize, pigeonpea and chickpea respectively for improved management practices (Fig. 6.9).

6.5.2 Increased water availability

Precise measurement of the water column depth in the check-dam was done by using a pressure transducer (Diver, make: Schlumberger Water Services, model-DI501) that was kept in the stilling well (constructed at the upstream side of the check-dam). Watershed villages received good amount of rainfall during September and October 2016 that resulted in high runoff leading to overflow of check-dams. Daily records of water column in check-dam obtained from diver and daily rainfall data from the weather station are shown in Fig. 6.10. The process to estimate the number of fillings of check-dam is presented in Table 6.7. The estimated infiltration rate was 19.1 cm/day. Total evaporation during the time when water was available in the check-dam was 12.9 cm. The total number

of fillings was 7.2. Thus, total water infiltrated from the check-dam was 7.2 times the storage capacity of the check-dam. Similar number of fillings was assumed for remaining check-dams to estimate amount of water infiltrated in the ground. The total estimated groundwater recharge from the check-dams was about 91,400 m³.

Groundwater levels were monitored in eight selected bore wells near check-dams using water-level indicator. The difference of groundwater levels during July and August was very less due to less amount of rainfall during this period. The heavy rainfall event occurred in the first week of September, which led to increase in groundwater table by 3–32 m (below ground level) during October (Fig. 6.11). Among these bore wells, those near check-dam in Bhanoor village showed highest rise in water table from 38 m in August to 21 m in September and 8 m in October (Fig. 6.11).

6.6 Way Forward

Scaling-up of the resource conservation technologies implemented in this watershed project to resource-poor and water-scarce rainfed agriculture will help to achieve the sustainable

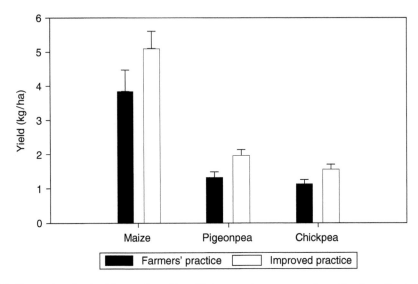

Fig. 6.9. Comparing standard farmers' practice with improved management practice for grain yield of three crops, 2016.

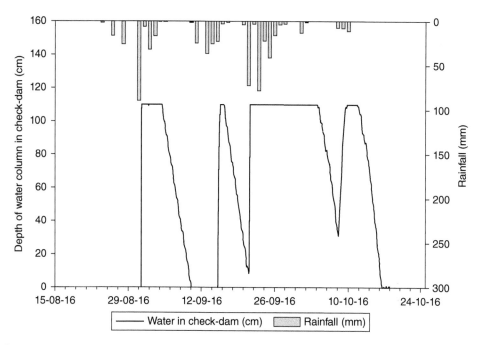

Fig. 6.10. Observed rainfall and runoff depth during the 2016 monsoon period.

Table 6.7. Process to estimate number of fillings of check-dam from well logger data in Bhanoor village.

Item	Method	Value
Maximum depth of water column (cm) (A)	–	110
Time to deplete water from full capacity to zero level (days) (B)	From well logger	5.8
Infiltration rate (cm/day) (C)	A/B	19.1
Number of days of water available in check-dam (D)	From well logger	41.3
Total evaporation during days of water available in check-dam (cm) (E)	From pan evaporimeter	12.9
Total depth of water infiltrated in check-dam (cm) (F)	C x D	788.8
Number of fillings (G)	F/A	7.2

development goals of zero hunger and reduced poverty. The learning from this project will be utilized to implement the technologies in upcoming watershed projects. For example, in the earlier project, ICRISAT in consultation with SABMiller had initiated provision of supplying spent malt from The Charminar breweries to Fasalvadi village (~40 km from Bhanur) with the aim of strengthening livelihood opportunities and financial security of the women's SHG by increasing milk yield and fat content since December 2011. Based on the success of pilot study, the activity was extended to another watershed area nearby at Kothapally. Similar activity is extended to Asian Paints Limited-ICRISAT watershed.

Acknowledgements

Authors acknowledge Asian Paints Limited for providing the funding support for implementing the watershed project, READ as an implementation partner, the village level watershed committee, SHGs and farmers for active participation in watershed activities, Mr D.S. Prasad Rao (ICRISAT) for coordinating the activities with village community, Mr Satya Vagu (ICRISAT) and Mr Mallesham (ICRISAT) for assisting in watershed project, and Dr VenkatRadha for developing soil fertility maps.

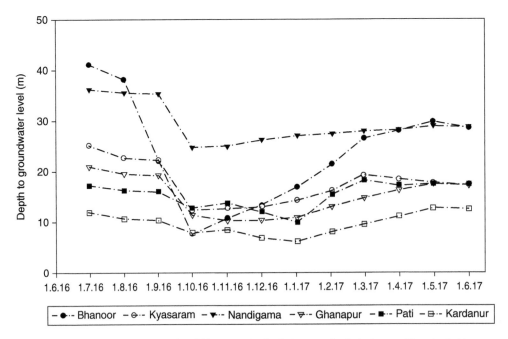

Fig. 6.11. Increase in groundwater level (decrease in depth to groundwater) observed in selected bore wells located near the check-dams in project villages, 2016–2017.

References

Dixit, S., Wani, S.P., Rego, T.J. and Pardhasaradhi, G. (2007) Knowledge-based entry point and innovative up-scaling strategy for watershed development projects. *Indian Journal of Dryland Agriculture and Development* 22(1), 22–31.

Gram Panchayats of respective villages (2015) Statistical abstract of Bhanur, Pati, Ghanapur, Nandigama, Kysaram, and Kardanur Gram panchayats, Patancheru Mandal, Sangareddy District, Telangana State, India.

Mandal Panchayat of Patancheru mandal (2015) Statistical abstract of Patancheru Mandal, Sangareddy District, Telangana State, India.

Sahrawat, K.L., Rego, T.J., Wani, S.P. and Pardhasaradhi, G. (2008) Stretching soil sampling to watershed: evaluation of soil-test parameters in a semi-arid tropical watershed. *Communications in Soil Science and Plant Analysis* 39, 2950–2960.

Wani, S.P., Singh H.P., Sreedevi, T.K., Pathak, P., Rego *et al.* (2003) Farmer-participatory integrated watershed management: Adarsha watershed, Kothapally, India, an innovative and upscalable approach. A case study. In: Harwood, R.R. and Kassam, A.H. (eds) *Research Towards Integrated Natural Resources Management: Examples of Research Problems, Approaches and Partnerships in Action in the CGIAR*. Interim Science Council, Consultative Group on International Agricultural Research, Washington, DC, pp. 123–147.

Wani, S.P., Sreedevi, T.K., Reddy, T.S.V., Venkateswarlu, B. and Prasad, C.S. (2008) Community watersheds for improved livelihoods through consortium approach in drought prone rainfed areas. *Journal of Hydrological Research and Development* 23, 55–77.

Wani, S.P., Sreedevi, T.K., Rockström, J. and Ramakrishna, Y.S. (2009) Rainfed agriculture – past trends and future prospects. In: Wani, S.P., Rockström, J. and Oweis, T. (eds) *Rainfed Agriculture: Unlocking the Potential*. Comprehensive Assessment of Water Management in Agriculture Series. CAB International, Wallingford, Oxfordshire, pp. 1–35.

7

Improving Water Availability and Diversification of Cropping Systems in Pilot Villages of North and Southern India

Kaushal K. Garg,[1]* Ramesh Singh,[2] Suhas P. Wani,[1] O.P. Chaturvedi,[2] Inder Dev,[2] Mukund D. Patil,[1] R. Sudi[1] and Anand K. Singh[1,2]

[1]*International Crops Research Institute for the Semi-Arid Tropics, Patancheru, India; [2]Central Agroforestry Research Institute (ICAR), Jhansi, India*

Abstract

Bundelkhand region of Uttar Pradesh and southeastern region of Karnataka (e.g. Kolar) are hot spots of poverty located in the semi-arid tropics. These regions are vulnerable to climate change and experience water scarcity and land degradation. Despite having moderate to good rainfall (700–850 mm), freshwater availability in these areas are declining due to over-extraction, poor groundwater recharge and change in land use. With realization of the importance of watershed development programme, the International Crops Research Institute for the Semi-Arid Tropics (ICRISAT) along with national partners (ICAR – Central Agroforestry Research Institute (CAFRI), Jhansi), NGO (MYRADA), district administration, state governments and local community started developing a model watershed with support of CSR funding of Coca-Cola India Foundation from 2011. The Parasai-Sindh watershed of 1250 ha with ICAR–CAFRI at Jhansi and Muduvatti watershed of 1340 ha with MYRADA in Kolar district were selected. From beginning of the project, science-led interventions comprising soil and water conservation practices, productivity enhancement, crop diversification and intensification through agroforestry interventions, integrated nutrient and pest management and other livelihood-based activities were implemented. This has resulted in improved groundwater table, crop intensification and increased rural income and livelihood. Low-cost rainwater harvesting structures at Parasai-Sindh watershed harvested minimum 250,000 m^3 of surface runoff annually and facilitated groundwater recharge, resulting in increased groundwater table by 2–5 m and increased cropping intensity and agricultural and livestock productivity by 30–50%. It is estimated that watershed interventions in pilot villages enhanced average annual family income from ₹50,000/year to ₹140,000/year in a short span of 3–4 years in Parasai-Sindh watershed. Similar results on increased groundwater table and crop intensification were observed in Muduvatti watershed in Kolar district.

7.1 Introduction

India has been recognized as a hot spot for poverty. In 2012, the Indian government stated that 22% of its population lived below its official poverty limit. In 2011, the World Bank, based on 2005 purchasing power parity initiative, the International Comparison Program, estimated that 23.6% of Indian population or about 276 million people lived on less than US$1.25 per day on

---

* Corresponding author: k.garg@cgiar.org

purchasing power parity. Agriculture is the largest sector, providing employment and a source of livelihood for more than 65% of the population in India. Out of a total of 141 million ha of agricultural land, 55% of total area is rainfed having current productivity level of 1–1.5 tons/ha. To achieve growth and sustainability, it is essential to enhance the agricultural productivity both in rainfed and irrigated areas. Current agricultural productivity has largely become either stagnant or is declining due to several reasons. Inappropriate use of natural resources resulted in increased water scarcity, land degradation and loss of various ecosystem services. Moreover, large uncertainty is arising on current and future water availability and other resource availability due to changing climatic situations. Extreme events like flash floods or longer dry spells, more frequent dry or wet years, change in crop water demand, and increasing temperature and pest/disease infestation (the clear evidence of climate change) are enhancing risk in agricultural system.

Despite a number of challenges, integrated watershed management approach has proved to be the suitable adaptation strategy to cope with the changing climatic situation and for achieving holistic development (Wani et al., 2009; Garg et al., 2011; Singh et al., 2014). Integrated watershed development programmes reduce water-related risks by improving the green and blue water availability, reduce land degradation and strengthen various ecosystem services (such as reduced soil loss, increased base flow, carbon (C) sequestration, etc.). International Crops Research Institute for the Semi-Arid Tropics (ICRISAT) and Indian Council of Agricultural Research – Central Agroforestry Research Institute (ICAR–CAFRI), Jhansi, India has long research and development experience in areas of natural resource management and also in designing and developing watershed technologies. ICRISAT along with consortium partners has developed a number of watersheds across India and also outside the country (e.g. China, Vietnam and Thailand) in regions with variation in rainfall, soil types and agroecology. Technologies demonstrated in these watersheds have not only helped farmers and the farming community directly in terms of enhancing agricultural productivity, income and livelihood (e.g. Adarsha watershed, Kothapally in Medak, Telangana; and

Garhkundar-Dabar watershed, Uttar Pradesh) but also influenced various stakeholders (development agencies, nongovernment organizations (NGOs), government and private agencies, policy makers, etc.) to scale-up and adopt further on a larger scale (Wani et al., 2009).

The Coca-Cola India Foundation has requested ICRISAT to undertake watershed activities in Parasai-Sindh watershed (adjoining three villages in Jhansi district, Uttar Pradesh) and Muduvatti watershed of 1340 ha in Kolar district, Karnataka under the corporate social responsibility (CSR) initiative. The Coca-Cola India Foundation, a company registered under Section 25 of the Companies' Act 2013, is committed to sustainable development and inclusive growth by focusing on issues relating to water, the environment, healthy living and social advance so that it can contribute to a strong and resolute India enabling the common people to build a better life. In order to promote the Foundation's objectives, monetary grants and other assistance will be provided to NGOs, beneficiary organizations, cooperatives, philanthropies and such others who can be suitable partners in implementing projects for social welfare across the country. The Foundation seeks to ensure project execution, maintenance and sustainability through the active involvement and direct participation of the beneficiary community at the grassroots level. The overall project goal in both the selected watersheds was to build resilience of the rural community against climate change (e.g. drought, dry spells, etc.) by enhancing groundwater recharge and introducing various natural resource management (NRM) interventions.

7.2   Bundelkhand Region of Central India

Bundelkhand region of Central India is a hot spot of water scarcity, land degradation, poverty and poor socioeconomic status. Due to poor groundwater potential, high temperature, and low and erratic rainfall, agricultural productivity in this region is very poor (0.5–1.5 t/ha). Most of the areas are single cropped and completely under rainfed conditions (Tyagi, 1997). Rainfall is highly erratic, both in terms of total amount and its distribution over time. Long-term weather data monitored at Jhansi station (nearby site) show that annual average rainfall in study region is 877 mm (standard deviation, σ = 251 mm) with about 85% during June to September. On an average, 42 rainy days during the monsoon and 13 rainy days during non-monsoon were recorded. Long-term data analysis showed that annual average rainfall has decreased from 950 mm between 1944 and 1973 as compared to 847 mm between 1974 and 2004 (Fig. 7.1). This reduction was mainly due to decreased number of low (0–10 mm) and medium rainfall (30–50 mm) events (Fig. 7.1). Similarly, total number of rainy days in a year also decreased.

Dry spells longer than 5–7 days are very common and occur several times (5–6 times) per season, whereas 10–15 days or longer dry spells also may occur during the monsoon period. The climate of the region is tropical monsoonal preceded by hot summer (minimum air temperature ranges between 17 and 29°C and maximum air temperature between 31 and 47°C in May) and is followed by cool winter (minimum

(a)

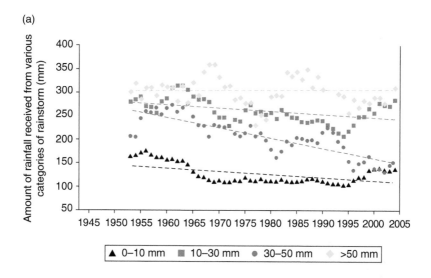

(b)

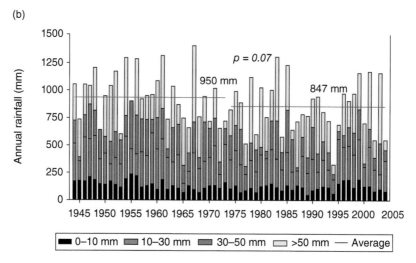

Fig. 7.1. Rainfall in Jhansi: (a) moving average (ten years) of rainfall received from various categories of rain events between 1944 and 2004; (b) comparison of annual rainfall between 1944–1973 and 1974–2004.

air temperature ranges between 2 and 19°C and maximum air temperature between 20 and 31°C in January). Soils in the region are reddish to brownish-red in colour (Alfisols and Entisols), coarse-gravelly and light-textured with poor water-holding capacity (80–100 mm/m). A large extent of the region is in degraded stage, and poor in organic matter and nutrient status. The geology of the targeted region is dominated by hard rocks of Archaen granite and gneiss and largely composed of crystalline igneous and metamorphic rocks (Tyagi, 1997), and aquifers are either unconfined or perched, having poor storage capacity (porosity of 0.01–0.05%). These aquifers were derived primarily from weathering and developed into two-layered system: (i) unconsolidated fractured layers derived through prolonged weathering of bedrocks within 10–15 m depending upon the topography, drainage and vegetation cover; and (ii) relatively impermeable basement starting from 15 to 20 m depth. In such hard rock aquifers with poor transmissibility, shallow dug wells of 5 to 15 m depth are the only primary source of water for domestic and agricultural use in this region (Singh *et al.*, 2014).

7.2.1   Pilot site: Parasai-Sindh watershed, Jhansi

Frequent droughts are common in Bundelkhand. More than 80% of open wells get dried out soon after monsoon period due to deficit rainfall and poor groundwater recharge. In the absence of drinking water availability and poor livelihood opportunity, a large number of the rural community usually migrate to nearby cities. Lack of availability of water has affected the agricultural sector.

The urban and rural communities largely depend on outside water source and private suppliers such as tankers for domestic use especially in summer. Cattle were abandoned due to shortage of water and less fodder availability. In such conditions, watershed development programme is considered to enhance groundwater recharge and reduce water scarcity with effective interventions. ICRISAT consortium, with ICAR–CAFRI, selected one of the mesoscale watersheds, Parasai-Sindh in Jhansi district to demonstrate the impact of watershed development interventions on

groundwater recharge and strengthening ecosystem services. This watershed is located in Babina block of Jhansi district, Uttar Pradesh and covers 1250 ha of geographical area. It comprises three villages, namely Parasai, Chhatpur and Bachauni located between 25°23′56″ to 25°27′9″ N and 78°19′45″ to 78°22′42″ E (Fig. 7.2). The watershed development programme of CSR initiative in selected villages was started in 2011 with the objectives: (i) to enhance groundwater recharge and reduce water stress situation; (ii) to enhance agricultural productivity and water use efficiency; and (iii) to improve livelihoods of rural community.

7.2.2   Baseline characterization

A baseline survey was conducted in all the three villages for understanding biophysical, social and economic condition of selected villages at inception of the project in 2011 (Table 7.1). The total population of the three villages in the watershed is 2896 persons (1550 male and 1346 female). Large farmers in the villages generate 80% income from agriculture and 20% from milk production. The source of income for small and marginal farmers is from agriculture and by sale of milk almost in equal proportion. Activities on daily wages are also a source of income for small and marginal farmers. Literacy status in the villages is poor. On average about 56% of the population is literate. Topography of the selected watershed is relatively flat with an average slope of 1–2%. This watershed is mainly dominated by agricultural land covering nearly 63% of total geographical area and a large portion (32%) is covered by barren and scrubland which is used mainly for animal grazing. Groundnut, black gram and sesame are the dominating *kharif* (rainy season) crops and wheat and chickpea are grown mainly in *rabi* (post-rainy) season. Average productivity of these crops in the project villages was: wheat 1677 kg/ha, barley 1725 kg/ha, black gram 189 kg/ha, green gram 169 kg/ha, chickpea 430 kg/ha, mustard 907 kg/ha, sesame 315 kg/ha and groundnut 1111 kg/ha.

Soils of the watershed are dominated by Alfisols and Entisols which are shallow (10–50 cm), coarse-gravelly, light-textured with poor water-holding capacity (80–100 mm/m), and

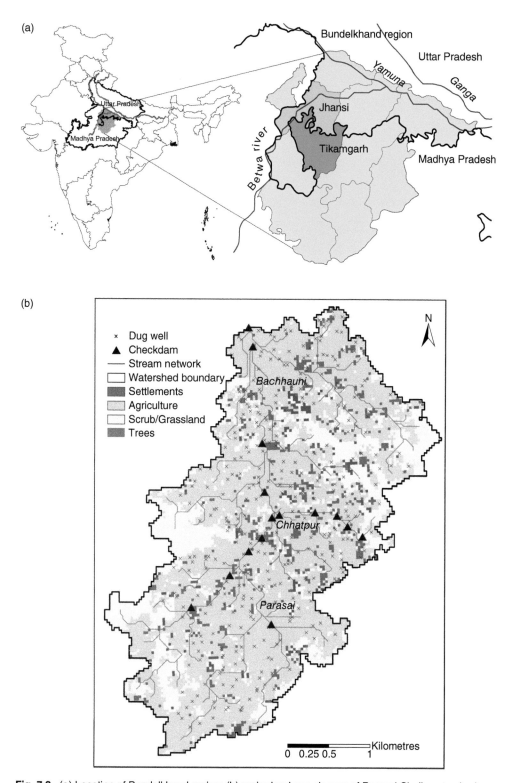

Fig. 7.2. (a) Location of Bundelkhand region; (b) major land use classes of Parasai-Sindh watershed.

Table 7.1. General characteristics and land use resources of Parasai-Sindh watershed.

Particulars	Data
Watershed characteristics	
Area (ha)	1250
Altitude (m above msl)	270 to 315
Relief (m)	45
Length (m)	6263
Width (m)	3994
Perimeter (km)	27.83
Drainage density (km/km^2)	2.11
Land use[a] (ha)	
Agricultural land	1105.5 (88.70)
Scrubland	66.00 (5.29)
Forest	5.60 (0.45)
Drain network	43.4 (3.60)
Road	14.30 (1.15)
Habitation	11.10 (0.89)
Resources	
Total population	2896
Population below 18 years age (%)	52
Literacy (%)	56
No. of households	417
No. of animals	2558
Average holding (ha/household)	3.12

[a]Figures in parentheses are percentage values.

low in nitrogen, phosphorus and organic carbon. There are 388 open wells (8–12 m deep) in the watershed and these are the primary source of water for domestic and agricultural use. Bore wells in this region do not work due to poor specific yields (<0.5% specific yield). Water in the open wells of the project villages was found safe for drinking. However, human health survey conducted during 2013, showed large-scale intestinal worm infection. This indicates the need for awareness building on safe use of water and food and hygiene.

7.3 Kolar District of Peninsular India

Kolar district in Karnataka lies between latitude 12°46′ to 13°58′ N and longitude 77°21′ to 78°35′ E. The district lies almost in the central part of peninsular India, which has immense bearing on its geo-climatic conditions. Kolar district falls in the eastern dry agroclimatic zone. It experiences a semi-arid climate, characterized by typical monsoon tropical weather with hot

summer and mild winter. The year is normally divided into four seasons: dry season during January-February, pre-monsoon season during March-May, southwest monsoon season during June-September and post- or northeast monsoon season during October-December. There is a general south to north decreasing trend in annual rainfall. The southwest monsoon contributes around 55% of the annual rainfall while the northeast monsoon yields around 30%. The balance of around 15% results from the pre-monsoon. September and October are the wettest months with over 100 mm monthly rainfall. Thunderstorms are common during May. The post-monsoon season often gets copious rains due to passing depressions.

As per the classification of the National Bureau of Soil Survey and Land Use Planning, Kolar area falls in the hot moist semi-arid agroecological subregion with medium to deep red loamy soils. Available water capacity is low (80–100 mm/m) and the rainfed length of growing period is about 120–150 days. Summer showers are experienced in May. Though the southwest monsoon sets by the first week of June, rainfall more than the potential evapotranspiration (PET) is received only during middle of September to third week of October. This period has potential for harvesting and storage of runoff water for use by *rabi* crops. First week of August is usually dry, but may not adversely affect the crops. During the period from last week of August to the first week of September, average rainfall is comparatively low and the rainfall expected at 60% probability is almost zero. This period coincides with the flowering and late flowering phase of several crops, which are likely to experience severe moisture stress. Annual PET is 1638 mm and the annual average rainfall is 711 mm.

7.3.1 Pilot site: Muduvatti watershed, Kolar

Muduvatti watershed comprises eight villages (Muduvatti, Jangalahalli, Konepura, Papenahalli, Shettiganahalli, Shettikothanur, Dandiganahalli and Nernahally) of Kolar district, Karnataka (Fig. 7.3). The total area of the eight selected villages of the project is 1340 ha, with a population of 5556 that has an average family

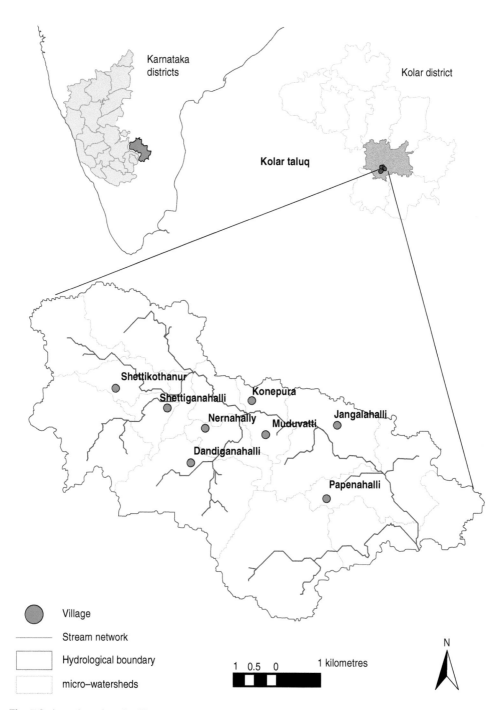

Fig. 7.3. Location of study villages, stream network and micro-watersheds of Muduvatti watershed.

size of 4.7 and population density of 4.01 persons per ha. These eight villages of Vakkaleri Hobli are in the vicinity of Kolar town about 6–16 km away.

7.3.2 Baseline characterization

Baseline of the selected villages is presented in Table 7.2. About 67% of households are in

Table 7.2. Baseline information of selected villages in Kolar watershed collected in 2013.

Particulars	Muduvatti	Jangalahalli	Konepura	Papenahalli	Shettiganahalli	Shettikothanur	Dandiganahalli	Nemahally
Population (2011)[a]								
Backward	704	78	33	NA	222	109	301	132
Others	1064	512	259	NA	695	874	110	209
Total	1768	590	292	NA	917	983	411	341
No. of households	368	98	45	17	116	210	82	72
Total geographical area (ha)	304	87	70	70	260	215	179	155
Common land (ha)	57	20.42	17.29	22.39	54.78	43.74	63.11	63.11
Agricultural land (ha)								
Irrigated	80.17	26.53	28.2	8.75	19.44	12.28	24.55	43.35
Unirrigated	90.36	15.45	12.26	8.3	152.4	138.41	53.17	14.07
Livestock (no.)								
Large ruminants	240	128	44	7	120	129	170	120
Small ruminants	800	610	140	0	470	320	700	420
Tubewells (no.)								
Total	206	66	81	1	91	97	95	75
Functioning	52	10	14	1	16	11	28	16
Defunct	154	56	67	0	75	86	67	59
Average depth of tubewells (ft)	1100	1000	1000	1100	1100	1100	1200	1000

[a]From: http://censusindia.gov.in. NA= Data not available in 2011 census.

small, 27% in medium, and 3% each in the large and landless category. The arable land in the watershed is about 55% of total geographical area. The common land which is about 25% is the source of grazing. Major land area is under rainfed agriculture, while with bore well as a main source vegetable cultivation is gaining importance. The present land use is 88% cultivated (46% rainfed, 31% under vegetable and irrigated annual crops) and 12% under other uses that includes habitat, forest, road and drains. The main agricultural crops grown are finger millet, paddy, pigeonpea, groundnut, castor, etc. The major horticultural crops grown in the villages are tomato, onion, cabbage, carrot, brinjal, beans, potato, green chilli, leafy vegetables, etc. The major fruits grown are mango, banana, guava, sapota and papaya. Tamarind, ginger, coriander are also grown. The main floriculture crops are marigold, *Crossandra* sp., jasmine and chrysanthemum. Mulberry is also quite a prominent crop grown for sericulture. Good animal population, particularly milch animals prevails in the villages.

7.4   NRM Interventions Implemented in Parasai-Sindh Watershed

7.4.1   Entry point activities

Formation of watershed committee

In 2011, an ICRISAT-led consortium along with ICAR–CAFRI, Jhansi, farmers and district administration selected Parasai-Sindh watershed for enhancing water resources availability and optimizing agricultural productivity. Villagers and watershed committee members were involved from the project inception stage. Watershed committee of pilot villages were formed to implement the watershed work. Farmers are the primary stakeholders and beneficiaries. Hence, involvement of community was important for successful execution of project activity/interventions and to ensure long-term sustainability of the project. Women, and Scheduled Caste/ Scheduled Tribe candidates and members from panchayat were also involved in the formation of watershed committee, as per common guidelines. The committee was constituted in an open

meeting and the objectives were briefed clearly. The committee members and villagers were involved at each and every stage of project planning and execution of proposed interventions. For example, selection and construction of water harvesting sites and types of structure, procurement of the materials, record keeping, verification of bills and payment delivery, etc. were handled by the watershed committee under the guidance of the consortium team. Transparency at every step established good rapport and resulted in large and active participation of the village community in watershed management and development. With the technical backstopping of CAFRI and ICRISAT scientists, potential locations for soil and water conservation structures were identified by the watershed committee and villagers themselves. Similarly, decisions on procurement of quality seeds, planting materials and other inputs were taken by the committee in open meetings. Right approach and knowledge-based entry point enabled the village community to take up the responsibility, bring transparency and accelerate the execution process.

Formation of environmental clubs

Environmental clubs were formed in the pilot villages. These clubs involved women and children participants and aimed to create awareness about conservation and better utilization of natural resources such as water, air and groundwater resources. The consortium team interacted with children and women groups (Fig. 7.4) and shared their knowledge on soil and water conservation. There were discussions on poor quality of drinking water and causes for water pollution. Water-quality analysis showed that groundwater in Parasai and Chhatpur villages is safe for human and animal consumption as all the quality parameters are found in permissible limit (Table 7.3). Formation of these environmental clubs was the entry point activity during the project initiation. The consortium team gathered at the centre of the village and interacted with children through various activities such as team building exercises (conducting games, quizzes, etc.). Winners were awarded books on environmental issues.

Further, 15 children were chosen to become members of an eco-club based on their knowledge and participation. These children belonged

Fig. 7.4. Members of the environmental club (women and children) interacting with an ICRISAT scientist in Parasai-Sindh watershed.

Table 7.3. Groundwater quality for drinking purpose in project villages in 2011.[a]

Parameter	Chhatpur	Parasai	Threshold
pH	7.45	7.51	6.5 to 8.5
EC (dS/m)	0.46	0.48	–
Total dissolved solids (mg/l)	307	320	Maximum 500
Alkalinity to phenolphthalein as $CaCO_3$ (mg/l)	Nil	Nil	–
Alkalinity to methyl orange as $CaCO_3$ (mg/l)	225	220	–
Total hardness as $CaCO_3$ (mg/l)	184	203	Maximum 300
Chloride as Cl (mg/l)	7	14	Maximum 250
Sulphate as SO_4 (mg/l)	2	2	Maximum 150
Nitrate as NO_3 (mg/l)	38	47	Maximum 45
Fluoride as F (mg/l)	0.7	1.5	0.6 to 1.2
Calcium as Ca (mg/l)	62	61	Maximum 75
Magnesium as Mg (mg/l)	7	12	Maximum 30
Potassium as K (mg/l)	1	1	–
Sodium as Na (mg/l)	11	19	–
Iron as Fe (mg/l)	0	0.1	Maximum 0.3
Cadmium as Cd (mg/l)	Nil	Nil	Maximum 1
Cobalt as Co (mg/l)	Nil	Nil	Maximum 0.05
Copper as Cu (mg/l)	Nil	Nil	Maximum 2.0
Lead as Pb (mg/l)	Nil	Nil	Maximum 0.5
Manganese as Mn (mg/l)	Nil	Nil	Maximum 0.1

[a]Five water samples were collected in first year of the project.

to diverse socioeconomic background, attended different schools and were in the age group between 10 and 14 years. The project team motivated them to circulate books, share the knowledge and meet regularly at the given venue and date. Formation of eco-clubs facilitated the consortium team to interact with farmers and women groups and also with village administration. Eco-club members sent a formal letter to the watershed committee requesting for plants which they could plant in their backyards. The survival rate of these fruit plants planted by the children was much more than those planted by adults. Members and non-members made miniature models with sand and tried to understand the watershed intervention being undertaken in their villages. There was a tremendous response even among girls who took active part in all such activities. Children were given chalk to write slogans on sanitation and water conservation in their villages.

During a visit to Chhatpur it was discovered that this village was not totally covered under the Integrated Child Development Services (ICDS) scheme, which provides young children with food and nourishment, and is sponsored by the central government. The project took cognizance of this and sent a request to the authorities to pursue the matter. Since 1 March 2013, an ICDS centre has been newly opened in the village benefiting 50 infants aged 7 months to 3 years, 68 children aged 3–6 years, 11 pregnant women and 15 nursing mothers and 3 young girls.

7.4.2 Rainwater harvesting

Groundwater recharge in Bundelkhand areas is generally poor due to hard rock geology and poor specific yield. The situation becomes critical during dry years and summer months. Construction of low-cost water-harvesting structures is one of the important interventions considered for groundwater recharge. These structures harvest a substantial amount of surface runoff, allow it to percolate into aquifer and facilitate groundwater recharge. A number of locations for harvesting surface runoff were identified by the watershed committee and village members. Nearly 115,000 m^3 of storage capacity was developed in watershed by constructing various water harvesting structures (Fig. 7.5). Water balance indicated that such water harvesting

structures can harvest surface runoff by a factor of two to three times of the developed storage capacity in a normal year (with average rainfall of 877 mm). Moreover, water table monitoring along with state-of-the-art runoff monitoring system showed that these structures harvested nearly 250,000 m^3 of surface runoff between June and October, resulting in high groundwater table. Water table in Parasai-Sindh watershed increased by 2.5 m on average, compared to that before implementation of watershed activities. Increase in water table was 5 m near stream location and 2 m at upstream areas.

7.4.3 Agroforestry interventions

Through agroforestry interventions in watershed a total of 22,210 (5380 fruit and 16,830 multipurpose trees) seedlings of different tree species were planted in farmers' fields, households and on bunds (Fig. 7.6). Effect of deep pitting and profile modification using black soil on survival and growth of teak was demonstrated. Teak plantation on field boundary has been adopted by more than 150 farmers. Survival of different tree species varied from 32% to 95% by the end of 2015. Apart from this, during 2012 to 2016, about 2100 *desi ber* (*Ziziphus mauritiana*) plants were budded with improved varieties with more than 80% survival. Sixty-seven households have guava, citrus and pomegranate in their homestead with survival more than 90%. Plantations in homesteads are meeting nutritional requirement of the households.

7.4.4 Productivity enhancement interventions

Yield gap analysis undertaken by ICRISAT revealed that large yield gap exists in the major rainfed crops grown in the semi-arid tropics. Further, there is a potential of increasing the productivity by two- to threefold using available technologies in farmers' fields (Wani *et al.*, 2009, 2012). Soils in rainfed areas have low moisture content and are deficient in essential nutrients. Soil analysis showed 65–80% of the farmers' fields were deficient in sulfur (S), zinc (Zn) and boron (B) (Table 7.4).

Fig. 7.5. Rainwater harvesting in watershed: (a, b) check-dams constructed at different locations; and (c, d) water harvested in check-dams during the rainy season 2013–14.

In this context, farmers' participatory trials were conducted in different years to demonstrate the impact of micronutrients (Zn and B) on groundnut yield. Farmers contributed 50% of fertilizer cost (agribor (B) and zinc sulphate ($ZnSO_4$)). Application of B and Zn increased groundnut yield by 15–20% (average yield 1825 kg/ha) over control plots (average yield 1510 kg/ha) in 2011. During *rabi* 2011, improved varieties of chickpea (Vaibhav), lentil (DPL 62) and mustard (Pusa Bold) were introduced in farmers' participatory trials at 14 locations. Crop yields of improved crop varieties increased by 18 to 33% over local crop varieties (Table 7.5).

In addition, groundnut yields and other agronomic parameters were evaluated in farmers' participatory trials and compared with traditional cultivar (*Jhumku*) (Fig.7.7). Improved groundnut variety (TAG 24) had highest number of pods (19.2 pods/plant). Correspondingly, this variety had highest kernel yield (1.68 t/ha) and pod yield (2.42 t/ha). Data showed that introducing improved variety of groundnut enhanced crop yield by 30–50% compared to the local cultivar.

Similarly, farmers' participatory demonstrations were conducted for wheat crop in different years. For example, crop demonstrations in 30 wheat fields (HI 1418, HI 1479, HI 1531 and HI 1544) and 15 chickpea fields (JG 11 and JG 130) were designed during *rabi* 2012–13. Farmers recognized a clear difference in crop growth and anticipated a 10–15% higher yield while crop harvesting. A total number of 76 participatory demonstrations (14 in Parasai, 44 in Chhatpur and 18 in Bachhauni) were laid out in farmers' fields with improved varieties during *rabi* in 2013–14. About 28% increase in yield was observed in barley cultivar RD 2552, while 17% increase was observed in mustard cultivar Maya over local varieties (Table 7.6).

Fig. 7.6. Agroforestry interventions in Parasai-Sindh watershed: (a–c) teak and other trees were planted along field bunds during June–July 2012; (d) tree of *desi ber* (traditionally grown) budded with improved variety.

Table 7.4. Soil fertility status in selected villages in Parasai Sindh watershed.[a]

Particulars	EC (ds/m)	Exchangeable K (mg/kg)	Olsen P (mg/kg)	Organic C (%)	Available Zn (mg/kg)	Available B (mg/kg)	Available S (mg/kg)
Average	0.16	83	11.12	0.51	0.75	0.23	5.47
SD	0.10	60	6.96	0.19	0.39	0.11	3.00
Maximum	0.54	335	36.00	1.10	2.50	0.64	19.95
Minimum	0.04	25	1.20	0.22	0.22	0.10	1.85

[a]A total of 80 soil samples were collected from the top 0–15 cm of soil.

7.4.5 Developing forage resource

Napier bajra hybrid (NBH) and guinea grass are the important pasture species suitable for higher forage production. These have profuse tillering and regeneration capacity, high leaf-stem ratio and provide highly nutritious fodder to the livestock. About 137,000 rooted slips of NBH and guinea grass were transplanted in an area of about 3 ha (on bunds, near check-dams and around *haveli*) during 2013 and 2014. During the initial year of establishment of these grasses two cuts could be harvested with biomass potential of 4.0 tons dry matter per ha. During 2015 farmers of the area transplanted the rooted slips obtained from well-established tussocks of NBH, thereby increasing the area under these pasture grasses to about 7 ha. Biomass potential has gone up to 7.2 tons dry matter per ha, whereby farmers are able to harvest 8–10 cuts in a year (Fig. 7.8).

7.4.6 Income-generating activities

Most families in the watershed have landholdings and cattle. Women work alongside their husbands in fields. Yet due to *purdah*, it was often difficult to communicate with the women in the beginning of the project. The need for a female field worker was felt and the project team was helped by one of the youngsters within the village to communicate with the women members. Young girls have taken responsibility to form

women self-help groups (SHGs) so that they can avail the benefits of government schemes.

Promoting agroforestry

Farmers of the villages Parasai, Chhatpur and Bachhauni were motivated to adopt agroforestry practices in their fields. Training programmes on *Z. mauritiana* (*desi ber*) budding were conducted for farmers and women SHGs in watershed villages.

Vermicomposting

Soil test results showed that soils in the watershed are deficient in micronutrients and poor in organic matter. Use of undecomposed manure may cause several pest problems and lead to poor crop productivity. Training on preparation of vermicompost from locally available materials (crop straw, biomass and cow dung) was conducted for farmers and women SHGs in watershed villages.

Introduction of dona-making machine

A one-day training programme on *dona* (platter) making was organized in August 2014 in Bachchauni village in Jhansi district in which tribal farmers from the village participated and six SHGs were formed.

Table 7.5. Performance of crop varieties in farmers' participatory trials in Parasai-Sindh watershed during *rabi* 2011.

Crop	Variety	Number of trials	Average grain yield (kg/ha)	Yield increase (%)
Chickpea	Vaibhav	5	1870	33
	Desi	–	1402	–
Lentil	DPL 62	6	1130	18
	Desi	–	960	–
Mustard	Pusa Bold	3	1470	25
	Desi	–	1180	–

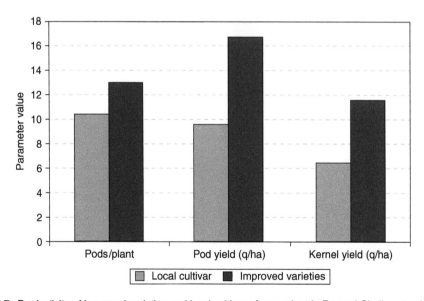

Fig. 7.7. Productivity of improved varieties and local cultivar of groundnut in Parasai-Sindh watershed.

Table 7.6. Participatory demonstrations at Parasai-Sindh watershed during *rabi* 2013–14 and 2014–15.

Crop	Varieties introduced	No. of demonstration trials				Av. yield (kg/ha)	
		Parasai	Chhatpur	Bachhauni	Total	Improved	Local
2013–14							
Barley	RD 2552	9	20	–	29	2400	1470
Mustard	Maya	4	8	6	18	1190	1020
Chickpea	JG 130	–	–	–	20	1400	820
2014–15							
Pigeonpea	ICPL 85063 (Lakshmi), ICPL 88039	3	3	–	6	760	630
Barley	RD 2552	11	7	–	18		
Chickpea	JG 130	–	6	2	8	1210	820
Mustard	NRC HB 101, NRC HB 506, NRC DR 02	2	8	–	10	1180	920
Wheat	HI 1532, HI 1544, HI 1418, HI 1479	8	12	8	28	4420	3450

Fig. 7.8. Napier bajra hybrid slips planted on bunds near stream network.

7.4.7 Capacity building

Exposure visits

A one-day exposure visit-cum-training programme was organized for villagers at Garhkundar-Dabar watershed and Domagaur-Pahuj to enhance their capacity. More than 50 farmers participated in this programme. Farmers observed various interventions including soil and water conservation measures, rainwater harvesting structures, well recharging, improved crop varieties and cropping systems, crop diversification with high value crops, productivity enhancement, livestock-based improvement and livelihood initiatives, and interacted with the local community. The visiting farmers were impressed with the salient impacts that resulted

due to the implementation of this model and appreciated the success due to collective action. They expressed that the visit provided an excellent learning opportunity. In 2012, farmers from Parasai-Sindh watershed also visited Indian Agricultural Research Institute (IARI), New Delhi to gain more knowledge on new and innovative technology (Fig. 7.9).

Field day

Field days were organized by the consortium team in the watershed to disseminate knowledge and to bring awareness about project activities and demonstrations. Farmers from all the three villages, including women members, participated in the programme. The community was reminded about the objectives of the project to increase

Fig. 7.9. Capacity development programmes for Parasai-Sindh watershed farmers: (a) exposure visit to IARI, New Delhi; (b) field day in project village; (c, d) health camp during November 2013.

surface as well as groundwater resources in the villages and its efficient utilization for increasing agricultural productivity and rural livelihoods. Farmers were explained about the soil fertility status and advised to adopt balanced nutrient application, including the deficient B, Zn and S, in addition to only nitrogen, phosphorus and potassium (NPK) fertilizers. Farmers participated in experimental trials and narrated their experiences with project technological interventions of improved varieties and balanced nutrition, including deficient secondary and micronutrients. The interactive session was followed by field visit to show the other farmers the effects of improved varieties and balanced nutrition in groundnut crop. As a result of the interactive session and field visit, the farmers realized the importance of balanced nutrient application and became motivated to use the technology in their fields to improve crop productivity (Fig. 7.9).

International Women's Day at ICRISAT

Five tribal women participated in International Women's Day at ICRISAT, Hyderabad during 2014. They also interacted with the SHGs of Adarsha watershed, Kothapally and were exposed to the best agricultural practices at the institute.

Human health camp

A human health camp was organized in Parasai-Sindh watershed during November 2013 with the support of the project fund. Five medical practitioners (one pediatrician, two gynaecologists, one pathologist and one surgeon) from an eminent medical college in New Delhi visited the watershed. Nearly 400 village members benefited from this camp; about ₹10,000 worth of medicines were distributed along with consultancy. A large number of children were found to be malnourished, women were diagnosed as anaemic, and many villagers complained about intestinal worm infestation and skin problems (Fig. 7.9).

7.4.8   Impact of watershed intervention on water resources availability and income

A number of water harvesting interventions and productivity enhancement activities, implemented at Parasai-Sindh watershed have made a significant impact on water resources availability, and income and livelihood of the farmers. Water, which was one of the limiting factors and a scarce commodity, was enhanced significantly. Both surface and groundwater were found in surplus amount even at the end of the summer period. Hydrological monitoring showed that nearly 250,000 m^3 of water was harvested in storage structures, which enhanced groundwater level by 2 to 5 m, with an average of 2.5 m compared to baseline status (before interventions) (Fig. 7.10). The NRM interventions have significantly changed the cropping pattern both in *kharif* and *rabi* seasons (Fig. 7.11).

Groundnut is the predominant crop in *kharif* along with black gram and sesame whereas wheat, mustard, chickpea, lentil and barley are being cultivated in the *rabi* season. More than 100 ha cultivable fallow land was brought under groundnut cultivation in *kharif* with increased water availability in open wells during the project period. Significant change also has been found in *rabi* crops. With increased and assured water availability, farmers who were cultivating lentil, chickpea and mustard have replaced these crops with barley and wheat. Also nearly 300 ha additional area which was left fallow in *rabi* especially at upstream locations were brought under wheat cultivation. This has made a significant contribution towards enhancing farmers' income in the villages during three to four years of NRM interventions. Figure 7.12 shows the NDVI (normalized difference vegetation index) values in Parasai-Sindh watershed before (February 2011) and after (February 2014 and 2015) the interventions. This is clear evidence of how the upland areas which were fallow have now been brought under cultivation due to groundwater

availability. High rainfall occurred in 2014 but rainfall in 2015 was deficit by 30% than normal. Despite low rainfall, farmers were able to cultivate *rabi* crop successfully in 2015.

With increased water availability, the cost of cultivation especially for wheat and barley has reduced. Before project interventions, farmers used to engage hired or family labour for more number of days for irrigation work due to poor availability of groundwater as water in open wells used to deplete completely within 2–3 hours of pumping. Increased water availability (2–5 m increased water table in open wells) after the project interventions has facilitated farmers to complete irrigation in few days as they can pump water for 8–10 hours per day and therefore enhance labour use efficiency. This has reduced the cost of production especially for barley and wheat by reducing labour engagement. In addition, by introducing improved cultivars and management practices, wheat yield increased from 1.7 t/ha to 2.7 t/ha (Fig. 7.13). This all together made a compounding effect in enhancing net profit from agricultural production (Table 7.7) significantly. Yield and household data collected from pilot villages clearly showed that agricultural sector alone contributed towards enhancing net income from ₹20.8 million/year to ₹58.4 million/year.

The NRM interventions further improved fodder and livestock productivity. The number of buffaloes in project villages increased from 950 to 1300 with increased milk productivity of 2–3 l/day/animal. Livestock income increased from ₹10.2 million/year to ₹21.2 million/year, i.e. additional gain of ₹11 million/year. Altogether, average household income in Parasai-Sindh watershed increased from ₹51,000 to ₹143,000 per household per year, clearly indicating that there exists a huge scope for enhancing farmers' income by more than double through implementation of various NRM interventions in the Bundelkhand region. In addition to agriculture and livestock sectors, project interventions also helped in enhancing other ecosystem services such as increased greenery, tree biomass and productivity and reduced soil erosion and carbon sequestration. Moreover, drudgery and migration levels have significantly reduced in pilot villages with increased domestic and agricultural water availability and livelihood opportunities.

Fig. 7.10. Watershed status (a–d) before interventions: (a, b) rainwater harvest locations; (c) *desi ber* budding for agroforestry; (d) noncultivable fallow area; and (e–h) after interventions: (e, f) harvested water in check-dams; (g) fruiting one year after budding; (h) wheat crop grown in fallow land due to enhanced availability of groundwater during 2013.

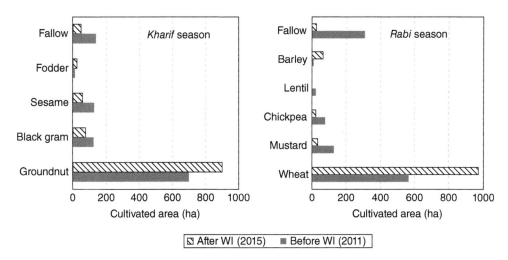

Fig. 7.11. Change in cropping pattern due to watershed interventions (WI) during *kharif* and *rabi* seasons.

7.5 NRM Interventions Implemented in Muduvatti Watershed

7.5.1 Entry point activity

Formation of watershed committee

Several village-level meetings were conducted with farmers and the watershed committee was formed with 15 members representing each village, women and small farmers. Along with watershed committee members, panchayat members and farmers participated in identification of constraints and preparation of work plan for the various possible watershed interventions to alleviate the constraints to enhance water resources and agricultural productivity while minimizing degradation of natural resources. Transparency at every step established good rapport and resulted in large and active participation of the village community in watershed management and development.

Soil fertility assessment

Soil health degradation is an important issue and studies show that most of the farmers are affected by it. As good soil health is a prerequisite to strengthen agri-based enterprises and this intervention fits well in the criteria of a good entry point activity, it may prove to be a very effective entry point intervention. Based on stratified soil sampling method (Sahrawat *et al.*, 2008), 70 soil samples were collected and analysed.

Farmers' fields were found severely deficient in organic carbon (84%), S (73%) and B (61%) (Table 7.8). Soil fertility status was shared with farmers through village-level meeting during awareness-building programmes and by writing the information on walls of common buildings. Further, soil fertility information was used to provide village-wise and crop-wise fertilizer recommendation. Moreover, demonstrations were conducted in farmers' fields with these recommendations.

7.5.2 Rainwater harvesting

Rainwater harvesting is the most-needed activity in this watershed to improve water recharge as well as groundwater quality. Various soil conservation and groundwater recharge structures were constructed (Fig. 7.14) and these included farm ponds (28), field bunding (8800 m), gully plugs (75) and ponds for cattle (Table 7.9). As the watershed has low potential of runoff in waterways, major focus was on construction of farm ponds to harvest the runoff from individual fields of farmers. These farm ponds have been very beneficial in terms of storage of water after percolation. All the water-harvesting structures constructed increased the storage capacity by 13,500 m³ resulting in total 33,750 m³ rainwater harvested (assuming 2–3 times filling) in a season depending on the rainfall during the year. A success story is described in Box 7.1.

Vegetation cover (February 2011)   **Vegetation cover (February 2014)**

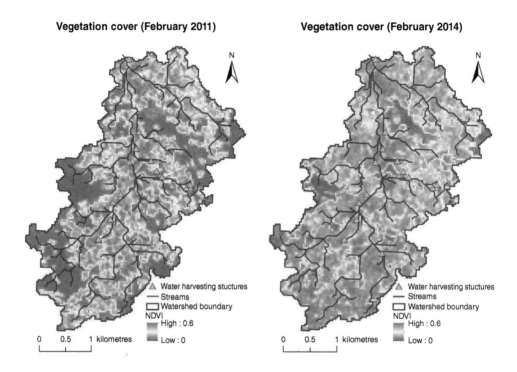

Vegetation cover (February 2015)

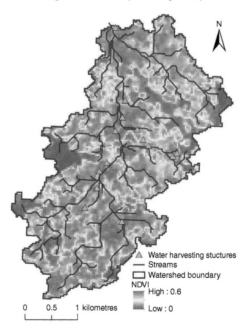

Fig. 7.12. Spatial maps of NDVI before NRM intervention (February 2011) and after intervention (February 2014 and February 2015) in Parasai-Sindh watershed. (Note: The dark red colour shows fallow area and green shows cropped area; triangles indicate various water-harvesting structures constructed across the stream network such as *haveli* renovation, check-dam and village pond.)

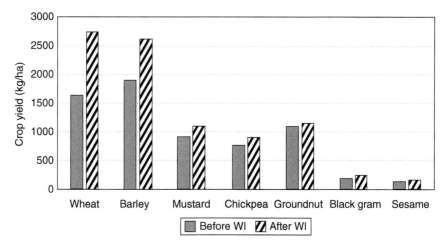

Fig. 7.13. Impact of watershed interventions (WI) on crop productivity.

Table 7.7. Impact of various natural resource management interventions on household (HH) income in project villages.

Details	Before interventions	After interventions	Difference
Kharif area under cultivation (ha)	968	1,057	89
Net income generated in *kharif* (₹ million)	13.8	20.3	6.5
Rabi area under cultivation (ha)	797	1,083	286
Net income generated in *rabi*[a] (₹ million)	−2.6	18.5	21.1
Total net income from agriculture (₹ million)	11.2	38.8	27.6
Buffalo population	950	1,300	350
Milk yield (l/day/animal)	6	8.5	2.5
Milk yield[b] (l/day)	2,850	5,525	2,675
Annual milk production cost (₹ million)	4.8	7.8	3
Annual income from livestock[c] (₹ million)	10.2	21.2	11
Total net income (₹ million/year)	21.4	60	38.6
Number of HHs	417	417	Nil
Average increase in income (₹/HH/year)	51,000	143,000	92,000

[a]Imputed cost of HH labour included.
[b]50% of the total buffaloes providing milk.
[c]150 days lactation period.

Table 7.8. Soil health status: percentage of farmer's fields deficient in nutrients in watershed villages.

Village	Percentage of farmers' fields deficient					
	Organic carbon	Phosphorus	Potassium	Sulfur	Zinc	Boron
Jangalahalli	75	0	0	75	0	38
Dandiganahalli	88	0	13	88	0	88
Konepura	100	0	13	100	0	88
Muduvatti	67	0	0	0	0	0
Nernahally	86	0	0	71	0	71
Papenahalli	80	0	0	20	0	20
Shettiganahalli	81	6	6	69	0	63
Shettikothanur	87	7	33	87	0	67

Fig. 7.14. Soil and water conservation structures established in project villages: (a) farm pond at Konepura; (b) trench bund at Dandiganahalli.

Table 7.9. Rainwater harvesting structures created in project villages.

Rainwater-harvesting structures	No. of structures				No. of beneficiaries
	2013–14	2014–15	2015–16	Total	
Farm pond	6	15	7	28	28
Cattle pond	1	1	–	2	65
Check-dam	–	–	4	4	40
Vermicomposting unit	–	3	26	29	29
Silage	–	–	4	4	4
Rooftop rainwater harvesting	–	–	3	3	3
Animal drinking water tank	–	–	7	7	350
Gully plugs	–	64	11	75	–
Bunding[a]	–	1800	7000	8800	–

[a]Bunding in m.

7.5.3 Productivity enhancement interventions

Field trials were conducted to demonstrate the impact of application of micronutrients (Zn and B) on groundnut and finger millet. Crop cutting experiments were conducted for estimating crop yield in improved and farmer-managed field practices. Farmers contributed 50% of fertilizer cost (agribor (B) and zinc sulphate ($ZnSO_4$)). Application of B and Zn increased crop yields by 23–26% over control plots (Table 7.10). Apart from field crops, bund plantation was done in the watershed with 3812 horticultural plants covering 15 ha benefiting 68 farmers and forestry species of about 4000 plants of silver oak, *Gliricidia* and neem covering 20 ha benefiting 30 farmers.

7.5.4 Livestock-related activities

Watershed villages had good number of milch animals so the watershed committee had suggested to provide assistance on livestock management for improving the milk yield. In this context, key initiatives started under the project were structures for drinking water storage, animal health camps, demonstrations of silage preparation, fodder production, etc. Forage production in the watershed improved through introduction of fodder purpose trees such as *Melia dubia* and silage for storing the fodder (see Box 7.2 for a success story). The Department of Animal Husbandry, Government of Karnataka has extended help through existing schemes for implementing these activities in the watershed villages.

Box 7.1. Watershed project helps farmer diversify activities and gain increased rewards.

In Jangalahalli village, progressive farmer Srinivas B, aged 40, proves the benefits of the watershed project through diversification in his farm. The farmer, who owns 2.4 ha of land in the village at present, is growing maize and napier grass in 0.6 ha, marigold in 0.2 ha and mango (Alphonso and Mallika varieties) in 1.6 ha. After the initiation of the project, the farmer decided to construct a farm pond through the project and the benefits have been extremely positive. After the farm pond construction, water availability improved drastically in comparison to other farmers' fields and Srinivas decided to grow fodder crops, such as maize and napier grass. He has also put a tarpaulin sheet as an impermeable lining in the farm pond to help retain more water.

Maize fodder and napier grass have increased the milk yield per cow by 3–4 l/day and from 5 milch animals the farmer could get about 100 litres per day, which resulted in net additional income of up to ₹27,600 per month. With 200 mango trees in 1.6 ha, the farmer now harvests about 2 tons per year, with net income of ₹43,000 per year.

Table 7.10. Impact of balanced micronutrient application with improved variety on groundnut and finger millet during *kharif*.

Variety	Treatment[a]	Yield[b] (kg/ha)	Year
Groundnut	Improved practice: ICGV 91114	1780 (14)	2012
	(RDF + agribor + zinc sulphate)	2450 (26)	2013
	Local variety: Farmers' practice (RDF)	1560	2012
		1950	2013
Finger millet	Improved practice: GPU 28 (with two irrigations)	2650 (17)	2012
	(RDF + agribor + zinc sulphate)	2860 (23)	2013
		740 (26)	2015
	Local variety: Farmers' practice (RDF)	2260	2012
		2320	2013
		580	2015

[a]RDF = Recommended dose of fertilizers.
[b]Figures in parentheses are percentage values of increase over control.

Box 7.2. Use of micronutrients and reduction of inorganic fertilizers helps farmer Muniswamy reap large rewards.

Muniswamy, a panchayat member and his wife, the watershed committee treasurer, have played pivotal roles in making the project a success. The couple, who own 2 ha of land in Konepura village, mainly practise dryland farming on their land and were dependent on finger millet for their income. After the project team visited their fields, they decided to apply micronutrients and used the recommended amounts of 12 kg zinc sulphate, 4 kg borax and 100 kg gypsum per hectare. The results have been phenomenal: the dependence on inorganic fertilizers such as diammonium phosphate has been reduced to 18 kg per ha from 100 kg per ha and urea to 36 kg per ha from 100 kg per ha.

The yield of finger millet increased by 1230 kg/ha and the farmer harvested 2470 kg/ha and sold at ₹21 per kg. Having had severe labour shortage, the farmer decided to share the labour in the field and thus expenditure on harvesting has reduced, spending only ₹24,700 per ha as overall expenditure. The net income generated for 2.02 ha is ₹65,000 for finger millet alone and earlier it used to be only ₹20,000–25,000 for 2 ha.

The project has also enabled the farmer to try methods such as mango–finger millet intercrop and with the increased income the farmer has diversified his goat-rearing business and also his small dairy unit. By selling the lambs, he earns almost ₹100,000 additional income per year and also after planting 50 *Melia dubia* saplings as a part of the project, milk yields have increased to 8 litres per day per cow after feeding the leaves as compared to 6 litres per day per cow before feeding *M. dubia* leaves. The monthly expenditure on the dairy unit is ₹15,000 and the net income generated from 4 HF crossbred cows is approximately ₹8000 to ₹10,000 per month.

7.5.5 Waste management: recycling, recovery and reuse

Composting the crop residue and animal waste

Along with multinutrient deficiencies, low levels of soil organic carbon due to soil mismanagement and misuse are the major stumbling blocks for realization of productivity potential. Soil organic carbon plays a major role in soil health improvement through influencing soil chemical, physical and biological properties. So practices that add organic matter into soil need to be promoted. Considering the availability of large quantities of on-farm wastes, there are opportunities to promote composting for soil health improvement and also cost-cutting of chemical fertilizers. Traditional composting (farmers' practices of heaping straw and dung) is very time-consuming and relatively less effective. In such a case, using half-decomposed compost/manure/plant residue creates many plant nutrient and pest-related problems rather than benefits. Vermicomposting (using earthworms) and aerobic composting (using microbial consortia culture) are tested technologies to effectively recycle on-farm wastes to produce quality compost for use in crop production. Vermicomposting has been done with 19 farmers with vermi-bed size of 3 m × 1 m × 1 m, which can prepare 10–12 tons of manure in 8–10 weeks.

Wastewater treatment and safe reuse of treated wastewater for improving water productivity

The rationale behind developing a decentralized wastewater treatment (DWAT) system is water scarcity, direct use of wastewater in agriculture is not good for farmers and consumers, disposal of untreated wastewater pollutes the environment, and all localities do not have sewage treatment plants. Wastewater treatment should be linked with integrated watershed development programme at field and community scale (500–1000 ha) (Wani *et al.*, 2015). A combination of wastewater treatment and integrated water resources management is helpful not only in enhancing crop production and income of smallholders but also in improving the water quality of groundwater wells and downstream water bodies and better soil quality through carbon sequestration. Phytoremediation technology in the form of constructed wetlands was adopted to treat the wastewater. The treatment capacity of the established constructed wetland is approximately 5 m³ per day (Fig. 7.15).

Fig. 7.15. Constructed wetland in Dandiganahalli for treating domestic wastewater.

7.5.6 Income-generating activities

Several SHG activities have been adopted to improve the livelihoods with convergence and linkage of banks to SHG members for financial support. The watershed project coordinated to train 13 SHG members on tailoring by Community Management Resource Centre of MYRADA and linked SHGs to banks for financial support to buy sewing machines to improve their livelihood. One such woman, Ms Pavitra, was linked to National Bank for Agriculture and Rural Development (NABARD) through the project and procured a loan to buy one sewing machine. She also obtained free training on tailoring for 3 months. During marriages and festivals, she gets many orders and her income has increased by ₹4000 per month due to stitching alone. Similarly, the watershed project has facilitated farmers (11 groups consisting of 15 members in each group) to avail themselves of a loan from NABARD for the purchase of milch animals. To encourage women farmers to improve home nutrition and additional income, 300 fruit plants were distributed on the occasion of the International Women's Day celebration.

7.5.7 Capacity building

Awareness among the village/farming community regarding the solutions to achieve food and water as well as environmental security was very poor. For example, majority of smallholders are following the traditional agricultural practices that are not sustainable to cope with climate change and increasing food demand. The awareness-building programmes such as farmers' field day, environment day in schools, exposure visits to progressive farming communities or research institutes, etc. were conducted to bring new knowledge to the community and to create supportive environment for introduction of new interventions (Table 7.11).

Farmer-to-farmer video dissemination

In addition to conventional methods of information dissemination a farmer-to-farmer dissemination route was explored through a farmer-centric video documentation (Fig. 7.16) in collaboration with Digital Green (http://www.digitalgreen.org) (Patil *et al.*, 2016). The processed videos were used for screening during the village-level meeting. The battery-operated portable projectors (PICO projector) along with necessary accessories were provided to NGO staff. The project team screened the video to a small gathering (20–30 farmers) in villages. At the end of the video, the farmer facilitator collected feedback from farmers regarding previous videos. The feedback system also captures the adaptation rate of screened technologies. Thirteen videos were produced by ICRISAT staff and were screened in target villages, which benefited 400 farmers.

Acknowledgements

Authors acknowledge the Coca-Cola India Foundation for providing the funding support at Jhansi and Kolar districts; also Ms Parvati Krishnan for support during project implementation phase. The authors acknowledge the village-level watershed committees and men and women farmers for their active participation; and CAFRI, ICRISAT and MYRADA scientists/staff for designing, implementation of various watershed interventions, monitoring and data recording.

Table 7.11. Capacity development programmes conducted in watershed villages.

Description	No. of programmes	No. of beneficiaries
Farmers' training	11	366
International Women's Day	2	350
World Environment Day	2	210
Video production and dissemination	13	401
National Women's Day at ICRISAT	1	13
Training to SHGs	29	486
Visit to Kamasamudra watershed (milk federation)	5	42
Visit to ICRISAT	1	14

Fig. 7.16. Project staff recording a video in a farmer's field.

References

Garg, K.K., Karlberg, L., Barron, J., Wani, S.P. and Rockström J. (2011) Assessing impacts of agricultural water interventions in the Kothapally watershed, Southern India. *Hydrological Processes* 26(3), 387–404.

Patil, M.D., Anantha, K.H. and Wani, S.P. (2016) Digital technologies for agricultural extension. In: Raju, K.V. and Wani, S.P (eds) *Harnessing Dividends from Drylands: Innovative Scaling up with Soil Nutrients*. CAB International, Wallingford, Oxfordshire, pp. 99–115.

Sahrawat, K.L., Rego, T.J., Wani, S.P. and Pardhasaradhi, G. (2008) Sulfur, boron and zinc fertilization effects on grain and straw quality of maize and sorghum grown on farmers' fields in the semi-arid tropical region of India. *Journal of Plant Nutrition* 31, 1578–1584.

Singh, R., Garg, K.K., Wani, S.P., Tewari, R.K. and Dhyani, S.K. (2014) Impact of water management interventions on hydrology and ecosystem services in Garhkundar-Dabar watershed of Bundelkhand region, Central India. *Journal of Hydrology* 509, 132–149.

Tyagi, R.K. (1997) *Grassland and Fodder, Atlas of Bundelkhand*. Indian Grassland and Fodder Research Institute, Jhansi, India.

Wani, S.P., Sreedevi, T.K., Rockström, J. and Ramakrishna, Y.S. (2009) Rainfed agriculture – past trends and future prospects. In: Wani, S.P., Rockström, J. and Oweis, T. (eds) *Rainfed Agriculture: Unlocking the Potential*. Comprehensive Assessment of Water Management in Agriculture Series. CAB International, Wallingford, Oxfordshire, pp. 1–35.

Wani, S.P., Garg, K.K., Singh, A.K. and Rockström, J. (2012) Sustainable management of scarce water resource in tropical rainfed agriculture. In: Lal, R. and Stewart, B.A. (eds) *Soil Water and Agronomic Productivity*. Advances in Soil Science. CRC Press, Boca Raton, FL, pp. 347–408.

Wani, S.P., Patil, M., Datta, A. and Tilak, A. (2015) Decentralized wastewater treatment system for safe reuse as rural business model in rural area. 26th Euro-mediterranean Regional Conference and Workshops (ICID), 12th–15th October, Montpellier, France.

8 Scaling-up of Science-led Development – Sir Dorabji Tata Trust Initiative

GIRISH CHANDER,* P. PATHAK, SUHAS P. WANI, G. PARDHASARADHI AND S.K. DASGUPTA

International Crops Research Institute for the Semi-Arid Tropics, Patancheru, India

Abstract

Soil health mapping in Sir Dorabji Tata Trust-supported initiative across 16 districts of Madhya Pradesh and Rajasthan, India showed widespread deficiencies of sulfur, boron, zinc and phosphorus. Soil test-based balanced nutrient management recorded yield benefit of 10–40%, while the integrated nutrient approach recorded still higher yield up to 20–50% along with 25–50% saving in chemical fertilizers through promotion of on-farm vermicomposting. Maximum yield advantage (90–200%) was realized with improved varieties and nutrient management. Other advantages included food/fodder nutrition, rainwater use efficiency, more food per kg of nitrogen or phosphorus, and residual benefits of micro/secondary nutrients and vermicompost. Promoting land-form management enabled farmers to cultivate rainy season fallows and harvest 1270–1700 kg/ha soybean. *In-situ* and *ex-situ* rainwater management interventions improved surface and groundwater availability and irrigated area with marked reduction in crop failures in the catchment areas. Women mainstreaming was targeted through livelihood options like nutri-kitchen gardens, fodder promotion for livestock, seed banks, composting and dal-processing. The initiative built capacities of about 30,000 farmers through direct interventions and of around 4–5 times more farmers through information dissemination.

8.1 Project Background

8.1.1 Why the project?

The actual yields from rainfed agriculture have remained quite low as compared to yields achievable because of the fact that rainfed regions have been bypassed since green revolution era (Wani *et al.*, 2016). Studies focused in Rajasthan, Madhya Pradesh and other semi-arid regions of India show that there are large yield gaps of 850 to 1320 kg/ha in soybean, 1180 to 2010 kg/ha in groundnut, 610 to 1150 kg/ha in chickpea, 680 to 1040 kg/ha in pearl millet, 460 kg/ha in mustard and 70 kg/ha in wheat (Bhatia *et al.*, 2006; Murty *et al.*, 2007; Aggarwal *et al.*, 2008). A long-term experiment (since 1976) at International Crops Research Institute for the Semi-Arid Tropics (ICRISAT), based at Patancheru, India has demonstrated a virtuous cycle of persistent yield increases up to 5 times through improved land, water and nutrient management in rainfed agriculture (Wani *et al.*, 2003, 2011a, 2015a).

* Corresponding author: g.chander@cgiar.org

In this context, Sir Dorabji Tata Trust (SDTT) supported ICRISAT to undertake farmer participatory action research for improving rural livelihoods and minimizing land degradation in dryland areas of assured rainfall ecoregion of Madhya Pradesh and Rajasthan. The specific objectives were as follows.

(i) To enhance productivity and reduce land degradation in target districts.
(ii) To use these sites as centres of learning for scaling-out the benefits.
(iii) Capacity building of lead farmers, development workers and consortium partners in the target region.

The initiative of the Tata-ICRISAT-ICAR (Indian Council of Agricultural Research) project during 2000 to 2013 demonstrated the power of science-led development model for improving agricultural productivity and income of the rural poor in India (see Chapter 2 in this volume). The initiative of the Tata-ICRISAT-ICAR project during 2000–2007 showed the proof of concept and piloted the power of science-led development model for improving agricultural productivity and income of the rural poor in three districts, namely Bundi in Rajasthan, and Guna and Vidisha in Madhya Pradesh. During the second phase, in addition to scaling-up in three districts, the programme was extended to nine districts in Madhya Pradesh and seven districts in Rajasthan

for developing the sites of learning and capacity building of stakeholders.

8.1.2 Pilot site details in Rajasthan and Madhya Pradesh

The target ecoregions for this project were the dryland areas of Madhya Pradesh and eastern Rajasthan with assured rainfall, with medium water-holding-capacity soils. Specifically, the seven target districts in Rajasthan were Alwar (Rajgarh block), Banswara (Kushalgarh block), Bhilwara (Jahajpur block), Bundi (Hindoli block), Jhalawar (Jhalarpatal block), Sawai Madhopur (Khandar block) and Tonk (Deoli and Newai blocks). The nine districts in Madhya Pradesh were Barwani (Barwani block), Guna (Madusudangarh block), Indore (Samer block), Raisen (Silwani), Rajgarh (Rajagarh block), Sagar (JC Nagar block), Sehore (Sehore block), Shajapur (Agar block) and Vidisha (Vidisha, Lateri blocks) (Fig. 8.1).

Agriculture is the predominant occupation of its inhabitants and the dismal state of affairs in agriculture is mainly responsible for poor farm-based livelihoods. Depletion of the resource base diminishes the capabilities of poor farmers to earn more and making them vulnerable to drought and other climate-related disasters. As there is evidence that every 1% increase in

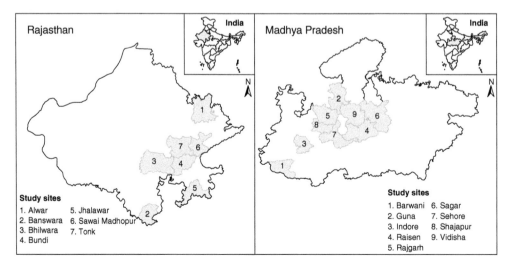

Fig. 8.1. Study sites in Rajasthan and Madhya Pradesh states of India.

agricultural yields translates to a 0.6% to 1.2% decrease in the percentage of absolute poor (Thirtle *et al.*, 2002), addressing the issue of agricultural development in these neglected regions is much more important today than ever before as agriculture in such regions has a key role to play in economic development and poverty reduction (Irz and Roe, 2000).

The rainfall in Madhya Pradesh varies from 770 to 1690 mm per year and soils are predominantly black soils (Vertisols and Vertic Inceptisols) and loamy soils (Alfisols) varying in soil depth. Major crops grown in the region are soybean, sorghum, maize, rice, pigeonpea, wheat and chickpea. The length of growing period (LGP) varies from 90 to 180 days and in some cases extends up to 210 days. This ecoregion has the potential to grow two crops (200% cropping intensity) with supplemental irrigation during the post-rainy season. However, irrespective of this, only 120–130% cropping intensity is observed in Madhya Pradesh. The groundwater table is depleting every year and at the same time causing severe land degradation. In Madhya Pradesh, due to perceived fear of waterlogging and risk of reduced yields of post-rainy season crops, farmers leave 2 million ha land fallow during the rainy season. In eastern Rajasthan, the soils are mostly red and black with the rainfall varying from 660 to 1025 mm per annum. The LGP in eastern Rajasthan varies from 90 to 150 days and the main crops grown are pearl millet, sorghum, maize, wheat, chickpea, mustard and sesame.

8.1.3 Cropping systems and production scenario in Rajasthan

In the cropping pattern of Rajasthan, pearl millet, maize, soybean and groundnut are important rainy season crops. In terms of pearl millet area (6.98 million ha) and production (8.06 million t) in India during 2015–16, Rajasthan stands on the top among all states by covering about 57.9% of total acreage and 43.8% of production at national level (Government of India, 2016). In spite of the highest acreage (4.04 million ha) and production (3.53 million t) of pearl millet in Rajasthan, low productivity is an issue of concern. Maize is grown in 0.88 million ha

with a production of 1.21 million t and contributes 10.1% in acreage and 5.55% in production to all India level, with lowest productivity compared to national level. For the country as such, soybean and groundnut together contribute about 60% of total oilseed production (Government of India, 2016). Rajasthan contributes 10.3% (1.20 million ha) in acreage and 11.6% (1 million t) in production of soybean at country level; and 11.4% (0.52 million ha) in acreage and 15.6% (1.06 million t) in production of groundnut in the country. Being the cheapest source of high quality protein (40%), soybean has potential to play an important role in mitigating the large-scale problem of protein malnutrition, particularly in children and women in the rural areas of the state. Its oil content (18%) is second only to groundnut among food legumes. Similarly, groundnut seeds contain high quality edible oil (50%), easily digestible protein (25%) and carbohydrates (20%). Moreover, both soybean and groundnut are legume crops which help in improving soil health, and hence have an important role in fitting in the cropping system mainly during the rainy season and sustaining soil fertility in the drylands of Rajasthan.

Among post-rainy season crops, wheat, rapeseed/mustard and chickpea are the most important crops of Rajasthan covering 3.11, 2.55 and 0.94 million ha respectively (Government of India, 2016). Mustard/rapeseed in India (5.76 million ha, 6.82 million t) is grown mainly in northern and eastern India. Only one-third of the total mustard area in India is rainfed. Rajasthan ranks highest covering about 44.3% area and 47.9% production at national level, which indicates the importance of the crop in the state. The leguminous crop chickpea has been a preferred crop in low-input traditional production systems because of its minimal dependence on monetary inputs of nitrogen (N) and phosphorus (P) fertilizers, irrigation and agrochemicals in general. It is a valuable source of protein for the poor population and a source of livelihood for the small and marginal farmers in India and other developing countries. Also, chickpea is a suitable legume crop for the cropping system during the post-rainy season and thus contributes to soil health improvement and sustains soil fertility, particularly in drylands.

8.1.4 Cropping systems and production scenario in Madhya Pradesh

In the cropping pattern of Madhya Pradesh, soybean, groundnut and mustard are the major oilseed crops (Wani *et al.*, 2016). Madhya Pradesh contributes the largest acreage (56%) and production (51%) of soybean at national level (Wani *et al.*, 2016). Low soybean productivity in the state in comparison to national level in spite of suitable agroclimatic conditions is a matter of concern. Groundnut is another important oilseed crop in India (5.31 million ha area, 6.93 million tons production) and Madhya Pradesh contributes significantly, about 4% of national acreage and about 5% of national production (Wani *et al.*, 2016). Among pulse crops, chickpea is one of the most important crops of India contributing about 44% of total pulse production, and Madhya Pradesh state contributes the highest (37%) to national chickpea acreage and 43% to national chickpea production (Wani *et al.*, 2016).

Among cereals, wheat, maize, rice and nutri (coarse) cereals fit in the cropping system in Madhya Pradesh, and their lower productivity mainly due to poor management is an issue of concern. Wheat is cultivated during the post-rainy season and Madhya Pradesh ranks after Uttar Pradesh in acreage and Uttar Pradesh, Punjab and Haryana in production; and contributes to about 16% of national acreage and 11% of national production (Wani *et al.*, 2016). Wheat yields in different states vary tremendously due to different technologies adopted by the farmers and the agroclimatic characteristics of the region. Maize and rice are other important cereal crops grown widely in the state during the rainy season.

8.2 Institutional Arrangements and Modalities of Scaling-up

This project adopted collective working with lead non-governmental organizations (NGOs) in the region to reach out to the large number of farmers. The NGOs, ICRISAT entered into partnership in Madhya Pradesh included, BAIF Development Research Foundation, BYPASS and CARD. Similarly, in Rajasthan, ICRISAT entered into partnership with BAIF Development Research Foundation and DEEP Development Research Foundation Institute. In Rajasthan and Madhya Pradesh enhancing water-use efficiency of rainy season and post-rainy season crop trials for the project supported by Ministry of Water Resources, Government of India were also converged with the on-going programme in the selected districts.

Other collaborative partners included universities like Maharana Pratap University of Agriculture and Technology, Udaipur; Rajasthan Agricultural University, Bikaner; Jawaharlal Nehru Krishi Vishwa Vidyalaya, Jabalpur; and Rajmata Vijayaraje Scindia Krishi Vishwa Vidyalaya, Gwalior. National research institutes as partners included Indian Institute of Soil Science, Bhopal; National Research Centre for Soybean, Indore; Central Institute of Agricultural Engineering, Bhopal; Central Arid Zone Research Institute, Jodhpur; Central Research Institute for Dryland Agriculture, Hyderabad; and National Research Centre for Agroforestry, Jhansi. Jain Irrigation Ltd was among the key private-sector partners.

A state level coordination committee of partners led by ICRISAT monitored implementation of the initiative. Annual reviews and planning meetings of all partners were put in place to review the previous year's progress and make plans for the incoming year based on the learnings and opportunities available. During the year, progress was monitored through half-yearly and annual reports. Responsible ICRISAT scientists from headquarters and on-ground staff coordinated among the partners on a day-to-day basis, and for orientation/capacity building and progress updates on monthly basis.

8.3 Major Interventions

8.3.1 Mapping soil fertility degradation and management

Soil health mapping

To diagnose soil fertility-related constraints, soil samples were collected from farmers' fields in Madhya Pradesh and Rajasthan by adopting participatory stratified soil sampling method (see Chapter 3 in this volume) and analysed for diagnosing soil fertility-related constraints in a state-of-the-art laboratory in ICRISAT headquarter at Patancheru.

A soil health assessment of crop fields across districts in Madhya Pradesh showed 47–100% fields having adequate levels of soil organic carbon (C) (Table 8.1; Wani *et al.*, 2016). Except for the Sehore district, most (>50%) fields in general were sufficient in soil organic C and available N also. Similarly, most fields (55–75%) in Indore and Shajapur had adequate P levels; while the rest of the districts of Barwani, Guna Raisen, Rajgarh, Sagar, Sehore and Vidisha had only 8–40% fields sufficient in available P, indicating thus, deficiency in most of the fields. Available potassium (K) was sufficient in 95–100% fields and so not really a limiting nutrient to productivity enhancement. Across the districts, relatively few fields in general had adequate levels of sulfur (S) and micronutrients boron (B) and zinc (Zn), or, in other words, deficiency in most fields, which farmers are not aware of and that is not part of their fertilizer management practices, and so apparently holding back the realization of higher yields. Specifically, S was in adequate amounts in most fields in Indore (91% fields) and Shajapur (75% fields), but in the rest

of the districts only 4–47% fields had adequate S. Similarly, B was in adequate amounts in most fields in Indore (83% fields), while rest of the districts had only 5–50% fields with adequate B levels. Micronutrient Zn was in adequate amounts in most fields (60–78%) in Indore, Rajgarh, Sagar and Shajapur; while few fields (3–48%) had adequate Zn in Barwani, Guna, Raisen, Sehore and Vidisha.

In contrast to Madhya Pradesh, Rajasthan soils were relatively poor in soil organic C, particularly in Alwar, Sawai Madhopur and Tonk districts, where only few fields (16–33%) were adequate in soil organic C, and thus indicating deficiency in most fields and also low levels of available N (Table 8.1). The other districts of Banswara, Bhilwara, Bundi and Jhalawar had most fields (57–93%) with sufficient levels of soil C. Soils were critical in available P in Bundi, Sawai Madhopur and Tonk where only 27 to 47% fields tested with adequate amounts of P. Most fields (50–90%) in Alwar, Banswara, Bhilwara and Jhalawar were however, having adequate levels of P. Similar to Madhya Pradesh, the soil fertility-related degradation due to S, B and Zn was widespread in the districts in Rajasthan. Leaving aside Bhilwara district, only

Table 8.1. Soil health status of farmers' fields indicating sufficiency/adequacy of essential nutrients in Madhya Pradesh and Rajasthan states of India. From: Chander *et al.* (2013a,b); Wani *et al.* (2016).

District	No. of farmers	% of fields with adequate C	% of fields with adequate available nutrients				
			P	K	S	B	Zn
Madhya Pradesh							
Barwani	20	55	30	100	45	20	25
Guna	38	79	21	100	13	50	5
Indore	23	91	61	100	91	83	78
Raisen	20	70	10	100	10	10	10
Rajgarh	30	87	40	100	47	27	73
Sagar	32	91	22	100	37	9	66
Sehore	19	47	16	95	26	5	5
Shajapur	20	90	75	100	75	20	60
Vidisha	72	68	8	100	4	7	3
Rajasthan							
Alwar	30	33	90	100	37	13	17
Banswara	30	57	50	83	30	0	20
Bhilwara	30	83	60	83	57	53	63
Bundi	36	61	47	50	28	28	33
Jhalawar	30	93	70	100	13	23	40
Sawai Madhopur	44	16	27	93	14	48	59
Tonk	78	28	45	68	21	36	6

13–37% fields tested adequate in S, and 0–48% fields in B. Similarly with exception of Bhilwara and Sawai Madhopur, only 6–40% fields tested adequate in available Zn. In Bhilwara district, however, majority fields tested with adequate levels of S (57% fields), B (53% fields) and Zn (63% fields); while in Sawai Madhopur most fields (59%) tested had adequate levels of Zn.

In other parts of semi-arid tropics (SAT) also, soil fertility-related degradation (Sahrawat *et al.*, 2010; Wani *et al.*, 2011b; Chander *et al.*, 2012; Wani *et al.*, 2015a,b, 2016), in addition to water scarcity, has been identified as the main cause for low crop yields and inefficient utilization of production resources. This corrective fertilizer management strategy to address soil fertility-related degradation apparently is the building stone to realize achievable yields. Lack of awareness about soil health status leads farmers into fertilizer use which rarely matches soil needs and hence an uneconomic and inefficient practice from a sustainability point of view as well.

Soil health management for enhanced crop and water productivity

Based on soil analysis results and variable soil fertility across the region, fertilizer recommendations were developed and promoted in the target regions. In this initiative, soil test-based fertilizer recommendations were designed at block level by considering practical aspects such as available infrastructure, human power and economics in research for impact for smallholders in the Indian SAT. The deficient secondary and micronutrient inputs were arranged on 50% incentives for the participatory trials/demonstrations with the farmers, which were applied by following either of two options, i.e. full dose once in two years or half dose every year. For soil C building, recycling of on-farm wastes through composting was promoted and also to bring in 25–50% saving in chemical fertilizers by the farmers. Around 1000–1500 trials/demonstrations were conducted in target regions during the project period during each of the rainy and post-rainy seasons and random crop cuttings were done along with data collection from farmers to evaluate the benefits.

The first phase during 2002–7 showed proof-of-concept and pilot testing of benefits of soil test-based balanced nutrition (BN) in crops, while during the second phase (2008–12), it was scaled-up to develop sites of learning in adjoining districts. In Madhya Pradesh, soybean productivity significantly increased with BN over farmers' practice (12–25%) (Table 8.2; Chander *et al.*, 2013a). However, the substitution of 50% of chemical fertilizers with vermicompost as integrated nutrient management (INM) further increased yields over BN with nutrients applied solely through chemical fertilizers. Soybean productivity increased by 17% to 50%, as compared

Table 8.2. Effect of nutrient management on soybean grain yield, benefit–cost ratio and rainwater use efficiency under rainfed conditions in Madhya Pradesh during 2010 and 2011.[a] From: Chander *et al.* (2013a).

District	Grain yield (kg/ha)				Benefit–cost ratio		Rainwater use efficiency (kg/mm/ha)		
	FP	BN	INM	LSD (5%)	BN	INM	FP	BN	INM
2010									
Guna	1270	1440	1580	34	1.31	4.58	1.76	1.99	2.19
Raisen	1360	1600	1600	115	1.85	3.55	1.76	2.07	2.07
Shajapur	1900	2120	2410	69	2.99	10.2	3.45	3.85	4.38
Vidisha	1130	1410	1700	640	2.16	8.43	1.48	1.84	2.22
2011									
Guna	1370	1560	1600	169	1.47	3.4	0.83	0.95	0.97
Shajapur	1220	1400	1510	44	2.45	5.8	1.12	1.28	1.38
Vidisha	1190	1380	1460	91	1.47	3.99	0.88	1.02	1.08

[a]Note: FP = Farmers' practice (application of N, P and K only); BN = Balanced nutrition (FP inputs plus S + B + Zn); and INM = Integrated nutrient management (50% BN inputs + vermicompost).

with farmers' standard practice. A cost–benefit analysis showed BN as an economically remunerative option and INM as a still better option. Rainwater use efficiency (RWUE) which indicates quantity (kg) of food produced per unit (mm) of rainfall per unit area (ha) also enhanced under improved management. The INM practice recorded 0.97 to 4.38 kg/mm/ha followed by BN at 0.95 to 3.85 kg/mm/ha as compared with farmers' practice with lowest RWUE of 0.83 to 3.45 kg/mm/ha. Similar benefits were recorded with other crops in the region. Water is a scarce resource and chief determinant of poverty and hunger in rural dryland areas. So improving RWUE is important for achieving food security and better livelihoods. Lack of good rainwater and other management practices in the target region is one of the factors for low RWUE. Soil fertility degradation is also one of the major

limitations to effectively use available rainwater and other resources in crop production leading to low rainwater and other resource use efficiency. The results from the present on-farm study thus proved very clearly that soil fertility management, with a purpose to increase proportion of water balance as productive transpiration, is one of the most important rainwater management strategies to improve yields and water productivity (Rockström et al., 2010).

Similarly, in Rajasthan, BN showed significant yield advantage of 15–40% in maize, 10–20% in pearl millet, 14–17% in groundnut and 6–22% in soybean (Table 8.3; Chander et al., 2013a). The INM option either maintained the yields at par with balanced nutrition solely through chemical fertilizers or increased over it. An economic analysis showed the benefit-cost ratio of BN in the range of 1.59–4.28 for

Table 8.3. Effect of nutrient management on crop yield, benefit–cost ratio and rainwater use efficiency under rainfed conditions in Rajasthan.[a] From: Chander et al. (2013a).

District	Grain yield (kg/ha)			LSD (5%)	Benefit–cost ratio		Rainwater use efficiency (kg/mm/ha)		
	FP	BN	INM		BN	INM	FP	BN	INM
2010									
Maize									
Banswara	2850	3390	3620	780	2.45	5.8	4.85	5.77	6.16
Sawai Madhopur	1560	2180	2530	268	4.28	8.24	2.31	3.23	3.75
Tonk	2840	3350	3560	280	2.32	5.08	4.21	4.96	5.27
Pearl millet									
Sawai Madhopur	1410	1590	1700	234	1.12	2.42	2.09	2.36	2.52
Tonk	2210	2560	2800	325	1.43	3.66	3.27	3.79	4.15
Groundnut									
Tonk	820	960	1060	107	1.78	5.84	1.21	1.42	1.57
Soybean									
Jhalawar	1700	1810	2020	82	0.85	3.96	3.04	3.23	3.61
2011									
Maize									
Banswara	2410	3290	3140	1456	4	5.5	2.44	3.33	3.18
Sawai Madhopur	2330	2700	3000	324	2.55	5.69	3.12	3.61	4.02
Tonk	2410	2760	3060	378	1.59	4.59	3.07	3.51	3.89
Pearl millet									
Sawai Madhopur	1340	1470	1610	73	0.81	2.26	1.79	1.97	2.16
Tonk	1720	2060	2280	365	1.39	3.47	2.19	2.62	2.9
Groundnut									
Tonk	1340	1530	1660	142	2.42	7.79	1.7	1.95	2.11
Soybean									
Jhalawar	1940	2370	2620	307	3.32	8.42	1.85	2.26	2.5

[a]Note: FP = Farmers' practice (application of N, P and K only); BN = Balanced nutrition (FP inputs plus S + B + Zn); and INM = Integrated nutrient management (50% BN inputs + vermicompost).

maize, 0.81–1.43 for pearl millet, 1.78–2.42 for groundnut and 0.85–3.32 for soybean, while the benefit:cost ratio of INM option was far better than BN, viz. 4.59–8.24 for maize, 2.26–3.66 for pearl millet, 5.84–7.79 for groundnut and 3.96–8.42 for soybean. The INM practice also resulted in the most efficient use of scarce water resources by crops like maize, pearl millet, groundnut and soybean with RWUE of 1.57–6.16 kg/mm/ha. Balanced nutrition solely through chemical fertilizers was the next best option from RWUE point of view at 1.42–5.77 kg/mm/ha, while farmers' practice showed the lowest RWUE of 1.21–4.85 kg/mm/ha.

In participatory trials, soil test-based nutrient management showed resilience building of production system as evident from residual benefits of secondary and micronutrients. As an example, in Madhya Pradesh districts, the plots with applied S, B, Zn and vermicompost as BN and INM during the rainy season of 2010 showed significant residual benefits during the succeeding post-rainy season 2010–11 and rainy season 2011; the benefits were, however, more under INM. During post-rainy season 2010–11, wheat yields were higher by 12–26% and chickpea by 14–39% in the plots with INM (Chander *et al.*, 2013a). Similarly, in the rainy season 2011, soybean yields were higher by 9–33% under INM-treated plots. In target districts in Rajasthan, the residual benefits of rainy season 2010, applied S, B, Zn and vermicompost as BN and INM were studied in succeeding post-rainy season wheat and chickpea. As such, yield increase of 7–97% was recorded in INM-applied plots and 11–54% under BN-applied plots (Chander *et al.*, 2013a). The results clearly showed that the adoption of improved management of INM and BN options not only are economically remunerative during the season of application but also

lead to production system resilience building resulting in benefits in the succeeding seasons.

In this initiative, linkages with soil health and plant quality and soil health management served as an effective strategy to address micronutrient malnutrition through agronomic fortification of crops. Balanced nutrition and INM interventions in general tended to increase soybean grain nutrient contents over farmers' practice; the differences however, were insignificant except for S and Zn contents under the INM option (Chander *et al.*, 2013a).

8.3.2 Integrated rainwater management

Integrated rainwater management is one of the critical components for increasing and sustaining productivity in the project areas of Rajasthan and Madhya Pradesh. Currently only 40–60% of the rainfall is effectively used for crop production. Therefore, large numbers of *in-situ* (broad-bed and furrow (BBF), conservation furrow and contour cultivation) and *ex-situ* soil and water management interventions were implemented and evaluated in several districts of Madhya Pradesh (Raisen, Sagar, Vidisha, Bhopal, Indore and Guna) and Rajasthan (Bundi, Alwar and Sawai Madhopur). On-farm trials on *in-situ* water management of Vertisols of Central India revealed that BBF system resulted in a 35% yield increase in soybean during rainy season and yield advantage of 21% in chickpea during post-rainy season when compared with farmers' practice. Similar yield advantages were recorded in maize and wheat rotation under BBF system (Table 8.4). Yield advantage in rainfall use efficiency was also reflected in cropping systems involving soybean–chickpea, maize–chickpea and soybean/maize–chickpea under improved

Table 8.4. Effect of land configuration on productivity of soybean and maize-based system in the watersheds of Madhya Pradesh, 2001–2005.

| Watershed location | Crop | Grain yield (t/ha) | | Increase in yield (%) |
		Farmers' practice	BBF system[a]	
Vidisha and Guna	Soybean	1.27	1.72	35
	Chickpea	0.80	1.01	21
Bhopal	Maize	2.81	3.65	30
	Wheat	3.30	3.25	16

[a]BBF = Broad-bed and furrow.

land management systems. The rainfall use efficiency ranged from 10.9 to 11.6 kg/ha/mm under BBF system across various cropping systems compared with 8.2 to 8.9 kg/ha/mm with flat-on-grade system of cultivation on Vertisols (Table 8.5). Based on these findings about 675 improved farm implements and 32 training programmes at different locations were provided to farmers for scaling-up *in-situ* water management interventions on large areas of Madhya Pradesh.

Several *ex-situ* water management interventions (check-dams, percolation tanks, gully plugs, farm ponds, gabion structures, earthen check-dam, bore well and open well recharge pits, etc.) were implemented and evaluated in different watersheds of Madhya Pradesh and Rajasthan. These interventions have significantly improved both surface and groundwater availability in different cropping seasons (Fig. 8.2). It has resulted in significant increase in the irrigated area particularly during the post-rainy and summer seasons. There is a threefold increase in the mean pumping duration and substantial improvement in recovery or recharge period and the total area irrigated by wells during post-watershed interventions period (Table 8.6).

The integrated watershed management intervention at the Gokulpura-Goverdhanpura watershed in Bundi made significant impact on land use pattern (Table 8.7). It is evident that the area under irrigation had increased by 66% due to the increased water availability in the wells after the implementation of *in-situ* and *ex-situ* water management interventions. Area with supplemental irrigation increased drastically. This resulted in a marked reduction in crop failures in the watershed area and gave greater confidence to farmers to use improved agricultural inputs. In addition to this, about 35 ha land was brought under high-value horticulture with irrigation facility.

Table 8.5. Rainfall use efficiency (kg/ha/mm) of different cropping systems under improved land management practices in Bhopal, Madhya Pradesh.

Cropping system[a]	Flat-on-grade	Broad-bed and furrow
Soybean–chickpea	8.2	11.6
Maize–chickpea	8.9	11.6
Soybean/ maize–chickpea	8.9	10.9

[a]– = Sequential system; / = Intercropping system.

8.3.3 Improved crops, varieties and cropping systems

Promoting farmer-preferred crop varieties

Prevalence of low-yielding crop cultivars is one of the major reasons for low crop yields in target regions, and varietal replacement is a big opportunity for enhancing productivity and income levels of farmers. Under the initial phase of the

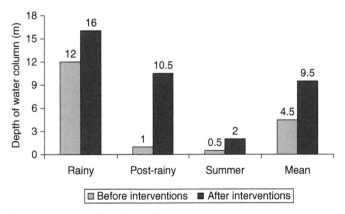

Fig. 8.2. Effect of various *ex-situ* water interventions on depth of water column in open wells during different cropping seasons in Gokulpura-Goverdhanpura watershed, Bundi, Rajasthan.

Table 8.6. Effect of watershed interventions on the performance of open wells in Gokulpura-Goverdhanpura watershed Bundi, Rajasthan.[a]

Season	Pumping duration (h)		Recharge/recovery period in well (h)		Area irrigated by one well (ha)	
	BWI	AWI	BWI	AWI	BWI	AWI
Rainy	4	11	13.5	10	1	2.5
Post-rainy	1.5	6.5	21	16	0.5	1.5
Summer	0	1	30	21	0	0.2
Mean	1.83	6.2	21.5	15.7	0.5	1.4

[a]BWI = Before watershed interventions; AWI = After watershed interventions.

Table 8.7. Land use pattern in Gokulpura-Goverdhanpura watershed, Bundi, Rajasthan.[a]

Land use system	Before watershed interventions (ha)	After watershed interventions (ha)
Irrigated	207 (15)	343 (25)
Rainfed	327 (24)	209 (15)
Pasture	167 (12)	114 (8)
Horticulture	0	35 (3)
Forest	360 (27)	360 (27)
Dwelling and river	294 (22)	294 (22)
Total	1355	1355

[a]Figures in parentheses are the percentage values of total area.

project, the benefits of improved cultivars were recorded in farmers' fields. Therefore, improved crop cultivars along with good management practices were promoted under the project initiative to bridge yield gaps in the target regions.

Participatory trials in Rajasthan showed that with maize crop across the districts, maize grain yield with farmers' standard practice (local cultivar and application of only NPK fertilizers) was 1150–2990 kg/ha (Table 8.8; Chander *et al.*, 2013b). Replacement of local cultivar with improved cultivar increased maize grain yield by 22–68%. But the practice of adopting the improved cultivar along with BN recorded the highest increase in grain yield, which varied from 92% to 204% over farmer's practice. It is thus evident that impoverished soils in the drylands need to be rejuvenated to harness the yield potential of improved cultivars. The benefit–cost ratio of the best technology in maize crop varied from 3.33 to 8.03, indicating economic viability for adoption at farm level. The additional profit

in adopting the best practice varied from ₹9910 to ₹29,890 per ha. The RWUE of existing farmers' cultivars with applied N and P in maize varied from 3.36 to 7.39 mg/kg/ha. The introduction of improved cultivar in on-farm trials in target districts increased RWUE from 5.43 to 10.8 mg/kg/ha, and thereby proved the ability of improved cultivar to best utilize the limiting water resources. The integrated approach involving soil test-based addition of secondary and micro-nutrients to improved cultivar, however, recorded the maximum RWUE (8.20 to 16.2 mg/kg/ha). The best practice also recorded increased stover yield of 58–165% over farmers' practice (Chander *et al.*, 2013b). Stover is used as cattle fodder, and thereby increased fodder availability translated into beneficial impacts on cattle-based livelihoods. Improvement in stover productivity in monetary terms ranged from ₹3500 (US$77.3) to ₹8100 (US$179) with an average of ₹6300 (US$139) per ha (Chander *et al.*, 2013b).

Similarly, the replacement of local pearl millet cultivar with improved cultivar increased grain yield by 46% in Tonk district and 54% in Sawai Madhopur district (Table 8.8; Chander *et al.*, 2013b). The adoption of best practice, however, enhanced pearl millet yield by 166% in Tonk and 115% in Sawai Madhopur. Similar yield improvement (150%) was also recorded with best practice in groundnut as compared with farmers' practice in Tonk district. Considering the net additional returns and benefit–cost ratio, pearl millet seems to be the best crop compared to groundnut for Tonk and Sawai Madhopur region because of low rainfall. The net additional returns with best practice varied from ₹6110 to ₹7620 for pearl millet and ₹1350 for groundnut cultivation. As in maize crop, the RWUE in pearl millet also increased from 2.72 to

Table 8.8. Effects of improved crop varieties and nutrient management practices on crop yield, benefit-cost (BC) ratio and rainwater use efficiency (RWUE) under rainfed conditions in Rajasthan, India.[a] From: Chander et al. (2013b).

District	Yield (kg/ha)					RWUE (kg/mm/ha)			
	FP	IC	IC+BN	LSD (5%)	BC ratio	FP	IC	IC+BN	LSD (5%)
Maize									
Tonk	1150	1930	3160	280	4.26	3.4	5.52	9.13	0.73
Sawai Madhopur	1430	2030	3000	420	3.33	4.1	5.77	8.59	0.95
Bundi	1380	2180	4240	714	6.05	3.6	5.68	10.93	1.68
Bhilwara	2990	4340	6510	860	7.45	7.4	10.8	16.15	1.69
Jhalawar	2550	3520	4960	316	5.11	4.2	5.82	8.2	0.52
Udaipur	2530	3090	6320	509	8.03	4.5	5.43	11.11	0.89
Pearl millet									
Tonk	810	1180	2160	212	3.4	2.7	3.93	7.2	0.59
Groundnut									
Tonk	300	550	750	140	1.15	0.9	1.69	2.28	0.38
Pearl millet									
Sawai Madhopur	1010	1560	2170	225	2.92	2.9	4.49	6.27	0.51

[a]Note: FP = Local cultivar + farmers' practice of application of N, P and K; IC = Improved cultivar + farmers' practice of application of N, P and K; and BN = Balanced nutrition (FP inputs plus S + B + Zn).

2.90 kg/mm/ha with farmers' practice to 6.27–7.20 kg/mm/ha under best management. In groundnut, RWUE increased from 0.92 kg/mm/ha under farmers' practice to 2.28 kg/mm/ha with best practice. A relative analysis of RWUE by crop plants in Rajasthan revealed that C4 crop plants (maize and pearl millet) are more efficient in contrast to counterpart C3 plants (groundnut) for better water productivity.

Intensification of rainy season fallows

There are regions in Madhya Pradesh where no crop is grown during rainy season primarily due to waterlogging (Wani et al., 2002, 2016). Traditionally farmers grow a secured post-rainy season crop on stored soil moisture and keep the fields fallow during rainy season. Three fundamental barriers to cropping in black soil region are: (i) threat of flooding of the rainy season crop due to heavy rains; (ii) difficulty of soil preparation prior to the monsoon for timely sowing of a rainy season crop; and (iii) reduction in available soil moisture for the post-rainy season crop. Soil degradation is also an important issue to be considered to take two good crops in a year. It is estimated that 2.02 million ha, accounting for

6.57% of the total area of the state, remains under rainy season fallows (Sreedevi et al., 2009). Madhya Pradesh in Central India is endowed with Vertisols and associated soils along with assured rainfall (700–1200 mm). The Vertisols contain high (40–60%) montmorillonite clay and exhibit typical swelling and shrinking characteristics under moist and dry conditions. Vertisols have poor hydraulic conductivity, and consequently are frequently poorly drained. Madhya Pradesh is endowed with well-distributed rains. Vertisols with good moisture-holding capacity can be used to grow short-duration soybean by adopting sound land management practices. This will help increase income to farmers besides preventing land degradation due to runoff erosion.

In rainy season fallow regions, the project interventions of landform management coupled with soil test-based balanced fertilization enabled farmers to grow and harvest good soybean yields during the rainy season (Table 8.9; Wani et al., 2016). The BBF landform management tended to prove superior over contour furrow. In the same plots, after taking rainy season crop with recommended technology, post-rainy season wheat and chickpea crops were also grown.

Table 8.9. Effects of landform management and balanced nutrition on soybean yield in rainy season fallow regions in Madhya Pradesh, rainy season 2010.[a] From: Wani *et al.* (2016).

District	No. of trials	Grain yield (kg/ha)			Straw yield (kg/ha)		
		CF + BN	BBF + BN	LSD (5%)	CF + BN	BBF + BN	LSD (5%)
Guna	21	1350	1450	210	2110	2310	226
Raisen	26	1270	1360	59	1930	2300	70
Indore	5	1600	1700	231	1730	1810	158
Vidisha	5	1340	1520	511	1440	1830	748

[a]Note: CF = Conservation furrow at 4–5 m distance; BBF = Broad-bed and furrow (1 m raised bed followed by 0.5 m furrow); and BN = Balanced nutrition (N, P, K plus S, B, Zn).

Results showed increased wheat and chickpea grain yields in rainy season fallow plots as compared to farmers' practice of growing only one crop (wheat or chickpea) in post-rainy season. These results are expected due to improved soil health as a result of soil test-based balanced nutrition during rainy season and more moisture storage due to appropriate landform management.

8.3.4   Forage production for promoting livestock-based livelihoods

On-farm fodder promotion

Rearing livestock is a common practice by farmers in target regions. However, fodder shortage is a major drawback for low productivity. Therefore under this project, seeds of forage crops such as fodder sorghum, lucern and berseem were distributed for forage cultivation. This helped to provide good quality fodder to animals. A large number of farm demonstrations (~25–75 each year) were arranged under this activity wherein farmers learnt to grow good quality fodder for their cattle and increase milk production which is especially in the domain of women and thus, contribute to increasing their incomes.

Wasteland management

Under the Tata–ICRISAT–ICAR initiative funded by SDTT, efforts were undertaken to demonstrate combating land degradation in Bundi district during the year 2000. The soils in selected pilot site in Thana, Govardhanpura and Gokulpura cluster of villages in Bundi district, eastern Rajasthan, India are degraded due to overgrazing. The total geographical area of this cluster is 1356 ha, of which common grazing land is 95 ha. BAIF Institute of Rural Development, an NGO partner, initially recognized the problem and engaged the community to demonstrate wasteland development interventions in half (45 ha) of the common grazing land. Villagers contributed labour to erect stone fencing in around 45 ha and construct soil and water conservation structures like gully plugs, percolation pits, contour and staggered trenches. With a rainwater-harvesting structure in place, useful grasses and saplings were planted, resulting in the establishment of good plantation despite consecutive droughts between 2000 to 2003.

A participatory assessment later showed that this management has led to abundance of grasses/fodder in the area and such conservation initiative has benefited all sections of society (Dixit *et al.*, 2005). In addition, biodiversity in the conserved plot increased tremendously. Rehabilitated grazing land got richer in floristic diversity as it contained 56 plant species (20 woody taxa, 36 herbacious species), while there were only 9 species in open degraded land. In addition, below ground microbial biodiversity assessed through collecting surface (0 to 0.15 m) soil samples recorded 32% higher microbial biomass carbon (460 vs 288 μg C g^{-1} soil) in rehabilitated land as compared to the degraded land. Biomass nitrogen was 37% higher (37.8 vs 25.4 μg N g^{-1} soil) in rehabilitated land. Similarly, the population of bacteria (10 × 10^4 vs 8.8 × 10^4 cfu g^{-1} soil), fungi (37 × 10^3 vs 15 × 10^2 cfu g^{-1} soil), actinomycetes (57 × 10^3 vs 35 × 10^3 cfu g^{-1} soil) were found significantly higher in rehabilitated grazing lands than in degraded grazing lands. Further higher diversity in microbial population was found in samples from rehabilitated land compared to the degraded land.

8.3.5 Other income-generating activities

Along with strengthening natural soil and water resources, efforts were placed to strengthen livelihoods of farmers and especially mainstreaming of women through certain targeted activities. Women farmers were trained in kitchen gardens, recycling agricultural wastes through vermicomposting, raising nurseries for biological N fixing-trees, producing improved seed and establishing a village seed bank, dal processing, etc. All these activities were promoted through women collectively as self-help groups (SHGs) and thrift saving activities. Major livelihood activities promoted in project sites to show these as learning sites were kitchen gardening, vermicomposting and biomass generation, and seed bank.

Kitchen gardening

Under this activity, especially the women farmers were guided and supported to grow vegetables in a small area or as kitchen garden (10–100 m²) to improve family nutrition and capture the market-led opportunities. The demand-driven seeds of vegetables such as brinjal, tomato, okra, cabbage, cauliflower, etc. were provided during the initiative by ICRISAT along with required capacity building and other inputs like soil test-based nutrients. Demonstrations of vegetables along with needs-based micro/secondary nutrients were done with 200 new women farmers every year to strengthen their skills which resulted in high yields and benefits in income and family nutrition.

Vermicomposting and biomass generation

Vermicompost pits (~100 functioning) were constructed at project locations as sites of learning and farmers were encouraged to apply the produced vermicompost in their fields to maintain soil health. The benefits were documented as increased crop yields and savings in chemical fertilizers.

Under the SDTT project, biomass generation was promoted in villages which had less population of cattle and thereby having less dung and compost. Seeds of *Gliricidia* were provided to farmers each year to grow seedlings to cover 10–50 ha as learning sites. Leaves of

Gliricidia contain N (2.4%), P (0.1%), K (1.8%), calcium and magnesium and they add various plant nutrients and organic matter to the soil, and increase crop productivity of unproductive soils.

Seed bank

In an effort to counter the timely availability of sufficient quantities of improved seed, seed bank activities were initiated in Madhya Pradesh (Sehore) and Rajasthan (Tonk) districts. Farmers were trained in seed production of crops like groundnut, chickpea, soybean and wheat, and seed grading and storage. This intervention has not only ensured availability of quality seed to farmers but also made available village-wise livelihood option for them.

Strengthening livestock-based livelihoods

The partner NGO BAIF has expertise in maintaining cattle health and breed improvement. And thereby large number of animal health camps were organized for deworming and breed improvement of livestock (~2000–3000 every year) in the project regions. Also the farmers were organized through SHGs and supported to purchase and expand livestock.

8.4 Capacity Building

To ensure sustainability of science-led development, due focus was on capacity building of stakeholders.

8.4.1 Capacity building under the initiative

Without appropriate training and knowledge sharing, no technology can percolate down to grassroots level for adoption. Thus farmers were oriented to better crop production technology and their capacity was built by organizing various types of training on new technology and better farming practices. Some of the major interventions were technical training conducted in villages, planning exercises, training of SHGs for management of seed banks, exposure visits and farmers' days. Capacity building of various stakeholders and farmers has been an important component of the SDTT project. Various capacity-building activities were taken up for the effective implementation of productivity enhancement through sustainable management of natural resources in Madhya Pradesh and Rajasthan. During the project period, annual workshops, training during crop seasons and field days were targeted activities. During the project period, capacity of about 20,000–30,000 farmers was improved directly through hands-on training and demonstrations and 4–5 times through field days.

In this initiative, ICRISAT also conducted capacity-building courses for the senior policy makers from Rajasthan and Madhya Pradesh in integrated watershed management programme implemented by the Department of Land Resources, Ministry of Rural Development. To further boost the efforts to sensitize the senior policy makers in the country, a National Symposium for Enhancing the Impact of the Integrated Watershed Management Program was held in New Delhi during 2010.

Capacity building of ultimate stakeholders, the farming community, is a core feature of any development project and SDTT is no exception. Sharing of knowledge in a village community is an essential means of spreading new technology. This was done by interactive group discussions, field visits, demonstrations and farmers' days where farmers could interact with scientists in exchanging ideas, views and experience. Hands-on training was a major benefit to the farmers. Soil health management, micronutrients, seed treatment and pest management were some of the hands-on training programmes regularly imparted to farmers in the project locations. Other major points of group discussions were water-use efficiency and enhancing productivity through various interventions. Thus the project created a common platform for information sharing to access information and resource and also disseminated information in the neighbourhood cluster of villages.

8.4.2   Important principles of capacity building followed

Quality of training, developing training material, content development and delivery of a programme are some aspects which affect any capacity-building programme. Seldom is there any quality check, especially where an assessment is to be done as to whether the training objectives were met. All capacity-building programmes need to address these basic issues to make the training an effective tool for transferring new technologies, so that it really benefits the ultimate stakeholder. Any capacity-building programme has primarily two objectives: transfer of technology and knowledge and skill development.

As the training flows from top-level functionaries of a state department/organization to the farm level, training becomes more skills-based for applications rather than principles and concept. Accordingly, training methodologies change, become more participatory and results-oriented. Awareness of this among the planners and policy makers is important so that the training pedagogy is relevant to the audience/participants.

Training is not a one-time event but should be sustainable in the long term. Development objectives are not a single intervention, but rather a continuous effort towards a long-term perspective and goal. Any training programme needs to be highly interactive, participatory and results-oriented. This needs the training to take a systems approach for better impact and technology transfer. There is no common prescription for all the training programmes in a project. It needs constant innovation in delivery mechanisms, wide consultations with the stakeholders and proactive steps in planning process. In other words, training has to be dynamic and systems-oriented if there is to be a change in the lives of millions of farmers to give them a better quality of life. Training has to be an agent for change – a change for the better. This has been a guiding principle in capacity-building efforts in the project.

8.5   Summary and Key Findings

The pilot initiative supported by SDTT has demonstrated widespread deficiencies of S, B and Zn in the semi-arid regions in Madhya Pradesh and Rajasthan states of India, which farmers should consider and include in their fertilizer management strategies. The on-farm evaluation results in pilot sites suggest the need to promote the use of vermicompost in food production for higher productivity and net returns. Vermicompost use for food production may be economical and practical only if it is produced on-farm from available wastes. Varietal replacement, rainy season fallow cultivation, wasteland management and developing livelihood opportunities like village seed banks, fodder promotion for livestock productivity and nutri-kitchen gardens are other big opportunities to improve incomes and productivity. *In-situ* and *ex-situ* rainwater management is critical in water augmentation and enhancing water-use efficiency, leading to higher production, incomes and reduced instances of crop failures. The smallholders in the rainfed SAT in India are unaware of such issues and available technologies and are not in a position to implement the science-led strategy on their own. So, there is a strong need for desired policy orientation by the respective governments to promote capacity strengthening and soil test-based INM and BN strategies through appropriate incentives for poor smallholders in the SAT in India.

Acknowledgements

The support from SDTT in Mumbai, India for undertaking the presented work is gratefully acknowledged. Authors also acknowledge help from NGOs BAIF, BYPASS and CARD in Madhya Pradesh and BAIF and DEEP in Rajasthan for reaching out to farmers and collecting data. Help in mapping pilot sites from Mr K. Srinivas is acknowledged.

References

Aggarwal, P.K., Hebbar, K.B., Venugopalan, M.V., Rani, S., Bala, A. *et al*. (2008) *Quantification of Yield Gaps in Rain-fed Rice, Wheat, Cotton and Mustard in India*. Global Theme on Agroecosystems Report No. 43. International Crops Research Institute for the Semi-Arid Tropics, Patancheru, India.

Bhatia, V.S., Singh, P., Wani, S.P., Kesava Rao, A.V.R. and Srinivas, K. (2006) *Yield Gap Analysis of Soybean, Groundnut, Pigeonpea and Chickpea in India Using Simulation Modeling*. Global Theme on Agroecosystems Report No. 31. International Crops Research Institute for the Semi-Arid Tropics, Patancheru, India.

Chander, G., Wani, S.P., Sahrawat, K.L. and Jangawad, L.S. (2012) Balanced plant nutrition enhances rainfed crop yields and water productivity in Jharkhand and Madhya Pradesh states in India. *Journal of Tropical Agriculture* 50(1–2), 24–29.

Chander, G., Wani, S.P., Sahrawat, K.L., Kamdi, P.J., Pal, C.K. *et al*. (2013a) Balanced and integrated nutrient management for enhanced and economic food production: case study from rainfed semi-arid tropics in India. *Archives of Agronomy and Soil Science* 59(12), 1643–1658.

Chander, G., Wani, S.P., Sahrawat, K.L., Pal, C.K. and Mathur, T.P. (2013b) Integrated plant genetic and balanced nutrient management enhances crop and water productivity of rainfed production systems in Rajasthan, India. *Communications in Soil Science and Plant Analysis* 44, 3456–3464.

Dixit, S., Tewari, J.C., Wani, S.P., Vineela, C., Chaurasia, A.K. and Panchal, H.B. (2005) *Participatory Biodiversity Assessment: Enabling Rural Poor for Better Natural Resource Management*. Global Theme on Agroecosystems Report No. 18. International Crops Research Institute for the Semi-Arid Tropics, Patancheru, India.

Government of India (2016) *Agricultural Statistics at a Glance 2016*. New Delhi: Directorate of Economics and Statistics, Ministry of Agriculture. Available at: http://eands.dacnet.nic.in/latest_2006.htm (accessed 19 April 2018).

Irz, X. and Roe, T. (2000) Can the world feed itself? Some insights from growth theory. *Agrekon* 39, 513–528.

Murty, M.V.R., Singh, P., Wani, S.P., Khairwal, I.S. and Srinivas, K. (2007) *Yield Gap Analysis of Sorghum and Pearl Millet in India Using Simulation Modeling*. Global Theme on Agroecosystems Report No. 37. International Crops Research Institute for the Semi-Arid Tropics, Patancheru, India.

Rockström, J., Karlberg, L., Wani, S.P., Barron, J., Hatibu, N. *et al*. (2010) Managing water in rainfed agriculture – the need for a paradigm shift. *Agricultural Water Management* 97, 543–550.

Sahrawat, K.L., Wani, S.P., Pardhasaradhi, G. and Murthy, K.V.S. (2010) Diagnosis of secondary and micronutrient deficiencies and their management in rainfed agroecosystems: case study from Indian semi-arid tropics. *Communications in Soil Science and Plant Analysis* 41, 346–360.

Sreedevi, T.K., Wani, S.P., Rao, A.V.R.K., Singh, P. and Ahmed, I. (2009) New science tools for managing community watersheds for enhancing impact. *Journal of SAT Agricultural Research* 7, 1–19.

Thirtle, C., Beyers, L., Lin, L., McKenzie-Hill, V., Irz, X. *et al.* (2002) *The Impacts of Changes in Agricultural Productivity on the Incidence of Poverty in Developing Countries.* DFID Report No. 7946. Department for International Development, London.

Wani, S.P., Dwivedi, R.S., Ramana, K.V., Vadivelu, A., Navalgund, R.R. and Pande, A.B. (2002) *Spatial Distribution of Rainy Season Fallows in Madhya Pradesh: Potential for Increasing Productivity and Minimizing Land Degradation.* Global Theme on Agroecosystems Report No. 3. International Crops Research Institute for the Semi-Arid Tropics, Patancheru, India.

Wani, S.P., Pathak, P., Jangawad, L.S., Eswaran, H. and Singh, P. (2003) Improved management of Vertisols in the semi-arid tropics for increased productivity and soil carbon sequestration. *Soil Use and Management* 19, 217–222.

Wani, S.P., Rockström, J., Venkateswarlu, B. and Singh, A.K. (2011a) New paradigm to unlock the potential of rainfed agriculture in the semi-arid tropics. In: Lal, R. and Steward, B.A. (eds) *World Soil Resources and Food Security.* CRC Press, Boca Raton, FL, pp. 419–470.

Wani, S.P., Sahrawat, K.L., Sarvesh, K.V., Mudbi, B. and Krishnappa, K. (2011b) *Soil Fertility Atlas for Karnataka.* Patancheru, India: International Crops Research Institute for the Semi-Arid Tropics.

Wani, S.P., Chander, G., Sahrawat, K.L. and Pardhasaradhi, G. (2015a) Soil test-based balanced nutrient management for sustainable intensification and food security: case from Indian semi-arid tropics. *Communications in Soil Science and Plant Analysis* 46(S1), 20–33.

Wani, S.P., Chander, G. and Uppal, R.K. (2015b) Enhancing nutrient use efficiencies in rainfed systems. In: Rakshit, A., Singh, H.B. and Sen, A. (eds) *Nutrient Use Efficiency: From Basics to Advances.* Springer, New Delhi, pp. 359–380. DOI: 10.1007/978-81-322-2169-2_23.

Wani, S.P., Chander, G., Sahrawat, K.L., Pal, D.K., Pathak, P. *et al.* (2016) Sustainable use of natural resources for crop intensification and better livelihoods in the rainfed semi-arid tropics of Central India. *NJAS – Wageningen Journal of Life Sciences* 78, 13–19.

9

Increasing Agricultural Productivity of Farming Systems in Parts of Central India – Sir Ratan Tata Trust Initiative

GAJANAN L. SAWARGAONKAR,* GIRISH CHANDER, SUHAS P. WANI, S.K. DASGUPTA AND G. PARDHASARADHI

International Crops Research Institute for the Semi-Arid Tropics, Patancheru, India

Abstract

Soil health mapping was adopted as entry point activity in the initiative supported by Sir Ratan Tata Trust in Jharkhand and Madhya Pradesh states of India which emphasized on developing soil test-based fertilizer recommendations at block level. In Jharkhand, yield benefit with balanced nutrition was 27–44% in paddy, groundnut and maize with benefit–cost (BC) ratio varying from 7.36 to 12.0. In Madhya Pradesh, balanced nutrition increased crop productivity by 11–57% in crops like soybean, paddy, green gram, black gram and groundnut with BC ratio of 1.97 to 9.35. Water harvesting through farm ponds (~500) helped in supplemental irrigation during critical crop stages besides serving as reservoir for fish cultivation. Efforts were made to promote off-season cultivation of vegetables, crop intensification, vermicompost units (~200) and seed bank in pilot villages and capacity development was carried out for ~15,000 farmers through direct demonstrations and around 2–3 times more through field days.

9.1 Background

With the growing population, achieving food security in the 21st century has become a daunting challenge due to increase in water scarcity and land degradation, and extreme variation in weather, which is further expected to aggravate due to impact of climate change. In this scenario, to meet the Millennium Development Goal (MDG) of halving the number of food-insecure poor people could not be met by India. In order to meet the food demand and reduce poverty, there is an urgent need to unlock the potential of rainfed agriculture by enhancing soil productivity, and resource use efficiency through integrated approach. During the past six decades, agricultural research emphasized mainly on component and commodity-based research involving development of crop varieties, animal breed, farm implements, machinery, fertilizer use, and other production and protection technologies. These technologies were mostly conducted in isolation and at the institute level which enabled the farmers to grow more but at the same time

---

* Corresponding author: g.sawargaonkar@cgiar.org

over-exploited the resources. It resulted in de-creasing factor productivity and resource-use efficiency and ultimately less farm productivity and profitability. The greatest challenge for In-dian agriculture is to increase the production in agriculture and allied sectors, while minimizing environmental impact. This necessitates conser-vation and protection of quality of the present resources that determine the performance of agriculture like land, water and air.

Reduction in yield, although determined by many factors, may be partially a consequence of land and water exploitation. Land degradation and water scarcity are among the major con-straints for Indian agriculture and are largely re-sponsible for the reduction in crop yield (Chadha *et al.*, 2004). By the early 1980s approximately 173.6 million ha (53%) of India's geographical area had been considerably degraded either by human or natural causes (due to water and wind erosion) (GoI, 2001); 15% is degraded cul-tivable wasteland (NRSA, 2000); waterlogging affected about 6% of the cultivated area, while alkaline and acidic soils both affected about 3%. It is further complicated by national problems such as environmental degradation, groundwater contamination and entry of toxic substances into the food chain (Gill *et al.*, 2009).

Thus, because of the ever-increasing popula-tion and decline in per capita availability of land, there is practically no scope for horizontal expan-sion of land for agriculture. Only vertical expan-sion is possible by integrating farming components requiring lesser space and time and ensuring rea-sonable returns to farm families (Kuruvilla and Mathew, 2009). The declining size of landhold-ings without any alternative income augmenting opportunity is resulting in a decrease in total farm income and causing agrarian distress, whereas a large number of smallholders have to move to non-farm activities to augment their income.

9.1.1 Sir Ratan Tata Trust Initiative

For harnessing the potential of dryland agriculture through available scientific technologies and ap-proaches for improving rural livelihoods on a sustainable basis, Sir Ratan Tata Trust (SRTT) supported the International Crops Research Institute for the Semi-Arid Tropics (ICRISAT),

Patancheru, India through an impact-oriented development project in Central India. ICRISAT was invited for technical backstopping and em-powerment of all the stakeholders to improve their livelihoods through increased agricultural productivity and livelihood opportunities by sus-tainable use of natural resources.

9.1.2 Project locations

The target districts were Gumla and Saraikela districts in Jharkhand and Jhabua and Mandla in Madhya Pradesh, India (Fig. 9.1). These dis-tricts in general are dominated by an agrarian economy. Soil fertility degradation is one of the major factors holding back the realization of large potential yields in these regions (Wani *et al.*, 2003; Sahrawat *et al.*, 2007; Chander *et al.*, 2013a,b, 2014). Rice fallow (practice of keeping extensive tract of lands fallow after rainy season crops) is another important issue and presents considerable scope for crop intensi-fication and increasing farmers' incomes. Hence, for achieving high productivity and profitability, a farming system approach was adopted which helped to integrate farm as a unit targeted for adoption of modern management practices per-taining to seeds, water, labour, capital or credit, fertilizers and pesticides usage and its further linking with other agriculture allied activities for efficient resource management and enhancing system's profitability.

9.1.3 Project goal and objectives

The overall objective of this project was to increase the impact of the development projects in Cen-tral India through technical backstopping and empowerment of stakeholders to improve liveli-hoods through increased agricultural productiv-ity and livelihood opportunities by sustainable use of natural resources.

The specific objectives of this technical as-sistance programme were as follows.

● To establish a holistic participatory integrated genetic and natural resource management (IGNRM) model for the convergence of activities in four nucleus clusters (five

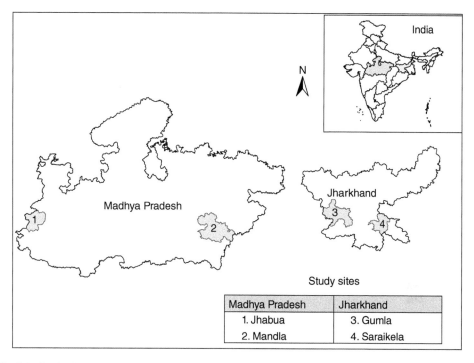

Fig. 9.1. Study sites in Madhya Pradesh and Jharkhand states of India.

villages in each cluster) encompassing suitable technical, institutional, gender equity and policy options for enhanced agricultural productivity and crop-livestock management systems to alleviate poverty.

• To provide technical know-how to farmers, landless rural people in the target districts and partner nongovernment organizations (NGOs) supported by SRTT in the region through empowerment by bringing together learnings from the national and international experience.

9.2 Methodology

9.2.1 Yield gap analysis for increasing system productivity in project location

Globally rainfed areas are hot spots of poverty, malnutrition and degradation of natural resources. Modern agriculture begins on the research station, where researchers have access to all requirements, i.e. fertilizers, pesticides and labour at appropriate time. But when the package is extended to farmers, even the best performing farms cannot match the yields obtained by researchers. Similarly, Barman *et al.* (2003) reported that the partial factor productivity of the crops for fertilizers and manures, irrigation and pesticides has been declining over the past decade and there is good scope to introduce better management practices using holistic farm management approach to increase the production by reducing yield gaps (attainable yield minus actual yield), namely 48, 30, 35 and 52% for rice, wheat, maize and mustard respectively.

Studies undertaken by many researchers revealed that the crop yields in dryland areas of Central India are quite low (1–1.5 t/ha) which are lower by two- to fivefold of the achievable potential yield (Fig. 9.2) largely due to low (35–45%) rainwater as well as resource use efficiency (Rockström *et al.*, 2007; Singh *et al.*, 2009; Wani *et al.*, 2009; Jha *et al.*, 2011). ICRISAT and its partners have demonstrated that large yield gap exists for different dryland crops in different parts of the country as well as in the region. The current farmers' yields of rainfed crops are lower by two- to fourfold than the yield from researcher-managed or commercial plots.

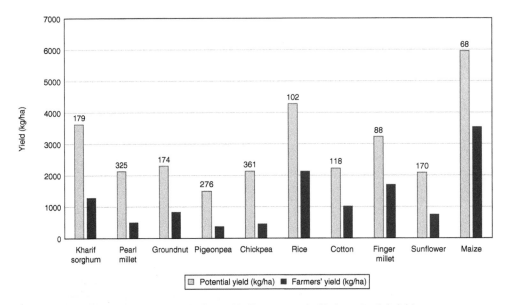

Fig. 9.2. Crop yields in farmers' fields in Central India compared with the potential yield.

9.2.2 Assessing the challenges for increasing system productivity

In the project area of Madhya Pradesh, in addition to the problem of soil erosion and waterlogging, particularly in lowland, Vertisols and associated soils, a large tract of land is kept fallow during the rainy season. The rainy season fallow area is about 16,400 ha in the two target districts of Madhya Pradesh despite relatively fertile soils and assured rainfall. Similarly, an extensive tract of land in Jharkhand is kept fallow after harvest of the rainy season crop, although sufficient stored moisture remains in the soil for growing a post-rainy season crop. However, nutrient depletion is a common problem across these rainfed areas. Thus, the potential for double cropping in these areas remains untapped due to the lack of availability of proper technology for soil, water, nutrient and crop management, and improved crop cultivars.

9.2.3 Soil health mapping as an entry point activity

Soil and water are vital natural resources for human survival. The burgeoning world population and increased standard of living are placing tremendous pressure on these resources. Because the soil and water resources are finite, their optimal management without adverse environmental consequences is necessary, if human survival is to be assured and development is to be sustained. In India, severe soil infertility problems in the rainfed systems (Rego *et al.*, 2007; Bekunda *et al.*, 2010; Sahrawat *et al.*, 2010b) and managing water stress alone cannot sustainably enhance the productivity of rainfed systems; hence for achieving sustainable gains in rainfed productivity both water shortage and soil fertility problems need to be simultaneously addressed through effective natural resource management practices (Wani *et al.*, 2009; Sahrawat *et al.*, 2010a).

Indian soils show deficiency of not only primary nutrients (nitrogen (N), phosphorus (P) and potassium (K)) but also secondary nutrients (sulfur (S), calcium and magnesium) and micronutrients (boron (B), zinc (Zn), copper and iron) in most parts of the country. Field studies carried out by different researchers clearly indicate that integrated nutrient management comprising soil test-based nutrient management approach can be an important entry point activity and also a mechanism to diagnose and manage soil fertility in practical agriculture (Wani, 2008). Research at ICRISAT and several on-farm benchmark watersheds demonstrated that soil testing is a useful tool for diagnosing the nutrient deficiencies in farmers' fields (Sahrawat *et al.*, 2010a). Therefore soil sampling and its chemical analysis assumes greater importance for developing soil test-based fertilizer recommendation more precisely at micro level.

Thus, soil health mapping was adopted as entry point activity under the SRTT initiative to strengthen the soil resource base. Farmers' fields in target regions were found seriously mined of S, B and Zn. In Jharkhand, 69–100% farms were low in S, 93–98% in B and 71–73% in Zn (Table 9.1). Similarly in Madhya Pradesh, 43–95% farms were low in S, 69–91% farms in B and 5–19% farms in Zn. Some farmers' fields also showed low levels of soil organic carbon (C), available P and K; however, in general, the majority of fields had their normal levels. Saraikela district, by contrast, had a majority of farms with low levels of P (80%) and K (58%). The results revealed relatively serious land degradation in Jharkhand as compared with Madhya Pradesh.

9.2.4   Institutional arrangement

To reach out to a large number of farmers for developing sites of learning and scaling-out best practices, ICRISAT entered into agreements with local NGOs such as Tata Rural Development Trust, Jamshedpur and PRADHAN, Gumla in Jharkhand and Gramin Vikas Trust, Jhabhua and Foundation for Ecological Security, Mandla in Madhya Pradesh. In addition to the NGO partners, other important partners collaborated for collective action, such as integrated watershed management programmes in target states, state agricultural universities (SAUs) (Jawaharlal Nehru Krishi Vishwa Vidyalaya, Jabalpur; Birsa Agricultural University, Ranchi), national research institutes (Indian Institute of Soil Science, Bhopal; and National Research Centre for Soybean, Indore), All India Coordinated Research Project for Dryland Areas and Jain Irrigation Ltd, Jalgaon.

9.2.5   Capacity building

Training assessment

In the SRTT project, efforts were made to understand the variability of different factors affecting crop productivity, its sustainability and thereby livelihood of the farmers, and accordingly training modules were designed for capacity building

of all the stakeholders. The first and foremost aspect targeted at the beginning of the project was to assess the need for training and conduct training programmes. To provide quality training, efforts were placed on developing training material and content, and delivery of a programme and targeting the right stakeholder for the particular training.

Capacity building under the initiative

Capacity building of various stakeholders and farmers has been an important component of the SRTT project. For the successful technology transfer to grassroot level, capacity building is very important as without it no technology can percolate down to grassroot level. Thus farmers were oriented towards better crop production technology and their capacity was built by organizing various types of training on new technology and better farming practices. Some of the major interventions were technical training conducted in villages, planning exercises carried out, self-help groups (SHGs) trained for management of seed banks, field exposure visits and farmers' days. Apart from this, training was provided on soil sampling (Fig. 9.3), use of multipurpose bullock-drawn toolbar – tropicultor; planting of *Gliricidia* on bunds, balanced nutrient management including secondary and micronutrients, seed priming, vermicomposting, nursery raising and seed bank development. Various capacity-building activities were taken up for effective implementation of productivity enhancement through sustainable management of natural resources in Jharkhand and Madhya Pradesh. Along with this initiative, ICRISAT conducted capacity-building courses on integrated watershed management and best practice management options for senior policy makers from the states as well as from the NGO Central India Initiatives (CINI) and other NGO staff. Lectures on methodology of designing and delivery mechanisms were followed by demonstration and hands-on training and skills development, which resulted in increased adoption of the technologies with high degree of success. The primary stakeholders were marginal and small farmers from the project districts. During the project period, annual workshops, training during crop seasons and field days were conducted with targeted activities. During the project period, around 5371 farmers were trained on different agro-techniques

Table 9.1. Soil fertility status of farmers' fields in target districts in Jharkhand and Madhya Pradesh states of India. From: Chander *et al.* (2012).

State	District	pH	OC	P	K	S	B	Zn
					% deficiency[a] (Range of available contents[b])			
Jharkhand	Gumla	5.0–7.1	33 (0.28–1.13)	23 (1.4–72.4)	27 (29–247)	100 (2.0–9.6)	93 (0.06–0.80)	73 (0.30–2.90)
	Saraikela	4.5–7.4	45 (0.19–0.99)	80 (0.0–18.2)	58 (8–194)	69 (1.3–50.0)	98 (0.06–0.80)	71 (0.24–2.50)
Madhya Pradesh	Jhabua	6.4–7.4	0 (0.58–1.53)	45 (0.2–42.2)	0 (88–506)	95 (2.7–28.2)	91 (0.26–0.76)	5 (0.66–3.18)
	Mandla	5.9–7.4	3 (0.45–2.62)	32 (1.0–147.5)	0 (82–1846)	43 (2.0–74.2)	69 (0.06–1.02)	19 (0.40–5.50)

[a]Critical values adopted for delineating % deficiency are 0.5% for OC, 5 mg/kg for P, 50 mg/kg for K, 10 mg/kg for S, 0.58 mg/kg for B and 0.75 mg/kg for Zn.
[b]Figures in parentheses indicate the range of available contents (% for OC and mg/kg for P, K, S, B and Zn).

Fig. 9.3. Soil sampling training to farmers of: (a) Jojo village of Saraikela district, Jharkand; (b) Katangsivani village of Nivas block of Mandla district of Madhya Pradesh.

directly by ICRISAT and partners whereas capacities of more than 20,000 farmers were improved through indirect measures, namely field exposure visits, results of demonstrations and field days during the cropping season.

9.2.6 Dissemination

The learnings from the project were disseminated and spread in the neighbourhood cluster of villages. For disseminating the results of the interventions, field exposure visits of nearby villagers were targeted as an important activity under this initiative. This helped in training as well as straightforward transfer of technology, knowledge transfer and skills development to different stakeholders. Thus, there was no intermediary and this helped farmers to learn directly from the live demonstrations and knowledge providers (scientists, field staff, NGOs, ICRISAT, SAU partners, etc.). The project partner NGOs were active in their respective areas and conducted field-level training, field days, field exposure visits and farmers' days with active help and guidance from ICRISAT scientific staff.

9.3 Integrated Approach for Livelihood Improvement

An integrated livelihoods framework is essential for increasing agricultural productivity, income and sustainable use of natural resources by adopting the participatory and holistic farming system approach. In order to bridge the yield gap, ICRISAT and its partners have adopted integrated genetic natural resource management (IGNRM) guided by an inclusive market-oriented development strategy, linking farmers with markets and reaping the benefits of productivity enhancement initiative. The aim is to bridge the gap between the 'desired' and 'achieved' and to bring quantitative as well as qualitative improvement in fulfilling the food needs in parts of Central India, so as to sustain the agricultural resource base and to provide livelihood security to millions of rural citizens.

9.3.1 Soil test-based balanced nutrient management

Balanced nutrient management is the timely application of all essential plant nutrients (which include primary, secondary and micronutrients) in readily available form, in optimum quantities and in the right proportion, through the correct method, suitable for specific soil/crop conditions. It includes judicious use of chemical fertilizers based on deficient soil nutrients as established by soil testing in conjunction with other sources of plant nutrients such as organic manures and bio-fertilizers. Use of soil amendments for acidic/alkaline soils also need to be promoted to improve soil health and its fertility thereby ensuring adequate availability of nutrients in soils to meet the requirement of plants at critical stages of growth and thus ensuring adequate soil humus to improve physico-chemical and biological properties of the soil. Researchers have reported that soils below the critical limits of the nutrients evaluated responded to the application of nutrients although the overall crop response was regulated by the rainfall received during the cropping season (Rego *et al.*, 2007; Sahrawat *et al.*, 2007, 2010b).

Thus, based on analysis of results, fertilizer recommendations were designed for a cluster of villages called a block, a lower administrative unit in a district and promoted in the pilot sites. In Jharkhand, the yield benefit with soil test-based fertilization was 27–44% in crops such as paddy, groundnut and maize as compared to that under farmers' standard practice (Table 9.2). The benefit–cost (BC) ratio of adopting balanced nutrition (BN) was 11.5–12.0 for paddy, 7.36–12.0 for maize and 9.92 for groundnut. Similarly, in Madhya Pradesh, BN increased crop productivity when compared with farmers' practice by 11–57% in crops like soybean, paddy, green gram, black gram and groundnut. The BC ratio of adopting BN in Madhya Pradesh varied between 1.97 and 9.35, a profitable proposition to promote BN.

9.3.2 Weather monitoring

A rain gauge with a dual recording system (manual and using a data logger) was installed in all the pilot sites for recording rainfall, minimum

Table 9.2. Crop yield improvement with balanced nutrition (BN) in Gumla district, Jharkhand and Jhabua district, Madhya Pradesh, India during the rainy season 2009–13.[a]

Crop	Yield (kg/ha)		BC ratio
	FP	BN	
Gumla			
Paddy	3442.5	4762.5	11.75
Groundnut	1997.5	2950	10.66
Maize	3785	4995	9.68
Jhabua			
Soybean	1495	1705	2.205
Paddy	2435	3230	5.215
Green gram	907.5	1292.5	7.135
Black gram	560	662.5	3.36

[a]FP = farmers' practice; BC = benefit–cost.

and maximum temperatures, and relative humidity (Fig. 9.4). The data was recorded daily for all the above parameters by the villagers, who were trained by ICRISAT on the working of the rain gauge and maintenance of the data set.

Rainfall data was recorded by farmers from the rain gauges installed at Teleya village for Gumla district and at Sherbida village for Saraikela district. Rainfall received in Gumla district was higher than normal during 2008 and 2011 (101.3% and 108.6% of normal rainfall respectively), whereas during 2009, 2010, 2012, 2013 and 2014, the rainfall ranged from 49.4 to 80.3% of normal rainfall (Fig. 9.5). Thus, except in 2008 and 2011, paddy as well as other crops suffered due to deficit rainfall and thereby recorded reduction in crop productivity. In Saraikela district, rainfall during 2008 was 97.5%, but during 2009 to 2014 there was only 36.3–85.4% of normal rainfall, which clearly affected the crop productivity in these areas. However, ICRISAT promoted a diversified cropping pattern in the pilot areas with the introduction of crops, namely maize, black gram and chickpea, which could be grown with less rainfall.

The rainfall deficit affected paddy cultivation, meaning that farmers incurred huge losses on raising paddy seedlings, as transplanting was not possible in many places. The rainfall information shared with the farmers helped them with better planning of growing upland crops and vegetables. Due to the variability in rainfall, coupled with its irregular distribution, farmers were advised to plant more upland crops which require less water than paddy, and they realized the usefulness of this change over monocropping of paddy. Thus, the farmers obtained considerable yield from the change in cropping pattern, promoted through both vertical and horizontal integration, and thereby obtained sufficient nutritional food security besides ensuring economic stability.

9.3.3 Water conservation and harvesting

In the target districts, the productivity enhancement practices available through integrated water resource management are used with participatory research and development approach for enhancing the overall productivity of farming

Fig. 9.4. Dual-purpose manual and recording type rain gauge with data logger installed at (a) Sherbida in Jharkand and (b) Hateyadeli in Madhya Pradesh.

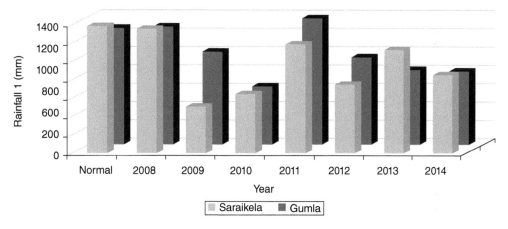

Fig. 9.5. Rainfall during 2008–14 in Gumla and Saraikela districts of Jharkhand.

systems. Water-shortage-related plant stress is the primary constraint to potential crop production and productivity in the rainfed systems in the semi-arid tropics (SAT), and consequently the importance of water shortage has been rightly emphasized globally (Wani *et al.*, 2002; Molden, 2007; Pathak *et al.*, 2009). In rainfed agriculture, demand for rainwater can be met through efficient rainwater conservation and management. For this both *in situ* and *ex situ* rainwater management play crucial roles in increasing and sustaining the crop productivity. The comprehensive assessment of water management in agriculture (Molden, 2007) describes a large untapped potential for upgrading rainfed agriculture and calls for increased water investments in the sector.

Water harvesting through the construction of farm ponds comprising small dugout structures with a capacity of 300–400 m³ and having a catchment area of around 1 acre was promoted in the project area (Fig. 9.6). These ponds were constructed on the land of farmers who had a landholding of 0.75–2 acre and with the active contribution from beneficiary farmers in kind. The construction cost was ₹10,000 per farm pond. Farm ponds supported supplemental irrigation during the critical crop growth stage besides serving as a reservoir for fish cultivation. Thus, 256 farm ponds in Gumla district (Fig. 9.7) and 30 farm ponds in Saraikela district were constructed with the farmers' contribution. In 2012–13 season, 500 g of fish seeds were released in each farm pond and each pond contributed

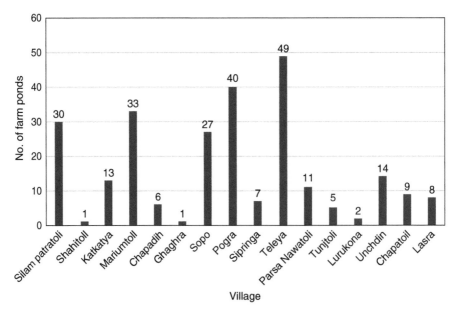

Fig. 9.6. Farm ponds constructed in villages in Raideh block, Gumla district, Jharkhand during 2010–14.

Fig. 9.7. Farm pond at Sipringa village in Gumla district, Jharkhand.

profit of ₹6000–7000 to beneficiary farmers. During 2013–14, the government also supported this activity by giving fish seeds and feed as a subsidy to farmers, who thus gained increased monetary benefits up to ₹10,000 from each pond. These farm ponds also provided drinking water for cattle and provided water for washing clothes.

9.3.4 Crop intensification

Rainy season fallow management

Vertisols and associated soils which occupy large areas globally (approximately 257 million ha) (Dudal, 1965) are traditionally cultivated during the post-rainy season on stored soil moisture. Due to poor infiltration rates and waterlogging, farmers were facing difficulties to cultivate during the rainy season. It is perceived that the practice of fallowing Vertisols and associated soils in Madhya Pradesh have decreased after the introduction of soybean. However, 2.02 million ha of cultivable land is still kept fallow in Central India, during *kharif* (rainy season) (Wani *et al.*, 2002; Dwivedi *et al.*, 2003). Therefore efforts were made to intensify the *kharif* fallow areas with suitable landform management options along with required change in cultivar selection. Accordingly, ICRISAT conducted on-farm soybean trials involving improved land configuration (broad-bed and furrow system) and short-duration soybean varieties during *kharif* and growing of chickpea with minimum tillage in *rabi* (post-rainy season), which had practically enhanced the cropping intensity in Guna, Vidisha and Indore districts of Madhya Pradesh. The results revealed that there was an increase in crop yields of 40–200% while income increased up to 100% with landform treatment, new varieties and other best practice management options (Wani, 2008) through crop intensification.

Rice fallow management
for crop intensification

To feed the burgeoning population, vertical expansion in dryland agriculture is being targeted by many stakeholders with the aim of increasing productivity. However, the other potential areas, particularly rice fallows in eastern and southern India (Jharkhand, Bihar, Chhattisgarh, Andhra Pradesh, Odisha and Assam) offer great scope for horizontal expansion of area by inclusion of a suitable pulse crop in the system and thereby enhancing cropping intensity and systems productivity. About 14.29 million ha (30% of the rice-growing area) rice fallows are available in the Indo-Gangetic Plains spread in Bangladesh, Nepal, Pakistan and India, of which 11.4 million ha (82%) are in the Indian states of Bihar, Madhya Pradesh, Chhattisgarh, Jharkhand, West Bengal, Odisha and Assam (Subbarao *et al.*, 2001). ICRISAT analysed rice fallows in pilot sites along with identification of various bottlenecks associated with effective and sustainable utilization of rice fallows (Subbarao *et al.*, 2001) and it was estimated that considerable amount of green water is available after the monsoon, especially in the rice fallow systems, which could be easily utilized by introducing a short-duration legume crop with simple seed priming and micronutrient amendments (Kumar Rao *et al.*, 2008; Wani *et al.*, 2009; Singh *et al.*, 2010). Taking advantage of the sufficiently available soil moisture after harvesting the rice crop, growing of early-maturing chickpea during the winter season in rice fallow areas with best management practices provides an opportunity for intensification (Harris *et al.*, 1999; Kumar Rao *et al.*, 2008).

Therefore efforts were targeted towards introducing appropriate legumes into rice fallows to have significant impact on the national economies through improved quality of nutrition for humans and animals, poverty alleviation, employment generation and contribution to the sustainability of the cereal-based production systems. ICRISAT adopted the strategy to develop a sustainable farmers' participatory seed production system for pulses by promoting improved agronomic (e.g. seed priming, soil test-based balanced fertilizer including micro- and secondary nutrients, biofertilizers, integrated management, etc.) and water conservation practices (e.g. zero/minimum tillage, relay planting) for better crop establishment in rice fallows. Similarly, suitable rice cultivars with appropriate crop duration were identified to help make use of residual moisture to promote short-duration pulses during *rabi*. This intensification combined early-maturing varieties of rice to best fit chickpea in sequence as there is time to sow a chickpea crop to take advantage of the residual moisture in the soil.

Earlier, the rice varieties cultivated were late maturing and were sown late, thereby increasing more area left as fallow. However, with ICRISAT intervention, the farmers started growing an extra crop on residual soil moisture. On-farm research in farmers' fields have clearly showed that short-duration pulses are suitable for cultivation in rice fallows and good yields can be obtained, provided suitable varieties and technologies including mechanization for crop establishment in rainfed rice fallows are made available. Participatory trials to demonstrate and evaluate chickpea cultivars (JG 11, JGK 9218 and KAK 2) in post-rainy fallow regions showed a yield of 1710–1900 kg/ha with KAK 2 and 1608–1728 kg/ha with JG 11 in Jharkhand (Table 9.3). Results clearly demonstrated that chickpea is a suitable crop to grow after rice in otherwise fallow regions and that is bringing dividends for the farmers through additional income as well as by enhancing rainwater use efficiency.

An economic analysis for the project sites revealed that growing legumes in rice fallows is profitable for farmers with BC ratio exceeding 3 for many legumes. In addition, utilizing rice fallows for growing legumes resulted in the generation of employment to the farmers, besides helping in tackling issues of nutrient deficiencies due to inclusion of pulses in the diet.

9.3.5   Farmer participatory varietal evaluation

Balancing productivity, profitability and environmental health is a key challenge for today's agriculture for ensuring long-term sustainability (Robertson and Swinton, 2005; Foley *et al.*, 2011). However, most crop production systems in the world are characterized by low species and management diversity, high use of fossil energy and agrochemicals, and large negative impacts on the environment. Therefore, there is urgent need to focus attention on the development of crop production systems with improved resource use efficiencies and more benign effects on the environment (Tilman *et al.*, 2002; Foley *et al.*, 2011). Cropping system design provides an excellent framework for developing and applying integrated approaches to management because it allows for new and creative ways of meeting the challenge of sustaining the agricultural productivity.

The main issue with the existing cropping system in the targeted districts was the recurrence in usage of low-yielding cultivars year after year, which was accompanied by low seed replacement rate, largely contributing to decrease in factor productivity and in turn low crop production. So efforts were made to focus on farmer participatory varietal evaluation programme in these pilot districts to test the suitability of new high-yielding climate smart crops and cultivars to prevailing climatic situations. The farmer participatory varietal evaluation programme works towards increasing farm productivity by facilitating the delivery of high-yielding, profitable varieties that are well adapted to a wide range of soil types, environments and farming systems. This is achieved by providing accredited, unbiased information to farmers on better adapted crop varieties, or new and better cultivars, at the earliest opportunity. In all targeted districts of Madhya Pradesh and Jharkhand, farmers were able to choose improved varieties of preferred dryland crops from the list of varieties provided to farmers' groups.

ICRISAT and SAUs released improved cultivars and proprietary hybrids of crops were evaluated in this mission programme with an objective to select cultivars having suitable traits for better adaptation to biotic and abiotic stresses to enhance or sustain productivity and further scaling-up the spread of these varieties to satellite taluks. Each demonstration was laid approximately on 0.5–1 acre of farmer's field. Best management practice included application of 70 kg diammonium phosphate, 100 kg urea, 5 kg borax, 50 kg zinc sulphate and 200 kg gypsum per ha for cereal crops and for legumes a reduction in urea application from 100 to 40 kg/ha. The layout of varietal trial was designed to assess the performance of local variety with traditional

Table 9.3. Evaluation of chickpea cultivars in rice fallows in Jharkhand during post-rainy season.

District	Block	Variety	Yield (kg/ha)
Gumla	Raideh	KAK 2	1900
		JG 11	1610
Saraikela	Saraikela	KAK 2	1710
		JG 11	1730

practice of input management. In this trial, there were two treatments: (i) farmers' practice with local/traditional cultivar + farmers' inputs; (ii) Improved cultivar + best practice inputs.

With these trials, farmers were exposed to several improved varieties of each crop grown in their villages and had the option of evaluating the performance of each variety more or less in the same climatic and soil conditions with different levels of input management. Participatory varietal selection trials were confined to two or three main rainfed cropping systems of the district/region during the crop season. During the rainy and post-rainy seasons, crops evaluated included cereals (sorghum and pearl millet), pulses (pigeonpea, chickpea and cluster bean) and oilseeds (groundnut, soybean and castor). The programme collects and delivers the data which not only assists farmers with their choice of suitable varieties but also facilitates the registration and commercialization of new cultivars by plant breeders. The experimental protocol has been established to evaluate the performance of improved varieties under BN against a common set of traditional varieties to characterize their yield, quality, disease resistance/tolerance and agronomic characteristics. The information on yield performance of the improved cultivars was collected through crop-cutting experiments by ICRISAT, NGOs and lead farmers in presence of agriculture department staff/officials.

9.3.6 Crop diversification

In Madhya Pradesh and Jharkhand, the agriculture sector is the important source of livelihood for over 65% of the total population that is dominated by small and marginal farmers. After independence, there was yield advantage in these regions due to irrigation expansion and Green Revolution technologies well supported with government policies. However during the course, especially in Jharkhand and partially in Madhya Pradesh, there was a tendency towards cereal specialization without inclusion of pulses and oilseeds in the cropping system, which in turn resulted in decline in factor productivity often coupled with more probability of crop failures. So attempts were made to come out of subsistence agriculture having dependence on single

crop and move towards diversified crops that have a larger potential for returns from land. For crop diversification in targeted sites, information was obtained on the potential benefits of diversifying cropping systems through efficient crop rotation as a means of controlling decrease in crop productivity while simultaneously enhancing other desirable agroecosystem processes (Karlen and Stott, 1994). The aim in diversifying the cropping system in these states, particularly in rainfed ecology, was to reduce the risk factor of crop failures due to drought or less rains or decline in market value. This process was triggered by inclusion of suitable pulses (namely pigeonpea, green gram, black gram, cowpea, etc.) and oilseeds (namely soybean and groundnut) to the existing cropping system either as vertical or horizontal integration which proved to be one of the safest cultivation practices to overcome the climate change effect. ICRISAT witnessed similar experiences from these states and also from Southeast Asian countries, which clearly revealed that diversification toward high-yielding cultivars leads to the development of innovative supply chains and opens new vistas for augmenting income, generating employment and promoting exports. Thus, if carried out appropriately, diversification can be used as a tool to augment farm income, generate employment, alleviate poverty and conserve precious soil and water resources.

Major driving forces for crop diversification were increasing income on small farm holdings, mitigating effects of increasing climate variability, balancing food demand, improving fodder for livestock, conservation of natural resources, minimizing environmental pollution, reducing dependence on off-farm inputs, decreasing insect pests, diseases and weed problems, and increasing community food security. Based on these aspects, pigeonpea was pilot-tested and evaluated at SRTT sites and results proved that it could be a potential crop for these regions (Table 9.4). The yield of important varieties was 760–880 kg/ha in Hazaribagh district whereas in Deoghar district, it ranged between 2050 and 2290 kg/ha.

9.4 Livelihood Improvement

Apart from targeting productivity enhancement interventions, efforts were also concentrated on

Table 9.4. Evaluation of pigeonpea varieties in Jharkhand, post-rainy season 2009–13.

District	Block	Variety	Yield (kg/ha)
Hazaribagh	Mandu	Asha (ICPL 87119)	790
		Laxmi (ICPL 85063)	880
		Puskar (ICPH 2671)	760
Deoghar	Palajor	Asha (ICPL 87119)	2050
		Laxmi (ICPL 85063)	2290

improving livelihood of resource-poor farmers in pilot districts of Jharkhand and Madhya Pradesh. Emphasis was especially given to empowering women through certain targeted activities, namely vermicomposting, kitchen gardening, raising nurseries for vegetable seedlings as well as for biological N-fixing trees, producing quality seed and establishing a village seed bank, etc. All these activities were promoted through women as well as youth clubs collectively as the SHGs with a focus on increasing the income to their family.

9.4.1   Vermicomposting

Vermicomposting activity was started in all the districts with demonstration of model units constructed at all locations. Training was provided to farmers for the preparation of vermicompost using crop and field organic waste and dung and earthworms. In Teleya village of Gumla district, 22 units were constructed in 2009 by active involvement of farmers. After realization of benefit of increased yield in vermicompost applied field of vegetables and agricultural crops, there was huge demand generated at local level. Therefore, vermicomposting was successfully promoted to each farmer in the pilot sites in Gumla district and many farmers' fields in other pilot districts (Fig. 9.8). Villagers in the surrounding areas also learnt this process and more than 50 units were established by farmers themselves by taking advice and guidance from the locally trained lead farmers from the pilot sites. The strategy was worked out with support from Government of Jharkhand and SRTT team so that in this initiative, the cost of material for tank construction was borne by the team whereas farmers invested in the shed. The cost of each unit was around ₹3000 and each unit had 2 or 4 chambers and

comprised internal walls with holes for the movement of earthworms from one chamber to the other.

With the project direct interventions, altogether 87 units were established in Gumla district in four villages, viz. Teleya, Sipringa, Tunjutoli and Parsa Novatoli and 27 units were established in Sherbida and Jojo villages of Saraikela district which are producing higher quantity of good-quality compost. In order to make better use of this activity, extensive training was given to the farmers on the approach, methodology and maintenance of vermicomposting units using crop and field organic waste with dung and earthworms. Each unit produces about 800–1000 kg of good quality of vermicompost. Similarly, farmers were encouraged to use the vermicompost for cultivation of vegetables, as it helps in improving the quality of produce besides obtaining increased productivity. The results clearly revealed that farmers cultivated vegetables such as cauliflower, tomato and pea using vermicompost and obtained 20–80% increase in quality produce compared to their general cultivation practices. Even after withdrawal of ICRISAT from the project in 2004, all the farmers are still active in vermicompost preparation and harvest 800–1000 kg of produce three times a year.

9.4.2   Vegetable cultivation

The farm ponds have sufficient water to support a considerable area, particularly in providing supplemental irrigation to crops both during the *kharif* and *rabi* seasons. With the additional water, farmers started cultivating vegetables like tomato, cauliflower, cabbage, brinjal, okra, peas, potato and other leafy vegetables during winter and summer. In order to use the available water efficiently, drip irrigation was promoted for vegetable cultivation in Teleya village in Gumla district with support from ICRISAT and team. The efforts towards off-season cultivation of these vegetables has enabled considerable economic gain to the farmers as they earn net profit of ₹8000 to ₹10,000/*bigha* land (1 *bigha* = 0.2 acre). After reaping such huge benefits, this watershed model now was extended to many villages in Gumla and Saraikela districts, where

Fig. 9.8. Vermicompost units at farmer's field in Gumla district, Jharkhand.

farmers are constructing farm ponds on their own land with the support from Government of Jharkhand, and technical guidance from ICRISAT and NGO partners involved in this project.

9.4.3 Biomass generation for soil fertility management

Considering the poor soil health due to indiscriminate use of fertilizers, efforts were concentrated on promoting green manuring activities in the project area. Accordingly, *Gliricidia* seeds were distributed to farmers who were then trained on raising the seedlings in nurseries and plantation on field bunds and boundaries. Farmers were encouraged to plant 3–4-month-old plants from the nursery or cuttings of tender branches of *Gliricidia* at 50 cm apart on field bunds. *Gliricidia* plants produce green leaf and succulent green branches abundantly, which are rich in N. The *Gliricidia* plants grown on

bunds not only strengthen the bunds while preventing soil erosion but also provide N-rich green biomass, fodder and fuel. *Gliricidia* can be harvested 2–3 times in a year and applied before sowing of rainy and post-rainy season crops. A study conducted at ICRISAT Center indicated that adding the N-rich green biomass from *Gliricidia* plants planted on bunds at a spacing of 0.5 m apart for a length of 700 m could provide about 30–45 kg N per ha per year. From the first year itself, farmers harvested the green leaf and loppings, leaving 1-m-high plants, and applied it to the top soil for enriching organic C and nutrients in the soil.

During 2008–14, 5–10 kg of *Gliricidia* seeds were supplied by ICRISAT to women SHGs and youth clubs to raise the seedlings at all the project locations. Seeds were treated with acid for removing dormancy and planted in polythene bags (supplied by ICRISAT) by adding soil mixed with fertilizer and vermicompost (Fig. 9.9). Women SHG and youth club members raised about 15,000–35,000 seedlings per year in

Fig. 9.9. *Gliricidia* seedlings raised in a nursery for transplantation into the main field at Teleya village, Jharkand.

Gumla district and 7000–15,000 seedlings per year in Saraikela district since 2008 and sold these seedlings to fellow farmers for planting on main field bunds at low price. Seedlings were planted during the rainy season as hedges on field bunds (Fig. 9.10) and inside the fence of mango orchards. Farmers also planted these seedlings on bunds as fences for vegetable fields. Loppings were placed in paddy and vegetable fields and around mango plants, which resulted in good crop yields besides a reduction in cost of fertilizer use. Apart from these project locations, about 1–2 kg seeds were supplied to different NGOs associated with project partners for promoting *Gliricidia* planting in different locations, namely Kunti, Keonjar, Mandu, Hazaribagh, Deoghar, Pravah Deoghar and RDA Ghatsila.

9.4.4   Seed bank

Considering the lack of quality seed available to farmers, efforts were targeted towards producing quality seed at farmer level and its preservation by SHGs at village level. Thus the concept of the seed bank was established in the pilot villages in Jharkhand and Madhya Pradesh. In Gumla, Jharkhand and Jhabua, Madhya Pradesh

seed banks were successfully established where in seeds of pigeonpea (Asha, Maruti variety) black gram (TAU 1, T 9 variety), chickpea (JG 11, JAKI 9218 variety) were established. Lead farmers were taking care of seed bank management and necessary precautions and care were taken by them to protect seeds from any pest damage. ICRISAT gave these farmers hands-on training in seed storage and its protection. The farmers were trained in seed production of crops such as black gram, chickpea and pigeonpea and also their grading and storage aspects. The seed bank concept helped farmers to earn a good profit by selling the stored seed at a premium price to fellow farmers.

9.4.5   Kitchen gardening

For this activity, the women farmers were guided and supported to grow vegetables in a small area (0.1 to 0.2 *bigha*) or as kitchen garden to improve family nutrition and capture the market-led opportunities. The demand-driven seeds of vegetables such as brinjal, tomato, okra, cabbage and cauliflower were provided during the initiative by ICRISAT along with required capacity building and other inputs like soil test-based nutrients.

Fig. 9.10. *Gliricidia* planted by farmers on farm bunds as a living fence in Sherbida village, Saraikela district, Jharkhand.

Vegetables were grown by around 100 women farmers every year and they obtained good yields and income.

9.5 Sustainability

In the project sites, a common practice of open grazing of animals prevails after the harvest of the paddy crop. Thus, concerted efforts were targeted on training and awareness building of stakeholders (including farmers and development agencies), strengthening formal and informal seed systems and increasing access to other inputs for enhancing adoption of improved cultivars and technologies. Along with technology demonstrations, for bringing awareness to stakeholders and policy makers, social engineering was focused to intensify crop production in these fallows. For effective implementation and scaling-up of interventions, a sustainable approach with efficient monitoring and evaluation system was followed. It was aimed to target and demonstrate crop intensification as well as other technologies on a pilot basis and further scale-out to a large number of farmers' fields in a phased manner. This initiative helped in strengthening various environmental benefits/ecosystem services such as improved land- and water-use efficiency and a more resilient rice-based cropping system with balanced fertilizer input and improved soil fertility. Apart from the increased income and livelihood, the project helped the community to address the issues of nutritional deficiency with increased domestic availability of chickpea and other pulses.

9.6 The Way Forward

The initiative supported by SRTT has demonstrated several agrotechniques for adoption by resource-poor farmers. The soil health status clearly reflected that there are widespread deficiencies of S, B and Zn in Jharkhand and Madhya Pradesh, which farmers should consider and include in their fertilizer management strategies. The on-farm evaluation results in pilot sites suggest the need to promote the use of vermicompost in vegetable production for higher productivity and net returns. Almost all farmers from Gumla district, and many farmers from other pilot districts, constructed vermicompost units in their fields and are judiciously utilizing them in vegetable as well as food grain production. Crop intensification with chickpea, black gram and short-duration pigeonpea has helped in horizontal expansion of cropping intensity in the area with additional net profit of ₹8000–15,000 per ha. Varietal replacement and increased livelihood opportunities like village seed banks, fodder promotion for livestock productivity and nutri-kitchen gardens are notable interventions for improving the incomes of farmers. The smallholders in the rainfed SAT of India are unaware of the issues and available technologies and are not in a position to implement the science-led strategy on their own. So, there is a strong need for desired policy orientation by the respective governments to promote capacity strengthening and soil test-based integrated and balanced nutrient management strategies through appropriate incentives for poor smallholders in the SAT of India.

Acknowledgements

The support from SRTT in Mumbai, India for undertaking the work presented is gratefully acknowledged. The authors also acknowledge the help of the lead partner NGO (CINI) and other NGOs, namely Tata Rural Development Trust, Jamshedpur and PRADHAN, Gumla in Jharkhand and Gramin Vikas Trust, Jhabhua and Foundation for Ecological Security, Mandla in Madhya Pradesh for reaching out to farmers and collecting data.

References

Barman, D., Datta, M., De, L.C. and Banik, S. (2003) Efficiency of phosphate solubilizing and phytohormones producing bacteria on the growth and yield of tuberose in acid soil of Tripura. *Indian Journal of Horticulture* 60(3), 303–306.

Bekunda, M., Sanginga, N. and Woomer, P.L. (2010) Restoring soil fertility in sub-Saharan Africa. *Advances in Agronomy* 108, 183–286.

Chadha, G.K., Sen, S. and Sharma, H.R. (2004) *State of the Indian Farmer: A Millennium Study. Volume 2: Land Resources*. Department of Agriculture and Cooperation, Ministry of Agriculture/Academic Foundation, New Delhi.

Chander, G., Wani, S.P., Sahrawat, K.L. and Jangawad, L.S. (2012) Balanced plant nutrition enhances rainfed crop yields and water productivity in Jharkhand and Madhya Pradesh states in India. *Journal of Tropical Agriculture* 50(1–2), 24–29.

Chander, G., Wani, S.P., Sahrawat, K.L., Kamdi, P.J., Pal, C.K. *et al.* (2013a) Balanced and integrated nutrient management for enhanced and economic food production: case study from rainfed semi-arid tropics in India. *Archives of Agronomy* 59(12), 1643–1658.

Chander, G., Wani, S.P., Sahrawat, K.L., Pal, C.K. and Mathur, T.P. (2013b) Integrated plant genetic and balanced nutrient management enhances crop and water productivity of rainfed production systems in Rajasthan, India. *Communications in Soil Science and Plant Analysis* 44, 3456–3464.

Chander, G., Wani, S.P., Sahrawat, K.L., Dixit, S., Venkateswarlu, B. *et al.* (2014) Soil test based nutrient balancing improved crop productivity and rural livelihoods: case study from rainfed semi-arid tropics in Andhra Pradesh, India. *Archives of Agronomy and Soil Science*. DOI: 10.1080/03650340.2013.871706 (accessed 15 July 2017)

Dudal, R. (1965) Dark clay soils of tropical and subtropical regions. *FAO Agricultural Development Paper* 83, 161.

Dwivedi, R.S., Ramana, K.V., Wani, S.P. and Pathak, P. (2003) Use of satellite data for watershed management and impact assessment. In: Wani, S.P., Maglinao, A.R., Ramakrishna, A. and Rego, T.J. (eds) *Integrated Watershed Management for Land and Water Conservation and Sustainable Agricultural Production in Asia*. Proceedings of the ADB-ICRISAT-IWMI Project Review and Planning Meeting, Hanoi, Vietnam, 10–14 Dec 2001. International Crops Research Institute for the Semi-Arid Tropics, Patancheru, India, pp. 149–157.

Foley, J.A., Ramankutty, N., Brauman, K.A., Cassidy, E.S., Gerber, J.S. *et al.* (2011) Solutions for a cultivated planet. *Nature* 478, 337–342.

Gill, M.S., Singh, J.P. and Gangwar, K.S. (2009) Integrated farming system and agriculture sustainability. *Indian Journal of Agronomy* 54(2), 128–139.

Government of India (GoI) (2001) *India: Nation Action Programme to Combat Desertification. Volume – I*. Ministry of Environment and Forests, New Delhi.

Harris, D., Joshi, A., Khan, P.A., Gothkar, P. and Sodhi, P.S. (1999) On-farm seed priming in semi-arid agriculture: development and evaluation in maize, rice and chickpea in India using participatory methods. *Experimental Agriculture* 35, 15–29.

Jha, Y., Subramanian, R.B. and Patel, S. (2011) Combination of endophytic and rhizospheric plant growth promoting rhizobacteria in *Oryza sativa* shows higher accumulation of osmoprotectant against saline stress. *Acta Physiologiae Plantarum* 33, 797–802.

Karlen, D.L. and Stott, D.E. (1994) A framework for evaluating physical and chemical indicators of soil quality. In: Doran, J.W., Coleman, D.C., Bezdicek, D.F. and Stewart, B.A. (eds) *Defining Soil Quality for a Sustainable Environment*. Soil Science Society of America, Inc., Madison, WI, pp. 53–72.

Kumar Rao, J.V.D.K., Harris, D., Kankal, M. and Gupta, B. (2008) Extending rabi cropping in rice fallows of eastern India. In: Riches, C.R., Harris, D., Johnson, D.E. and Hardy, B. (eds) *Improving Agricultural*

Productivity in Rice-Based Systems of the High Barind Tract of Bangladesh. International Rice Research Institute, Los Banos, Philippines, pp. 193–200.

Kuruvilla, V. and Mathew, T. (2009) Integrated farming systems for sustainability in coastal ecosystem. *Indian Journal of Agronomy* 54(2), 120–127.

Molden, D. (ed.) (2007) *Water for Food, Water for Life: A Comprehensive Assessment of Water Management in Agriculture.* Earthscan, London and International Water Management Institute, Colombo.

NRSA (2000) *Wastelands Atlas of India.* NRSA, Department of Space, Government of India, Balanagar, Hyderabad, India.

Pathak, P., Sahrawat, K.L., Wani, S.P., Sachan, R.C. and Sudi, R. (2009) Opportunities for water harvesting and supplemental irrigation for improving rainfed agriculture in semi-arid areas. In: Wani, S.P. Rockström, J. and Oweis, T. (eds) *Rainfed Agriculture: Unlocking the Potential.* Comprehensive Assessment of Water Management in Agriculture Series. CAB International, Wallingford, Oxfordshire, pp. 197–221.

Rego, T.J., Sahrawat, K.L., Wani, S.P. and Pardhasaradhi, G. (2007) Widespread deficiencies of sulfur, boron and zinc in Indian semi-arid tropical soils: on-farm crop responses. *Journal of Plant Nutrition* 30, 1569–1583.

Robertson, G.P. and Swinton, S.M. (2005) Reconciling agricultural productivity and environmental integrity: a grand challenge for agriculture. *Frontiers in Ecology and the Environment* 3, 38–46.

Rockström, J., Hatibu, N. and Oweis, T. (2007) Managing water in rain-fed agriculture. In: Molden, D. (ed.) *Water for Food, Water for Life: A Comprehensive Assessment of Water Management in Agriculture.* Earthscan, London and International Water Management Institute, Colombo, Sri Lanka, pp. 315–348.

Sahrawat, K.L., Wani, S.P., Rego, T.J., Pardhasaradhi, G. and Murthy, K.V.S. (2007) Widespread deficiencies of sulphur, boron and zinc in dryland soils of the Indian semi-arid tropics. *Current Science* 93(10), 1428–1432.

Sahrawat, K.L., Wani, S.P., Pardhasaradhi, G. and Murthy, K.V.S. (2010a) Diagnosis of secondary and micronutrient deficiencies and their management in rainfed agroecosystems: case study from Indian semi-arid tropics. *Communications in Soil Science and Plant Analysis* 41(3), 346–360.

Sahrawat, K.L. Wani, S.P., Pathak, P. and Rego, T.J. (2010b) Managing natural resources of watersheds in the semi-arid tropics for improved soil and water quality: a review. *Agricultural Water Management* 97, 375–381.

Singh, P., Aggarwal, P.K., Bhatia, V.S., Murty, M.V.R., Pala, M. *et al.* (2009) Yield gap analysis: modelling of achievable yields at farm level. In: Wani, S.P., Rockström, J. and Oweis, T. (eds) *Rainfed Agriculture: Unlocking the Potential.* Comprehensive Assessment of Water Management in Agriculture Series. CAB International, Wallingford, Oxfordshire, pp. 81–123.

Singh, P., Pathak, P., Wani, S.P. and Sahrawat, K.L. (2010) Integrated watershed management for increasing productivity and water use efficiency in semi-arid tropical India. In: Kang, M.S. (ed.) *Water and Agricultural Sustainability Strategies.* CRC Press, Leiden, The Netherlands, pp. 181–205.

Subbarao, G.V., Kumar Rao, J.V.D.K., Kumar, J., Johansen, C., Deb, U.K. *et al.* (2001) *Spatial Distribution and Quantification of Rice-fallows in South Asia – Potential for Legumes.* International Crops Research Institute for the Semi-Arid Tropics, Patancheru, India.

Tilman, D., Cassman, K.G., Matson, P.A., Naylor, R. and Polask, S. (2002) Agricultural sustainability and intensive production practices. *Nature* 418(8), 671–677.

Wani, S.P. (2008) Taking soil science to farmers' doorsteps through community watershed management. *Journal of the Indian Society of Soil Science* 56, 367–377.

Wani, S.P., Pathak, P., Tam, H.M., Ramakrishna, A., Singh, P. and Sreedevi, T.K. (2002) Integrated watershed management for minimizing land degradation and sustaining productivity in Asia. In: Adeel, Z (ed.) *Integrated Land Management in the Dry Areas.* Proceedings of Joint UNU-CAS International Workshop, 8–13 September 2001. Beijing. United Nations University, Tokyo, pp. 207–330.

Wani, S.P., Pathak, P., Jangawad, L.S., Eswaran, H. and Singh, P. (2003) Improved management of Vertisols in the semiarid tropics for increased productivity and soil carbon sequestration. *Soil Use and Management* 19, 217–222.

Wani, S.P., Sreedevi, T.K., Rockström, J. and Ramakrishna, Y.S. (2009) Rainfed agriculture – past trends and future prospects. In: Wani, S.P., Rockström, J. and Oweis, T. (eds) *Rainfed Agriculture: Unlocking the Potential.* Comprehensive Assessment of Water Management in Agriculture Series. CAB International, Wallingford, Oxfordshire, pp. 1–35.

10 Sustainable Development of Fragile Low-rainfall Regions – Power Grid Corporation of India Initiative

PRABHAKAR PATHAK,* R. SUDI, SUHAS P. WANI, AVIRAJ DATTA AND NAGARAJU BUDAMA

International Crops Research Institute for the Semi-Arid Tropics, Patancheru, India

Abstract

Rainfed agriculture in low-rainfall areas of Andhra Pradesh and Karnataka is characterized by high risks from drought, degraded natural resources and pervasive poverty, food insecurity and malnutrition. Under corporate social responsibility, Power Grid Corporation of India Limited, Gurugram, Haryana has been supporting International Crops Research Institute for the Semi-Arid Tropics (ICRISAT), Patancheru, Telangana in implementing farmer-centric watershed management in Kurnool district, Andhra Pradesh and Vijayapura district, Karnataka for improving rural livelihoods and reducing degradation of natural resources. This innovative model of watershed management uses holistic approach with science-led development in participatory mode with farmers. The watershed interventions have increased water availability by 25–30%, increased irrigated area by 15–25%, improved cropping intensity by 20–30%, increased crop yields by 15–35%, increased area under high-value crops by 10–15%, increased income, improved livelihoods and reduced runoff, soil loss and environment degradation. Innovative low-cost village-based wastewater treatment units were established at benchmark watersheds to increase the water availability for irrigation and improve the surface and groundwater quality.

10.1 Project Background

10.1.1 Why the project?

In most drylands, increasing population pressure, lack of investment and technological progress are taking a heavy toll on the quality of productive natural resource base. Water scarcity, land degradation and productivity loss are major challenges to the eradication of poverty. Depletion of the resource base diminishes the capacity of the small farmers to earn their livelihood and makes them more vulnerable to drought and other natural disasters (Pathak *et al.*, 2013). In these regions particularly in rural areas, majority of population does not get access to sanitation facilities and safe drinking water services. For such regions, local strategies are needed to tackle the challenges considering locally available resources with people's participation (Wani *et al.*, 2012). Integrated watershed management approach proved to be the suitable strategy for

---

* Corresponding author: p.pathak@cgiar.org

achieving holistic development in such regions through collective action (Wani *et al.*, 2003). The very purpose of the watershed development programmes is to reduce water-related risks in rainfed agriculture by improving surface and groundwater availability through implementing both *in-situ* and *ex-situ* soil and water management interventions. Since water and soil are important components of agricultural development, proper management of these resources is crucial to build the resilience of these systems to cope with varying climatic risks and improve livelihoods (Wani *et al.*, 2009; Sahrawat *et al.*, 2010).

As a part of corporate social responsibility, Power Grid Corporation of India Limited (POWERGRID), Gurugram, Haryana has been supporting International Crops Research Institute for the Semi-Arid Tropics (ICRISAT), Patancheru, Telanagana to undertake farmer-centric integrated watershed management for improving rural livelihoods and reducing environmental degradation at two sites, one at Bethamcherla mandal, Kurnool district of Andhra Pradesh and another at Ukkali village, Vijayapura district of Karnataka. The overall goal of this initiative is to increase agricultural productivity and improve the livelihoods of rural poor in fragile dryland areas on a sustainable basis by enhancing the impact of integrated watershed management programmes in the selected region through capacity-building initiatives using site of learning in low-rainfall agroecoregions. The specific objectives of the initiative are as follows.

- To establish 'Model Sites of Learning' in Andhra Pradesh and Karnataka for harnessing the potential of rainfed areas by adopting the integrated water resource management approach.
- To enhance water availability and its use efficiency for diversifying the livelihood systems in the target villages.
- To build capacity of the farmers in the region for improving rural livelihoods through knowledge sharing and dissemination.

The two selected benchmark sites for this project have low annual rainfall (<700 mm). Both the project sites are the hot spots of water scarcity, poverty, malnutrition and land degradation, which are critical factors that affect farmers' livelihoods. Agriculture in the two regions where project sites are located needs special attention and requires holistic development for improving rural

prosperity. To address these issues, an innovative self-sustaining farmer-centric integrated watershed was initiated at both project sites in 2014. The integrated watershed project is expected to be completed by 2019. This chapter discusses the achievements and impact made during 3 years (2014–17) of the project.

10.1.2   Location details of benchmark watersheds

The Bethamcherla watershed in Kurnool district of Andhra Pradesh comprises ten villages in four revenue villages of Pendekal, Muddavaram, Emboy and Bugganipalli in Bethamcherla mandal. It is located (latitude 15°28′25″ to 15°33′48″ N and longitude 78°03′20″ to 78°10′57″ E) about 45 km from Kurnool town (Fig. 10.1). The second benchmark watershed in Vijayapura district of Karnataka is located in Ukkali village (latitude 16°43′02″ N and longitude 75°53′17″ E) in Basavana Bagewadi taluk (Fig. 10.1). This watershed is about 25 km from Vijayapura district headquarter.

10.1.3   Benchmark watersheds in Andhra Pradesh and Karnataka

Bethamcherla watershed has 4113 households with total population of 20,213, covering a geographical area of 6402 ha. The analysis of household categories reveal that 71% of households are small farmers, 20% are medium farmers and 9% are large farmers (Table 10.1). The land use information of watershed villages is given in Table 10.2. Out of a total geographical area of 6402 ha only 2962 ha (46%) are under cultivation. The general socioeconomic conditions of farmers in the watershed villages is extremely bad mainly due to low rainfall, recurring droughts and crop failures. In the watershed, red soils are the major soils (85%) with depth ranging from 0.5 m to 1.25 m and black soils (15%) with a depth of 1.0–1.5 m. Average annual rainfall in the watershed area is about 675 mm. Major crops grown in the watershed villages are maize, groundnut, pigeonpea and sorghum. Farmers with bore wells grow cotton, chilli, paddy and onion. Average crop yield (t/ha) of maize under rainfed condition is 2.15,

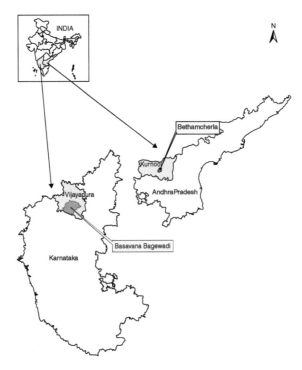

Fig. 10.1. Project sites of POWERGRID–ICRISAT watersheds in Andhra Pradesh and Karnataka.

Table 10.1. Household category of farmers in Bethamcherla watershed, Kurnool, Andhra Pradesh.

Village	Household (no.)	Small farmers (no.)	Medium farmers (no.)	Large farmers (no.)	Landless farmers (no.)
Pendekal	1290	929	232	120	9
Muddavaram	1545	1004	386	143	12
Mandlavanipalli	340	272	48	20	0
Bugganipalli	938	722	150	56	8
Total	4113	2927	816	339	29

Table 10.2. Land use in Bethamcherla watershed, Kurnool.

Village	Geographical area (ha)	Forest (ha)	Uncultivable land (ha)	Land under non-agri uses (ha)	Fallow area (ha)	Current fallow area (ha)	Net cultivated area (ha)
Pendekal	1264	39	207	63	44	475	436
Muddavaram	2599	147	635	74	178	60	1505
Mandlavanipalli	589	0	130	60	0	54	345
Bugganipalli	1950	3259	455	314	516	45	676
Total	6402	3445	1427	511	738	634	2962

pigeonpea 1.1, groundnut 1.15 and paddy 2.7. Water scarcity and drought are the common features of this area and water is the most limiting factor for increasing agricultural productivity. About 90% of the area is rainfed. Most of the irrigation is from bore wells, ponds and open wells. The current rainfall use efficiency is about 45–55% and there is good potential to increase

the rainwater efficiency and double the agricultural productivity.

The Ukkali watershed in Vijayapura district, Karnataka has 2950 households with total population of 18,000 and covers a geographical area of 8436 ha. The forest area is 383 ha, rainfed area is 7653 ha, irrigated area is 400 ha and net cultivated area is 8053 ha. In this watershed most of the area is under cultivation (96% of total geographical area). The watershed village has 19% small farmers, 41% medium farmers, 24% large farmers and about 16% landless. The soil in the watershed is predominantly medium-to-deep black with a depth ranging from 0.6 m to 1.8 m. The general topography is flat to moderate slope (<1.5%). Average annual rainfall of the district is 625 mm. Major crops grown in the watershed are pearl millet, pigeonpea, chickpea and *rabi* (post-rainy season) sorghum. Now the farmers are showing keen interest in horticultural crops. During *kharif* (rainy season) about 40% of area is cultivated and in *rabi* 60% of total area is cultivated. Average crop yield (t/ha) of pearl millet is 0.85–0.90, pigeonpea 0.68–0.72, chickpea 0.8–1.0 and *rabi* sorghum 0.8–0.9. Most of the crops are grown under rainfed conditions. Due to very low annual rainfall, water scarcity and drought are common features of this area. There is good potential to double the crop yields and improve the rainfall use efficiency by adopting integrated watershed management approach.

10.2 Strategy for Execution and Process

Some of the key features of the project strategy, which has been used in implementing this project at both benchmark watersheds are as follows.

- Select target villages in Kurnool in Andhra Pradesh and Vijayapura in Karnataka.
- Establish site of learning of about 5000 ha encompassing holistic community watershed management approach.
- Establish field laboratory for students to undertake strategic research in target agroecoregion in the area of community watershed management.
- Holistic and integrated approach for sustainable development of rainfed areas through

conservation, enhancement and efficient use of natural resources by using watershed management as an entry point for improving rural livelihoods.

- Develop innovative and effective mechanisms to share the knowledge with different stakeholders and build community-based institutions for sustainable development.
- Harness public–private partnerships for backward and forward linkages, for improving the incomes of the farming community.
- Establish rain gauges and hydrological monitoring stations at sites of learning watersheds, which will provide strategic data on hydrological parameters for planning watershed interventions in specific agroecoregions with varying soil types.
- Develop natural resource management based income-generating activities for improving livelihoods of vulnerable groups.
- Demonstrate improved management options for enhancing productivity on sustainable basis.
- Train lead farmers to serve as trainers in the district.
- Initiate wastewater treatment and its reuse in agriculture to address the issues of water quality and scarcity.
- Diversify the sources of livelihoods for the families to build their resilience against the impacts of climate change.

10.2.1 Partnerships

The partners were carefully selected based on the need of the project and their expertise. Also organizations which could assist in scaling-up of the technologies in large areas were considered. Key partners in the project are as follows.

- Power Grid Corporation of India Limited, Haryana
- International Crops Research Institute for the Semi-Arid Tropics, Patancheru, Telangana
- Watershed committees at benchmark watersheds in Andhra Pradesh and Karnataka
- Rural Study and Development Society, Dhone, Kurnool, Andhra Pradesh
- Shri Banashankari Mahila Mattu Makkala Abhivruddhi Samsthe, Vijayapura, Karnataka
- Department of Agriculture, Government of Andhra Pradesh and Karnataka

- Department of Horticulture, Government of Andhra Pradesh and Karnataka
- District Watershed Development Agency, Government of Andhra Pradesh
- Watershed Development Department, Government of Karnataka

10.2.2 Entry point activity

Knowledge-based entry point activity was undertaken based on the need and important constraint of the benchmark watersheds that should benefit the farmers in watershed development-related activities, which will also help to build rapport and confidence with farmers. ICRISAT has used baseline soil characterization as knowledge-based entry point activity successfully in the past. Baseline soil characterization has benefited farmers in implementing balanced fertilization to increase productivity while saving money on wastage of fertilizers and to maintain soil health and environment.

To diagnose soil fertility-related constraints, soil samples were collected from farmers' fields in Bethamcherla, Kurnool and Ukkali, Vijayapura watersheds by adopting participatory stratified soil sampling method (Sahrawat *et al.*, 2008). Under this method, target villages in the watersheds were divided into three topo-sequences. At each topo-sequence location, samples were taken proportionately from small, medium and large farmholding sizes to address the

variations that may arise due to different management practices because of different economic status in each farm size class. Within each farm size class in a topo-sequence, the soil samples were chosen carefully to represent all possible soil fertility variations as judged from soil colour, texture, cropping system and agronomic management. The soil samples were processed and analysed in ICRISAT laboratory for organic carbon, phosphorus, potassium, sulfur, boron and zinc following the standard procedures. Soil health assessment of Bethamcherla and Ukkali watershed villages clearly shows moderate to severe deficiencies in critical elements including micronutrients (Table 10.3).

10.2.3 Institutional arrangements

Institutions play a critical role in effective implementation, monitoring, scaling-up and sustaining the impact of watershed programme. In this initiative for social mobilization and implementation of various watershed interventions ICRISAT has entered into agreement with two local non-governmental organizations (NGOs), namely Rural Study and Development Society, Bethamcherla, and Shri Banashankari Mahila Mattu Makkala Abhivruddhi Samsthe, Ukkali. These NGOs supported in implementing the various watershed interventions and day-to-day monitoring. They provided necessary local support in all the watershed activities. At each watershed site one

Table 10.3. Percentage of farmers' fields deficient in soil nutrients in Bethamcherla and Ukkali watersheds.

Village	OC	Av P	Av K	Av S	Av Zn	Av B	Av Fe	Av Cu	Av Mn	Ca	Mg
Bethamcherla watershed											
Emboy	18	0	0	36	73	0	0	0	0	18	0
M. Pendekal	17	6	0	94	78	39	0	0	0	78	0
Mandlavanipalli	85	0	15	100	85	54	0	31	0	100	0
Marrikunta	75	33	33	92	92	75	0	33	0	100	0
Muddavaram	50	23	3	65	58	18	15	0	0	70	0
Musalai Cheruvu	46	8	0	77	77	23	0	15	0	100	0
Pendekal	50	20	5	55	60	30	5	0	0	70	0
Rudravaram	67	0	17	83	100	44	0	17	0	94	0
Veeraiah Pally	45	30	10	95	80	50	0	35	0	100	0
Venkatagiri	50	25	0	75	100	50	0	0	0	50	0
Mean	50	15	8	76	75	35	4	12	0	80	0
Ukkali watershed											
Ukkali	49	89	0	71	94	16	8	0	0	0	0

watershed committee (WC) was established. The WC comprised of all the sections of the community, including women representatives, proportionately small, medium, large and landless farmers and represented all the communities. The WC was responsible for conducting *gram sabha* (village meeting with all farmers) at monthly intervals or when needed to identify the activities, execution and monitoring of works in the watershed. At each watershed, user groups were formed for active participation and maintenance of various interventions, namely water harvesting structures, etc. Self-help groups (SHGs) were formed and supported for various activities through revolving fund to benefit smallholder women farmers to generate additional family income.

Several state government departments (Watershed Development, Agriculture, Horticulture and Animal Husbandry) were actively involved in the development of watersheds at both benchmark sites. Several government-funded schemes were effectively converged to strengthen the various watershed activities and impact.

10.2.4   Capacity building

In any integrated watershed management programme, capacity building plays a key role in successful implementation of watershed programme and enhancing the entrepreneurial skills and knowledge of various stakeholders. In this initiative, capacity-building activity has been focused to strengthen the capacity of all stakeholders from partner institutions and farmers. Farmers were oriented on better crop production technology and their capacity was built by organizing various types of training on new technology and better farming practices. Need-based training was conducted on major interventions, namely soil sampling, construction of soil and water management structures, implementation of *in-situ* water management technologies, cultivation of high-value crops, integrated pest management, livestock improvement, construction and management of village-based wastewater treatment unit and farm machinery. Self-help group members were trained on various income-generating activities, namely vermicomposting, tailoring, goat rearing, dal mill and other interventions.

Several capacity-building programmes (76 events benefiting 2375 participants in Bethamcherla and 124 events benefiting 2961 participants in Ukkali) were conducted to create awareness about the watershed programmes and its various activities such as watershed community formation, participatory soil sampling, soil health, action plan preparation, use and application of micronutrients, improved crop productivity technologies, and integrated pest management. Some of the key capacity building programmes conducted include the following.

- Training to the members of WC about their roles and responsibilities, planning on various interventions, budgeting, and monitoring and evaluation.
- Interactive group discussions, field visits, demonstrations, farmers' days where farmers could interact with scientists in exchanging ideas, views and experience.
- Training workshops to enhance awareness about some specific technical skills, combining indoor training and practical application in the field through interactive sessions as formal and informal events.
- Field demonstrations through participatory mode.
- Field days, a core part of the project, where farmers would come together to share details of on-farm research and demonstration and learn from each other in a spirit of openness and curiosity.
- Learning/exposure visits cum study tours to new successful technologies.

10.3   Watershed Interventions

10.3.1   Integrated soil and water management interventions

Soil and water are two most important natural resources for rural livelihoods with agriculture as the key occupation. In rainfed agriculture, the constant risk of drought increases the vulnerability to livelihoods. Both the benchmark watersheds are located in very low annual rainfall region and there is strong demand from the watershed community for interventions which can improve the surface and groundwater availability. Several field-based soil and water management interventions such as conservation furrows, contour cultivation, field bunding, loose boulder structures, compartmental bunding and others were undertaken on large numbers of farmers' fields. These interventions increased the rainwater infiltration and improved soil moisture. On average, these interventions increased the crop yields by 13–25%.

To improve the surface and groundwater availability large numbers of water harvesting and groundwater recharging structures have been constructed in participatory mode with the community. Some of these structures which were constructed in benchmark watersheds are

check-dams, farm ponds, percolation tanks, bore well and open well recharging pits, rock-fill dams, loose boulder structures, field bunding, gully plugs and sunken pits (Fig. 10.2; Table 10.4).

Due to these structures the surface and groundwater availability increased by 25–30%. Several of the bore wells and open wells which were dead became functional. This activity has significantly increased irrigated area by 15–25% and thereby crop yields. It has also reduced risk to drought and crop failure. A success story about water harvesting and groundwater recharging structures is presented in Box 10.1.

Fig. 10.2. *In-situ* and *ex-situ* soil and water management interventions implemented at POWERGRID–ICRISAT watersheds: (a) check-dam at Bugganipalli, Bethamcherla, Kurnool; (b) broad-bed and furrow system at Ukkali, Vijayapura.

Table 10.4. Soil and water conservation works done at benchmark sites during 2014–17.

Works	Kurnool	Vijayapura
Farm/dugout pond (no.)	22	17
Check-dam (no.)	8	8
Check-wall (no.)	2	–
Rock-fill dam (no.)	16	–
Loose boulder structures (no.)	28	–
Open well and bore well recharge system (no.)	4	4
Mini-percolation tank (no.)	4	4
Land development (stone removal and silt spreading) (ha)	7	–
Stone field bunding (ha)	12	–
Wastewater treatment unit (no.)	1	1
Diversion (feeder) channel (running per metre)	50	–
Gully plugs (no.)	–	2
Sunken pits (no.)	–	5
Field bunding (ha)	–	550
Silt removal from existing tank (no.)	–	1

Box 10.1. Bore well recharge helps the farmer rejuvenate land and gain increased income.

Kallanagouda A. Patil from Ukkali village has 2.4 ha of land with two bore wells. During the summer, due to a shortage of water, he was forced to remove the lemon trees from his land before the watershed project. During 2014–15 POWERGRID–ICRISAT initiated a watershed project in Ukkali village. Technical team visited his field and analysed the water problem due to drying of the bore well and suggested the farmer to construct a bore well recharge pit beside one of the bore wells.

After the guidance from project staff, he constructed a bore well recharge pit of 2 x 2 x 2 m filled with gravel and sand (see figure below, left). From the bottom of the recharge pit, a PVC pipe was connected to the bore well so that the filtered and drained rainwater from pit directly flows to the bore well and thus efficiently recharging it. Now the farmer has planted grapes in 0.8 ha of land and has gained an income of ₹250,000 from grapes only (see figure below, right).

10.3.2 Productivity enhancement through improved crop varieties and nutrient management

In 2014, when the watershed project started, most crop yields were extremely low. This was mainly due to lack of water, poor soil health and use of low-yielding crop varieties. Yield gap analysis clearly shows that there is good potential to double the yields of most crops. Large trials/numbers of demonstrations and participatory trials on balanced nutrient management, improved crop varieties and other improved agricultural practices were carried out at both Bethamcherla and Ukkali watersheds.

At Bethamcherla watershed, 267 farmer participatory trials were conducted to evaluate improved crop management practices including soil test-based fertilizer recommendations. The results showed productivity improvement by 22% in maize, 25% in pigeonpea, 10% in groundnut, 35% in foxtail millet and 9% in paddy (Table 10.5). Around 50 farmers every year were encouraged to plant pigeonpea on the periphery of field bunds in the watershed. An average of 1 ha field which was planted with pigeonpea has given an additional yield of 80–100 kg with an economic gain of ₹4000–5000 without any additional expenditure on fertilizer or irrigation.

At Ukkali watershed, Vijayapura district of Karnataka, 376 participatory trials on productivity enhancement were conducted. The yield increase and economic returns from these interventions are shown in Table 10.6. Apart from this under convergence with Department of Agriculture, Karnataka under Bhoochetana initiative soil test-based nutrients management was covered on 2000 ha, wherein average yield increase of 8–10% was recorded in various crops. A success story from this activity is discussed in Box 10.2.

10.3.3 Cultivation of high-value crops for increasing income and water productivity

With improved availability of surface and groundwater in watershed villages the farmers were encouraged to grow high-value crops, namely

Table 10.5. Increase in crop yields and economic gain due to improved practice (IP) at Bethamcherla watershed, Kurnool district.[a]

Crop	Average % increase in IP over farmers' practice	Additional yield gain (kg/ha)	Additional economic gain (₹/ha)
Maize (65 ha)	22	750	7500
Groundnut (35 ha)	10	150	6800
Pigeonpea (350 ha)	25	220	8800
Paddy (50 ha)	9	250	4500
Foxtail millet (200 ha)	35	400	8800

[a]IP includes *in-situ* moisture conservation and *ex-situ* water conservation, improved crop varieties, balanced fertilization, etc.

Table 10.6. Increase in crop yields and economic gain due to improved practice (IP) at Ukkali watershed, Vijayapura district.

Crop	Yield with IP[a] (t/ha)	Yield with farmers' practice (FP) (t/ha)	% yield increase with IP over FP	Additional economic gain (₹/ha)
Maize (100 ha)	5.88	5.03	17	8,500
Groundnut (40 ha)	1.08	0.91	19	8,500
Pigeonpea (200 ha)	1.55	1.35	15	10,000
Chickpea (70 ha)	1.34	1.10	22	7,200

[a]IP includes *in-situ* moisture conservation and *ex-situ* water conservation, improved crop varieties, balanced fertilization, etc.

vegetables and other horticultural crops (Fig. 10.3). At Bethamcherla watershed, farmers have undertaken mango plantation and cultivation of onion, chilli and tomato. Similarly, at Ukkali watershed farmers have undertaken floriculture and are also growing grapes and pomegranate and brinjal. Necessary training and exposure visits were conducted for watershed farmers to improve their skills. At Bethamcherla watershed, 50 farmers were provided improved vegetable seeds along with micronutrients. These farmers got 18–24% increase in vegetable yields (Table 10.7). A success story from Ukkali watershed is presented in Box 10.3.

10.3.4 Kitchen gardening

Women farmers from Bethamcherla and Ukkali watersheds were encouraged, guided and supported to grow vegetables in a small area as kitchen garden to improve family nutrition and capture market-led opportunities. The demand-driven seeds of vegetables such as brinjal (100 g), tomato (200 g), okra (1500 g), cluster bean (3400 g), bitter gourd (300 g), ridge gourd (100 g), bottle gourd (100 g), common bean (200 g) and leafy vegetables (3900 g) were provided by the project along with required capacity building and other inputs like soil test-based nutrients. Vegetables were grown by around 40 women farmers at both watersheds of Bethamcherla and Ukkali by using improved cultivation practices which resulted in high yields and benefits. At Ukkali watershed, by selling the vegetables, daily income of the women increased from ₹125 to ₹240 per day. A success story from this intervention is presented in Box 10.4.

10.3.5 Livestock improvement

With help from government department, large number of animal health camps were organized for deworming and breed improvement of livestock. In watershed villages, shortage of fodder is the key issue for improving livestock productivity. Therefore, fodder promotion was taken up in the watershed villages. Fodder promotion translates into improving livestock-based productivity including milk, which is generally in the domain of women and thus leads into their

Box 10.2. Productivity-enhancement activities increased the income and help the farmer to cope with vagaries of nature.

Before the watershed project, Ayyaswamy from Marrikunta village in Kurnool district cultivated local variety of pigeonpea and foxtail millet as intercrop and received only 1000 kg/ha yield of each crop. He would sell the produce depending on the market rate and gain a net income of ₹25,000–30,000 from the two crops.

After initiation of the watershed project, the farmer decided to try and test the use of micronutrients in his land. With the help of ICRISAT staff and the local NGO staff, he applied 250 kg of gypsum per ha, 25 kg of zinc sulphate per ha and 2.5 kg agribor (boron) per ha. He also used improved varieties such as pigeonpea Asha and foxtail millet Suryanandi (see figure below). With these two crops, the farmer received 1500 kg/ha yield of each crop. He is extremely happy with the yield and has stored the produce and is waiting for the market price to increase so that he can reap a higher net income and earn about ₹90,000-100,000 from the two crops.

Fig. 10.3. Cultivation of high-value crops for increasing farmers' income: (a) mango at Bethamcherla; (b) rose cultivation at Ukkali.

empowerment. Improved variety of sorghum fodder and agroforestry was implemented in the watershed villages to enhance the availability of green fodder. At Bethamcherla watershed, daily milk production has increased significantly compared to start of the project (Table 10.8). The daily milk production from the local buffalo breed has increased from 1.5 to 2.8 l/day mainly

Table 10.7. Yield of vegetables with different practices at Bethamcherla watershed, Kurnool.

Vegetable crop	Yield (t/ha) with improved practice (IP)	Yield (t/ha) with farmers' practice (FP)	% yield increase with IP over FP
Onion	26.25	21.25	24
Tomato	16.25	13.75	18

Box 10.3. Vegetable cultivation with watershed project interventions increased the farmer's income.

Ramesh Harake from Ukkali village in Vijayapura district has 3.2 ha of land of which 1.61 ha is irrigated. It was after the initiation of the watershed project by Power Grid Corporation of India Limited with the support of ICRISAT, the farmer was provided information on vegetable cultivation.

The farmer was provided with improved variety of brinjal seeds and was provided guidance about cultivation of vegetables using bed landform sowing technology (see figure below). Earlier he would get an income of ₹1500 per week by growing brinjal but with improved variety, the farmer now gets an income of ₹3000 per week by selling 100 kg of the vegetable.

---

due to the increased availability of quality green fodder in the watershed villages.

10.3.6   Strengthening livelihood through income-generating activities

In very low-rainfall dryland regions in which benchmark watersheds are located, non-agriculture-based income-generating activities are required to improve and sustain the livelihoods of the community. Several income-generating activities, such as sewing, food processing, dal mill, goat rearing, improving the local goat breeds through crossbreeding with Sirohi goats, vermicomposting, nursery and home gardening, photocopying, small grocery shops and photo studios were taken up by women SHGs (Fig. 10.4). Success stories from two benchmark sites are discussed in Box 10.5 and Box 10.6.

10.3.7   Low-cost decentralized wastewater treatment system

The potential of constructed wetland to improve rural wastewater management was validated through setting-up of decentralized wastewater

---

Box 10.4. Kitchen garden helps self-help groups benefit from increased income.

Reshma Abdul Makanadar from Ukkali village has 1.61 ha of land and was not making sufficient income from agriculture due to severe drought and low water availability. After initiation of the watershed project by Power Grid Corporation of India Limited with the support of ICRISAT and the local NGO, Shri Banashankari Mahila Mattu Makkala Abhivruddhi Samsthe, she was given information on self-help groups (SHGs) and their formation. The staff noticed that land beside her residence was barren and suggested growing a kitchen garden in the area. After clearing the land, the staff provided vegetable seeds to her group and trained them in land preparation, methods of sowing and use of household water. After few months, she sold the vegetables in the weekly market and gained an income of ₹500 per week. At present, Reshma manages to sell more and makes an income of ₹800–1000 per week (see figure below).

Table 10.8. Increase in milk production due to watershed intervention (WI) with improved multi-cut variety of sorghum fodder at Bethamcherla, Kurnool district.

		Milk production (l/day)			
		Local breed buffalo		Crossbreed buffalo	
Name of the farmer	Village	Before WI	After WI	Before WI	After WI
Giddaiah	Veeraipalli	1.5	2.5	6	10
Lyyaswamy	Marrikunta	1.5	3.0	6	11
Balaiah	Muddavaram	1.5	3.0	6	10.5
Suneetha	Veeraipalli	1.5	2.5	6	10
Giddaiah	Repalle	1.5	3.0	6	11
Average		1.5	2.8	6	10.5

treatment (DWAT) unit comprising a field scale subsurface flow constructed wetland at the Pendekal village in Kurnool district of Andhra Pradesh and at the Ukkali village in Vijayapura district of Karnataka. Pendekal village, Bethamcherla mandal has 400 households with a population of 1800 individuals. An initial survey of possible site locations was carried out and an area where wastewater flows under natural gradient and collects near a piece of panchayat land at the village periphery was selected for the construction of the DWAT unit. Wastewater analysis was conducted using the standard methods and consistently high concentrations of inorganic nitrogen (ammoniacal as well as nitrate) and phosphate were observed. Further village-level meetings were conducted to disseminate the

Fig. 10.4. Income-generating activities for women SHG members at benchmark watershed sites: (a) dal mill at Bethamcherla; (b) sewing at Ukkali.

Box 10.5. Increased benefits for self-help groups after watershed activities.

Ms Padmavathamma, a self-help group (SHG) beneficiary and watershed committee member from Muddavaram village, has been handling 21 SHGs in her village. After observing her dedicated efforts, the watershed committee decided to enrol her as a member and provided ₹30,000 as a revolving fund to the Madhuri group, a group that is run by Padmavathamma. Under the revolving fund, the group was supported to buy ram lambs to improve the livelihoods in addition to agricultural income (see figure below). Each member purchased a ram lamb at ₹2500–3000 and sold them at a rate of ₹7000 per lamb.

---

concept of DWAT to end users. The DWAT unit was designed based on the average wastewater flow (51 m³/day) and average inlet wastewater characteristics. The wastewater flow was estimated from the population data and guided by the supplied water data for the village. The designed hydraulic retention time of the unit was three days. The DWAT unit comprised an upstream inlet and flow equalization tank (length: 2 m, width: 3 m and depth: 2.25 m) followed by a subsurface constructed wetland (length: 56 m, width: 3 m and depth: 0.8 m) divided in three equal and hydraulically connected cells. An outlet tank (length: 1 m, width: 3 m and depth: 0.8 m) was provided downstream of the constructed

> **Box 10.6.** Business flourishes after formation of self-help group.
>
> Ms Kaveri Prakash Bashetti has been running a photo studio in Ukkali village and was earning an income of ₹200–300 per day. It was not sufficient to maintain her household expenses and she was finding it difficult to meet the needs of the family. After initiation of the watershed project, she was given information on self-help groups (SHGs) and their formation.
>
> After training, ten members together formed a group named Shri Annapoorneshwari Mahila Swa Sahaya Sangha, in Ukkali and were given an amount of ₹30,000 as a revolving fund from watershed project. From the revolving fund, Kaveri requested other SHG members and borrowed an amount of ₹10,000 from the SHG. With the money, she purchased a colour printer and scanner. She has started developing photos, scanning, designing and printing and is now getting an income of ₹600 per day (see figure below). She also manages to save ₹200 per day and is sending her children to an English-speaking school.
>
>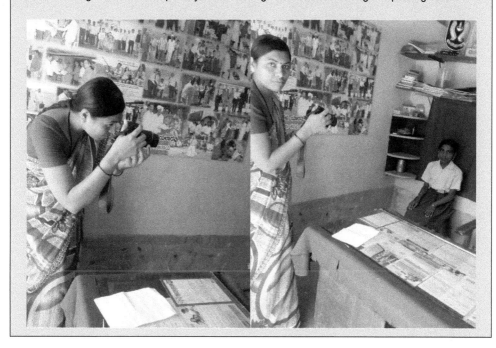

wetland to maintain the subsurface flow regimen. The treated wastewater was stored in a storage pond located further downstream of the outlet tank (Fig. 10.5). The DWAT unit was vegetated with *Canna indica*. The period during which plants get established in the constructed wetland is known as stabilization period. During this phase the plant roots get established and the microbial biofilm in the rhizosphere of these plants undertakes biodegradation of pollutants from the wastewater. *Canna indica* plants got established within a period of 35 days at this location. The DWAT unit at present is exhibiting an average removal efficiency of 54% for chemical oxygen demand, 47% for sulphate, 67% for inorganic nitrogen and 86% for suspended solids concentration. Treated water can be used for agriculture during water scarcity and it can also help in increasing the efficiency of domestic wastewater treatment leading to improved health and hygiene of the village. A similar decentralized wastewater treatment unit has been established in Ukkali village in the Vijayapura district of Karnataka, which is at same stage of implementation. In coming years, these two DWAT units are expected to provide extra water for irrigation as well as significantly contribute to improving quality of drinking water in the villages.

10.4   Impact and Outcome from the Integrated Watershed Project

During the three years of the project, Bethamcherla, Kurnool and Ukkali, Vijayapaura watersheds have made significant impacts on economic gain,

Fig. 10.5. Different phases in construction of decentralized wastewater treatment DWAT unit in Pendekal village: (a) construction of tanks; (b) planting of *Canna indica*; (c) fully constructed DWAT unit during stabilization phase.

social and environmental parameters (Fig. 10.6). Watershed interventions have increased surface and groundwater availability, irrigated area, cropping intensity and crop yield and reduced runoff and soil loss and improved water quality. These two watershed programmes will continue for another two years (up to 2019) and are expected to make much greater impact and outcome.

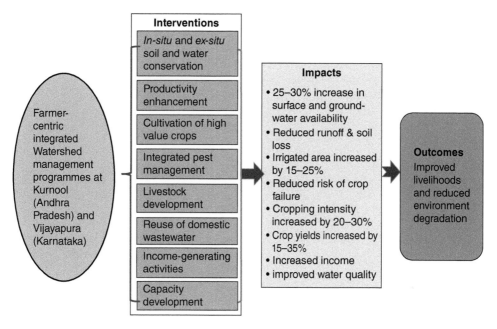

Fig. 10.6. Flow chart of interventions, impact and outcome from farmer-centric integrated watershed management programmes at benchmark sites in Bethamcherla, Andhra Pradesh and Ukkali, Karnataka.

10.5 Sustainability

Success of any watershed programme depends on sustainability of the various watershed interventions. From the beginning emphasis has been laid on capacity building and empowerment of various stakeholders. Community-based organizations (CBOs) have been established, trained and strengthened to continue development and management. Economic activities will be sustained through community participation. Participatory research and development approach along with demand-driven interventions will reduce dependency on subsidies. Through community contributions for all the activities, watershed development fund is being built and the CBOs are trained to run watershed as business model. The economic activities and tangible economic benefits along with empowerment and hand-holding from the consortium partners is empowering the CBOs to develop and sustain the watershed activities after project phase. Also with active involvement of various state government departments, various long-term funded schemes are being effectively converged in the watershed

programmes to further strengthen and sustain the watershed activities after the project phase.

10.6 Scaling-up Process

To scale-up the benefits from the innovative farmer-participatory consortium model, necessary strategies are being identified. In the process of scaling-up, the watershed implementing NGO becomes the pilot trainer for other NGOs in the districts as well as in the region. In addition, the pilot NGOs transfer the lessons learnt from these model watersheds to other watershed projects implemented by their staff in the area and thus promote knowledge dissemination. New science tools such as remote sensing, geographical information system (GIS) and digital terrain modelling are being used. These tools provide the capabilities for extrapolating and implementing technologies to other potential areas.

This project has already been running for three years and in the next two years the scaling-up process will start. It is also envisaged that the district watershed departments who are closely involved in this watershed project will assist in scaling-up this farmer-centric integrated watershed management model in the districts as well as in the region. It is expected that this watershed model will potentially benefit large numbers of the watershed programmes which are being implemented in the low-rainfall areas of Andhra Pradesh and Karnataka.

10.7   Summary and the Way Forward

The farmer-centric integrated watershed management model implemented by ICRISAT along with its partners could be effectively used for improving rural livelihoods and reducing environment degradation in low-rainfall regions of Karnataka and Rayalaseema region of Andhra Pradesh. This initiative of POWERGRID and ICRISAT could go a long way in addressing the key issue of rural poverty in low-rainfall dryland areas on sustained basis. The project should now focus more on organizing field exposure visits of officials from private companies, watershed departments and other development agencies to sensitize and bring more awareness about the impact of this approach. In the next two years of the project, the focus should gradually shift from development phase to consolidation phase, considering the sustainability of these watersheds after project phase. All efforts should be made to make these two watersheds as learning sites to benefit large numbers of watersheds implemented by other agencies.

Acknowledgements

The support from Power Grid Corporation of India Limited, for undertaking the presented work is gratefully acknowledged. Authors also acknowledge the help from NGOs (Rural Study and Development Society and Shri Banashankari Mahila Mattu Makkala Abhivruddhi Samsthe), for providing local support in implementing the various project activities and collecting data. The full support, participation and cooperation of farmers, community-based organizations and of various government departments, namely District Watershed Management Agency, Department of Agriculture, Department of Horticulture and others is gratefully acknowledged.

References

Pathak, P., Chourasia, A.K., Wani, S.P. and Sudi, R. (2013) Multiple impact of integrated watershed management in low rainfall semi-arid region: a case study from eastern Rajasthan, India. *Journal of Water Resource and Protection* 5(1), 27–36. Available at: https://doi.org/10.4236/jwarp.2013.51004 (accessed 12 December 2012).

Sahrawat, K.L., Rego, T.J., Wani, S.P. and Pardhasaradhi, G. (2008) Stretching soil sampling to watershed: evaluation of soil-test parameters in a semi-arid tropical watershed. *Communications in Soil Science and Plant Analysis* 39(19–20), 2950–2960.

Sahrawat, K.L., Wani, S.P., Pathak, P. and Rego, T.J. (2010) Managing natural resources of watersheds in the semi-arid tropics for improved soil and water quality: a review. *Agricultural Water Management* 97(3), 375–381. Available at: https://doi.org/10.1016/j.agwat.2009.10.012 (accessed 20 October 2009).

Wani, S.P., Singh, H.P., Sreedevi, T.K., Pathak, P., Rego, T.J. *et al.* (2003) Farmer-participatory integrated watershed management: Adarsha watershed, Kothapally, India – an innovative and upscalable approach. *Journal of SAT Agricultural Research* 2(1), 1–27.

Wani, S.P., Singh, P., Boomiraj, K. and Sahrawat, K.L. (2009) Climate change and sustainable rain-fed agriculture: challenges and opportunities. *Agricultural Situation in India* 66(5), 221–239.

Wani, S.P., Dixin, Yin, Li, Zhong, Dar, W.D. and Chander, G. (2012) Enhancing agricultural productivity and rural incomes through sustainable use of natural resources in the semi-arid tropics. *Journal of the Science of Food and Agriculture* 92(5), 1054–1063. Available at: https://doi.org/10.1002/jsfa.4721 (accessed 20 April 2018).

11 Farmer-centric Integrated Water Management for Improving Livelihoods – A Case Study of Rural Electrification Corporation Limited

R. Sudi,* Girish Chander, Suhas P. Wani
and G. Pardhasaradhi

International Crops Research Institute for the Semi-Arid Tropics, Patancheru, India

Abstract

Rural Electrification Corporation Limited (RECL) supported an ICRISAT-led consortium to establish two watershed learning sites in Penukonda mandal (4 villages, 3150 ha of cultivated land and home to 8700 people) of Anantapur district in Andhra Pradesh and Wanaparthy mandal (4 villages, 3968 ha of cultivated land and home to 11,726 people) in the Mahabubnagar district of Telangana. The community and farm-based rainwater conservation have created a net storage capacity of about 18,000 m^3 with total conservation of about 50,000 m^3/year of surface runoff water in Anantapur watershed, and 27,000 m^3 storage capacity with conservation of about 54,000 m^3/year of surface runoff water in Mahabubnagar watershed. Soil health improvement with soil test-based addition of macro- and micronutrients and carbon building, and varietal replacements are promoted with farmers in the watershed. The science-led management has resulted in increasing and sustaining crop and livestock productivity and diversification leading to increased incomes to farmers. The RECL–ICRISAT watershed sites have provided a proof of concept and a good learning site for holistic solutions to harness the system productivity and strengthening of livelihood.

11.1 Project Background

11.1.1 Why the project?

To achieve food security, minimize the water conflicts and reduce poverty, it has become essential to harness potential of rainfed systems, as globally 80% of agriculture is rainfed and current productivity on farmers' fields is lower by two- to fourfold than achievable potential. A long-term study since 1976 at the International Crops Research Institute for the Semi-Arid Tropics, Patancheru, India demonstrated a virtuous cycle of persistent yield increase with an average annual productivity of 5.1 t/ha through improved watershed management (land, water and crop management, etc.) in rainfed agriculture as compared with 1.1 t/ha

---

* Corresponding author: s.r.rao@cgiar.org

(Wani *et al.*, 2003a, 2012). In India, the rainfed regions or drylands where water scarcity is a major limiting factor, currently cover majority (54%, 76 million ha) of cultivable land and are projected to still cover 45% (63 million ha) of area by 2050, and thus, need due focus on enhancing rainwater use efficiency (Amarasinghe *et al.*, 2007; Wani *et al.*, 2016). Rainfed regions are also hot spots of poverty and malnutrition with potential opportunities in unexploited two- to fourfold yield gaps (Wani *et al.*, 2009). Further, the projected climate change scenario has increased the chances of water uncertainty and land degradation leading to the vulnerability of food production in tropical countries like India. This necessitates the need for resilience building of production systems through sound water and land management practices. In this scenario, developing rainfed agriculture needs to be a priority for directly benefiting masses to make food and nutrition secure, and enhance economic empowerment.

In rainfed areas, management at watershed scale is one of the most trusted approaches to manage rainwater and other natural resources for increasing food production, improving livelihoods, protecting environment, addressing gender and equity issues along with biodiversity concerns (Wani *et al.*, 2014). Therefore, the Rural Electrification Corporation Limited (RECL), Hyderabad, India has supported the ICRISAT-led consortium to develop 'Model Watershed Sites of Learning' in Mahabubnagar district of Telangana and Anantapur district in Andhra Pradesh with the aim of sustainably increasing agricultural productivity and improving livelihoods of the rural poor in vulnerable rainfed areas. Major focus was on enhancing the water availability and its (green and blue water) use efficiency for intensification and diversification of the livelihood systems and capacity building of stakeholders.

11.1.2   Pilot site description and selection process

The selection of watershed location was the first major activity taken up with the coordination of the District Water Management Agency (DWMA), Department of Agriculture and the local non-governmental organizations (NGOs). The following criteria were considered in the selection of sites for the watershed project.

- Representative in terms of soil, landscape (slope and terrain), rainfall, crops and socioeconomic conditions.
- Farmers who were cooperative and willing to take an active part in the watershed programme.
- Good potential for increasing the agricultural productivity, income and conservation of natural resources.
- Strong need for the watershed programme.
- Major area under rainfed agriculture.
- Good accessibility even during the rainy season.

Considering the above key criteria, two potential sites for the watershed project were identified in Anantapur district in Andhra Pradesh and Mahabubnagar district in Telangana (Fig. 11.1). The ICRISAT team and Watershed Development Department officials visited the proposed sites. At each site, farmers' meetings were conducted, and interactions were held with the local institutions and community members. Based on these discussions and observations followed by a transect walk, the final selection of sites for the watershed project was done.

The RECL–ICRISAT watershed project implemented in Penukonda mandal of Anantapur district in Andhra Pradesh covers four villages, namely Kondampalle, Gonipeta, Settipalle and Cherlopalle with a total geographical area of 6810 ha, including 3150 ha of area under cultivation covering 1480 households with population of 8700. The important crops cultivated are groundnut, maize, paddy, finger millet and sunflower.

In Wanaparthy mandal in Mahabubnagar district of Telangana, the project was implemented in four villages, namely Rajapet, Kadukuntla, Peddagudem and Mentapalle with a total geographical area of 5400 ha, including 3970 ha of area under cultivation, covering 2285 households with population of 11,726.

The baseline analysis showed lower crop yields, and identified good potential for improvement in productivity and livelihoods. About 315 open wells and 600 bore wells were found in Penukonda watershed. Only 35 open wells were found seasonally functional and depth of bore well for water extraction ranged between 300 feet

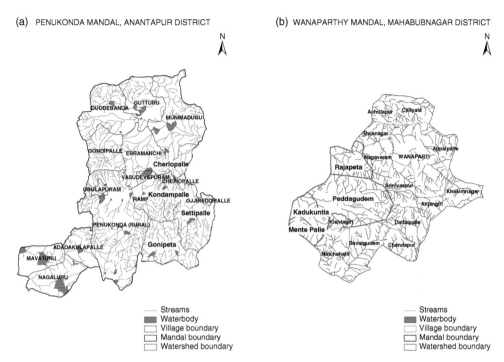

(a) PENUKONDA MANDAL, ANANTAPUR DISTRICT

(b) WANAPARTHY MANDAL, MAHABUBNAGAR DISTRICT

— Streams
▨ Waterbody
☐ Village boundary
☐ Mandal boundary
☐ Watershed boundary

Fig. 11.1. Watershed map with drainage network: (a) Penukonda mandal, Anantapur district; (b) Wanaparthy mandal, Mahabubnagar district.

and 500 feet. Similarly, in Wanaparthy watershed, the survey showed 350 open wells and 950 bore wells and most open wells were defunct and the depth of bore wells ranged between 300 feet and 600 feet.

11.2 Institutional Arrangement

For effective implementation and periodic monitoring, appropriate institutional arrangement is essential. Proper periodical monitoring mechanism is an essential facet for successful implementation of watershed programme. Regular monitoring of the project was carried out at each stage of development by adopting community participatory approach for planning, execution, monitoring and evaluation.

Baseline characterization was undertaken through participatory rapid rural appraisal and detailed household survey by adopting stratified random sampling approach for socioeconomic survey on productivity, land use, inputs use, income source of livelihoods, constraints, etc. For social mobilization and implementation of

interventions under the project, ICRISAT entered into agreement with local NGOs like Samatha in Anantapur and BAIF in Mahabubnagar. Work plans were discussed by the watershed committee and NGO partner with the community.

The expert team supported villagers in unanimously nominating and establishing the watershed committee. The watershed committee consisted of 19 members in Anantapur and 13 members in Mahabubnagar and that included the representatives from all the villages. The watershed committee comprised all the sections of the community, including women representatives, proportionately small, medium, large and landless farmers. The watershed committee is responsible to conduct *gram sabha* (village meeting with all farmers) at monthly interval or as and when needed to identify the activities, execution and monitoring of works in the watershed. Community watersheds are implemented purely in a participatory mode, wherein the watershed committee and farmers are involved at every stage of watershed works right from planning and execution, implementation and monitoring of various activities in consultation and supported by the technical expertise from ICRISAT-led consortium for effective implementation of the project.

User groups are formed for active participation and maintenance of interventions, viz. water harvesting structures, etc. Self-help groups (SHGs) are formed and supported for various activities through revolving fund to benefit small farmers to generate additional family income. All payments to the SHGs are made through the watershed committee bank account cheque withdrawal signed by the NGO representative and the watershed committee members (Chairman/Treasurer).

The monitoring system includes GIS (geographical information system) or remote sensing data with on-the-ground monitoring including a household survey, focus group discussions, participatory observations, thematic studies and case studies. It measures quantitative and qualitative indicators before, during and at the end of the project as well as after project completion. Periodical monitoring is done through weekly, monthly, half-yearly and annual progress reports, utilization certificates, audited statement of accounts, etc. Any further instalment is released only when the unspent balance is less than 30% of the last instalment released to the watershed committee and subject to the satisfactory physical progress as per work plan. Further the watershed project is subjected to mid-term evaluation for any corrections. ICRISAT conducts evaluation study of project and impact assessment studies to assess the overall impact of the programme at village/watershed level.

The staff structure involved in planning, implementation and monitoring of watershed project is as follows.

Project coordinator/director, ICRISAT Development Center: Responsible for overall project management; to provide direction to all the scientists and staff in the project, liaise with donors/stakeholders, guide in planning, and review and monitor the progress (physical, financial and administrative) of the project.

Project implementation committee: Comprises of one member each from RECL and ICRISAT to monitor the planning and implementation of interventions on scientific lines.

Nodal officer: Responsible for all day-to-day affairs for the implementation of works as per the approved action plan and progress report preparation; and overall coordination for on-ground

implementation of project and to liaise with stakeholders.

Multidisciplinary scientific team: Inputs of scientists such as the agronomist, soil scientist, entomologist, pathologist, hydrologist and socio-economist are taken to guide in the specific activity planning, implementation and capacity building of the community in the watershed project.

Scientific officer: Responsible for guiding the research technician to implement the interventions, data collection and tabulation and reporting to site in-charge scientist/manager.

Research technician: Responsible to carry out the activities on the ground, data collection and community mobilization in the watershed; place of posting is in the work site; and weekly progress of work is reported to the coordinator.

Local NGO: A local NGO is involved in community mobilization, construction of water harvesting structures, implementation of action plan on ground and data collection and reporting.

Watershed committee: It is a working committee elected by the community representing all the farmers in the watershed, and is responsible for coordination in planning, implementation and monitoring of watershed interventions at all stages of project development activities.

11.3 Major Interventions

11.3.1 Integrated rainwater management

Rainwater is the main source of water for agriculture, but its current use efficiency for crop production ranges only between 30 and 45%. Annually 300–800 mm of seasonal rainfall is not used productively as it becomes surface runoff or deep drainage. ICRISAT's long experience in partnership with national agricultural research systems in integrated watershed management has clearly demonstrated that areas with good soils in the semi-arid tropics (SAT) in Asia can support double cropping while surplus rainwater could recharge the groundwater. In the integrated watershed approach the emphasis is on *in-situ* conservation of rainwater at farm or community level with the excess water taken out from the fields safely through community drainage channels and stored in suitable low-cost structures. The stored water is used as surface irrigation or for recharging ground-water (Wani *et al.*, 2003b). Rainwater conservation and management has been broadly classified into two types: blue water augmentation (*ex-situ* water management) and green water management (*in-situ* water management).

Blue water augmentation (ex-situ water management)

Currently in most of the watershed programmes in India, community-based soil and water conservation play the key role in improving surface and groundwater availability and controlling soil erosion. Studies conducted by ICRISAT have shown that the cost of water harvesting and groundwater recharging structures varies considerably with type of structures and selection of appropriate location. Large variation is found in the cost of water harvesting in different structures. Selection of appropriate location for structures also can play a very important role in reducing the cost of structures.

In RECL–ICRISAT watershed sites, the rainwater harvesting structures are low-cost and constructed throughout the topo-sequence to achieve equity and access to water. These low-cost structures are proven for sustainability, equity as well as cost-effectiveness. The number of rainwater harvesting structures and storage capacity were determined based on the water availability and through water budgeting approach using simulation modelling with historical weather data sets. In the watershed sites, various rainwater harvesting and groundwater recharge structures such as check-dams, farm

ponds, percolation tanks, bore well recharge pits and sunken pits were constructed (Table 11.1; Fig. 11.2). The rainwater harvesting and groundwater recharging structures constructed have created a net storage capacity of 17,800 m³ resulting in total conservation of about 49,500 m³ of surface runoff water in 2–3 fillings in Anantapur watershed, while in Mahabubnagar watershed, 26,500 m³ resulted in total conservation of about 53,600 m³ of surface runoff water in 2–3 fillings. The rainwater harvested has helped in providing supplemental irrigation in critical crop growth stages during extended dry spell. It also helped in recharging groundwater, while reducing soil loss. The additional availability of water has resulted in increasing and sustaining crop and livestock productivity and diversification to high-value vegetable crops. Water-based works have led to various success stories in RECL–ICRISAT watersheds (see Box 11.1).

Table 11.1. Soil and water conservation works done in watershed sites in Anantapur and Mahabubnagar districts during 2015–17.

	No. of structures	
Works	Anantapur	Mahabubnagar
Farm ponds	37	68
Check-dams	6	10
Rock-filled dams	47	62
Sunken pits	11	2
Bore well recharge pits	15	1
Dugwell recharge pits	25	31
Farm pond with plastic lining and drip	2	1

Fig. 11.2. Farm ponds in Penukonda watershed villages: (a) Gonipeta; (b) Kondampalle.

Box 11.1. Farmers in Mahabubnagar reap the benefits of farm ponds.

Mahabubnagar district is a drought-prone area. Huge rainfall variability, in both quantity and distribution, during the growing season is a major challenge and threatens farmers' livelihoods. Due to erratic and undependable rainfall, farmers used to incur huge crop losses especially with groundnut crop where seed cost is a big investment. So, farmers are facing a high risk in cultivating a groundnut crop. In such a situation, a nearby water-harvesting system in a farmers' field such as a farm pond plays a major role through increased access to water for critical irrigation to check yield losses.

Under the RECL–ICRISAT watershed programme, Mr Lokya Naik of Rajapeta village in Mahabubnagar watershed constructed a small low-cost farm pond (10 x 10 x 2 m) to harvest rainwater and used it for irrigation of his groundnut crop. He shared his experience of significant yield advantage (up to 60%) and net additional benefit of about ₹19,000 with farm pond in cultivating groundnut crop during 2016–17 (see table below). He stated that it not only prevented groundnut crop losses during drought spells, but enabled him to cultivate vegetables in a 500 m² area and enhance his income.

Construction of farm ponds, thus, has proved a promising option for rainwater storage that allows for critical and vital irrigation of crops as well as other activities, such as planting of vegetables, fodder and fruit orchards that can supplement diets and incomes. The construction of farm ponds in RECL–ICRISAT pilot sites has enhanced farmers' risk-taking abilities to effectively adopt market-oriented development.

Net additional benefits with farm pond.

Details	Without farm pond	With farm pond
Crop	Groundnut	Groundnut
Area cultivated (acres)	4	4
Cost of cultivation (₹)	51,100	60,000 (plus irrigation and micronutrients)
Yield (q/4 acre)	32.0	52.5
Gross income at 4200 per q (₹)	134,400	220,500
Net benefit for 4 acre (₹)	83,300	160,500
Net additional benefit from groundnut with farm pond (₹/acre)		19,300
Benefit–cost ratio (based on operational cost excluding fixed cost and family labour)	2.63	(40% increase)

Green water management
(in-situ water management)

In-situ soil water conservation measures are important for effective conservation of soil and water at the field level. The main aim of these practices is to either reduce or prevent water erosion, while conserving the desired moisture for sustainable production. The suitability of any *in-situ* soil and water management practice depends greatly upon soil, topography, climate, cropping system and farmers' resources. Some of the promising *in-situ* soil and water conservation practices adopted in RECL watershed are broad-bed and furrow, contour cultivation and border strips (Fig. 11.3). Broad-bed and furrow system has resulted in 22% increase in groundnut yields compared with farmers' practice in Mahabubnagar district, while the border strip system in Anantapur has also been found beneficial in terms

of moisture conservation and increased yield (28%) over conventional flat cultivation.

11.3.2   Soil health mapping and need-based recommendations for enhancing productivity

For systematic soil health mapping, stratified geo-referenced soil samples were collected from watershed sites in Anantapur (220 samples) and Mahabubnagar (210 samples) districts. Results of soil analysis showed widespread deficiencies of secondary and micronutrients such as sulfur (S), boron (B) and zinc (Zn) along with macronutrients and low levels of soil carbon (C). In Anantapur watershed, 69% fields were deficient in phosphorus (P), 15% in potassium (K), 77% in S, 94% in Zn, 77% in B, 44% in manganese (Mn),

Fig. 11.3. Broad-bed and furrow (BBF) system of landform for *in-situ* water conservation in RECL–ICRISAT watershed, Mahabubnagar district: (a) preparation of BBF; (b) groundnut cultivated on BBF.

29% in calcium (Ca) and 7% in iron (Fe) along with low soil organic C level in 87% of farmers' fields (Table 11.2). Similarly, in Mahabubnagar watershed, 46% of fields were deficient in P, 14% in K, 83% in S, 81% in Zn, 73% in B, 39% in Mn, 38% in Ca and 10% in Fe, along with low C levels in 81% fields (Table 11.3).

Based on soil analysis results, soil test-based fertilizer recommendations were developed at village level and promoted in RECL–ICRISAT watershed sites. Deficient secondary and micronutrients were also included in recommendations by contrast to general practice of farmers, who are not aware of such deficiencies and do not add these nutrients into their fields. Considering risks of dryland agriculture, fertilizer recommendation included full dose of secondary and micronutrients in case of >50% deficient fields in the village, ½ dose in case of 25–50% deficiency, ¼ dose in case of 10–25% deficiency and nil if only <10% fields were deficient in micro and secondary nutrients. The yearly full dose was 15 kg/ha of S, 5 kg/ha of Zn and 0.25 kg/ha in case of B. Participatory trials/demonstrations with soil test-based fertilizer application showed 25–27% yield benefit in crops like groundnut and paddy in Anantapur watershed (Table 11.4). Similarly, the yield benefit in groundnut crop was 22% in Mahabubnagar watershed. A success story is given in Box 11.2.

11.3.3 Improved crops and varieties for intensification and diversification

As varietal replacement is a big opportunity in watershed sites, farmer participatory field demonstrations were set up to persuade the farmers to adopt climate-smart high-yielding crop cultivars. With the climatic variations observed in the past few years, the farmers are finding it difficult to get a good groundnut crop. In this context, the varieties ICGV 91114, ICGV 350 and ICGV 351 were evaluated in watershed sites and these proved superior over local cultivar with yield advantage of 15–36%. Similarly, in pigeonpea, the hybrid ICPH 2740 showed yield benefit of 96% and the variety ICPL 87119 showed 13% yield increase (Table 11.5).

With augmentation of water resources in the watershed, farmers have started vegetable cultivation by using about 1000–4000 m² land for high-value agriculture. Around 250 farmers in Mahabubnagar have started cultivating high-value crops such as tomato, leafy vegetables, brinjal and okra, and selling the vegetables in local market. Thus farmers' incomes have increased and they also earn at regular intervals.

11.3.4 Livelihood improvement through strengthening income-generating activities

Various income-generating activities, such as sheep rearing, improving the local goat breeds through crossbreeding with Sirohi goats, vermicomposting, nursery and home gardening were undertaken by women SHG members with financial support from the revolving fund.

Farm activities

SHEEP AND GOAT REARING. Rearing of small ruminants like sheep and goat supports subsistence

Table 11.2. Soil health status of farmers' fields in Penukonda watershed, Anantapur, Andhra Pradesh.[a]

Villages	pH	EC	% of fields with low organic C	% of fields deficient in available nutrients									
				P	K	Ca	Mg	S	Zn	B	Fe	Cu	Mn
Cherlopalle	7.0	0.12	88 (0.26)	80 (4.3)	43 (65)	68 (975)	0 (151)	90 (7.0)	98 (0.31)	90 (0.26)	3 (9.71)	68 (0.44)	78 (6.99)
Gonipeta	8.1	0.12	95 (0.24)	80 (4.0)	8 (78)	30 (1595)	0 (164)	95 (35)	93 (0.39)	93 (0.27)	10 (5.76)	0 (0.59)	38 (4.97)
Kondampalle	8.0	0.25	92 (0.31)	46 (8.5)	12 (75)	20 (1566)	0 (249)	68 (18.3)	92 (1.0)	76 (0.46)	12 (5.63)	0 (2.06)	58 (5.16)
Settipalle	8.4	0.23	78 (0.34)	73 (4.1)	3 (88)	12 (2225)	0 (322)	63 (9.5)	93 (0.41)	58 (0.48)	3 (8.00)	0 (0.88)	58 (5.67)
Mean	7.9	0.19	87 (0.29)	69 (5.3)	15 (78)	29 (1656)	0 (234)	77 (10.0)	94 (0.54)	77 (0.39)	7 (7.26)	0 (1.04)	44 (5.66)

[a]Figures in parentheses indicate mean of nutrient contents in ppm and percentage values in case of organic C.

Table 11.3. Soil health status of farmers' fields in Wanaparthy watershed, Mahabubnagar, Telangana.[a]

Village	pH	EC	% of fields with low organic C	% of fields deficient in available nutrients										
				P	K	Ca	Mg	S	Zn	B	Fe	Cu	Mn
Mentepalle	7.09	0.10	87 (0.36)	32 (8.33)	0 (148)	52 (1189)	0 (299)	84 (7.78)	87 (0.47)	84 (0.38)	6 (7.12)	0 (0.79)	39 (8.52)
Peddagudem	7.74	0.10	80 (0.35)	21 (10.89)	5 (129)	51 (1231)	1 (332)	83 (7.24)	85 (0.56)	64 (0.52)	19 (4.93)	0 (0.63)	60 (5.27)
Rajapeta	7.92	0.10	79 (0.38)	83 (3.34)	29 (84)	20 (1771)	1 (363)	80 (8.81)	75 (0.76)	76 (0.37)	3 (13.47)	0 (0.86)	16 (2.85)
Kadukuntla	7.85	0.09	90 (0.32)	0 (7.25)	0 (129)	40 (1287)	0 (323)	100 (4.48)	70 (0.98)	90 (0.39)	10 (5.53)	0 (0.64)	50 (9.10)
Mean	7.71	0.12	81 (0.36)	46 (7.30)	14 (114)	38 (1441)	1 (338)	83 (7.80)	81 (0.65)	73 (0.43)	10 (8.69)	0 (0.75)	39 (5.04)

[a]Figures in parentheses indicate mean of nutrient contents in ppm and percentage values in case of organic C.

Table 11.4. Crop yields (t/ha) with soil test-based balanced nutrient management (average of 2015–17).

Crop	Improved practice (IP) (t/ha)	Farmers' practice (FP) (t/ha)	% yield increase in IP over FP
Anantapur watershed, Andhra Pradesh			
Groundnut	1.780	1.400	27
Paddy	2.180	1.750	25
Mahabubnagar watershed, Telangana			
Groundnut	1.902	1.556	22

Box 11.2. Groundnut yield increased with soil test-based nutrient management.

Mr Krishna Naik, a small farmer from Settipalle village of RECL–ICRISAT watershed in Anantapur im-plemented integrated nutrient management practice in groundnut crop (see figure below). After land preparation, he applied 6 tons of farmyard manure to his 2 acres of land. In 1 acre of land, he followed soil test-based fertilizer recommendation including micro- and secondary nutrients like zinc sulphate (10 kg/acre basal), borax (1 kg/acre basal) and gypsum (200 kg/acre, half as basal and half at flower-ing), while in the other piece of land, he followed his practice without soil test-based micro- and sec-ondary nutrients. These micronutrients were provided through the project on a 50% cost-sharing basis. Other cultivation practices were common in both the plots. The seed rate was 60 kg/acre and seeds were treated with *Trichoderma* and mancozeb. At harvest, Mr Krishna got around 14% yield advantage in the plot where deficient micro- and secondary nutrients were added as compared to the plot where these were not added (5.6 q per acre vs 4.9 q per acre). In economic terms, at full costing, it means an additional return of ₹2800 per acre for a cost of around ₹1200 per acre, i.e. a benefit–cost ratio of 2.33, plus additional benefit of soil health rejuvenation and other ecosystem services.

agriculture and livelihoods in drought-prone areas of Anantapur and Mahabubnagar dis-tricts. Hence sheep- and goat-rearing activity was strengthened in RECL–ICRISAT watersheds with financial support from the revolving fund to SHG members. The SHG members who availed themselves of the loan returned the money in ten monthly instalments with reasonable inter-est decided by the members. Each SHG was provided ₹30,000 to benefit the SHG members on rotational basis. The SHG members as a group decided the priority of beneficiaries to avail themselves of the facility. Around 120 members from watershed villages in Anantapur availed themselves of this benefit and this initia-tive proved effective for farmers to increase their family income. A success story is described in Box 11.3.

Table 11.5. Crop yields with improved cultivars in Anantapur and Mahabubnagar (average of 2015–17).

Improved crop variety	Improved practice (IP) (t/ha)	Local variety	Farmers' practice (FP) (t/ha)	% yield increase in IP over FP
Groundnut in Anantapur watershed				
ICGV 9114	1.975	K6	1.750	29
ICGV 351	2.250	K6	2.075	15
ICGV 350	1.725	K6	1.525	36
Pigeonpea in Mahabubnagar watershed				
ICPH 2740	1.91		0.97	96
ICPL 87119	1.03		0.97	13

FORAGE PRODUCTION ACTIVITY AND LIVESTOCK IMPROVEMENT. Considering the fodder scarcity, fodder promotion is a targeted activity in the watershed villages. Fodder promotion translates into improving livestock-based productivity, including milk, which is generally in the domain of women and thus leads to their empowerment. Moreover, the benefits of soil health-based management are realized not only in increased grain yield but also in straw which is major fodder for cattle. Soil health management has also brought improvement in fodder quality in terms of micro- and macronutrients along with quantity as such. Specifically, *Stylosanthes hamata* fodder, which is rich in protein, was promoted in the watersheds along the sides/bunds of water-harvesting structures. Sorghum CSH 24 MF, a high-yielding multi-cut fodder variety has been introduced in the watersheds. A success story is described in Box 11.4.

KITCHEN GARDENING. With an objective to improve family nutrition and mainstreaming of women farmers, nutri-kitchen gardens were promoted as a women-centred activity in the backyards or a small piece of land. The farmers were trained in good management practices and about 1000 women farmers were provided with inputs, mainly seeds of vegetable crops such as tomato, brinjal, cluster bean, okra, bitter gourd and leafy vegetables to cultivate in the backyard in an area of 5–20 m² in both the watersheds (Anantapur and Mahabubnagar) that support for home consumption and the excess was sold in the market. In addition to this, around 1000 households were provided with 4–5 fruit plants for planting in the backyard as a perennial source to improve nutrition.

COMPOSTING AND BIOMASS GENERATION. Vermicomposting and aerobic composting are income-generating activities as well as produce manure for farmer's use in the field.

Nonfarm activities

Watershed villages have considerable population belonging to Schedule Tribe community who have very little farmland or are landless. To improve livelihoods of such households, several activities like tailoring and petty shops were supported. This initiative has benefited about 173 households with an average income of ₹2000–3000 per month. A success story is given in Box 11.5.

11.3.5 Capacity building

Capacity building plays a key role in any project for successful implementation and ensuring sustainability. This activity has been focused in RECL–ICRISAT watersheds to strengthen the capacity of all stakeholders. Need-based capacity-building activities were identified and assessed considering the current level of capacity/knowledge, gaps and priorities targeting the right topics at right time with right participants. These activities were also converged with Agricultural Technology Management Agency/department training programmes, wherein Krishi Vigyan Kendra scientists and department officials were also involved as resource persons.

Several capacity building programmes (90 events benefiting around 3000 participants in Anantapur district and 55 events benefiting around 1500 participants in Mahabubnagar district) were conducted to create awareness about

Box 11.3. Additional income through promoting livestock rearing for the SHGs.

In RECL–ICRISAT Watershed in Anantapur district, 120 farmers who were living below the poverty line collectivized in 20 SHGs across 4 watershed villages. They were supported with ₹3000 per member for ram lamb rearing as an income-generating activity to enhance their livelihoods through revolving fund. The SHG members bought ram lambs at the rate of ₹3000 each and reared them for 4–5 months (see figure below). After 4–5 months they sold the lambs at a profit of ₹2400–3200 (see table below).

Participating farmers have expressed satisfaction with this activity of the project as it supplemented their family income. Such developmental assistance enables farmers to earn more, and improve livelihoods and also reinvest for further gains. Such initial small investments slowly increase the resilience of smallholders to manage risks and harness markets.

Benefits of lamb rearing.

Name of SHG	Name of farmer	Date purchased and amount	Date sold and amount	Benefit (₹)
Shiridi Sai SHG	Ms P. Kavitha	02.01.2015; ₹3000	27.05.2015; ₹5800	₹2800
Janshi Mahila SHG	Ms Lakshmi Bai	02.01.2015; ₹3000	27.04.2015; ₹6200	₹3200
Ganesh SHG	Ms Santhi Bai	06.01.2015; ₹3000	01.05.2015; ₹5400	₹2400

Box 11.4. Promoting green fodder increased milk yield and farmer's income.

Mr Adikeshava Naidu from RECL–ICRISAT watershed in Anantapur district has achieved reasonably good success by cultivating fodder sorghum (CSH 24 MF) for his dairy animals. He has 2 milch buffaloes that yield only 4 litres milk/buffalo/day with fat content of 7%.

As a part of the watershed project, he was guided and provided with the multi-cut fodder sorghum CSH 24 MF. He sowed fodder crop in 0.1 acre of land and has been reaping rewards ever since. With the required quantity and quality of fodder, the average milk yield of buffalo increased to 6 litres milk/buffalo/day (see figure below). The fat content has also increased to 7.5% and that is fetching a higher price. With this simple intervention, Mr Adikeshava's net additional income increased by ₹2400/month/buffalo, and a total of ₹4800/month from 2 milch animals. Moreover, with increased fat content, he sells milk at a better price of ₹40/litre.

the watershed project on various aspects such as community formation, participatory soil sampling, soil health, action plan preparation, improved crop productivity initiatives and integrated pest management. Various capacity-building programmes were included as below.

- Training workshops to enhance awareness or technical skills.
- For specific technical skills, combining indoor training and practical application in the field through interactive sessions as formal and informal events.
- Field demonstrations through participatory mode.
- Field days have been a core part of the project, where farmers came together to share details

of on-farm research and demonstrations and learn from each other in a spirit of openness and curiosity.

- Learning/exposure visits cum study tours to new successful technologies.

11.4   Impact of Watershed Interventions

11.4.1   Productivity and economic benefits

Farmer participatory trials to evaluate improved crop management practices, including soil test-based fertilizer recommendations, improved

---

Box 11.5. Nonfarm-based activities enhanced income for landless in the watersheds.

Ms Ansuya belongs to Settipalle village in Anantapur watershed. She has her family of two children and elderly parents to take care of, but does not own any land. She was looking for a livelihood opportunity. Her parents suggested that she learn tailoring and supported her training. She took out a loan from the local moneylender to buy a sewing machine and tailoring materials with a high interest rate. Later, she approached the watershed committee for financial help to repay the loan through a revolving fund. The watershed committee decided to give a loan of ₹5000 from the revolving fund with repayment through ten instalments.

Ansuya is now working in tailoring and embroidery in the village and earning an income of ₹5000 to ₹6000 per month. She has repaid her entire loan. She is now selling stitched garments to shops and she has been able to send her children to school. She is very happy that her family income has improved and she is able to take care of her children and give them a good education, and take care of other family needs (see figure below). Thus she expresses gratitude to the watershed project for the needed timely support.

cultivars and rainwater management have shown significant productivity benefits with improved incomes for the farmers. Other livelihood programmes have resulted in significant improvement in income of the people with profit of ₹1000–6000 per month under different interventions (Table 11.6).

events in large numbers. Empowerment of women SHGs has enabled landless women to have additional income to support the family as well as improve social status. Vegetable cultivation in backyards or a small area of the field has helped in improving family nutrition as well as income with surplus.

11.4.2 Social benefits

Formerly, women farmers' participation in watershed meeting and development works was very low, but now they are participating in development activities with increased awareness. Now women are actively participating in watershed activities and attending meetings and

11.4.3 Environment benefits

Soil and water conservation interventions have reduced runoff by 50% and soil loss significantly. This initiative has strengthened climate resilience. Avenue and bund plantation has increased greenery and improved soil C sequestration. Forest tree species, namely teak, red sandal and

Table 11.6. Income generation through various livelihood activities in Anantapur and Mahabubnagar watersheds.

Intervention	Net gain (₹)
Ram lamb rearing (120 persons)	2400–2800 per lamb[a]
Sewing machine (2 persons)	4000–5000 per month
Petty shops (173 persons; tea shop and cloth shop)	2000–3000 per month
Carpentry (one power saw)	5000–6000 per month
Vermicomposting (20 persons)	1000–1200 per month

[a]During 4–5 months.

Gliricidia (20,000 plants) were also planted by farmers in project villages on field bunds and wasteland. Organic manure (vermicompost and aerobic compost) is available for farm use and thus reduces the use of chemical fertilizers while improving soil health.

11.4.4 Technological benefits

Soil and water conservation interventions created a storage capacity of about 50,000 m³ of rainwater in Anantapur watershed and 54,000 m³ in Mahabubnagar watershed, otherwise this would have been lost as runoff leading to soil erosion. The additional availability of water has served as climate resilient production system under prevailing climate change scenario to stabilize the production system on the farm.

Groundwater level has increased by 1.5–2.0 m. Along with groundwater yield, the period of water availability has also improved. Capacity of farmers and stakeholders in improved crop production technologies has increased.

11.5 Summary and Key Findings

The RECL–ICRISAT watershed sites in Penukonda mandal of Anantapur district in Andhra Pradesh and Wanaparthy mandal in Mahabubnagar district of Telangana are exemplary sites of learning for harnessing potential of rainfed agriculture. This has provided a proof of concept that farmers' incomes can be doubled through integrated resource management and end-to-end holistic solutions. Within these watersheds, the benefits need to be scaled-up to a large number of farmers in the watershed, and backed with policy, these simple technical solutions need to be scaled-up to farmers in the large tracts of drylands in the country. This has provided the way forward not only for uplifting drylands, but also to corporates to leverage social responsibility in mainstreaming the underprivileged, while contributing to food security and ecosystem services as such.

Acknowledgements

Authors duly acknowledge corporate social responsibility partner RECL for supporting and funding to develop the sites of learning in Anantapur and Mahabubnagar districts. The NGO partners, Samatha in Anantapur and BAIF in Mahabubnagar are acknowledged for reaching out to the farmers. Also Mr B. Nagaraju is acknowledged for technical support in field work.

References

Amarasinghe, U.A., Shah, T., Turral, H. and Anand, B.K. (2007) *India's Water Future to 2025–2050: Business As-usual Scenario and Deviations.* IWMI Research Report 123. International Water Management Institute, Colombo, Sri Lanka.

Wani, S.P., Pathak, P., Jangawad, L.S., Eswaran, H. and Singh, P. (2003a) Improved management of Vertisols in the semi-arid tropics for increased productivity and soil carbon sequestration. *Soil Use and Management* 19, 217–222.

Wani, S.P., Pathak, P., Sreedevi, T.K., Singh, H.P. and Singh, P. (2003b) Efficient management of rainwater for increased crop productivity and groundwater recharge in Asia. In: Kijne, W., Barker, R. and Molden, D. (eds) *Water Productivity in Agriculture: Limits and Opportunities for Improvement.* CAB International, Wallingford, Oxfordshire, pp. 199–215.

Wani, S.P., Sreedevi, T.K., Rockström, J. and Ramakrishna, Y.S. (2009) Rainfed agriculture – past trends and future prospects. In: Wani, S.P., Rockström, J. and Oweis, T. (eds) *Rainfed Agriculture: Unlocking the Potential*. Comprehensive Assessment of Water Management in Agriculture Series. CAB International, Wallingford, Oxfordshire, pp. 1–35.

Wani, S.P., Dixin, Y., Li, Z., Dar, W.D. and Chander, G. (2012) Enhancing agricultural productivity and rural incomes through sustainable use of natural resources in the SAT. *Journal of the Science of Food and Agriculture* 92, 1054–1063.

Wani, S.P., Chander, G. and Sahrawat, K.L. (2014) Science-led interventions in integrated watersheds to improve smallholders' livelihoods. *NJAS – Wageningen Journal of Life Sciences* 70/71, 71–77.

Wani, S.P., Chander, G., Sahrawat, K.L., Pal, D.K., Pathak, P. *et al.* (2016) Sustainable use of natural resources for crop intensification and better livelihoods in the rainfed semi-arid tropics of Central India. *NJAS – Wageningen Journal of Life Sciences* 78, 13–19.

12 Improving Rural Wastewater Management

AVIRAJ DATTA,* MUKUND PATIL AND SUHAS P. WANI

International Crops Research Institute for the Semi-Arid Tropics, Patancheru, India

Abstract

Improved sanitation and hygiene through proper wastewater management is critical for sustainable growth of rural communities. Traditional wastewater treatment technologies experience low penetration in the resource-poor semi-arid tropical villages with limited or no access to good quality electricity and skilled supervision. The substandard wastewater treatment efficiencies of traditional effluent treatment plants, even in the urban centres, are testimony of their unviability in rural India. Constructed wetland (CW) is an age-old, low-cost, decentralized wastewater treatment technology. The absence of heavy metal and other xenobiotics in rural grey water highlights their reuse potential for growing jute, flower, teak plantation, etc. Lack of field-scale study with real wastewater thus far has made policy makers and professionals working in the sanitation sector sceptic about the long-term reliability of CWs with respect to wastewater treatment efficiencies. This chapter is an attempt to present the potential and real-life challenges of CW implementation.

12.1 Significance of Decentralized Wastewater Treatment

Water, food and energy securities are emerging as increasingly important and vital issues for India and the world. Most of the river basins in India and elsewhere are experiencing moderate to severe water shortages due to the simultaneous effects of agricultural growth, industrialization and urbanization. One in every nine persons in the world today does not have access to safe and clean drinking water. There is a need to enhance the water use efficiency in the agricultural sector which consumes about 70% of the total anthropogenic withdrawal of 3928 km³/year (WWAP, 2017). Research and resources are thus necessary to find a more efficient, productive,

equitable and environmentally friendly way of using wastewater in agriculture, so that quality of crop, soil and human health is not compromised. There needs to be focused effort to maximize the potential of wastewater as a valuable and sustainable resource.

12.1.1 Rural wastewater as a sustainable resource

About 80% water supplied to a household comes out as wastewater; thus as long as households and human habitats exist, wastewater generation will take place. It is worth mentioning, as often the obsession with groundwater and rainwater statistics prompts us to declare cluster of

---

* Corresponding author: a.datta@cgiar.org

villages as 'dry' and hence no wastewater management activity is viable. Unfortunately the sheer number of such villages in the semi-arid tropics is large and the marginalized population living there is in need of wastewater management, at least for better health and hygiene. Often the wastewater generated from these resource-poor households is easily biodegradable and simple low-cost technology like constructed wetland (CW) can abate the environmental degradation. On a macro-scale, the effect of such small-scale scientific interventions cumulatively has the potential to influence major environmental degradation. Here it has to be mentioned that often local contractual engineers, and sanitation and rural health professionals do not prefer small-scale interventions for reasons pertaining to financial profit rather than environmental concern. Post-independence the focus of rural development in India has been on establishing schools, health care facilities, housing and drainage network. In the absence of a proper wastewater management scheme, however the health and hygiene of rural India has suffered. Pest- and vector-borne diseases such as malaria, chikungunya, etc. are impossible to eradicate in the absence of a proper wastewater treatment scheme. In recent years sanitation and cleanliness has received unprecedented attention of the Government of India through the Swachh Bharat mission. Good drainage network is the prerequisite of any rural wastewater management scheme. Moreover, maintaining proper slope of the drains and proper village-level maintenance of the drains are important and should be the starting point for any rural wastewater management scheme.

12.1.2 Impact of improper rural wastewater management on health and hygiene

The link between wastewater management and health is well documented. In developing countries as much as 80% of illness is linked to inaccessibility of good quality potable water. In 2012, an estimated 842,000 deaths in middle- and low-income countries were caused by contaminated drinking water, inadequate hand washing facilities and sanitation services (WHO, 2014). Additionally, 361,000 deaths among children aged below 5 years could have been prevented through reduction of risks related to inadequate

hand hygiene, sanitation and water during the same year (Prüss-Üstün *et al.*, 2014). Raw wastewater discharge contributes towards water pollution and critically affects the actual availability of potable water and thus adversely impacts the ecosystem services (Corcoran *et al.*, 2010) through eutrophication, groundwater pollution, etc. Annual health cost per child in an untreated wastewater irrigated environment is estimated to be about ₹4000/annum (~US$60), which is 73% higher than for freshwater irrigated areas (Grangier *et al.*, 2012). Srikanth and Naik (2004) reported that the prevalence of giardiasis among farmers irrigating with wastewater in a suburb of Asmara, Eritrea was 45%. Based on hospital data they found that giardiasis prevalence was 7% among residents of the community who consumed only vegetables grown with untreated wastewater compared with 1% for residents in similar towns in Eritrea without wastewater irrigated crops. Melloul and Hassani (1999) found higher rates of salmonella infection in children living in wastewater-irrigated areas near Marrakesh, Morocco compared with those living in areas without wastewater irrigation (Chary *et al.*, 2008). Organic pollution which affects around one-seventh of all river stretches in Africa, Asia and Latin America (UNEP, 2016) can have severe impacts on the livelihoods of poor rural communities depending on fisheries or natural resources. For every US$1 invested in water and sanitation, there is an economic return of US$3 to US$4 (WHO, 2015). Planned and safe irrigation practices with wastewater will significantly help in nutrient recycling. For example, the phosphorus load of the wastewater when discharged in surface water bodies triggers eutrophication. Remarkably, the sources of extractable phosphorus are dwindling and is estimated to become scarce or exhausted in the next 50–100 years (Van Vuuren *et al.*, 2010). This makes phosphorus recovery from wastewater financially viable. Recycling human urine and faeces can provide steady supply chain for phosphorus for about 22% of the present anthropogenic demand (Mihelcic *et al.*, 2011). Phosphorus recycling to agriculture through decentralized wastewater treatment (DWAT) schemes is fairly straightforward. Moreover, such initiatives will reduce the input cost and chemical dependency of agriculture increasing the net income of farmers (Winblad and Simpson-Hébert, 2004). Treated grey water can be suitably utilized to produce bio-ethanol (both first and second generation) through sweet sorghum cultivation.

12.1.3 Wastewater irrigation: prevailing practice, potential and risks

Use of wastewater in agriculture is not new as its fertilizer value is well recognized; however, reliable estimates of projected wastewater use in agriculture are scarce in literature (Qadir et al., 2007). Moreover, these farming activities often remain informal and are not indicated in official statistics (Drechsel et al., 2006). Globally about 800 million farmers are engaged in urban agriculture, of whom about 200 million practise market-oriented farming on small peri-urban plots using wastewater. Sometimes farmers use raw wastewater, as it provides nutrients or is more reliable or cheaper than other water sources (Keraita and Drechsel, 2004). For example, in rural Sri Lanka, use of sewage and wastewater for irrigation is common particularly among livestock farmers; as farm size in most cases is less than 1 ha, the extent of wastewater use in agriculture is difficult to estimate (Udagedara and Najim, 2009). There are past instances where farmers resisted the treatment of wastewater which is being used for agriculture, fearing that it will reduce its fertigation potential, for example, in the Tula Valley in Mexico (Jimenez, 2005). The potential of planned use of wastewater to increase the water-use efficiency and nutrient recycling is well demonstrated in countries such as Australia, Mexico, China and USA. In countries which suffer from acute water stress, such as Jordan, treated wastewater irrigation has been promoted since 1977 and today 90% of the treated wastewater is being used for irrigation in this country. Israel represents a similar example, where treated wastewater contributes about 40% of irrigation water demand (OECD, 2011). However, one has to make a distinction between safe and unsafe irrigation practices regarding wastewater irrigation. In India, the irrigation standards are prescribed for only a few parameters and not well implemented, particularly with regard to soil types, agro-climatic zone and nature of the agricultural produce. There is a huge lack of awareness about the risks or the potential environmental consequences of raw wastewater irrigation. Moreover, there is no proper labelling practice for farm produce grown

on wastewater or freshwater making the consumer vulnerable. Consumers or stakeholders involved in the postharvest value chain (commonly termed 'farm to fork') often remain unaware of the health risk associated with raw wastewater-irrigated farm produce.

12.1.4 Economics of rapid spread of peri-urban vegetable farms

The surplus wastewater from the major Indian cities is utilized for irrigation in the peri-urban area to grow vegetables. Lack of infrastructure and unreliable electric supply has resulted in lack of refrigerated transport facility in India for perishable salad crops and vegetables, thus long-distance travel of these crops are often not economically viable. Growing vegetables utilizing urban wastewater (which is often the most cheap and reliable fertigation source for marginal farmers) in the vicinity of urban centres in the hot Indian climates thus reduces both input cost as well as transport cost and hence is economically lucrative. In most West African cities, 60–100% of the vegetables consumed are produced in urban and peri-urban areas (Drechsel et al., 2006). In Accra (Ghana, Africa), for example, thousands of farmers produced contaminated lettuce grown on wastewater for the urban food sector. This supports livelihood and food supply for more than 200,000 urban dwellers every day but at the cost of health risk (Obuobie et al., 2006; Amoah et al., 2007). Apart from the health risk from pathogen contamination, the presence of xenobiotic, heavy metals and endocrine disrupting agents in urban wastewater increases the cost and capacity of treatment and thus restricts the scope of safe reuse. Risk of pathogen contamination compromises fitness of raw wastewater irrigated farm produce for human consumption. A survey along the Musi River in Hyderabad, India revealed the transfer of metal ions from wastewater to cow's milk through para grass fodder irrigated with wastewater. Milk samples were contaminated with different metal ions like cadmium, chromium, nickel, lead and iron ranging from 12 to 40 times the permissible levels (Minhas and Samra, 2004). Leafy vegetables and salad crops tend to bio-accumulate certain metals, namely cadmium. Generally, metal concentrations in plant tissue increase with metal concentrations in irrigation water, and concentrations in roots usually are higher than concentrations in leaves. This challenge can be addressed only through wastewater treatment.

12.1.5   Limitations of traditional wastewater treatment technologies

Despite the growing number of wastewater treatment units around the world, about 80% of the wastewater generated by anthropogenic activities returns to the ecosystem without any treatment (FAO, 2017). At present, of the 62,000 million litres per day wastewater generated in major Indian cities only 23,277 million litres per day are treated (CPCB, 2015). The explosion of population in urban centres of India has triggered higher water demand and greater wastewater generation over the past few decades. Unfortunately, the gap between wastewater generation capacity and treatment capacity is increasing. Untreated urban sewage is one of the biggest causes of environmental pollution in India. Wastewater treatment plants in Class I or Class II cities often do not function at their designed capacity or efficiency, and hence do not achieve standards prescribed under the environmental (protection) rules for discharge into streams. There is lack of awareness about the importance of separating storm water from sewerage networks or for that matter separation of municipal sewage from industrial effluents. Complex social, political, technical and financial challenges have impacted adequate and efficient management of these wastewater treatment plants. Nevertheless an increased capacity for sewage treatment is difficult yet attainable in urban area where necessary skill sets, human resource and other resources required for sophisticated wastewater treatment technologies are available. Considering the situation of wastewater treatment in urban India, a sustainable solution to wastewater management situation in rural areas is speculative. The facts and figures from rural India at a macro-level have rarely been reported or considered while planning solid and liquid waste management programmes. This track record of conventional wastewater treatment technologies such as activated sludge process, sequential batch reactors or membrane bioreactors, etc. makes their penetration in resource-poor rural India (where electricity is often unavailable or reliable) doubtful. Thus there is a need for low-cost wastewater treatment technologies which are feasible in rural India.

12.2   Sustainable Off-grid Technology for Rural Wastewater Treatment

12.2.1   Constructed wetland as a low-cost wastewater treatment technology

Constructed wetland (CW) is a proven age-old wastewater treatment system. Despite the apparent simplicity of CWs, these are complex ecosystems driven by many physical, chemical and biological processes. The CWs involve basic biogeochemical processes such as filtration, sedimentation, plant uptake, phytoremediation and microbial degradation in removing contaminants from wastewater. Common gardening skills are sufficient to take care of such a wastewater treatment system. The CWs present a feasible solution to the wastewater menace for small rural communities with limited resources and power supply. The various types of CWs used over the past four decades can be grouped into two broad categories, namely free water surface (FWS) wetlands or subsurface flow (SSF) wetlands. In a nutshell, the former involves a pond whereas the latter involves a dry surface (as their names suggest). The SSF CWs, though slightly more expensive than FWS CWs owing to the filter media (made of sand and aggregates), are preferred to avoid mosquito and odour menace. The SSF wetlands provide a path through which wastewater can move, and surfaces on which microorganisms can live (Fig. 12.1). As wastewater flows through the porous media, the microbial biofilm developed on the media constituents feed on the waste materials, removing them from the water. The top layer of sand provides support for the plants growing in the wetlands.

12.2.2   Overview of the constructed wetland-based wastewater schemes

Land-based treatment systems such as CW are well suited to agricultural applications given

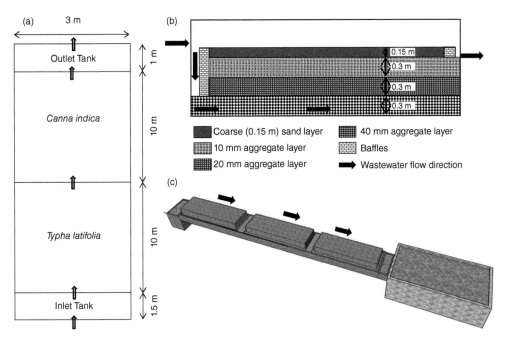

Fig. 12.1. General design of subsurface flow constructed wetland: (a) layout; (b) media constituents and flow regimen; (c) three-dimensional view of a typical DWAT unit.

their low cost and farmland availability (Carreau *et al.*, 2012). They are commonly used for the treatment of wastewater from on-farm slaughterhouses, dairies, piggeries, etc. (Bosak *et al.*, 2016). Despite the potential (Dunne *et al.*, 2015) application of full-scale FWS wetlands, these have been limited for community wastewater as these are notorious for mosquito and odour nuisance (Datta *et al.*, 2015). The SSF CWs are designed to minimize exposure of the wastewater to the ambient environment. Constructed wetlands reported in literature are predominantly horizontal SSF or vertical SSF types (Vymazal and Kropfelova, 2008). The technology is predominantly used to treat wastewater from small communities and is known for excellent removal efficiency for organic matter and total suspended solids. The removal of total nitrogen and total phosphorus as required to meet surface water discharge norms through CW is a land intensive option (Vymazal, 2010). Studies reported from Spain where horizontal SSF type CWs are widely used highlighted the limitations to removal of some pollutants such as nitrogen, organic matter and phosphorus (Puigagut *et al.*, 2007). The reason for poor removal

efficiency for nitrogen and phosphorus is because SSF-type CWs are anoxic systems with insufficient amount of dissolved oxygen in water (Vymazal, 2014); moreover, the traditional bed materials are not suitable enough to abate phosphorus as they lack sufficient calcium, magnesium, iron and aluminium ions (Vohla *et al.*, 2011). Energy-intensive solutions such as bed aeration (Fan *et al.*, 2013) or influent wastewater aeration (Rossmann *et al.*, 2013) using solar-powered aerators though will compromise the intrinsic operational simplicity of these systems. Such modifications should be limited to sites where skilled supervision is available at a reasonable cost. Specific bed materials to augment the natural bioremediation processes in a SSF type CW, such as blast-furnace slags or heated opoka (natural material from southeastern Poland composed of 50% of calcium carbonate, 40% of silicon dioxide and 10% of aluminium, iron and other oxides) may be utilized in a specific manner. In developed nations such as Spain, although CWs are listed in the Spanish reuse law (BOE, 2007) as adequate systems to maintain the quality of reclaimed wastewater during storage, they are not considered as suitable systems for secondary or tertiary treatment for further reuse. However, in the national guidelines of developing countries such as China and Mexico, the reuse of municipal wastewater treated with CWs for crop irrigation (Belmont *et al.*, 2004; Wang *et al.*, 2005) is allowed. In scarcely reported studies from the developed nations reuse of CW-treated urban wastewater by a hybrid CW system showed the reuse potential of the effluents (Ávila *et al.*, 2013). Nitrogen and phosphate recycling potential of CWs complements the irrigation potential for the treated water (Akratos and Tsihrintzis, 2007). The use of CWs to help recovering eutrophic water bodies has been reported in Europe and the numbers of such installations are increasing. The study carried out by Li *et al.* (2008) with three types of pilot-scale CWs (FWS, horizontal SSF and vertical SSF) in China gives a comparison of their nutrient removal potential. The difference of scale used in cited studies make sketching-up a general life cycle assessment difficult. Operation and maintenance of pump, pipe and overall functioning required for vertical SSF-type CWs makes them difficult to operate for the long term in rural environment. Bed media in SSF-type CWs are mostly made of gravel and sand (Zidan *et al.*, 2013). However, the use of shredded tyres (Collaço and Roston, 2006) and plastic pieces (Cordesius and Hedström, 2009) may be good media.

12.2.3   ICRISAT in-house research on constructed wetland

Performance of CW is being evaluated at field scale as part of ongoing Indo-European Union project named Water4Crops funded by the Department of Biotechnology, Government of India under the Seventh Framework Program (FP7). The project involved 22 European and 12 Indian partners. The field-scale experimental facility at the International Crops Research Institute for the Semi-Arid Tropics (ICRISAT), Patancheru, India provided the scope to compare the phytoremediation potential of several macrophytes in different combinations over a period of three years for the grey water generated by a nearby urban household.

A total of 12 CWs vegetated with different plant species, namely *Typha latifolia*, *Canna indica*, lemongrass (*Cymbopogon* sp.), napier grass

(*Pennisetum purpureum*), hybrid napier grass (*P. purpureum* × *P. americanum*), bamboo, para grass (*Brachiaria mutica*), and floating macrophytes such as water hyacinth (*Eichhornea crassipes*) and water lettuce (*Pistia stratiotes*) were evaluated (Table 12.1). The CWs were operated under identical hydraulic loading to evaluate the phytoremediation potential of these plant species at a field scale. Wastewater flow in each CW was about 3 m^3 per day which resulted in a hydraulic retention time of 4 days for each CW. The in-house research highlighted the tremendous potential of CWs in treating grey water (Tilak *et al.*, 2017). These studies also found plant nutrient uptake as well as plant growth rate combined is an effective measure to estimate the phytoremediation potential of these macrophytes (Datta *et al.*, 2015). The study found that the resilience of *Typha latifolia* and *Canna indica* combined with their high plant growth rate makes them superior in terms of their phytoremediation capacity and consistent performance compared to other plant species tested. The growth rate of both *Typha latifolia* and *Canna indica* showed very little seasonal variation in the semi-arid tropics which ensured minimal seasonal variation in the wastewater treatment efficiency of the CW vegetated with these two plant species. A weed species *Ageratum conyzoides* demonstrated higher nitrogen removal efficiency compared to *Typha latifolia* and *Canna indica* (Tilak *et al.*, 2017). However, their lower growth rate and long lag phase of growth following transplantation in CW sand media makes their field-scale application limited. Floating macrophytes showed tremendous wastewater treatment potential; however, their high moisture content severely restricts the dry biomass generation rate compared to terrestrial macrophytes limiting their overall phytoremediation potential.

As real wastewater was used for the evaluation of phytoremediation capacity, the inlet wastewater characteristics varied during the study period, hence removal efficiencies are better represented by range rather than any specific value (Tilak *et al.*, 2017). The study identified key wastewater parameters which are affected by CW; these are total suspended solids concentration (84–97%), chemical oxygen demand (56–70%), inorganic nitrogen (35–59%), sulphate (12–37%) and coliform count (72–88%). Low removal of phosphate was observed in the CWs. Virtually no removal of

Table 12.1. Average tissue concentration observed for nitrogen, phosphorus and potassium of different macrophyte species grown in the constructed wetlands at ICRISAT, Patancheru campus.

Plant species	Tissue concentrations (mg/kg)		
	Nitrogen	Phosphorus	Potassium
Ageratum conyzoides	26,958	3,251	15,398
Typha latifolia	21,219	3,520	22,370
Canna indica	21,633	3,558	25,786
Brachiaria mutica	24,761	6,498	19,266
Cymbopogon sp.	14,917	2,354	11,166
Bambuseae sp.	22,848	1,808	9,317
Pennisetum purpureum × *P. americanum*	20,324	2,999	14,828
P. purpureum	16,189	2,481	16,528
Pistia stratiotes	31,276	6,509	25,325
Eichhornea crassipes	25,378	6,238	20,621

sodium, potassium, calcium, magnesium, chloride and fluoride was observed in the CWs.

12.2.4 Impact indicators, advantages and disadvantages of DWAT

Based on the field-scale research on CW carried out as part of Water4Crops, a few key advantages and limitations of the technology were identified along with key impact indicators. Facilitating effective treatment of the wastewater flow has been selected as one of the key performance indicators for the DWAT systems implemented in different watersheds. However, wastewater treatment is only one of the impact indicators. Other impact indicators are self-sufficiency of villagers about the DWAT system maintenance activity. Sustainability of the DWAT system in terms of maintenance by its prime beneficiaries through work for treated wastewater or biomass access is also a key indicator which affects the longevity of the units implemented. Reuse of treated wastewater (at feasible locations), the final indicator of the utility of the DWAT system in terms of increased water- and nutrient-use efficiency is another key impact indicator. Making revenue out of treated wastewater reuse through energy or cash crop cultivation is the final impact indicator for this intervention. It is worth mentioning that some of these indicators are beyond technological provisions and involve considerable social engineering which often requires a systematic and patient approach as it takes longer to materialize on the ground. Probably inculcating a sense of pride and ownership among the villagers for the DWAT system implemented in their neighbourhood is the most important social-level intervention required for faster assimilation of the scientific intervention.

Advantages of DWAT system

- Devoid of chemicals or electricity; maintenance can be done by rural communities.
- Facilitates increased water-use efficiency of resource-poor rural communities.
- Income source during the construction, operation and maintenance activities.
- Enables recycling nitrogen, phosphates and other nutrients.
- Biomass generated in CW can be used for composting, biogas or ethanol production.

Limitations of constructed wetlands

- Requires lined drainage network.
- Incomplete removal of nutrients or coliforms.

12.2.5 Salient features of DWAT unit in ICRISAT watersheds in India

The DWAT system implemented by ICRISAT team utilizing funds available through various corporate social responsibility (CSR) initiatives typically consists of four components, namely an inlet tank, an SSF CW, an outlet tank and a storage pond (may or may not be lined). The inlet tank acts as flow equalization tank, whereas specific plants known for their phytoremediation potential such as *Canna indica* and *Typha latifolia* are grown on the sand layer of the SSF CW. The plant roots take up nutrients from the subsurface wastewater stream passing through their root zones to facilitate phytoremediation. Once the plants get established, the bulk of the pollutant removal takes place in the root zone by the biofilms present in the rhizosphere of these plants. The inlet tank and outlet tank help to maintain the SSF regimen by suitably placing the inlet and outlet pipes while utilizing the gravity flow. For sites where scope of reuse is restricted or the wastewater flow is not expected to irrigate 1 acre of land, the storage tank component may be omitted. The cost of the DWAT system varies from site to site based on the geometry, which in turn depends on the wastewater flow. A minimum 3-day hydraulic retention time is required to treat the wastewater effectively in DWAT system. The cost of filter media constituents, such as sand and aggregates, differ from place to place, thus affecting the cost. A typical DWAT system treating wastewater generated from rural communities costs ₹7–10 lakhs (US$10,000–15,000).

12.3 Field-scale Performance of Constructed Wetlands

12.3.1 Performance of DWAT units commissioned utilizing CSR funds

The scaling-up of CW outside ICRISAT campus in different village locations across the country was carried out as part of various developmental projects supported by the government and CSR projects. The DWAT units thus implemented range from 50 to 250 households in terms of

their designed capacity for wastewater treatment. The field-scale installation involved site selection, design and implementation by ICRISAT team, in partnership with local non-governmental organizations (NGOs) (e.g. Backward Integrated Rural Development Society (BIRD), Development Alternative (DA), Bharatiya Agro Industries Foundation (BAIF)) as well as through the government Panchayat Raj Engineering Department (PRED) in Karnataka. This critical next step generated further knowledge about challenges of scaling-up. To share the learnings about the diverse set of social, local and perceptional challenges, these were described as general learnings and site-specific learnings for the eight locations where DWAT units were established to treat rural wastewater, utilizing the CSR fund as a watershed development activity (Tables 12.2, 12.3 and 12.4).

12.3.2 Few general learnings from scale-up

The journey from proof of concept to field-scale installations, often referred as the 'science of delivery', gave abundant lessons of which the key learnings are listed below.

- The SSF CW is preferred over FWS CW despite the additional cost of media for the former as it avoids mosquito, pest and foul odour nuisance in the absence of free wastewater surface.
- Both *Canna indica* and *Typha latifolia* are suitable for field-scale units because of their short stabilization phase post-transplantation, tolerance to both water stress and abundance conditions, as well as high phytoremediation potential.

Table 12.2. Location of field-scale DWAT systems in India implemented through CSR fund.

Village	District	State	Capacity (m³/day)	Collaboration work[a]
Pendakal	Kurnool	Andhra Pradesh	51	ICRISAT, NGO, Power Grid Corp
Mentapalle	Wanaparthy	Telangana	20	ICRISAT, RECL, NGO
Rajapeta	Wanaparthy	Telangana	25	ICRISAT, RECL, NGO
Dhikoli	Jhansi	Uttar Pradesh	10	ICRISAT, CAFRI, NGO
Dandiganahalli	Kolar	Karnataka	10	ICRISAT, NGO, Coca Cola
Doddanthapur	Bellary	Karnataka	12	ICRISAT, NGO, JSW Foundation
Ukkali	Bijapur	Karnataka	90	ICRISAT, NGO, Power Grid Corp
Bhanoor	Medak	Telangana	56	ICRISAT, NGO, Asian Paints

[a]RECL = Rural Electrification Corporation Limited; CAFRI = Central Agroforestry Research Institute.

Table 12.3. Average inlet wastewater characteristics of different field-scale DWAT units in eight villages.[a]

Parameters[b]	Pendakal	Mentepalle	Rajapeta	Dhikoli	Dandiganahalli	Doddanthapur	Ukkali	Bhanoor
Alkalinity (mg/l as $CaCO_3$)	1044	440.00	196.00	634	168.00	153.00	567.00	197.00
Arsenic (mg/l)	0.02	0.01	0.01	BDL	0.01	BDL	0.01	BDL
Boron (mg/l)	3.45	0.14	0.12	2.13	0.06	0.03	0.31	0.09
Calcium (mg/l)	121	148.00	47.00	154	102	24.5	78	77
COD (mg/l)	121	400.00	160.00	216	88	89	456	720
Chlorides (mg/l)	1280	214.22	141.94	149	120	78	487.3	286.5
Chromium (mg/l)	BDL	BDL	BDL	BDL	BDL	BDL	BDL	BDL
Detergents (mg/l)	0.206	0.79	0.57	0.62	0.18	0.22	BDL	BDL
EC (mS/cm)	6.183	2.96	1.7	2.19	0.98	1.12	1.32	3.55
Fluorides (mg/l)	1.884	1.56	1.43	1.31	1.294	290	1.68	2.13
Faecal coliform (per 100 ml)	712	139	234	923	109	349	203	323
Hardness (mg/l as $CaCO_3$)	640	1000.00	490.00	530	320	56.8	360	360
Magnesium (mg/l)	90	126.00	82.00	32	43	11.6	22.3	113
N as ammonia (mg/l)	64.68	55.96	15.06	65	27	21.9	58.13	103.57
N as nitrate (mg/l)	3.086	3.84	12.01	3	2	1.8	1.9	16.68
pH at 25°C	8.47	8.30	8.47	7.98	8.14	7.67	6.81	8.62
Phosphates (mg/l)	1.38	0.96	BDL	1.88	0.7	0.72	1.86	1.32
Potassium (mg/l)	569	34.05	14.69	31	24	15	27.5	12.3
Sodium (mg/l)	844	218.22	148.05	102	67	107	112.3	49.8
Sulphate (mg/l)	2.55	121.17	84.04	6.2	8.5	4.1	234.36	17.2
Sulfur (mg/l)	1.62	35.00	26.00	3.8	4.9	2.3	73	9.42
TDS (mg/l)	4216	1774.00	1023.00	1123	57.9	892.3	2131	770
Total iron (mg/l)	BDL	0.02	BDL	0.02	0.04	0.01	0.17	0.16
TSS (mg/l)	40	80.00	138.00	67	32.3	8	2395	43.7
Zinc (mg/l)	BDL	0.07	0.05	BDL	BDL	BDL	0.07	0.01

[a]Concentrations for lead, manganese, nickel, cobalt, cadmium and copper were below detectable limit (BDL) for all samples. [b]COD = chemical oxygen demand; TDS = total dissolved solids; TSS = total suspended solids.

Table 12.4. Average removal efficiency of constructed wetlands (July 2014 to March 2017).[a]

Key parameters Parameter	Inlet (mg/l)	Removal efficiency (%)
Chemical oxygen demand	88–456	58–82
Inorganic nitrogen	27–120	43–67
Phosphate	BDL–1.88	19–48
Sulphate	1.6–73	37–72
Total suspended solids	8–2395	84–97
Faecal coliform	109–923[b]	72–88

[a]BDL = Below detectable unit. [b]No. per 100 ml

- Exact wastewater flow calculation in a village drain is a futile approach because of wide diurnal, seasonal and occasional variations. A better approach would be to estimate the flow based on the household number or total supplied water. Often, supply water is supplemented with innumerable village bore wells, so the former leads to better flow approximation.

- Information regarding household number, volume and frequency of water supply and length of cemented drainage network data is often available at the panchayat level. Updating and utilizing such data can help to approximate the wastewater flow.

- Rainwater data, terrain topography and land registration data can help not only to estimate storm water volume but also to check the availability of public land and its suitability for this activity.

- The number of households in the village may not be useful for deciding the design treatment capacity of CW as the village wastewater often flows in different directions through multiple drains, as per the terrain. A better approach would be to identify village drains which receive wastewater from at least 100 households for this activity.

12.3.3 Site-specific learnings from scale-up

Pendakal

At this site the seasonal variation of flow is quite high; hence during peak summer the unit experiences at least one week of dry period with no inflow. However, the SSF regimen as depicted in Figure 12.1b ensures that the root zone remains moist so that plants survive this period. The site also receives runoff from the nearby area during monsoon as lateral flow. Hence, to prevent ponding on the wetland sand surface, siltation and loss of top layer sand the side walls were raised and side drains were provided after initial months of operation.

Mentapalle

In Mentapalle village of Wanaparthy, Telangana, villagers were very accommodative of scientific interventions and their sincerity was evident through the clean and well-maintained village drains. The wastewater generated in the village is distributed in three main village drains. These three drains were joined with subsurface cemented pipe to channel the wastewater flow towards the inlet tank of the DWAT unit. Moreover, the required length of 23 m for the DWAT unit for all the components (as shown in Figure 12.2) was not available. Hence the design was modified and a storage tank was constructed on the side of the CW as shown in Figure 12.2. This is an example of the flexibility of the design for DWAT units. The general stepwise process of DWAT implementation is depicted in Figure 12.3.

Rajapeta

The wastewater from the nearby households was stagnated as a small wastewater sump (14 × 13 m). Because of the small available area the DWAT system was implemented as a circular unit with the storage tank at the centre (Fig. 12.4). The slope of the CW was adjusted to distribute the wastewater flow evenly.

Dhikoli

The village population was caste-sensitive and certain sections declined to do anything with wastewater. Also in the past, members of certain marginal classes did not have easy access to community tube wells. In subsequent years, through various government initiatives these lower-caste households were provided with individual tube wells at each household. This higher

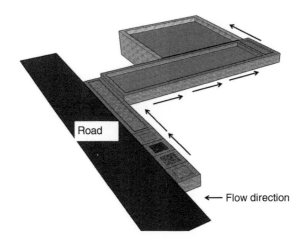

Fig. 12.2. Schematic diagram of the DWAT unit implemented at Mentapalle, Wanaparthy.

Fig. 12.3. Different phases of construction of the DWAT unit: (a) excavation; (b) concrete liner; (c) brick-masonry work; (d) plastering and curing; (e) fencing; (f) plantation.

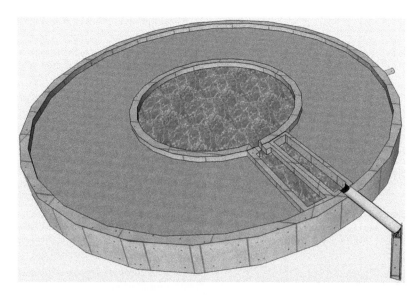

Fig. 12.4. Schematic diagram of the DWAT unit implemented at Rajapeta, Wanaparthy.

per capita water availability was probably the reason for higher wastewater flow in the drains which were in the proximity of these households. The members of these households were accommodative and receptive to the idea of improved wastewater management practices. Subsequently a village wastewater sump in Dhikoli was identified which receives wastewater from about 50 households (mostly belonging to the lower castes). The wastewater flow was about 2–3 m³/day. The wastewater samples collected by ICRISAT team from these drains were devoid of any heavy metal. Local NGO officials offered to help in monitoring the wastewater treatment efficiency for a few parameters based on water test-kit method. The land adjacent to the wastewater sump belongs to Mr Haricharan Paul with a plot size of 1.15 acre. He used to irrigate occasionally with the raw wastewater from the sump nearby. He had some school education (10th Pass) and could grasp the perils of raw wastewater irrigation during the team's interaction with him. As there was no public land available ICRISAT requested him to give a small patch (as the flow was very low) of land for the wastewater unit highlighting the prospect of a treated wastewater pond nearby his agricultural field. It took long hours of reasoning to convince him to give a portion of his land which was

uncultivable because of stone blocks. As the flow was very low, a small CW followed by a storage tank with 45 m³ capacity was finalized. The ICRISAT team got generous help from local officials of Development Alternative (Dr S.N. Pandey) and National Research Centre for Agroforestry (Dr Ramesh Singh and Mr Anand Kumar). The construction work was carried out in a short span (9 June 2015–6 August 2015). Good-quality construction practices were ensured through proper supervision and the unit cost was ₹172,000 (approximately US$2500). The expected minimum life of the unit is 7 years. Replacement of the filter media (gravel and sand) should rejuvenate the unit after this period. Establishing a demo-site for DWAT was the main motivation for the ICRISAT team in an attempt to gain the trust of the locals. In the subsequent summer, the village experienced severe water scarcity and the treated water available to Mr Haricharan Paul enabled him to irrigate his 1.15 acre land for fodder crop with an additional dry-season income of ₹8000. It also helped to mitigate the fodder crisis in the village and the small DWAT unit got increased attention. The farmer got approximately 230–260 kg (fresh weight) *Canna indica* biomass every 45 days throughout the year and used this nutrient-rich biomass as soil conditioner directly after sun-drying. The unit being small has been easy to construct and manage thus far by the locals. The site is an example of how even a limited quantity of treated wastewater can significantly influence the livelihood of marginalized small communities. Moreover, such small interventions even as demo-sites may lead to greater acceptance and faster assimilation of technological interventions.

Dandiganahalli

The CW in this location was commissioned in farmers' fields as no suitable public land was available. However, in subsequent years access to the DWAT site as well as equitable distribution of the treated wastewater became disputed among the local villagers. This site was a learning experience of the need to prepare proper documentation pertaining to transfer of the selected private land (with consent of the legal owner) to panchayat before the commissioning of the DWAT unit.

Doddanthapur

The local farmers here objected to the DWAT unit as they were utilizing raw wastewater irrigation as the pressure drop across the CW required pumping of the treated wastewater, whereas the raw wastewater flow was sufficient to irrigate the adjacent 2–3 acres of land. The farmers were made aware about the environmental and health impact of raw wastewater irrigation to resolve the problem. The problem could have been resolved by providing solar pumping system for the treated wastewater through panchayat. However, the farmer involved being a chronic alcohol addict made it difficult for the panchayat committee to place such expensive equipment in his custody. At present the farmer here is using the treated wastewater for cotton cultivation.

Ukkali

Local farmers who were irrigating with raw wastewater from the village main drain objected to its treatment through CW. Initially they dug up a sump inside the main drain at a location upstream to the DWAT unit, depriving it of any wastewater flow. The main objection was that

extra pumping power was required to fetch the treated water from the storage tank at the end of the CW. It took a three-month-long negotiation involving local villagers, school teachers and NGO to convince the upstream farmer to allow the wastewater flow to the DWAT unit. The local panchayat helped to resolve the issue by making the farmers understand the long-term adverse effect of such practice to human and soil health. This is an example why follow-up after the establishment of wastewater treatment unit is needed to ensure the longevity and sustainability of the scientific interventions. In this case the actual construction of the wastewater unit took less than 30 days, whereas convincing the local farmers took more than three months through multiple panchayat-level meetings. Sometimes, the sincerity and diligence of the people in the implementation of the project to convince the farmers gives them the confidence.

Bhanoor

Here the local villagers were unaware of the importance of wastewater treatment; in fact, the locals dump solid waste randomly at the DWAT site, severely impacting its performance. The awareness campaign and panchayat-level vigil to prevent waste dumping had proved inadequate to stop the solid waste dumping at this site. At present, fencing is being provided to this DWAT site to protect the unit. Moreover, construction of a proper waste-dumping site has started through panchayat in the vicinity to improve the situation.

12.4   Challenges and Way Forward

Despite the high wastewater treatment efficiency demonstrated by the DWAT installed (Fig. 12.5) there is a sense of apprehension among the villagers about the reuse of the treated wastewater in agriculture. After long deliberations in multiple locations about this perceptional issue, it seems utilizing the treated water for cash crop (namely jute, flowers, lemon grass or cotton) cultivation or orchard maintenance may be an easier option.

Fig. 12.5. The DWAT unit installed at Mentepalle, Wanaparthy in 2016.

References

Akratos, C.S. and Tsihrintzis, V.A. (2007) Effect of temperature, HRT, vegetation and porous media on removal efficiency of pilot-scale horizontal subsurface flow constructed wetlands. *Ecological Engineering* 29(2), 173–191.

Amoah, P., Drechsel, P., Abaidoo, R.C. and Henseler, M. (2007) Irrigated urban vegetable production in Ghana: microbiological contamination in farms and markets and associated consumer risk groups. *Journal of Water Health* 5, 455–466.

Ávila, C., Salas, J.J., Martín, I., Aragón, C. and García, J. (2013) Integrated treatment of combined sewer wastewater and stormwater in a hybrid constructed wetland system in southern Spain and its further reuse. *Ecological Engineering* 50, 13–20.

Belmont, M.A., Cantellano, E., Thompson, S., Williamson, M., Sánchez, A. and Metcalfe, C.D. (2004) Treatment of domestic wastewater in a pilot-scale natural treatment system in central Mexico. *Ecological Engineering* 23(4–5), 299–311.

BOE (2007) *Royal Decree 1620/2007*, of 7 December, that establishes the juridical regime of the reuse of treated waters. BOE No. 294 (in Spanish). Boletín Oficial del Estado (Official State Gazette), Madrid, Spain.

Bosak, V., VanderZaag, A., Crolla, A., Kinsley, C. and Gordon, R. (2016) Performance of a constructed wetland and pretreatment system receiving potato farm wash water. *Water* 8, 183.

Carreau, R., VanAcker, S., VanderZaag, A., Madani, A., Drizo, A. *et al.* (2012) Evaluation of a surface flow constructed wetland treating abattoir wastewater. *Applied Engineering in Agriculture* 28, 757–766.

Chary, S.N., Kamala, C.T. and Raj, D.S.S. (2008) Assessing risk of heavy metals from consuming food grown on sewage irrigated soils and food chain transfer. *Ecotoxicology and Environmental Safety* 69, 513–524.

Collaço, A.B. and Roston, D.M. (2006) Use of shredded tires as support medium for subsurface flow constructed wetland. *Engenharia Ambiental – Espírito Santo do Pinhal* 3(1), 21–31.

Corcoran, E., Nellemann, C., Baker, E., Bos, R., Osborn, D. and Savelli, H. (eds) (2010) *Sick Water? The Central Role of Wastewater Management in Sustainable Development.* UNEP, UN–Habitat, GRID–Arendal, Arendal, Norway.

Cordesius, H. and Hedström, S. (2009) *A Feasibility Study on Sustainable Wastewater Treatment Using Constructed Wetlands – An Example from Cochabamba, Bolivia.* MSc thesis. Division of Water Resources Engineering, Department of Building and Environmental Technology, Lund University, Sweden.

CPCB (2015) CPCB directs municipal bodies not to discharge untreated sewage into rivers. Available at: https://www.livemint.com/Politics/vqQbrfuwjhv7cHEaZ3dy7J/CPCB-directs-municipal-bodies-not-to-discharge-untreated-sew.html (accessed 26 April 2018).

Datta, A., Wani, S.P., Tilak, A.S., Patil, M.D. and Kaushal, M. (2015) Assessing the performance of free water surface constructed wetlands in treating domestic wastewater: a potential alternative for irrigation. Presented at the International Conference ICID2015 (26th ERC and 66th IEC) held during 11th–16th October 2015. Montpellier, France.

Drechsel, P., Graefe, S., Sonou, M. and Cofie, O.O. (2006) *Informal Irrigation in Urban West Africa: An Overview*. IWMI Research Report 102. International Water Management Institute, Colombo, Sri Lanka.

Dunne, E.J., Coveney, M.F., Hoge, V.R., Conrow, R., Naleway, R. *et al.* (2015) Phosphorus removal performance of a large-scale constructed treatment wetland receiving eutrophic lake water. *Ecological Engineering* 79, 132–142.

Fan, J., Zhang, B., Zhang, J., Ngo, H.H., Guo, W. *et al.* (2013) Intermittent aeration strategy to enhance organics and nitrogen removal in subsurface flow constructed wetlands. *Bioresource Technology* 141, 117–122. DOI: 10.1016/j.biortech.2013.03.077.

FAO (2017) Wastewater an opportunity being flushed away. Food and Agriculture Organization, 22 March 2017. Available at: http://www.fao.org/news/story/en/item/853565/icode/?platform=hootsuite (accessed 23 March 2017).

Grangier, C., Qadir, M. and Singh, M. (2012) Health implications for children in wastewater-irrigated peri-urban Aleppo, Syria. *Water Quality Exposure and Health* 4(4), 187–195.

Jimenez, B. (2005) Treatment technology and standards for agricultural wastewater reuse: a case study in Mexico. *Irrigation and Drainage* 54 (Supplement 1), S22–S33.

Keraita, B.N. and Drechsel, P. (2004) Agricultural use of untreated urban wastewater in Ghana. In: Scott, C.A., Faruqui, N.I. and Raschid-Sally, L. (eds) *Wastewater Use in Irrigated Agriculture*. CAB International, Wallingford, Oxfordshire, pp. 101–112.

Li, L., Li, Y., Biswas, D.K., Nian, Y. and Jiang, G. (2008) Potential of constructed wetlands in treating the eutrophic water: evidence from Taihu Lake of China. *Bioresource Technology* 99, 1656–1663.

Melloul, A.A. and Hassani, L. (1999) Salmonella infection in children from the wastewater-spreading zone of Marrakesh city (Morocco). *Journal of Applied Microbiology* 87(4), 536–539.

Mihelcic, J.R., Fry, L.M. and Shaw, R. (2011) Global potential of phosphorus recovery from human urine and feces. *Chemosphere* 84(6), 832–839. DOI: 10.1016/j.chemosphere.2011.02.046.

Minhas, P.S. and Samra, J.S. (2004) *Wastewater Use in Peri-urban Agriculture: Impacts and Opportunities*. Central Soil Salinity Research Institute, Karnal, India.

Obuobie, E., Keraita, B., Danso, G., Amoah, P., Cofie, O.O., Raschid-Sally, L. and Drechsel, P. (2006) *Irrigated Urban Vegetable Production in Ghana: Characteristics, Benefits and Risks*. IWMI-RUAF-IDRCCPWF, Accra, Ghana. Available at: http://www.cityfarmer.org/GhanaIrrigateVegis.html (accessed 25 March 2017).

OECD (2011) *OECD Environmental Performance Reviews: Israel 2011*. Organisation for Economic Co-operation and Development Publishing, Paris. Available at: http://www.oecd.org/env/oecd-environmental-performance-reviews-israel-2011-9789264117563-en.htm (accessed 5 April 2017).

Prüss-Üstün, A., Bartram, J., Clasen, T., Colford Jr, J.M., Cumming, O. *et al.* (2014) Burden of disease from inadequate water, sanitation and hygiene in low- and middle-income settings: a retrospective analysis of data from 145 countries. *Tropical Medicine and International Health* 19(8), 894–905.

Puigagut, J., Villaseñor, J., Salas, J.J., Bécares, E. and García, J. (2007) Subsurface-flow constructed wetlands in Spain for the sanitation of small communities: a comparative study. *Ecological Engineering* 30(4), 312–319.

Qadir, M., Wichelns, D., Raschid-Sally, L., Minhas, P.S., Drechsel, P. *et al.* (2007) Agricultural use of marginal-quality water – opportunities and challenges. In: Molden, D. (ed.) *Water for Food, Water for Life: A Comprehensive Assessment of Water Management in Agriculture*. Earthscan, London and International Water Management Institute, Colombo, Sri Lanka, pp. 425–457.

Rossmann, M., Matos, A.T., Abreu, E.C., Silva, F.F. and Borges, A.C. (2013) Effect of influent aeration on removal of organic matter from coffee processing wastewater in constructed wetlands. *Journal of Environmental Management* 128, 912–919.

Srikanth, R. and Naik, D. (2004) Health effects of wastewater reuse for agriculture in the suburbs of Asmara City, Eritrea. *International Journal of Occupational Environment and Health* 10(3), 284–288.

Tilak, A., Wani, S.P., Datta, A., Patil, M., Kaushal, M. and Reddy, K.R. (2017) Evaluation of *Ageratum conyzoides* in field scale constructed wetlands (CWs) for domestic wastewater treatment. *Water Science & Technology* 75(10), 2268–2280. DOI: 10.2166/wst.2017.119.

Udagedara, U.S.C. and Najim, M.M.M. (2009) Potential to enhance the extent of paddy cultivation using domestic and municipal wastewater harvesting – a case study from the dry zone of Sri Lanka. *Journal of Applied Irrigation Science* 44(2), 239–248.

UNEP (2016) *A Snapshot of the World's Water Quality: Towards A Global Assessment*. United Nations Environment Programme, Nairobi.

Van Vuuren, D.P., Bouwman, A.F. and Beusen, A.H.W. (2010) Phosphorus demand for the 1970–2100 period: a scenario analysis of resource depletion. *Global Environmental Change* 20(3), 428–439. DOI: 10.1016/j.gloenvcha.2010.04.004.

Vohla, C., Kõiv, M., Bavor, H.J., Chazarenc, F. and Mander, Ü. (2011) Filter materials for phosphorus removal from wastewater in treatment wetlands – A review. *Ecological Engineering* 37(1), 70–89.

Vymazal, J. (2010) Constructed wetlands for wastewater treatment: five decades of experience. *Environmental Science and Technology* 45(1), 61–69.

Vymazal, J. (2014) Constructed wetlands for treatment of industrial wastewaters: a review. *Ecological Engineering* 73, 724–751.

Vymazal, J. and Kropfelova, L. (2008) *Wastewater Treatment in Constructed Wetlands with Horizontal Sub-Surface Flow*. Springer Verlag, Heidelberg, Germany.

Wang, X., Bai, X., Qiu, J. and Wang, B. (2005) Municipal wastewater treatment with pond-constructed wetland system: a case study. *Water Science and Technology* 51(12), 325–329.

WHO (2014) *Preventing Diarrhoea through Better Water, Sanitation and Hygiene: Exposures and Impacts in Low- and Middle-income Countries*. World Health Organization, Geneva.

WHO (2015) *UN-Water GLAAS TrackFin Initiative: Tracking Financing to Sanitation, Hygiene and Drinking-water at the National Level*. Guidance document summary for decision-makers. World Health Organization, Geneva.

Winblad, U. and Simpson-Hébert, M. (eds) (2004) *Ecological Sanitation*. Revised and enlarged edition. Stockholm Environment Institute, Stockholm.

WWAP (2017) *The United Nations World Water Development Report 2016: Water and Jobs*. World Water Assessment Programme. United Nations Educational, Scientific and Cultural Organization (UNESCO), Paris.

Zidan, A.A., El-Gamal, M.A., Rashed, A.A. and Abd El-Hady, M.A. (2013) BOD treatment in HSSF constructed wetlands using different media (set-up stage). *Mansoura Engineering Journal* 38(3), 36–42.

13 Learnings and a Way Forward

Suhas P. Wani* and K.V. Raju

International Crops Research Institute for the Semi-Arid Tropics, Patancheru, India

13.1 Introduction

The mission of International Crops Research Institute for the Semi-Arid Tropics (ICRISAT) is 'to reduce poverty, malnutrition, hunger and environmental degradation in the dryland tropics'. The semi-arid tropics is a hot spot of poverty and malnutrition, as 850 million poor live in the region. In particular, the Indian subcontinent is a hot spot of malnutrition recording 3 million malnourished children below 5 years of age. This region is also water-scarce as the annual evapotranspiration demand is far higher than the available water in the region. As a result, agriculture largely depends on monsoonal rains and per capita availability of water particularly in India has declined from 5177 m³ in 1951 to 1450 m³ in 2015. Similar is the case for arable land availability, which is 0.11 ha per capita (in 2016). The region is also vulnerable to the impacts of climate change. In order to achieve sustainable development goal (SDG) of no poverty (SDG1), zero hunger (SDG2) including overcoming malnutrition through good health and wellbeing (SDG3) and responsible for production and consumption through sustainable management of natural resources (SDG12), ICRISAT in partnership with stakeholders undertakes science

with a human face through science of discovery to science of delivery.

In order to achieve the impacts of technologies and products developed by the researchers (ICRISAT and other researchers in the region), the ICRISAT Development Center has started addressing the issues of scaling-up by undertaking science-led development since 2002 to take the science of discovery to proof of concept and pilot stages to large impacts through number of innovations in terms of institutions, policies, partnerships, delivery mechanisms and input supply chain along with market linkages to achieve the impact. ICRISAT has developed a holistic, integrated participatory approach by adopting principles of the 4 'ICEs', i.e. 4 'Is': integrated, innovative, inclusive and intensive; 4 'Cs': consortium, collective action, convergence and capacity building; and 4 'Es': efficiency, equity, environmental protection and economic gain. This approach is intended to address the issues of enhancing profitability, building skills for increasing implementation, protecting environment by adopting inclusive market-oriented development (IMOD) approach. Scaling-up is undertaken by addressing the issues through science-led development to undertake corporate social responsibility (CSR) work as a win-win proposition for achieving the goals of sustainability,

* Corresponding author: s.wani@cgiar.org

©CAB International 2018. *Corporate Social Responsibility: Win-win Propositions for Communities, Corporates and Agriculture* (eds S.P. Wani and K.V. Raju)

environmental protection and improving livelihoods while achieving food security and nutrition
security. In this process, a number of corporates
like Sir Dorabji Tata Trust (SDTT), Sir Ratan Tata
Trust (SRTT), Jindal South West Foundation (JSW
Foundation), Asian Paints Limited, AB InBev
(earlier SABMiller India), Mahindra & Mahindra
Ltd, Coca-Cola India Inc., Power Grid Corporation of India Limited and Rural Electrification
Corporation Limited (RECL) have joined hands
with ICRISAT by providing funds through CSR
for rural development.

The main interventions undertaken through
this initiative are for improving rural livelihoods
through sustainable management of water resources, land resources and enhancing productivity and profitability of agriculture in the region.
The results of the CSR initiatives are remarkable
where the science-led development approach was
adopted with community participation in partnership with implementing non-governmental organization (NGO) partners. This is evident from
the number of families reached (>50,000) and
nearly 0.5 million m³ of rainwater storage capacity created in the rural areas. This has resulted
in the harvesting of 1 million m³ of water and
0.5–0.8 million m³ of groundwater recharge. In
addition to rainwater harvesting and increasing
groundwater recharge, the interventions also resulted in reducing soil erosion by 40–50%, increasing agricultural productivity from 13% to
56%. It also increased cropping intensity with improved water availability, resulting in reducing the
water footprint by 35% and increasing household
incomes up to 280%.

More importantly, in addition to the above
positive effects, tangible benefits and supportive ecosystem services such as improved water
quality, increased carbon sequestration along
with improved social capital through enhanced cooperation have also benefited the
community, because of the integrated holistic
approach. A number of income-generating
activities have benefited women and young
people in the villages, creating employment in
the rural areas. This win-win proposition for
corporates and research organizations and
the communities through CSR clearly highlights the need for science-led integrated holistic approach and linking farmers to markets
where corporates could play an important role.
This is one of the best models for sustainable

development through win-win proposition for
corporates and the communities.

13.2 Background

This initiative of development research or the concept of 'Science with a Human Face' underlines
the importance of achieving the impact of the
various technologies/products developed by researchers. However, on the ground, large yield
gaps currently exist between farmers' current
yields and achievable potential yields, which are
two- to fivefold higher than what farmers harvest.
At the same time, the potential achievable yield in
the rainfed situation has been established to be up
to 5–6 t/ha in Asia as well as in Africa (Rockström
et al., 2007; Wani et al., 2009). However, this potential is not realized, largely due to failure of delivery mechanism in terms of knowledge, about
the technologies and products as well as inputs,
credit and poor infrastructure. In order to bridge
this gap, ICRISAT has initiated scaled-up initiatives for all the technologies and products developed by researchers (national agricultural
research system (NARS), ICRISAT and other
international organizations) to achieve the impact
on a large number of farmers by bridging the gap
between the pilot scale and realizing impact. The
scientists undertake the 'discovery phase' as well
as 'proof of concept' and pilot scale, demonstrating the suitability of the technologies to several
hundreds or thousands of farmers. However, the
challenge in terms of the science of delivery,
through enabling institutions, policies and knowledge delivery systems, calls for innovations to
overcome the gaps to achieve the impact.

ICRISAT Development Center has undertaken the science of delivery to ensure that the
technologies/products developed by the researchers are made available to the farmers by
adopting the consortium approach. In this process, knowledge-generating institutions such as
ICRISAT, NARS, state agricultural universities
and other international centres are linked with
knowledge-transforming institutions such as
the Department of Agriculture of both national
and state levels, along with NGOs, besides building public–private partnerships to address different issues such as knowledge delivery, market
linkages and value addition by adopting the

IMOD approach and innovating, enabling institutions and policies to ensure the availability of the necessary infrastructure to achieve the impact (see Chapter 2 in this volume).

The CSR initiative is supported by corporates, particularly in terms of natural resource management, environment protection, livelihood improvement and skill development of the rural people to improve their livelihoods through increased productivity and profitability. This particular initiative builds on the four pillars of 4 'ICEs'. The strategy is built on *innovations* in the areas of not only technologies but also institutions, building partnerships and networking to ensure *inclusivity* for small and marginal farm holders, for sustainable *intensification* of the systems by adopting *integrated* approach. For building partnerships, IDC adopts the *consortium approach* by bringing different stakeholders such as knowledge-generating institutions with knowledge-transforming institutions, producers, processors and marketers with development partners together on one platform through *collective action* of the farmers, as well as other consortium members, to *converge* different interventions, and actions of the partners, resources and institutions through *capacity building* of all the consortium partners. Through innovations and partnership, ICRISAT aims for *economic* gain/ profitability through enhancing resource-use *efficiency* to address the issues of *equity* and *environmental* protection (see Chapter 2 in this volume).

The CSR initiatives have converged in the central place to help development with the Companies' Act 2013 of Government of India. With effect from 1 April 2014, every private limited or public limited company, which either has a net worth of ₹500 crore or a turnover of ₹1000 crore or a net profit of ₹5 crore, is required to spend on CSR at least 2% of its average net profit for the immediate preceding three financial years' activities.

This book provides an excellent insight into the early phase of CSR work undertaken by ICRISAT-led consortium for achieving the impacts and has gathered a number of learnings by working in partnership which can benefit development research as well as corporates to have a win-win proposition for improving the livelihoods, protecting the environment and building the skills in rural areas by undertaking science of delivery.

This also serves as a feedback loop for the scientists to undertake the discovery phase of research which is demand-driven and will benefit the farmers.

13.3 Learnings

ICRISAT has been working with corporates since 2002 and subsequently with the approval of the Companies' Act, a number of corporates and public-sector companies have come forward to help take science to the doorstep of the farmers to benefit through science-led development. In the process, the following lessons were learnt. Also, issues were raised on how to move forward and strengthen efforts to achieve large-scale impacts.

- The most important learning which emerged from this initiative is that most of the scientists are not keen to visit farmers' fields, as it is perceived that it is an extension job which needs to be done by the departments, at state or national level or by the NGOs. However, it is observed that neither the state Department of Agriculture nor the NGOs can keep themselves updated with the developments in the area of science as well as do the necessary refinements in the technology which scientists have worked on. Hence this new arena of research for development should be strengthened and the mindset of the scientists need to be changed so that it is a continuum from discovery to the proof of concept to the pilot stage to the impact. Scientists need to lead the partners to achieve the desired impacts, as it is their technologies and products which would benefit the farmers.
- It is observed that the best impact can be achieved by adopting the holistic and integrated approach and not to adopt compartmental approach while dealing with farmers, as they expect complete solutions for their problems from the scientists. In order to offer holistic solutions, a consortium approach should be adopted so as to build a partnership to resolve the issues faced by the farmers, namely scientific, availability of the products/inputs, knowledge, market information, market linkages, infrastructure and

all the solutions associated with agriculture and allied sectors such as horticulture, animal husbandry, fisheries, watershed management, etc. Unless a holistic and integrated approach is adopted, impacts cannot be seen on the ground; for example, ICRISAT had undertaken soil health mapping at the village level, and then scientists made recommendations to farmers using the soil health information. However, if the required inputs like micro- and secondary nutrients are not readily available at the right time and at the right price, farmers will not be able to make use of the knowledge or information provided to them about the soil test-based fertilizer recommendations. Hence the consortium needs to work with the concerned government departments as well as private companies to ensure availability of the recommended nutrients at the cluster/village level so that farmers do not have to travel long distances at the time of sowing, as farmers are really facing hardships to undertake timely sowing in their fields (see Chapter 3 in this volume).

- In the rainfed areas, water is the main limiting factor in agriculture and unless farmers are assured the availability of water during the cropping season, farmers generally do not take the risk to invest much in quality seeds, fertilizers as well as improved management practices as they do not have the capacity to bear the risk. Integrated watershed management approach which enhances the green water content through increased soil moisture, as well as excess rainwater harvested in small structures throughout the toposequence will benefit the farmers through seepage of water to the downstream areas, as well as providing lifesaving irrigation using the harvested rainwater or by increasing the availability of groundwater through groundwater recharge (see Chapters 5, 6, 7, 11 and 12 in this volume).
- Integrated watershed management approach has undergone a paradigm shift since 2009 where the watershed programmes which were dealing with soil and water conservation have been transformed into livelihood programmes in order to address the issues of women and landless people as traditional watershed programmes were land-based interventions so people who do not

own land were not the beneficiaries. Also, integrated watershed management ensures tangible economic benefits to the large number of farmers who do not have access to groundwater through *in-situ* moisture conservation and by enhancing water-use efficiency through improved cultivars, fertilizer management and improved soil crop-management practices for increasing crop productivity (Wani *et al.*, 2008).

- As it is evident from the work, productivity enhancement benefits not only farmers but also the market, as it is the market that determines the profitability for the farmers and the value chain or middle men who are involved in disposing the farmers' produce to the market. Hence collective action by the farmers through self-help groups (SHGs) or through farmers' cooperatives such as farmer producer organizations needs to be promoted to ensure that farmers have direct access to the markets and also the number of middle men is reduced so that farmers can get better benefit from the market price by directly dealing with the wholesalers/corporates who buy their products (see Chapters 2, 6, 9, 10 in this volume).
- The IMOD approach has to be adopted to ensure that every small farm holder is linked through cooperatives to the market or to the corporates so that corporates/wholesalers feel comfortable to deal with the producers and achieve full scale in their operations (see Chapter 2 in this volume).
- As farmers adopt mixed farming systems, a farming systems approach needs to be followed to provide solutions to the farmers rather than the compartmental approach of agriculture and allied sectors. Agriculture, horticulture, livestock, credit, market, etc. are the artificial boundaries created and through integrated holistic approach integrated solutions need to be provided to the farmers (see Chapters 2, 8, 9, 10 in this volume).
- Fifty per cent of the population in the villages is comprised of women. Hence women should be the integral part of various initiatives for livelihood and agriculture as they are involved in family decision making. The most important point is that issues such as food security and nutrition security of family

are better handled by women than men, and this strength needs to be harnessed by involving the women in integrated programmes through SHGs to handle value chain as well as income-generating activities and processing of the agricultural products in the rural areas (see Chapters 4, 5, 6, 7, 8, 9, 10 and 11 in this volume).

- There is an urgent need to strengthen knowledge delivery systems by using information and communication technology (ICT). About 137 million farm holders in India cannot be met through person-to-person contact methods of knowledge delivery. Hence simple ICT tools need to be developed and the youth should be trained for supporting the farmers through ICTs and also get interested in knowledge intensive technologies driven in the villages. Knowledge delivery system plays an important role and tools like farmer field school, farmer-to-farmer videos, tablet-based extension systems and mobile-based short-messaging systems need to be harnessed in addition to the para-agricultural workers who serve as a link between farmers and department staff or the scientists. Using the information about the soil as well as current rainfall and predictions for the next 5 days, sowing date application has been developed and has benefited farmers with increased crop yields. By undertaking the sowing of crops like groundnut, where the seed costs are very high, such simple applications using artificial intelligence and machine learning are very much needed to benefit the farmers for improving their livelihoods and profitability by minimizing their risk (see Chapters 2, 4, 6, 7, 9, 10 in this volume).

- Agriculture has become unprofitable largely because of the increased costs of inputs and labour. There is an urgent need to undertake mechanization of small farms through appropriate machinery like easy planters, seed dibber and other machines which can be provided through machine-hiring centres in the villages so that each small farmer does not have to own the machines, as these are economically not remunerative because of farm size.

- The access to improved seeds for the farmers needs to be ensured and by adopting farmer

participatory selection of cultivars, they should be able to take a decision about selection of cultivar based on the traits/parameters they prefer in terms of fodder, quality, size, colour, taste, marketability, etc., in addition to yield. Scientists need to provide the choice to the farmers of the improved cultivars by adopting farmer participatory selection approach and once the farmers have identified appropriate cultivars then seed systems particularly at the village level for varieties/cultivars need to be established. This ensures the supply of quality seeds at a reasonable price to the farmers as they themselves have seen the performance in their fields and at the same time, the SHGs can get livelihood opportunities also by establishing decentralized seed banks (see Chapters 4, 5, 9, 11 and 12 in this volume).

- In order to address the issue of integrated water scarcity and health, the perennial source of domestic wastewater in the villages needs to be harnessed through appropriate treatment by adopting decentralized wastewater treatment using filtration, microbes for bioremediation and phytoremediation for purification of domestic wastewater and making it safe for agricultural use. This initiative has benefited a number of villagers for producing fodder for the animals even during summer as well as producing other agricultural crops in small areas through SHGs. The decentralized wastewater treatment needs to be scaled-up across the country and can become part of the Swachh Bharat Mission, so that rural areas can be freed from health issues and address the issues of water availability for growing fodder, etc. (see Chapter 12 in this volume).

- In order to address the livelihood issues by adopting the farming systems approach, valuable trees like teak or fruit trees need to be planted on field bunds so that it benefits farmers in the long term by protecting the field bunds, producing increased income and also efficient use of water from the deeper layers which is not used by field crops (see Chapter 5 and 6 in this volume).

- Proper land-use planning is most important, based on the land capability and agroecological potential. Farmers should be encouraged through appropriate incentives to produce what the market needs. Market-led development will ensure that through collective planning at village/cluster of villages level, farmers will synchronize plantation and also produce the product/cultivars which are required by the corporates, for processing, etc. Generally, it is the normal scenario in Indian agriculture.

- The government also needs to ensure appropriate support mechanisms for farmers to produce food and should have in place the minimum support price mechanism as most of the agricultural activities in the country is driven by the state of national departments. Government support for crops like rice and wheat need to be extended to other crops which are grown by farmers.
- The impacts of climate change are very much evident now and appropriate adaptation and mitigation strategies based on the studies at micro-level of district/taluk need to be undertaken in order to build the resilience of farmers to the impacts of climate change. Farmers do not have the knowledge/information about the impacts of climate change in terms of change in the length of growing period, water availability and temperatures as well as natural disasters like drought, etc., and good information flow with prediction models need to be provided to the farmers (see Chapters 4, 7, 8, 9 and 10 in this volume).
- The science of soil analysis which has been known for the past 100 years has not benefited small and marginal farmers in Asia and Africa for the simple reason that the knowledge was not transformed into information and made available to the farmers. Soil health mapping and developing soil test-based recommendations for different crops are a good entry point activity to ensure tangible economic benefits to majority of the small farm holders in the project area. This simple knowledge-based entry point also helps in protecting the environment by reducing application of unwanted nutrients which result in pollution of water bodies and environment. In addition, it also helps in reducing the cost of cultivation for the farmers and increasing

farmers' income through increased productivity (see Chapter 3 in this volume).

13.4   The Way Forward

Based on the learnings from various CSR initiatives undertaken by the ICRISAT-led consortium as well as by others, there is a huge scope to channel the CSR funds for achieving the goals of no poverty (SDG1), zero hunger (SDG2) and responsible for production and consumption through sustainable management of natural resources (SDG12). However, a paradigm shift is needed to undertake the CSR initiatives, which should be science-led and integrated through building partnerships. Through CSR, ICRISAT has reached out to about 225 villages in different states of India covering about 100,000 ha benefiting 65,000 families and 325,000 people through improved food and nutritional security, and by improving their livelihoods and protecting the environment through various soil and water management and livelihood interventions. The following propositions are suggested for future CSR work.

- In order to achieve larger impacts through CSR, the group of companies should have crowd funding and undertake various development initiatives in the target area in an integrated manner through efficient management of financial resources and building partnerships which will benefit each other and also the community. A consortium of companies can be formed which can be led by an independent organization and by bringing together a reputed implementing agency, the programmes can be implemented which will benefit a large number of farmers in the country.
- The CSR funding has a huge potential to alleviate the agrarian distress in the country by channelling the funds and through convergence of actions/activities along with different government schemes. Corporates can play a leading role to establish novel models and innovations and undertake skill development which will be a win-win proposition for the corporates as well as for the rural people and the government.

- Corporates can harness the opportunities of building sustainable business through CSR by adopting the philosophy of 'whatever is given to society, society gives it back to you' so that it becomes a win-win proposition and also develop goodwill among the masses.
- The targeted initiatives to benefit women and the youth using scientific approaches and tools like mechanization, ICT and value-chain approach can create good number of jobs in the rural areas which will meet the requirement of the corporates in a cost-effective manner and help the rural people to improve their livelihoods.
- Scientific organizations like state agricultural universities, national agricultural research institutes and international institutions need to take lead to develop science-led development approach to benefit rural masses as well as achieve the larger impacts through CSR funding.
- Convergence of CSR funding with appropriate government schemes can be achieved through public–private partnerships and can result in a win-win proposition for the government programmes to achieve the targets through improved implementation and monitoring and evaluation through CSR programmes. The corporates need to procure the required products from agriculture, and the input supply chain can be established through the collective action of farmer cooperatives/farmer producer organizations.
- Infrastructure development through CSR for the value chain can be a good proposition to benefit the farmers, as well as create jobs for the young people in rural areas and also minimize postharvest losses.

References

Rockström, J., Nuhu, H., Oweis, T. and Wani, S.P. (2007) Managing water in rainfed agriculture. In: Molden, D. (ed.) *Water for Food, Water for Life: A Comprehensive Assessment of Water Management in Agriculture*. Earthscan, London and International Water Management Institute, Colombo, Sri Lanka, pp. 315–348.

Wani, S.P., Sahrawat, K.L., Sreedevi, T.K., Piara Singh, Pathak, P. and Kesava Rao, A.V.R. (2008) Efficient rainwater management for enhanced productivity in arid and semi-arid drylands. *Journal of Water Management* 15(2), 126–140.

Wani, S.P., Sreedevi, T.K., Rockström, J. and Ramakrishna, Y.S. (2009) Rainfed agriculture – past trends and future prospects. In: Wani, S.P., Rockström, J. and Oweis, T. (eds) *Rainfed Agriculture: Unlocking the Potential*. Comprehensive Assessment of Water Management in Agriculture Series. CAB International, Wallingford, Oxfordshire, pp. 1–35.

Index

CABI – who we are and what we do

This book is published by **CABI**, an international not-for-profit organisation that improves people's lives worldwide by providing information and applying scientific expertise to solve problems in agriculture and the environment.

CABI is also a global publisher producing key scientific publications, including world renowned databases, as well as compendia, books, ebooks and full text electronic resources. We publish content in a wide range of subject areas including: agriculture and crop science / animal and veterinary sciences / ecology and conservation / environmental science / horticulture and plant sciences / human health, food science and nutrition / international development / leisure and tourism.

The profits from CABI's publishing activities enable us to work with farming communities around the world, supporting them as they battle with poor soil, invasive species and pests and diseases, to improve their livelihoods and help provide food for an ever growing population.

CABI is an international intergovernmental organisation, and we gratefully acknowledge the core financial support from our member countries (and lead agencies) including:

Ministry of Agriculture People's Republic of China

Australian Government
Australian Centre for International Agricultural Research

Agriculture and Agri-Food Canada

Ministry of Foreign Affairs of the Netherlands

Schweizerische Eidgenossenschaft
Confédération suisse
Confederazione Svizzera
Confederaziun svizra
Swiss Agency for Development and Cooperation SDC

Discover more

To read more about CABI's work, please visit: **www.cabi.org**

Browse our books at: **www.cabi.org/bookshop**,
or explore our online products at: **www.cabi.org/publishing-products**

Interested in writing for CABI? Find our author guidelines here:
www.cabi.org/publishing-products/information-for-authors/